306.483 BAT V.2

Battleground sports /

PALM BEACH COUNTY
LIBRARY SYSTEM
3650 SUMMIT BLVD.
WEST PALM BEACH, FLORIDA 33406

BATTLEGROUND
SPORTS

BATTLEGROUND

SPORTS

VOLUME 2 (P–Z)

Edited by Michael Atkinson

GREENWOOD PRESS
Westport, Connecticut • London

Library of Congress Cataloging-in-Publication Data

Battleground sports / edited by Michael Atkinson.
    v. cm.
  Includes bibliographical references and index.
    ISBN 978-0-313-34024-6 ((set) : alk. paper) — ISBN 978-0-313-34025-3 ((vol. 1) : alk. paper) — ISBN 978-0-313-34026-0 ((vol. 2) : alk. paper)
  1. Sports—Social aspects—Encyclopedias. 2. Sports—Economic aspects—Encyclopedias. I. Atkinson, Michael, 1971–
    GV706.5.B375   2009
    306.483—dc22   2008030544

British Library Cataloguing in Publication Data is available.

Copyright © 2009 by Michael Atkinson

All rights reserved. No portion of this book may be reproduced, by any process or technique, without the express written consent of the publisher.

Library of Congress Catalog Card Number: 2008030544
ISBN: 978-0-313-34024-6 (set)
      978-0-313-34025-3 (vol. 1)
      978-0-313-34026-0 (vol. 2)

First published in 2009

Greenwood Press, 88 Post Road West, Westport, CT 06881
An imprint of Greenwood Publishing Group, Inc.
www.greenwood.com

Printed in the United States of America

The paper used in this book complies with the Permanent Paper Standard issued by the National Information Standards Organization (Z39.48–1984).

10 9 8 7 6 5 4 3 2 1

CONTENTS

Guide to Related Topics ix
Series Foreword xiii
Introduction [vol. 1] xv

Entries

Academic Misconduct Among Athletes	1
Adventure Racing	7
Animal Blood Sports	12
Antidoping Rules and Policies	18
Antitrust Violations in Professional Sports	22
Athlete Unions	29
"At-Risk" Youth in Sports	37
Biology and Athlete Performance	43
Cheating During Competition	53
Collective Protests and Social Movements	60
Commercializing Ethnic Athletes	65
Cool Pose	72
Corporate Branding	76

Corporate Stadiums	83
Criminal Violence During Competition	88
Disability Sports	97
Drafting Amateur Athletes	103
Eating Disorders	111
Environmental Impacts of Sports	117
Equipment Manufacturing in the Third World	125
Ergogenics	131
Erythropoietin (EPO)	138
Ethnic Coaches, Managers, and Owners	143
Field Invasions	151
Funding Equality Legislation	156
Gambling	161
Gay Games	167
Gender and Educational Opportunities	171
Gender and Game Rules	177
Gene Manipulation	185
Governments, Laws, and Gambling	191
Government Sponsorship of Teams	197
Hazing	203
Homophobia	208
Hooliganism	215
Illness	221
International Olympic Committee (IOC)	228
Labor Migration	235
LGBT Sports Leagues	240
Marijuana, Alcohol, and Illicit Drugs	247
Marketing Female Athlete Sexuality	253
Mascots	260
Media Broadcasting Rights	266
Media Coverage of Women's Sports	271

Men in Women's Sports	278
Militarism and the Olympics	284
Missile Throwing	289
Openly Gay Athletes	295
Parent Misconduct	301
Parkour (Free Running)	307
Partner Abuse Among Athletes	312
Player–Fan Fighting	317
Postevent Riots	321
Private vs. Public Sports Spaces	326
Pseudosports	331
Publicity in Sports	336
Racial Profiling and Stacking	343
Rape and Sexual Assault	348
Referee Abuse	354
Religious Expression	360
Rights of Young Athletes	366
Salaries of Professional Athletes	371
Sexual Abuse Among Athletes	377
Skateboarding	383
Snowboarding	389
Soccer Tragedies	398
Sports Doctors, Trainers, and Drugs	403
Sports for All	407
Steroid Use By Athletes	412
Surfing and "New" Water Sports	418
Taunting	425
Terrorism and the Olympics	430
Ticket Distribution and Scalping	436
Transsexual Athletes	443
Ubersexuality	449

Ultraendurance Running	454
Urban Planning and Gentrification	459
Video Games	465
Virtual Sports	472
Whistle-Blowers and Drugs	477
Women and the Apologetic	482
Women Coaches and Owners	488
Women in Men's Sports	491
Women Sportscasters	498
X Games	503
Yoga and Alternative Fitness	509
Bibliography	*515*
About the Editor and Contributors	*535*
Index	*539*

GUIDE TO RELATED TOPICS

ALTERNATIVE SPORTS
Adventure Racing
Parkour (Free Running)
Pseudosports
Skateboarding
Snowboarding
Surfing and New Water Sports
Ultraendurance Running
X Games
Yoga and Alternative Fitness

DRUGS
Antidoping Rules and Policies
Ergogenics
Erythropoietin (EPO)
Marijuana, Alcohol, and Illicit Drugs
Sports Doctors, Trainers, and Drugs
Steroid Use by Athletes
Whistle-Blowers and Drugs

ECONOMICS
Antitrust Violations in Professional Sports
Corporate Branding
Corporate Stadiums
Gambling

Governments, Laws, and Gambling
Marketing Female Athlete Sexuality
Salaries of Professional Athletes
Ticket Distribution and Scalping

EDUCATION
Academic Misconduct Among Athletes
Funding Equality Legislation
Gender and Educational Opportunities

GENDER
Gender and Educational Opportunities
Gender and Game Rules
Men in Women's Sports
Women and the Apologetic
Women Coaches and Owners
Women in Men's Sports
Women Sportscasters

HEALTH AND WELLNESS
Biology and Athlete Performance
Disability Sports
Eating Disorders
Illness

MEDIA
Media Broadcasting Rights
Media Coverage of Women's Sports
Publicity in Sports
Women Sportscasters

OLYMPICS
International Olympic Committee (IOC)
Militarism and the Olympics
Terrorism and the Olympics

POLITICS, IDEOLOGY, AND PUBLIC POLICY
Drafting Amateur Athletes
Government Sponsorship of Teams
Labor Migration
Militarism and the Olympics
Private vs. Public Sports Spaces
Religious Expression
Urban Planning and Gentrification

RACE AND ETHNICITY
"At-Risk" Youth in Sports
Commercializing Ethnic Athletes
Cool Pose
Ethnic Coaches, Managers, and Owners
Labor MigrationRacial Profiling and Stacking

RIGHTS MOVEMENTS
Athlete Unions
Collective Protests and Social Movements
Environmental Impacts of Sports
Equipment Manufacturing in the Third World
Rights of Young Athletes
Sports for All and Fair Play Leagues

SEXUALITY
Gay Games
Homophobia
LGBT Sports Leagues
Openly Gay Athletes
Transsexual Athletes
Ubersexuality

SPECTACLES
Cheating During Competition
Field Invasions
Mascots
Missile Throwing
Publicity in Sports
Taunting

TECHNOLOGY
Biology and Athlete Performance
Gene Manipulation
Video Games
Virtual Sports

VIOLENCE
Animal Blood Sports
Criminal Violence During Competition
Hazing
Hooliganism
Missile Throwing
Parent Misconduct

Partner Abuse Among Athletes
Player–Fan Fighting
Postevent Riots
Rape and Sexual Assault
Referee Abuse
Sexual Abuse Among Athletes
Soccer Tragedies

SERIES FOREWORD

Students, teachers, and librarians frequently need resources for researching the hot-button issues of contemporary society. Whether for term papers, debates, current-events classes, or to just keep informed, library users need balanced, in-depth tools to serve as a launching pad for obtaining a thorough understanding of all sides of those debates that continue to provoke, anger, challenge, and divide us all.

The sets in Greenwood's *Battleground* series are just such a resource. Each *Battleground* set focuses on one broad area of culture in which the debates and conflicts continue to be fast and furious—for example, religion, sports, popular culture, sexuality and gender, science and technology. Each volume comprises dozens of entries on the most timely and far-reaching controversial topics, such as abortion, capital punishment, drugs, ecology, the economy, immigration, and politics. The entries—all written by scholars with a deep understanding of the issues—provide readers with a non-biased assessment of these topics. What are the main points of contention? Who holds each position? What are the underlying, unspoken concerns of each side of the debate? What might the future hold? The result is a balanced, thoughtful reference resource that will not only provide students with a solid foundation for understanding the issues, but will challenge them to think more deeply about their own beliefs.

In addition to an in-depth analysis of these issues, sets include sidebars on important events or people that help enliven the discussion, and each entry includes a list of "Further Reading" that help readers find the next step in their research. At the end of volume 2, the readers will find a comprehensive Bibliography and Index.

PARENT MISCONDUCT

Parent misconduct, often called parental sports rage, in youth sports refers to any disruptive, abusive, or violent behavior parents engage in on and around sports playing fields. Such behaviors may be directed at other parents, officials, or even child athletes. Typical examples of parent misconduct include fist-fighting, throwing objects at others, and shouting obscenities or other forms of aggressive speech. Parent misconduct is one of the least systematically studied, but clearly patterned, aspects of violence in North American sports. Furthermore, there are no official databases or records kept in North American athletic organizations that precisely indicate the extent of the problem of parent misconduct in youth sports.

BACKGROUND

Newspapers and television programs have anecdotally documented how fights during Little League baseball games, attacks on soccer referees, and the verbal abuse of football coaches by parents is happening more frequently. Overzealous, misplaced, and even violent reactions by parents to children's athletic activities are, indeed, a complex sociocultural problem in sports that is often swept under the proverbial rug of sports cultures.

Lay explanations of parent violence offered by sports insiders or media critics focus on a number of well-worn explanations. One of the most popular explanations of the behaviors is based on a model of social imitation. Critics using this explanation believe that the cause of especially violent outbursts by parents in and around sports fields is our increased exposure to violence in professional sports. Almost every type and level of professional sports, it is argued, offers numerous examples of sports legends and icons using profanity, hitting fellow players, and attacking referees. The logic of the explanation follows that if sports can be a battleground at the professional level, it certainly can be a similar battleground at the youth level. The media are at times blamed for literally modeling cultures and structures of violence in youth sports.

A second prominent explanation of parental misconduct at sports venues posits that because parents often live vicariously through their children's activities, they develop strong ego attachments to events involving their children. When parents are projecting, in this case, their own (often failed in youth) athletic dreams and fantasies onto their children, then when a child fails, is injured, or is treated unjustly the parent interprets the event as an insult or slight to themselves. Frustration in the parent results, and disruption on the field may occur.

Finally, and certainly related to both of these explanations, fathers are believed to be especially tolerant of rough physical play in and around sports fields as a tool for building a young boy's sense of masculinity. If a boy is failing to perform as a stereotypically macho young man, a father may seek to provide an important role model in the sports context by acting out and asserting a level of male dominance for the boy to emulate.

Experts in the field of sports pedagogy and coaching add that one of the root problems of parent violence in sports is that adults too often establish the form and structure of youth sports. Specifically, youth sports is designed to mimic highly competitive and authoritarian adult versions of professional or elite amateur sports. From this perspective, watching in youth sports satisfies a thirst adults have for the various professional sports watched on television. When parents and coaches spend all their time focused on the scoreboard, concentrate on developing player skills similar to those found at the professional level, and seek to control the games, they are bound to lose sight of, arguably, the main purposes of youth sports, that is, to teach and guide young athletes in skill development in their sport of choice, to provide encouragement and support, to build self-esteem, and to allow children to have fun while exercising.

On the more violent side of parents sports rage, there are increasing numbers of cases reported throughout North America every year. Psychologists fear that not only will injury and attrition rates in most youth sports continue to rise (as they have been in football, ice hockey, and baseball since 1999) but that parents' violent behaviors will produce long-term emotional suffering and damage in children. Or, those children will themselves become violent adults by modeling their behaviors after their parents.

To combat these trends, a growing number of youth and amateur sporting associations are struggling to maintain control of overly aggressive parents at youth sports events. They are looking to enforce new systems that would set forth guidelines of behavioral conduct and seriously restrict how parents can act in and around the playing field. The Parents Association for Youth Sports (PAYS) program offered through the National Alliance for Youth Sports (NAYS) is essentially a training program for parents with children in a full range of sports. Under program rules, parents attend a 30-minute clinic where they view a training video, meet other parents who are concerned about safety in youth

A GLIMPSE INTO PARENTS' ATTITUDES ABOUT ABUSIVE BEHAVIOR

Survey USA took a poll of 500 sports parents in Indianapolis, Indiana, in May 2001. Parents were asked about their views on and experiences with violence in youth sports.

- 55 percent of parents say they have witnessed other parents engaging in verbal abuse at youth sporting events.
- 21 percent say they have witnessed a physical altercation between other parents at youth sporting events.
- 73 percent believe that parents who become verbally or physically abusive during games should be banned from youth sports.
- 22 percent would allow aggressive parents to remain in the stands.
- 5 percent are not sure what to do about parents who are prone to sports-induced tantrums.
- 27 percent think silent spectating (where no cheering is allowed by parents) is a good idea.

sports, participate in discussions, and sign the "Parents' Code of Ethics" pledge. The main goal of the PAYS program is to prevent incidents from happening in the first place through a harms-reduction educational approach. Including parents in this voluntary program offers a very proactive approach to parent rage control. Currently, more than 450 local communities across the United States have implemented the PAYS program, and more than 30,000 parents have been through the training.

KEY EVENTS

Extreme cases of parent violence in North America have mushroomed over the past decade. A number of internationally mass-mediated cases have called attention to the seriousness of the problem and have encouraged sports policy-makers to redraw lines of acceptable behavior for sports parents.

Among the most tragic of recent cases involved two ice hockey fathers, Thomas Junta and Michael Costin. On July 5, 2000, 44-year-old truck driver Thomas Junta fatally beat Michael Costin to death while at their sons' hockey practice in Reading, Massachusetts. The case is perhaps the most vicious instance of parental misbehavior in sports and epitomizes the burgeoning problems associated with parents' codes of conduct within minor or little league sports.

Junta claimed he killed Michael Costin, age 40, in self-defense after they argued over rough play during their sons' practice. The confrontation between Costin and Junta began when Junta became angry about incidents of stick slashing and cross-checking at what was supposed to be a noncontact hockey scrimmage, which Costin was supervising. Junta saw another player elbow his son in the face. Witnesses to the event said that when Junta yelled at Costin repeatedly for not controlling the rough play. The two men then got into a scuffle near the

THE SPORTS PARENT CODE OF CONDUCT

Preamble

The essential elements of character-building and ethics in sports are embodied in the concept of sportsmanship and six core principles: trustworthiness, respect, responsibility, fairness, caring, and good citizenship. The highest potential of sports is achieved when competition reflects these "six pillars of character."

I therefore agree:

1. I will not force my child to participate in sports.
2. I will remember that children participate to have fun and that the game is for youth, not adults.
3. I will inform the coach of any physical disability or ailment that may affect the safety of my child or the safety of others.
4. I will learn the rules of the game and the policies of the league.
5. I (and my guests) will be a positive role model for my child and encourage sportsmanship by showing respect and courtesy, and by demonstrating positive support for all players, coaches, officials and spectators at every game, practice, or other sporting event.
6. I (and my guests) will not engage in any kind of unsportsmanlike conduct with any official, coach, player, or parent such as booing and taunting; refusing to shake hands; or using profane language or gestures.
7. I will not encourage any behaviors or practices that would endanger the health and well-being of the athletes.
8. I will teach my child to play by the rules and to resolve conflicts without resorting to hostility or violence.
9. I will demand that my child treat other players, coaches, officials, and spectators with respect regardless of race, creed, color, sex, or ability.
10. I will teach my child that doing one's best is more important than winning, so that my child will never feel defeated by the outcome of a game or his/her performance.
11. I will praise my child for competing fairly and trying hard and make my child feel like a winner every time.
12. I will never ridicule or yell at my child or other participant for making a mistake or losing a competition.
13. I will emphasize skill development and practices and how they benefit my child over winning. I will also deemphasize games and competition in the lower age groups.
14. I will promote the emotional and physical well-being of the athletes ahead of any personal desire I may have for my child to win.
15. I will respect the officials and their authority during games and will never question, discuss, or confront coaches at the game field, and will take time to speak with coaches at an agreed upon time and place.
16. I will demand a sports environment for my child that is free from drugs, tobacco, and alcohol, and I will refrain from their use at all sports events.

17. I will refrain from coaching my child or other players during games and practices, unless I am one of the official coaches of the team.

I also agree that if I fail to abide by the aforementioned rules and guidelines, I will be subject to disciplinary action that could include, but is not limited to the following:

- Verbal warning by official, head coach, and/or head of league organization
- Written warning
- Parental game suspension with written documentation of incident kept on file by organizations involved
- Game forfeit through the official or coach
- Parental season suspension

Parent Signature: _____

---

locker rooms, but it was quickly broken up by bystanders. The minor altercation ended, and Junta left the arena.

Junta returned, however, to collect his children from the locker room, and he restarted the fight with Costin. Junta said that he tried to avoid fighting with Costin, but he fought back after the 156-pound Costin threw a "sucker punch" at him, jumped on him, and continued to hit and kick him after the two men fell to the floor. Junta claimed he threw punches but did not land any on Costin during the scuffle. Other witnesses to the fight said that Junta, in fact, struck Costin repeatedly in the head while pinning him to the thinly matted floor of the Burbank Ice Arena in Reading. Junta ignored several parents' pleas to stop hitting Costin. Costin suffered brain and heart damage that killed him. The fatal fight was witnessed by about a dozen children, including Junta's son and Costin's three sons, aged between 11 and 14.

Junta was arrested, tried, and convicted of involuntary manslaughter. On January 25, 2002, he was sentenced to 6–10 years imprisonment by Judge Grabau; nearly twice the recommended sentence established by state law. Critics of the case and the relative leniency of the sentence have argued that the jury was not privileged to important information about Junta and instead were regaled with stories about the tough culture of ice hockey. For example, Junta's wife, Michelle, was granted a restraining order against her husband in 1991 when she alleged he beat her continuously in front of their two children and another child. In 1992, police arrested Junta on charges that he punched a Boston police officer and ripped a gold chain off his neck. Junta was not convicted, but a Boston Municipal Court judge ordered him to pay the officer $250 in restitution. Equally, however, jurors in Junta's trial never heard about Costin's own troubled past, which included seven prison stints between 1983 and 1995 on charges of breaking and entering, drunken driving, and assaulting a police officer.

State legislators in Massachusetts relied on the potential deterrence effect of the verdict on parental behavior in sports cultures. It seems a body of legislators did not buy into the "let sports police itself" argument or the idea that harsh punishments for sports crimes would serve to alter the course of violence in games. On September 23, 2000, more than 30 heads of Massachusetts' chapters of national sports and medical associations, educational organizations, and professional associations met at Children's Hospital in Boston to participate in a consensus meeting to develop a "parent code of conduct" for youth sports in the entire state. The meeting was convened by the Massachusetts Governor's Committee on Physical Fitness and Sports and the National Youth Sports Safety Foundation. As a result of the meeting, the group produced the Sport Parent Code of Conduct (SPCC). The SPCC drew national and international media attention as one of the first explicit codes of conduct that parents would be asked to sign.

Despite the state's positive and innovative efforts to hold parents accountable for their actions, the NAYS has argued that many parents learned relatively nothing since the deadly encounter between Junta and Costin. While there are no official statistics on the amount of violence involving parents at youth practices or amateur or professional sporting events, the NAYS believes the problem of violence has not changed course. In November of 2004, for example, a Sarasota, Florida, father was arrested after storming the field and punching the referee during his son's flag football game. Other nationally documented and mediated incidents involving bad parental sportsmanship in 2006 included: a brawl involving approximately 30 adults following a youth soccer tournament in Los Angeles, California; two Salt Lake City, Utah, women allegedly beating a woman unconscious after a youth baseball game; and a Madison, Wisconsin, father hitting a coach's 10-year-old son during practice.

Still, other U.S. states have produced their own codes of parent conduct and produced other initiatives designed to improve and enhance sports parents' knowledge of proper fan conduct. In 2004, New Castle County Football League of Delaware instituted a new rule that demanded parents attend mandatory training spectator classes, which included a video on proper behavior at youth sports functions and team practices. The video is based on the training video volunteer coaches are required to see before being allowed to take over a team. If parents did not attend the class and did not show a "parent awareness card" certificate that proved their attendance, their children could not receive any football equipment. The mandatory classes and no-tolerance policy toward parental misconduct yielded positive results by reducing parent–parent, parent–player, and parent–official altercations.

In a program called "Time Out! For Better Sports for Kids," NAYS and the National Recreation and Parks Association proposed an idea in 2006 that would require volunteer parents and coaches who use any public parks and facilities for games and practices to undergo training in the proper behavior at youth sporting events. A professionally trained youth sports administrator would oversee a parent-run league, and parents and coaches would be required to follow a code of conduct. In the scheme, parents, coaches, and their children would be held accountable if they did not undergo their training. Children of parents who refuse to undergo training may not be allowed to play in the games.

On the heels of the Junta incident, the development of youth sports codes in the United States, and a wider critique of violence in the sport of ice hockey, Hockey Canada and USA Hockey (the two national governing bodies of the amateur sport in North America) organizations partnered for the 2002–2004 hockey season by launching a new series of integrated public service announcements under the banner of "Relax, it's Just a Game." As much a tactic of image repair as one of safety enhancement within the sport, the public service campaign was designed to raise awareness and promote discussion about the continuing problem posed by adults (parents, coaches, and fans) who put too much pressure on young players involved in amateur hockey and other sports. The clever television and print campaign attempted to expose the problem of parent violence through a role-reversal format, with children yelling and screaming at their parents over rather trivial everyday tasks. The advertisements attempted to illustrate how ridiculous some parents sound when they pressure their children at play. The Canadian Hockey Association (CHA) followed this initiative with other grassroots educational programs for hockey parents including "Standard of Play," "Safe and Fun Hockey," the "Parent Program," and a series of day camps, workshops, and clinics to help establish and promote parameters of acceptable behavior in the sport. The CHA even established a sports magazine titled *Proud Hockey Parent* to showcase how parents in the country can be positive role models in the sport.

FUTURE PROSPECTS

Preventing parents from becoming overly obsessed with youth sports, restructuring youth sports to be child-centered rather than adult-oriented, and disrupting violence modeling behavior in youth sports is not an easy task with a series of quick fixes. Clearly, youth sports is a battleground where parents' egos, statuses, and dreams meet with codes of toughness and character building in sports. The results can be deadly, and if more prohibitive measures are not instituted by amateur sports leagues on the continent, one can only anticipate that more instances of parent rage will occur. Codes of conduct and parent educational programs are important first steps, but if the cultural attitude toward youth sports as a symbolic playing ground for adults is not changed, they may have little long-term impact.

See also "At-Risk" Youth in Sports; Criminal Violence During Competition; Hooliganism; Missile Throwing; Player–Fan Fighting; Referee Abuse; Rights for Young Athletes.

Further Reading: David, P. (2005). *Human Rights in Youth Sport*. London: Routledge; Lineberry, W. (2005). *Breaking and Implementing the Parent Code in Sports*. Longwood, FL: Xulon Press.

Michael Atkinson

PARKOUR (FREE RUNNING)

Over the past 20 years, major cities such as New York, Los Angeles, Vancouver, and Toronto have become social hotbeds for a gymnastic practice called *parkour*. As innovated by French "free runners" David Belle and Sébastien Foucan in the

1990s, parkour is a style of athleticism that focuses on uninterrupted gymnastics over, under, around, and through obstacles in urban settings such as buildings, park benches, statues, parked cars, and walls. Parkour moves come in the form of running, jumping, falling, climbing, or a combination of these techniques. Practitioners engage in what they call timed or distance-measured "jams" across the city. Because the practice takes place in public and on and through public property, it has fallen under some scrutiny by police in the recent past.

BACKGROUND

The roots of parkour date back more than 100 years. The modern manifestation of parkour is a particular offshoot of a style of physical training called *Hébertism*. Hébertism emerged in the early twentieth century in France through the athletic philosophies and practices of French naval officer George Hébert. A lifelong advocate of exploring intense physical training as a means of developing personal virtue, Hébert was particularly impressed by the physical development and body–environmental oneness of indigenous peoples he encountered across the African continent. Hébert was stationed in St. Pierre, Martinique, during 1902, when the town fell victim to a volcanic eruption. Hébert himself coordinated the evacuation of nearly 700 people from a local village. The experience had a profound effect on him and reinforced his belief that athletic strength and skill must be combined with courage and altruism in order to be civically useful. Hébert came to believe that the pursuit of physical perfection and communion with one's local environmental surroundings is a technique for developing one's sense of place in the physical and social environment and as a vehicle for bringing forth the underlying essence of one's humanity.

Upon his return to France in 1903, Hébert tutored at the College of Rheims where he innovated a path-breaking physical cultural lifestyle. He designed a series of apparatuses and exercises to teach what he dubbed the "Natural Method" of training. Hébert believed that individuals should train in the open environment as an unfettered animal species traversing a variety of landscapes and obstacles. Hébert's physical cultural method eschewed remedial gymnastics and the Swedish methods of athletic training popular in France at the time. For Hébert, these methods seemed unable to develop the human body harmoniously with nature or to prepare students for the moral requirements of everyday life (i.e., courage, confidence, truth, calmness, and oneness). Hébert believed that by concentrating on competition and performance within "fake" environmental spaces (such as a gymnasium), mainstream sports cultures negatively impacted the physical and social development of youth.

Hébert's Natural Method typically placed practitioners in a wooded setting, wherein they would be instructed to run a course ranging from 5–10 kilometers. Practitioners were simply told to run through the woods, over bushes, through streams, climb up and down trees, and traverse fields. Students were also instructed, at particular time or distance points, to lift fallen logs, carry and throw heavy stones, or even hang from trees. Hébert believed that by challenging his students to practice basic human muscular–skeletal movements in uncontrolled settings, they would develop qualities of strength and speed toward being able to walk, run, jump, climb, balance, throw, lift, defend oneself, and swim in practically any geographic landscape. Hébert felt that Natural Method practitioners would progressively learn to encounter and control any emotions or social situations they encountered in life. The Natural Method demanded that one possess sufficient energy, willpower, courage, coolness, and *fermeté* (firmness, strength) to conquer any physical or mental obstacle. In a moral sense, by experiencing a variety of mental and emotional states (e.g., fear, doubt, anxiety, aggression, resolve, courage, and exhaustion) during training, one cultivated a self-assurance that would lead to inner peace.

Hébert became the earliest proponent of what the French call the *parcours* (obstacle course) method of training. Modern woodland challenge courses and adventure races—comprising balance beams, ladders, rope swings, and obstacles—are often described as Hébertisme courses both in Europe and North America. It is even possible to trace a full array of modern children's playground equipment to Hébert's original *parcours* designs of the early 1900s. The French government named Hébert "Commander of the Legion of Honor" in 1995 for his life-long commitment to physical and social pedagogy.

KEY EVENTS

The contemporary name *parkour* derives from Hébert's use of the term *parcours(e)* and the French military term *parcours du combattant*. Hébert's Natural Method of training had a special impact on French military training in the 1960s. French soldiers during the Vietnam War were inspired by Hébert's method and philosophy of physical and emotional development, and they employed the Natural Method as a technique for honing their jungle-warfare skills. Among the French soldiers exposed to the Natural Method was Raymond Belle.

After his tour of duty in Vietnam, Belle taught his son David the principles of the Natural Method. The younger Belle had participated in martial arts and gymnastics as a young teen and immediately took to the method. After moving to the Paris suburb Lisses, David Belle further explored the rigors and benefits of the Natural Method with his friend Sébastien Foucan. By the age of 15, Belle and Foucan developed their own sub-urban style of the Natural Method they termed *parkour*. In the 2003 BBC documentary *Jump London*, Foucan described his initial construction of parkour as a physical and spiritual lifestyle of movement in which, "the whole town [Lisses] was there for us; there for 'free running.' You just have to look and you just have to think like children. This is the vision of parkour."

Belle and Foucan gathered followers across Europe through the 1990s. By the end of the decade, the media in France, the UK, and The Netherlands had documented the emerging lifestyle movement. Media reports predictably framed the practice as a vacuous and style-oriented urban youth counterculture. Belle later referred to parkour's insertion into the media as part of a generational "prostitution of the art" (BBC, 2003). As a result of media attention, widespread youth interest, the commercialization of parkour images and identities, and movement

BASIC PARKOUR MOVES

Cartwheel: This is begun by extending both arms straight above the head. One foot is pointed in the desired direction of the cartwheel. The arms reach for the floor in symmetry with the foot that is being used for pointing (if pointing with the right foot, reach with the right hand). The other hand follows in this motion, keeping it over the head. As the first hand goes down, the opposite foot goes up in the air. The hands should touch the floor in a straight line. The other leg is lifted by kicking off from the ground. The free runner should already be standing on his/her hands at this point momentarily as the motion continues forward.

Roundoff: A roundoff is almost like a cartwheel; the difference is in the landing. After the second hand touches the ground, land on both feet at the same time. The final position should be facing in the opposite direction of the starting position.

Roll: This technique starts from an elevated position. Jump from the elevated area toward the ground while holding the body upright, as if free falling. Land on both feet with your knees bent, letting the resistance of the ground flow through (not bending your knees will result in serious injury). Then lean the head and either one of your shoulders forward toward the ground. Push off with both feet to roll on the ground using the back. The momentum is enough to carry you back into a standing position coming off the roll; continue moving forward to keep yourself balanced.

Monkey Vault: This can be done either from a static position or a run up to the rail/wall. Grab the obstacle with both hands. The hands should be spaced on the obstacle at more than the shoulder width so that the feet and the rest of the lower body can pass between the hands. Jump with both feet, and tuck the knees into the chest. In mid-air, push back with both arms to thrust the body straight forward; this then lands you on both feet.

Superman or Dive Roll: Run toward the obstacle. When the obstacle is only about a step away, jump forward with both feet. The midsection should be arched over the obstacle. Hold both arms in front to anticipate the landing in a diving motion. Both hands should land simultaneously before leaning the head forward on the ground. In a smooth motion, the upper back touches the ground, and the rest of the body follows in a roll. The momentum should carry you back to a standing position; continue to run.

---

away from the spiritual to the spectacular aspects of parkour, Foucan and Belle disagreed vehemently over the vision and purpose of parkour. Belle continued, at least for a time, to adhere to the original principles of parkour and the essence of the Natural Method. Belle pioneered a more dare-devilish and aesthetically oriented lifestyle of Parkour now globally referred to as "urban freeflow" or "freerunning."

The ideological split between Belle and Foucan and severing of their original Lisses crew into separate parkour factions is rather stereotypical for a youth lifestyle or subculture movement, especially in the wake of the lifestyle's mass mediation and popularity (i.e., parkour clothing, language, moves, and jargon). Interestingly, Belle and his followers attempted to police the Hébertisme essence of parkour by publicly denouncing its popularity as a style/commodity culture.

Foucan and his converts, by contrast, now sell parkour to global audiences through television commercials and documentaries, movies, clothing lines, training schools, video games, and even international parkour competitions. While Belle's loyalists remain somewhat resistance-oriented and purist, Foucan's brand of parkour continues to undergo the transformation into a mainstream sport that so many other alternative youth sports have fallen prey to over the past 30 years.

Since the late 1990s, some parkour crews in cities such as Toronto and New York have been referred to as thugs, gangs, or mere street criminals. Critics in government and on the police force have used conservative crime theorists Kelling and Wilson's (1982) inner-city "broken windows" theory to justify a series of public and media campaigns intent on making parkour an official crime. Kelling and Wilson published an article in the *Atlantic Monthly* advocating this theory, which states, "If the first broken window in a building is not repaired, then people who like breaking windows will assume that no one cares about the building and more windows will be broken. Soon the building will have no windows" (1982, 29). The theory suggests that crime results from ineffective and haphazard policing of broken windows in urban settings. From the broken windows vantage point, strict and consistent law enforcement is the primary ingredient for establishing safe communities. Kelling and Wilson argued that if loitering youths (or in this case, running and jumping youths) are left unchallenged, their behavior will likely evolve into more socially consequential offenses such as theft, assault, and drug use. Other targeted broken windows populations in Kelling and Wilson's theoretical model include panhandlers, beggars, muggers, pickpockets, and alcoholics. Serious street crime flourishes in areas in which disorderly behavior goes unchecked. The unchecked panhandler is, in effect, the first broken window. Muggers and robbers, whether opportunistic or professional, believe they reduce their chances of being caught or even identified if they operate on streets where potential victims are already intimidated by prevailing conditions.

If left in disrepair, a single broken window (such as parkour members, the police have argued) causes local neighborhood inhabitants to lose community pride and respect. Because of the residents' collective retreat into their homes

---

REFERENCES TO PARKOUR IN POPULAR CULTURE

Films: *Jump London*, *Banlieue 13*, *Yamakasi*, *Jump Britain*, *Casino Royale*, *Live Free or Die Hard*, and *The Bourne Ultimatum* all contain parkour chase scenes.

Video games: *Lara Croft Tomb Raider: Legend*; *Lara Croft Tomb Raider: Anniversary*; *Æon Flux*; *Free Running*; *Assassin's Creed*; *Tony Hawk's American Wasteland*; *Ninja Gaiden*; *Rayman DS*; *Prince of Persia*; *Crackdown*; *Prototype*; *Getting Up: Contents Under Pressure*.

Television: Free runners have appeared on the British shows *Top Gear* and *Britain's Got Talent* and on U.S. shows *The Friday Night Project*, *Modern Marvels*, *Heroes*, and *Taurus World Stunt Awards*.

and decreased civic participation, other windows break. Beginning with youth disorder and disobedience (i.e., parkour), crime levels rise. The effort and cost to fix the condition becomes insurmountable in the eyes of the police, and the community is lost as a culture of deviance takes root. If youth disorder and disobedience are broken windows, then parkour can be understood as at least a cracked pane. Seemingly harmless youth misbehaviors such as jumping over park statues or running down stair railings cannot be tolerated for fear of escalating behaviors. Local police and city officials in Toronto have condemned local residents who allow parkour to exist in their neighborhoods. City councillors in Toronto and New York have implied that city members who complain about drugs, guns, and youth violence need only to examine their own tolerance of broken windows (such as Parkour and other youth groups) to understand why urban crimes are flourishing. Between 2004 and 2006, governmental critics of parkour as a "broken window" quickly suggested how shifting the cause of crime and the responsibility for crime reduction from the state to everyday citizens obfuscates broader crime-related problems such as unemployment, unequal access to education, race and ethnic discrimination, and cultural intolerance.

FUTURE PROSPECTS

If the historical analysis of subcultures in sports teaches anything, it is that once an alternative youth group enters into sports worlds, it becomes assimilated into normative cultural practice therein relatively quickly. The case of parkour appears to be scarcely different in this regard. The corporatization and mass commercialization of the practice has already begun, and as scores of youth begin to buy into the sport, much of the traditional aspects of the parkour philosophy have been either rejected or forgotten. Pockets of traditionalists may hold fast to earlier parkour ideologies and techniques of practice, but the global parkour movement has already been transformed into a full-fledged mainstream youth sport.

See also Cool Pose; Skateboarding; Snowboarding; Surfing and New Water Sports; X Games; Yoga and Alternative Fitness.

Further Reading: BBC. (2003). *Jump London.* Originally aired September 9; Delaplace, J.-M. (2005). *George Hébert: Sculpter du Corps.* Paris: Vuibert; Kelling, G., and Wilson, J. (1982). Broken Windows. *Atlantic Monthly* 249: 29–38.

Michael Atkinson

PARTNER ABUSE AMONG ATHLETES

Does violence against women increase during the Super Bowl? While this is a popular myth, there is little evidence to support that rates of domestic violence increase on game day. In all likelihood, the myth emerged in 1993, when domestic violence advocates convinced NBC to run a Public Service Announcement (PSA) during the game. What is clear is that rates of domestic violence are already alarmingly high; nearly one-third of women report being physically or sexually abused by a husband or boyfriend at some point in their lives. According to the National Coalition Against Domestic Violence, 61 percent of female homicide victims are killed by spouses or intimate acquaintances, with an estimated 1,300 women killed each year. Statistics also reveal that abuse starts at a young age: 40 percent of girls between the ages of 14 and 17 years old report that they know someone who has been hit, beaten, or slapped by their boyfriend. And, as with sexual assault, athletes are overrepresented as batterers.

BACKGROUND

The first women's suffrage movement of the mid-to-late 1800s saw the first semiorganized attempts to draw attention to abuse in the home, a phenomenon that has been recorded in ancient historical documents. Spokespersons for this movement, including Elizabeth Cady Stanton, backed the temperance movement in large part because they lived through husbands who got drunk and came home violent. In 1871, Alabama and Massachusetts were the first states to criminalize all forms of physical assaults by husbands against their wives, and by World War I, all states had outlawed wife beating. Yet, laws were still enforced irregularly, and women who were abused generally lacked other resources to help. Although abuse by athletes in these earlier eras is not well-documented, there is some suggestion that baseball great Ty Cobb abused his wife.

In the 1970s, the second wave of feminists brought more attention to the problem of partner abuse, naming it domestic violence and helping to establish increased legal and police protection as well as shelters and resources for victims. Before 1976, only a few states had adequate provisions for arresting or removing batterers from their homes. Yet still, persons with fame, money, and influence were unlikely to be arrested and convicted of domestic violence, hence little is known about cases involving athletes. In 1983, Tracey Thurman's husband stabbed her 13 times and stomped on her head, all in front of her children. She was left partially paralyzed. She won a $1.9 million suit against the Torrington, Connecticut, police because they had failed to respond to Tracey's repeated calls. This case was pivotal and prompted dramatic change in police response, including mandatory arrest policies in many states.

In the mid-1990s, a spate of domestic violence allegations against professional athletes prompted national attention to the issue. Between 1990 and 1996, 150 formal complaints were issued against Division I or professional athletes for domestic violence, with 77 of those complaints filed in 1995 and 1996. All but seven of the allegations involved football or basketball players. In seven of the cases, the victims were pregnant. Abusers were convicted in only 28 of the 150 cases, and many of those involved plea bargains. Jeff Benedict researched criminal complaints of domestic violence involving National Basketball Association (NBA) players for his 2004 book, *Out of Bounds: Inside the NBA's Culture of Rape, Violence & Crime.* He found 33 complaints during the 2001–2002 season but suggested that was a significant underreport.

Unfortunately, domestic violence and sexual assault are underreported, in particular in cases involving athletes. It is estimated that victims call the police not after the first but after five incidents. Reporting is even worse among certain demographic groups, with estimates as low as 5 percent of incidents of rape or domestic violence occurring on college campuses being reported. Still, some believe that athletes may be targeted by women seeking money or fame. Or they simply do not believe that their favorite star could be an abuser. Boston Celtics star Robert Parrish was abusive to his wife, Nancy, who kept quiet about it for years. Nancy said she thought no one would believe her because Robert was considered to be a "gentleman" on the court.

Athletes may have a difficult time understanding how to behave at home when they are immersed on a daily basis in what is essentially a violent culture. In the United States, males in general are told that to be masculine is to be tough and aggressive, and nowhere is this more true than in athletics. The male peer culture that forms in sports, in particular those with some element of contact, has been found to reinforce antifemale attitudes. It also encourages silence so that athletes who hear their peers denigrating women or know about abusive behavior generally do not speak up. Even today, many people understand domestic violence as a "woman's issue" and tend to look to individual, or micro-level, explanations. That is, they say men who abuse are sick or only did it because they are drunk. Other abuses by men are chalked up to "boys will be boys." This is exacerbated in cases involving athletes, as these are our heroes, "our guys," as one author explained. We don't want to believe that there may be something about the way we as a society socialize males in general, and male athletes in particular, that contributes. Yet, research has demonstrated that there are likely several elements of the training high-level athletes receive that make them more likely to be biased against women and gays. One way to demonstrate your superiority over these groups is to act out violently.

Additionally, athletes may receive far more leniency from the criminal justice system than do others accused of criminal offenses, as many of the cases listed in this entry demonstrate. While the average male arrested for domestic violence typically goes through the criminal justice system, many times athletes are able to avoid serious sanctions based on their finances, notoriety, and connections.

KEY EVENTS

By no means an exhaustive list, the following cases illustrate the scope of the problem as well as the responses to it. Examples come from all the major sports. In June of 1988, just four months after former heavyweight champion Mike Tyson married Robin Givens, the actress and her family accused Tyson of abuse. He responded, "Anyone with a grain of sense would know that if I punched my wife I would rip her head off. It's all lies. I have never laid a finger on her." On September 20, 1988, Givens said on national television that she feared her husband. Only a week later, Givens filed for divorce. In a one-week period in December of the same year, two different women accused Tyson of grabbing them inappropriately. One of the women was awarded a pathetic $100 by a New York civil court. Tyson's problems escalated when, in 1991, Miss Black America pageant contestant Desiree Washington accused Tyson of rape. He was convicted in 1992 and sentenced to 10 years in prison. He served 3 years total.

Consider some of the most widely publicized cases of abuse between 1992 and 1995: former Portland Trailblazer's guard Rod Strickland was arrested when he gave a former girlfriend a black eye; a day after scoring four touchdowns for the University of Nebraska, Laurence Phillips was charged with assaulting his girlfriend; former National Football League (NFL) Man of the Year Warren Moon publicly apologized for repeatedly assaulting his wife.; Kansas City Chiefs running back Harvey Williams was arrested for domestic violence twice in 1993, then again in 1995 after he had been traded to the L.A. Raiders; Chiefs receiver Tim Barnett was arrested twice for battering his wife; in 1993, 310-pound Houston Oiler Doug Smith choked, head-butted, and punched his wife, Rebecca, in the eyes so hard she needed head surgery; and, Louisville Basketball player Troy Smith slammed his fianceé, Kelly Dwyer, to the ground when an argument "got out of hand."

The most well-publicized case of domestic violence involving an athlete was that of O.J. Simpson. In 1995, Simpson was found not guilty of murdering his former wife, Nicole Brown Simpson, and her friend Ronald Goldman. Throughout the investigation and during the trial, evidence emerged that Simpson had battered his former wife. Jurors heard a 911 tape made by Nicole Brown Simpson in which O.J. shouted at her while she pleaded for help. They also saw pictures of Nicole with her face terribly bruised. Many domestic violence advocates found the case to be full of mixed messages. While it did succeed in drawing the public's attention to domestic violence in general, as well as abuse perpetrated by athletes, Simpson's acquittal may have sent the message that battering men can get away with it. In San Diego, Sgt. Ann O'Dell reported that some batterers would threaten their partners by saying, "I'll O.J. you."

Homerun king Barry Bonds was arrested in 1993 for threatening his wife, choking her, and allegedly throwing her against a car and kicking her while she was on the ground. In 1997, Wil Cordero of the Boston Red Sox was arrested for spousal abuse. Although he was released by the Red Sox, he was contracted with the Pittsburgh Pirates for a not-paltry $9 million contract. Baseball player Jose Canseco has been in court numerous times for domestic violence charges.

On January 28, 2000, Colorado Rockies Pitcher Pedro Astacio pleaded guilty to third degree assault for punching his wife. Barely a week later, Bobby Chouinard, middle receiver for the Arizona Diamondbacks, was released from the team after admitting he choked, slapped, and held a gun to the head of his wife, Erica. In 2000, Colorado Avalanche goaltender Patrick Roy was arrested for domestic violence just days after he set the record for career victories by a National Hockey League (NHL) goalie. Roy admitted to police that he ripped two doors off their hinges during an argument in the couple's bedroom. His wife called 911 fearing what else he might do. The charges against Roy were ultimately dropped.

In 2001, New Jersey Nets star Jason Kidd pleaded guilty to assaulting his wife. Kidd was fined $200 and ordered to take anger management classes. His record was later expunged. Afterwards, he was heckled on the court as a wife beater, but the NBA did not reprimand him. In 2007, Kidd shocked sports fans when he took out a restraining order against his wife, Joumana Kidd. He accused Joumana of extreme cruelty and alleged she physically and mentally abused him over the course of their 10-year marriage. In addition, Kidd alleged that his wife's behavior negatively impacted their children.

Between September 11, 2001, and January 2002, the White Ribbon Campaign, a Canada-based, male-led movement to end domestic violence, documented 11 allegations involving athletes. In 2002, Milwaukee Bucks All-Star forward Glenn Robinson, suspecting his ex-fiancee Jonta French had been with another man, arrived visibly drunk at the home she shared with their 3-year-old daughter and badgered French to let him in. Upon entering the home, Robinson grabbed her hair, dragged her through the home, slammed her head against a wall, and banged her body against other objects. He then forced her onto the bed and left her, terrified, while he went to the master bedroom to obtain the gun he had left at the home a week earlier. French had hidden the weapon so the toddler wouldn't find it, which enraged Robinson. French managed to run out of the home, screaming, and Robinson was arrested. Little media coverage addressed the case because, according to Jeff Benedict, the media was more concerned with the domestic violence allegations against an even bigger star. Only three days before Robinson's arrest, Philadelphia police arrested the NBA's 2001 Most Valuable Player Allen Iverson based on a call they received from a man stating that Iverson had thrown his wife, Tawanna, out of their home naked. Iverson was also accused of entering the home later that same evening with a gun in the waist of his pants, threatening the same man who had called the police earlier and demanding to know where his wife was. Iverson was charged with 14 counts, including false imprisonment, criminal trespass, conspiracy, making terroristic threats, and a variety of gun offenses. At trial, the judge dismissed 12 of the 14 charges, then later the remaining 2.

In March 2003, former heavyweight champion Riddick Bowe was arrested on charges of second-degree assault against his wife. This was less than a week before Bowe was to begin serving prison time for abducting his first wife and their five children. Former Junior lightweight and lightweight champion Diego Corrales, who passed away in May 2007, served 14 months in prison for beating his pregnant wife. In 2002, Filmmaker Spike Lee released his second HBO documentary, this one on football great Jim Brown, who once threw a woman he was dating off a balcony during an argument and, at the time of filming, was serving a six-month sentence for domestic violence.

FUTURE PROSPECTS

In 1996, two members of Congress proposed legislation requiring athletes to spearhead a national campaign against domestic violence. The National Collegiate Athletic Association (NCAA) opposed the legislation, arguing it unfairly suggests that athletes bear responsibility for the problem. One NCAA official even called the legislation racist, suggesting that it was a way to target blacks, who are overrepresented in college and professional athletics. The legislation did not pass. The NFL expressed that it was committed to helping reduce the problem of domestic violence, but they did not feel this bill was the best way to do so.

There are, however, a number of excellent programs that address the problem of athletes and domestic violence. One of the most successful is Mentors in Violence Prevention (MVP), which uses a bystander approach and realistic scenarios relevant to both students and athletes to empower people to intervene in helpful ways when they hear about or witness abuse. The Family Violence Prevention Fund offers great materials on coaching boys into men, including curricula and downloadable posters. In 2001, Green Bay Packers guard Marco Rivera and his wife, Michelle, worked with Verizon Wireless to create a domestic violence PSA. In 2002, New York Yankees Manager Joe Torre founded the Joe Torre Safe at Home Foundation, which provides educational programs to help end the cycle of domestic violence.

See also Rape and Sexual Assault.

Further Reading: Benedict, J. (1997). *Public Heroes, Private Felons.* Boston, MA: Northeastern University Press; Benedict, J. (1998). *Athletes and Acquaintance Rape.* Thousand Oaks, CA: Sage; Benedict, J. (1998). *Pros and Cons: The Criminals Who Play in the NFL.* New York: Grand Central Press; Benedict, J. (2004). *Out of Bounds: Inside the NBA's Culture of Rape, Violence & Crime.* New York: HarperCollins; Finley, P., Fountain, J., and Finley, L. (2008, forthcoming). *Sport Scandals.* Westport, CT: Praeger; Katz, J. (2006). *The Macho Paradox.* Naperville, IL: Sourcebooks, Inc; Kimmel, M., and Messner, M. (Eds.). (2001). *Men's Lives.* Boston, MA: Allyn & Bacon; McBride, J. (1995). *War, Battering, and Other Sports: The Gulf Between American Men and Women.* Atlantic Highlands, NJ: Humanities Press.

Laura L. Finley

PLAYER–FAN FIGHTING

Player–fan fighting is one of the rarest forms of sports violence. In general, player–fan altercations involve fist-fights, missile throwing, verbal abuse, and quite frequently, injury to one or both parties. These events occur within stadium grounds, typically during the course of play or during an intermission. Males are predominantly involved in player–fan fighting, and participants are almost always institutionally reprimanded for the events. A review of North American sports history reveals that baseball, ice hockey, and basketball have been "hotbeds" for player–fan fighting.

BACKGROUND

Player–fan altercations are indeed difficult to systematically predict or control. Some simplistically attribute fan alcohol consumption or their criminal (genetic) predispositions to the cause of player–fan fighting, but historical evidence seems to suggest that episodes of player–fan violence require more in-depth analysis. Modern stadiums have been architecturally designed to distance players from fans as a first measure of protection and limits have been placed on the quantity of alcohol fans may consume during games. Yet, player–fan outbursts continue.

Perhaps with the increased media coverage of sports over the past 50 years and the public's appetite for controversy in sports worlds, the problem of player–fan fighting has never been more publicly visible or debated.

Experts often emphasize the biopsychological causes of sports violence using the Freudian-inspired "instinct theory." Instinct theory, which was popularized by Konrad Lorenz in the book *On Aggression* (1963), explains violence and aggression as Darwinian struggles between people for social superiority. Player–fan violence and aggression occur naturally in any competitive context, and Lorenz attributes aggression in competition to its critical role in clarifying the ranking of the members of a group. Lorenz and other instinct theorists also suggest that aggression is a motivator to participate in close, hand-to-hand struggles as a form of instinctual release (i.e., the release of emotions in players of fans that are built up in their everyday lives). Given all of the social rules that limit the use of aggression and violence in everyday life and the degree to which the instinct to aggress continues to underpin the human psyche, contexts such as sports allow individuals to release their naturally aggressive tendencies.

A second major explanation of player–fan violence is more social rather than individualistic in its orientation. This includes Gurr's (1970) relative deprivation theory, originally made popular in his book *Why Men Rebel*. Relative deprivation has been used to explain grievance, social hostility, and aggression. Gurr defines relative deprivation as "actors' perception of discrepancy between their value expectations and their value capabilities" (p. 24). In other words, relative deprivation is the gap between that "to which people believe they are rightfully entitled" and that which "they think they are capable of getting and keeping" (p. 24). Deprivation leads to frustration and aggression and is not based on wants or needs alone but on wants and needs that people feel they deserve. Therefore, a fan who feels that his wants and needs for his team's victory should be met within a contest will also feel a sense of entitlement to that outcome. If his team's success is not realized (if, for instance, the players do not perform as the fan expects or wants) then the individual feels personally deprived by the outcome, and violence may result toward the source of the perceived deprivation, such as a particular player.

Albert Bandura's (1973) even more social account of aggression is summarized in the book *Aggression: A Social Learning Analysis*. Bandura uses what he calls "learning theory" to describe how punishment and reward play an important role in the modeling of all behaviors. He argues that violence and aggression, like any other behavior, are learned through observation and imitation. Bandura believed that people also learn to aggress by observing the consequences of others' actions. Quite simply, fans learn to be violent from other fans and model their violent outbursts after watching violence committed by players on the field. Proponents of this theory have used it to explain why player–fan violence occurs most frequently in contact or quasicontact sports. The basis of the theory, then, is fans will imitate what they see players do on the field. If aggression is defined as pleasing or rewarding for the fan over time, it will continue.

While each of these theories has been used by policymakers in North American sports, none of them seem to predict (with any consistency) how and when player–fan violence will erupt.

KEY EVENTS

On November 19, 2004, National Basketball Association (NBA) basketball players Ben Wallace of the Detroit Pistons and Ron Artest of the Indiana Pacers started a brawl during a game that drew attention to the enduring problem of player–spectator violence in professional sports. The game took place in Auburn Hills, Michigan, and the brawl started when Artest fouled Wallace late in the game. Wallace, upset at being fouled hard when the game was effectively over (the Pacers led 97–82), responded by shoving Artest. The two started a skirmish near the scorer's table. Artest walked to the sideline but fell down onto the scorer's table. Pistons fan John Green then threw a cup of beer at Artest, hitting him on the shoulder. Artest jumped into the front-row seats and confronted the man he believed to be responsible, which then started a brawl between Pistons fans and several of the Pacers. Artest returned to the basketball court and punched Pistons fan A. J. Shackleford, who was apparently taunting Artest verbally. This fight resulted in the game being stopped with less than a minute remaining. Artest and teammates Jermaine O'Neal and Stephen Jackson were suspended indefinitely the day after the game, as was Wallace. On November 21, the NBA announced that Artest would be suspended for the remainder of the season (73 games plus playoff appearances)—the longest nondrug or betting-related suspension in NBA history to date (losing an estimated $5 million in wages as a result). Eight other players (four Pacers and four Pistons) received suspensions without pay that ranged from 1 to 30 games. Each of the Pacers players involved were levied fines and ordered by police to perform community service. Several fans were also charged and were barred for life from attending events at the Palace arena.

Later in 2004, Frank Francisco of the Texas Rangers baseball team was arrested after hitting two fans with a thrown chair during a game against the Oakland Athletics. Francisco was arrested on a charge of aggravated battery after he threw a chair into the right-field box seats near the Rangers' bullpen. The chair hit a man in the head then bounced and struck a woman on her left temple. The year proved to be pivotal in the world of professional sports in North America because on the heels of these events, the NBA, Major League Baseball (MLB), the National Hockey League (NHL), and the National Football League (NFL) all instituted new codes of conduct for players and stiffened institutional penalties for any players fighting with fans. Critics have argued, though, that too much emphasis has been placed on players' actions and not those of fans.

The cases in the sidebar illustrate that, despite popular belief in Western sports cultures and media, problems of player–fan violence are not isolated to European or South American sports cultures. Especially in the case of professional baseball, there seem to be patterns of player–fan violence that require further study and explanation. Standard policy and practice has been to either deny or ignore the systematic nature of sports as a cultural battleground for players and fans. Offenders are described as atypical fans, and events are viewed as isolated episodes in a sport.

NOTORIOUS CASES OF PLAYER–FAN VIOLENCE

2001—NHL player Tie Domi doused some Philadelphia Flyers fans with water and wrestled another while in the penalty box.

2000—Chicago Cubs fans showered the Los Angeles Dodgers bullpen with beer and attempted to steal catcher Chad Kreuter's baseball cap. Dodgers coaches John Shelby and Rick Dempsey joined Kreuter and a slew of other Dodgers and went into the stands to retaliate. Nine days later, 16 players and 3 coaches were handed suspensions for their involvement in the melee.

1999—In an Astros–Brewers game in Milwaukee, a 23-year-old fan ran onto the field and jumped Houston right fielder Bill Spiers. As Spiers tried to shake him off, his teammates came to the rescue. Spiers suffered whiplash and was bloodied and bruised. The fan was arrested and held on $250,000 in bail on charges of battery and disorderly conduct.

1995—With the Houston Rockets basketball team on the way to a 120–82 loss, Vernon Maxwell of the Rockets lost his cool and plunged 12 rows deep into the stands in order to punch a fan who had been heckling him. Maxwell got a 10-game suspension and $20,000 fine from the NBA.

1991—Chicago White Sox player Albert Belle, who disliked being called "Joey" by fans, was playing against the Cleveland Indians in the Cleveland Stadium when fan Jeff Pillar yelled from the left-field stands, "Hey, Joey, keg party at my place after the game, c'mon over." Belle retaliated by picking up a foul ball and throwing a perfect strike at Pillar's chest from about 15 feet away, leaving Pillar with a weltering souvenir. Belle received a one-week suspension from play.

1984—Atlanta Braves pitcher Pascual Perez hit San Diego Padres batter Alan Wiggins on the first pitch to set off a beanball war in the game. Brawls between Atlanta and San Diego players erupted in the second, fifth, eighth, and ninth innings. Late in the game, Atlanta fans participated in the brawls. One threw a mug of beer at Padres' player Kurt Bevacqua's head, and Bevacqua climbed onto the top of the dugout in pursuit before police got in his way. Another fan was wrestled to the ground by Atlanta's Chris Chambliss and Jerry Royster near the third-base line. Five fans in all were led away from the action in handcuffs.

1979—During an NHL game in New York, Boston Bruins and New York Rangers fans engaged in a brawl during the last moments of the third period. They fought one another and threw objects onto the ice. One of them punched Boston player Stan Jonathan, setting off a melee with Bruins players charging into the stands. Terry O'Reilly and Gerry Cheevers of the Bruins went into the crowd to fight, and other players from both teams followed. Rangers' fan John Kaptain was beaten over the head with his shoe, a woman was slapped across the face, and other fans were punched. Four Rangers fans were arrested for their part in the brawl.

1922—Babe Ruth was booed by New York Yankee fans during a game after he had been ejected for arguing calls with an umpire. On his way off the field, he paused to bow before the fans. Fans heckled him a while longer, and Ruth jumped onto the dugout roof and into the stands, chased a heckler until he was too far out of reach, then returned to the dugout roof. Ruth got a brief suspension and a $200 fine for the episode.

1912—A couple of day's worth of heckling by New York Yankees fans finally got to Ty Cobb of the Detroit Tigers. During a game, Cobb vaulted into the stands behind the Tigers' bench and went right after a man identified, pseudonymously, as "Otto Blotz." Cobb severely beat Mr. Blotz and was suspended for one week.

FUTURE PROSPECTS

At a bare minimum, it has been argued that all sports leagues must institute and use stringent, zero-tolerance policies that prohibit any and all forms of physical interaction between players and fans. Equally, there is strong evidence to suggest that while police intervention does not appear to have a deterrence effect, anyone involved in player–fan fighting should be criminally prosecuted. Given the precipitating causes of most of the player–fan altercations highlighted in this chapter, leagues and stadiums might do well to strongly enforce antiabuse language policies. Finally, a publicly unpopular suggestion has been to either limit the alcohol consumption of any fan to one unit or prohibit alcohol from being served in sports stadiums in which player–fan fights have occurred.

See also Criminal Violence During Competition; Missile Throwing; Postevent Riots; Taunting.

Further Reading: Bandura, A. (1973). *Aggression: A Social Learning Analysis.* Englewood Cliffs, NJ: Prentice Hall; Gurr, T. (1970). *Why Men Rebel.* Princeton, NJ: Princeton University Press; Lorenz, K. (1963). *On Aggression.* San Diego, CA: Harcourt Brace.

Michael Atkinson

POSTEVENT RIOTS

Postevent riots may be defined as collective forms of civil disobedience occurring directly after a sports contest. Often referred to as celebratory riots, a pattern of them has crystallized in the past 20 years. Celebratory riots most typically follow the final game of a playoff championship and are characterized by fan vandalism, looting, nudity and sexuality, fist-fighting, and public drunkenness. Not to be confused with fan rioting that occurs in the wake of highly controversial on-field calls or political events in sports, celebratory riots are typically the misplaced and illegal expression of fan excitement and jubilation.

BACKGROUND

Postevent, celebratory riots are yet another poorly understood form of social deviance in sports. The problem of fan rioting is generally ascribed by sports experts and agents of social control to English soccer hooligans and dismissed as a feature of the North American sports world. But a closer inspection of fan behavior in North America reveals that consistent patterns of celebratory rioting cut across many professional sports. Less evident, though, is how and why celebratory riots occur and what institutional means may be employed to contain them.

The leading explanations of celebratory riots in sports derive from collective psychology, especially the theories of crowd behavior developed by Sigmund Freud, Gabriel Tarde, and Gustav le Bon. In their respective theories, riotous forms of celebration occur when base human emotions are stimulated by an event and then allowed to run freely in a large group; individuals "disappear" into the crowd, and their social responsibilities are loosened. People in the crowd are not led by any single individual nor does the mob have a single cultural logic underpinning its collective action. Instead, people come to "herd" around others who are engaged in dangerous activities in a relative pack mentality. It is not well known how, when, or why people's base human emotions and instincts are triggered when in sports mobs. At a basic level, though, we must appreciate that sports is a social context where base emotions and instincts are deliberately stimulated as a routine part of the games.

Sports have been historically regarded as a social timeout from the stresses and emotional strictures of everyday life. Sports offers one of the few social spaces where boisterous and publicly displayed forms of emotion are permitted among large groups of people. Part of sports' allure, then, is the degree to which emotions among fans are purposefully pushed to the limits; antagonisms between rival fans are accentuated, fan loyalties develop into strong feelings of pride and shame related to team's winning or losing streaks, and immense joy or sorrow results among fans when the symbolic wars in sports come to an end. Playoff or championship sports events are especially noteworthy here because emotions are deliberately stirred up by event organizers and commercial industries promoting sports as a means of encouraging investment in the contests.

Viewed from these perspectives, sports is a scheduled form of Saturnalia for fans and spectators. Being in a crowd and being exposed to the emotional thrill-ride that sports can provide manifests into a *sui generis* feeling, wherein people often describe "losing themselves" in collective joy, agony, anger, fear, anxiety, or relief. Participants purposefully immerse themselves in the world of sports to indulge in deep-seated emotions that are otherwise pushed behind the scenes of normal public life. When the majority of people in a crowd are there to directly experience emotionality along these lines, it creates a highly charged atmosphere that is often described as electric. In le Bon's terms, these are the classic conditions of crowd contagion that lead to most forms of public rioting.

A problem for sports teams and organizers is how to create atmospheres of excitement in sports but eliminate the potential for crowd contagion. Contagion theory teaches that sports riots emerge rather spontaneously after people have been almost hypnotized by common, powerful emotional sentiment in a crowd. If people are emotionally "charged up," view sports as a site for releasing penned-up emotions in their life, and are exposed to an event at a game that stimulates the unbridled release of their emotions, then crowd disorder may occur. From this theoretical vantage point, being a member of a sports crowd potentially exposes a person to a situation in which dangerous social emotions and instinctual tendencies (resting underneath the thin veneer of people's learned capacity for self-control) are likely to be released.

On the other hand, hordes of spectators might actually come to sports, or near to where sports victories will be celebrated or defeats mourned, to purposefully create a "bother" and instigate riots. Jack Katz (1998) refers to how individuals pursue "sneaky thrills" in these ways and others. Katz's explanation jibes with what psychologists refer to as convergence theory. Convergence theory suggests that crowd behavior is not a product of emergent features and emotions in the crowd itself but rather a handful of like-minded people deliberately bring their interests in doing social deviance to crowds, thus, crowds amount to a convergence of like-minded individuals. While the crowd contagion theories of Freud, le Bon, and others state that the feeling of being in a crowd actually causes people to act in a base (or what they called "leveled") way, convergence theory says the opposite: that people who wish to act in a certain way come together to form crowds. In the case study of celebratory sports riots, both explanations seem to have empirical credibility.

KEY EVENTS

Riotous behavior among fans gained wider public attention in the 1970s around several high-profile events. At an October 18, 1977, NFL game at Schaefer Stadium in Foxboro, Massachusetts, between the New England Patriots and the New York Jets broadcast nationally on *Monday Night Football,* fans engaged in celebratory rioting while the game still progressed. The New England Patriots took a large lead in the fourth quarter of the game, and fans were jubilant at first. But their joy turned to anger quickly as a fight between rival fans in the stadium lead to a collective melee in the stands. Fans jumped onto the field, disrupting the game; items were hurled onto the field, and interpersonal violence escalated. Over 30 spectators were taken to the hospital for minor injuries, and one was treated for a critical stab wound. Two fans lost their lives during the riot; each suffered a heart attack. While attempting to resuscitate one of them at the event, a police officer was urinated upon by several fans. Forty-five fans were arrested for their varied involvement in the riot.

The lion's share of celebratory sports rioting does not, however, take place in the confines of a stadium. Celebratory riots generally unfold near a stadium directly following a game and can involved thousands of fans. There have been large-scale, postevent riots in each the following cities: Detroit (October 1968, October 1984, June 1990), Pittsburgh (October 1971, January 1975), Toronto (November 1983), Montreal (December 1955, May 1986, June 1993), Hamilton (November 1986), Chicago (June 1992), Dallas (June 1993), and Vancouver (June 1994). The escalation of their occurrence through the late 1980s and early 1990s in all of the four major professional sports in North America gave support to convergence-theory proponents who believed that rioters were intentionally staging planned disobedience after playoff games.

The city of Montreal has been the site of some of the most notorious and destructive celebratory riots in Canadian sports. In 1986, 5,000 people rampaged through downtown Montreal following the team's Stanley Cup victory over the Calgary Flames. Strangely enough, no one had anticipated a postevent riot, and the Montreal police were so poorly prepared to stop the violence that Quebec courts ruled the police criminally negligent. With the Canadiens poised to win another cup on June 9, 1993, Montreal authorities deployed close to 1,000 police officers, many of them helmeted riot troopers. The city had been lulled into a potential sense of false security, potentially, after the Canadiens Stanley Cup loss to the Flames in 1989 that occurred without civil disobedience in Montreal. Moments after the final game ended in 1993 (with the Canadiens winning), thousands of people descended onto Ste-Catherine Street in Montreal, setting bonfires, overturning cars, breaking windows, and looting stores. By the next morning, 15 city buses and 47 police cars had been destroyed; 168 people had been injured, including 49 police officers; and 115 people were jailed. Damage to city property was estimated at more than C$10 million.

Only a year later, police in Vancouver had learned very little about crowd control from the Montreal debacle. One of the ugliest postevent riots in hockey history was triggered not by the overindulgent celebration of a team victory but by a defeat. On the night of June 14, 1994, following the Vancouver Canucks' loss to the New York Rangers in the seventh game of the Stanley Cup finals, an angry mob of 75,000 filled the streets of downtown Vancouver. The mood of the crowd was initially upbeat, but in classic contagion theory model, things turned ugly when drunken brawls broke out among rival fans at the corner of Robson and Thurlow streets. More than 50 glass windows at the downtown Eaton's clothing store were smashed. It took nearly five hours before 540 Vancouver police and Royal Canadian Mounted Police officers could restore order. Dozens of people were arrested, and more than 200 were injured. The most seriously injured was 17-year-old Ryan Berntt, who was accidentally shot in the head by police with a rubber bullet. He spent nearly a month in the hospital and suffered permanent brain damage. Berntt later spent 9 months in jail for his part in the riot.

When the Lakers beat the Indiana Pacers in Los Angeles to win the National Basketball Association (NBA) Championship in 2000, the city's first major pro sports championship in 12 years, a mob of postevent celebrators staged a mini riot after the game. Riot police fired rubber bullets to disperse the crowd, and many fled south through city streets, shattering windows and looting stores. At least 74 vehicles at 7 car dealerships were damaged. Most of those involved in the violence came from a crowd of about 10,000 that had watched the game on a giant screen monitor outside the arena on 11th Street, near the Staples Center. One group tore branches from trees and stuffed them into a car before setting it on fire. A city bus, two police cars, a van, and other vehicles were also torched. As the night went on, groups of men formed conga lines around scattered fires and danced in circles, while some occasionally leaped over the flames. As police forced rioters away, the crowds moved down quiet city streets only to spontaneously unite again in smaller, more numerous groups. By midnight, most of the crowds had dispersed. Estimated total damage to Los Angeles property was nearly $1 million.

FLAMES' GIRLS GONE WILD

During the 2004 playoffs, Calgary Flames fans poured onto 17th Avenue in Calgary nightly. During a typical evening's events, female fans, party revelers, and passers-by were asked to expose their breasts by male fans in a mardi gras fashion. The men developed specific chants and cheers to encourage them, such as "shirts off for Kiprussof" (the name of the Calgary Flames goaltender). Women were often thrown beads for taking their shirts off, had their pictures taken by people while flashing, and even participated in "best chest" contests staged by sports bars in the area. Women often told press agents that they have never flashed in public before. Entire Web sites were created to showcase either scantily clad or partially nude "Flames girls." Many of the Web sites were shut down or altered after female fans and police protested. City councillors were outraged by the flashing/sexual tradition on the Red Mile and begged for it to stop. The Calgary Flames organization was noticeably quiet on the subject, neither supporting nor condemning the practice outright.

In 2004, the Calgary Flames qualified for the Stanley Cup playoffs for the first time since 1996. In the early stages of the playoffs, Flames fans gathered to watch televised broadcasts of the games in bars and restaurants on 17th Avenue (a street leading directly to the Saddledome where the Flames play). After the matches, fans would mill about, cheer, honk car horns, and sing songs if the Flames had won. After their first playoff round victory over the Vancouver Canucks, a spontaneous party developed on the streets, drawing thousands of fans (many of whom had not even watched the final game on television). As the team progressed through the playoffs, more people gathered on 17th Avenue nightly (irrespective of when the games were being held) to engage in hockey-related partying. The street quickly became dubbed the Red Mile, in reference to the color of the Flames' team jersey. Each night saw the number of people increase and the party atmosphere intensify. Social norms were progressively relaxed during evening-long parties, including an internationally mediated tradition of flashing among female fans. Dozens of local merchant complaints regarding riotous, sexually explicit, and drunken behaviors on the Red Mile flooded the police, and by the third round of the playoffs, the police started to close the street off and enforce local noise and behavioral by-laws. While the crowds grew increasingly boisterous, a dominating police force surveilled the Red Mile until the Flames were ousted from the playoffs in the semifinals. In 2005 and 2006, the Red Mile tradition resurfaced (even during regular season play), forcing the police to boost their control efforts as minor instances of violence had cropped up during celebrations that routinely involved more than 10,000 participants.

In 2006, Edmonton Oilers' fans copied their provincial counterparts by starting a Blue Mile in the city on Whyte Avenue during that year's playoffs. Dissimilar to Calgary, however, violence plagued postgame celebrations almost immediately, including 2 stabbings, over 30 fist-fights, and 15 separate incidents of vandalism. By the time the Oilers' reached the Stanley Cup finals, police had effectively shut down the Blue Mile. After nearly 50 years of precedents in ice hockey, city officials finally saw fit to contain crowds before the end of a playoff series.

FUTURE PROSPECTS

In the wake of events in Los Angeles, Calgary, and Edmonton, a new lockdown era in the city planning for and staging of mega-events in professional sports has commenced. Authority agents in cities who host professional sports playoffs or one-time mega-events are far less tolerant of displays of mass spectator emotion than in the past. At the request of business owners, insurance companies, urban residents, and other concerned citizens, zero-tolerance rules and policies about postevent celebrations are being tabled in cities across the continent. But much of the evidence on celebratory rioting indicates that riots may be difficult to predict with pinpoint precision and, when they commence, both practically and politically difficult to contain. Spectators and fans who seek open forms of collective celebration of their teams' victories as a form of social bonding, collective identification, and "institutional time out" from everyday stress argue that the tight social control will undoubtedly shift the meaning of mass sports rituals in North America.

See also Collective Protests and Social Movements; Criminal Violence During Competition; Field Invasions; Hooliganism; Missile Throwing; Soccer Tragedies; Taunting.

Further Reading: Elias, N., and Dunning, E. (1986). *Quest for Excitement: Sport and Leisure in the Civilizing Process.* New York: Basil Blackwell; Katz, J. (1988). *Seductions of Crime.* New York: Basic Books; Young, K. (2002). Standard Deviations: An Update on North American Sports Crowd Disorder. *Sociology of Sport Journal* 19: 237–275.

Michael Atkinson

PRIVATE VS. PUBLIC SPORTS SPACES

One of the most important determinants of participation in sports and physical recreation is access to space and facilities, and this is also one of the more enduring struggles that exist in sports and recreation: between those who own land and sports facilities and wish to keep them to themselves (or profit from their ownership) and those who cannot afford to own such land and facilities but are seeking access to participate in sports and recreation. These struggles have been played out over urban parks and playgrounds, ocean beaches and lake shores, national parks and wilderness areas, and urban and suburban facilities such as golf courses, tennis clubs, swimming pools, and so on. The struggles are usually related to social class, but those seeking access to sports and recreation have also been excluded on the grounds of gender, race/ethnicity, age, and religion. Some access to recreational and sporting space has been provided by charities and service organizations, but the main struggles involve public space—space that is available to all.

BACKGROUND

Until the eighteenth century in many Western societies, large areas of land were collectively owned; because they were held in common and available to all for grazing animals, collecting firewood, and for recreation, they were often known as *commons*. (The name is still evident in places such as Boston Common.) The Agricultural Revolution that occurred in the second part of the eighteenth century, combined with increasing individualization and privatization, led wealthy landowners to claim and enclose (with fences and hedges) large tracts of common land for private grazing, forestry, cultivation, hunting, and other forms of private recreation. By the first part of the nineteenth century, with the Industrial Revolution well under way, there were massive population shifts from rural areas to urban centers; those who had lost access to common land for their livelihood were moving to the newly industrialized cities to seek work in the new factories.

The new industrial workers had only one free day (Sunday) each week and very little access to recreational space. They often played, socialized, gambled, and drank in the streets, but business owners complained about the effects on trade, so workers were barred from congregating and playing in the streets. In some cities, cemeteries were the only open green spaces, and in cities such as Boston they became popular sites for picnics and for walking.

The newly industrialized cities became notoriously unhealthy places; many of the factory owners lived on the outskirts of cities—in what is now often referred to as the "greenbelt"—to avoid the polluted air, smells, and lack of sanitation. As urban reformers began to take steps to introduce clean water and sewage systems, they also began to introduce a new form of public space—parks.

It is fitting that the idea of public parks should have originated in England, where the Agricultural and Industrial Revolutions also started. When American Frederick Law Olmstead traveled to England and visited Birkenhead Park in 1850, he was surprised at this unprecedented use of land. Olmstead wrote that the park was: "entirely, unreservedly, and for ever, the people's own. The poorest British peasant is as free to enjoy it in all its parts as the British queen ... Is it not a grand, good thing?" Olmstead went home to create Central Park and Prospect Park in New York City, the city of Buffalo parks system, and parks on Mount Royal (Montreal) and in Niagara Falls, Canada.

Concerns about low-income children and youth in urban areas, especially with regard to their (mis)behavior in public places, led to the introduction of spaces and programs to occupy their time. Church-affiliated organizations such as the Young Men's Christian Association (YMCA) began to introduce evening sports programs just as good indoor lighting (gas and then electric) started to become available. Basketball and volleyball were invented at the YMCA-affiliated Springfield College in Massachusetts precisely to occupy the evenings of urban youth in active and useful ways. Parental demand, combined with urban reform in what came to be known as the rational recreation movement, resulted in the allocation of public space for children's playgrounds.

With the growth of public education, schools began to supplement these spaces. Gymnasiums for physical education classes eventually expanded into playing fields for school sports. In some school boards (e.g., Toronto), agreements between the municipality for cost sharing and public use led to the creation of additional facilities, such as a widespread system of swimming pools, many housed in schools. Pools were also built by municipalities as a part of their

SOME KEY EVENTS IN WINNING PUBLIC SPACE FOR SPORTS AND RECREATION

1847 Birkenhead Park, Birkenhead, UK—first publicly funded park; provided the inspiration for many well-known urban parks in North America.

1872 First national parks, Yellowstone and Yosemite, opened in the United States; historians have suggested that the parks, designated on what was considered to be "useless land," were a result of "monumentalism," that is, feelings of inferiority in the United States at not having spectacular architecture as in European cities and the consequent desire to preserve America's "natural monuments."

1885 Banff national park designated—Canada was the third country to develop national parks but for far more utilitarian reasons than the United States—the desire to promote passenger traffic on the newly completed trans-Canada railroad.

1890s Flourishing of the urban playground movement in the United States.

1932 Mass trespasses in the English Peak District to demand access to moorland that is only used by wealthy people for grouse hunting during a few days in August each year.

1951 Peak National Park, the first British national park, was designated as a direct result of public demand and an indirect result of civil disobedience (mass trespasses) in the period before World War II.

2000 Countryside and Rights of Way Act passed in England—after over 100 years of struggle, the English won a modified form of *allemansrätten*, one that is currently being introduced in stages.

---

growing parks and recreation programs—people who could not afford pools at home or at private clubs could learn to swim in safety, enjoy recreational swimming, learn to be lifesavers, or even swim competitively as the sport democratized because of low-cost access to pools.

Access to recreational space also grew in countryside and wilderness areas, although some countries in Scandinavia (and Scotland) continued to enjoy access to the countryside even after enclosure of the commons. Common law in those countries gave people the right to walk wherever they wanted so long as they did not damage crops or property or invade the personal privacy of landowners. The traditions of hiking and long distance skiing in the Scandinavian countries owe much to that right, known in Sweden as *allemansrätten*, everyman's right. In other countries, the idea of national parks granted access to wilderness areas. The first national parks were in North America (Yosemite and Yellowstone in the United States in 1872; Banff in Canada in 1885) and Australia (Royal in 1879).

KEY EVENTS

Sports are, by their very nature, exclusive. Clubs are formed to bring like minded people together, but the fact of membership is also used to exclude—that exclusion has frequently been taken to mean "people not like us," people of the wrong gender, race, religion, social class, sexuality, athletic ability, and so on. Such exclusions have been maintained even when they became illegal (e.g., the Augusta National golf club's troubles over race and gender exclusions). Also, very few competitions are actually open to all who are interested in participating. Athletes must be registered, they must survive selection processes, and those who fail to meet whatever criteria are established are excluded.

But people enjoy participating in sports and physical recreation—hence the struggles to win those opportunities for themselves and their children. It has often been claimed that public playgrounds and playing fields were a result of lobbying by liberal reformers to establish such spaces for the poor. Historians have recently shown that this was only half of the story and that the poor actively lobbied municipal councils to provide safe places for their children to play.

Most of these struggles involved individuals, small groups, or communities. They were not dramatic or even newsworthy, and it is only since the 1980s that historians have begun to discover the extent to which people were not only *granted* play space and access by benevolent donors and politicians but also *demanded* and *won* that space in a series of struggles. However, one of those struggles was dramatic and newsworthy. In the 1930s, when hiking was very popular in Britain, large areas of moorland in the North of England were owned by major landowners—access was restricted and enforced by armed gamekeepers because the land was used for hunting grouse for a few days in August each year. Workers in the North of England organized two mass trespasses in 1932 to protest the lack of access, and despite a show of force by police and gamekeepers, the trespasses took place with 600–800 people participating. Six trespassers were arrested, and five were given prison sentences of two to six months. The actions forced Parliament to begin to reconsider the right to roam on nonagricultural land—the British version of *allemansrätten*. Their deliberations ended in 1939 because of World War II, but the socialist government that introduced public health care and a number of other reforms following the War designated the land that had been the subject of the mass trespasses as the first British national park.

Olmstead argued that "the people's own" parks (and playgrounds) were "a grand, good thing," but that is open to question. Given the alternative between access to parks, play areas, and sports facilities and no access, they are "a grand, good thing." But in the struggles and negotiations that resulted in winning these spaces, people gave up something very important—the power to determine and control the forms of sports and recreation that could occur in those spaces. Thus, the powerful in society not only control the form and meaning of activities practiced in their own private spaces but also the form and meaning of activities in so-called public spaces.

For example, public parks control and limit the behavior of users with a series of proscriptive rules. These may include: no picking flowers, no walking on the grass, no cutting wood, no motorcycles/snowmobiles/motorboats, no loud music, no alcohol, no dogs, no skateboarding, no playing sports, and so on. Although some of the restrictions may have been introduced by users themselves in order to ensure their mutual enjoyment of the space, they were often imposed without consulting the users. Thus, individuals are not always permitted to participate in the leisure activities of their own choosing. The notorious nineteenth-century Sunday Blue Laws in North America, which lasted in varying and more limited forms until the 1970s, initially proscribed the opening of bars, businesses, and places of entertainment on Sundays and also attempted to prevent people from playing sports in public parks. Because Sunday was the only free day for most workers, the rules against sports were widely ignored and eventually dropped from the statutes.

Thus, people not only had to struggle to win space; they then had to struggle to determine the use of that space. Some people were actually arrested in the latter part of the nineteenth century for playing sports in parks on a Sunday.

FUTURE PROSPECTS

The struggles continue. Demands for access to countryside and wilderness areas in England were finally met with the introduction and phasing in of a modified form of *allemansrätten* in 2000 (see sidebar on p. 328).

New forms of struggle concern the use of public funds to build private stadiums or public sports facilities. In Colorado, for example, the community of Colorado Springs spent $6 million in 2000 to construct a youth sports complex with 12 baseball/softball/T-ball fields, 10 soccer/football fields, 6 volleyball courts, an in-line skating rink, a batting cage, and a number of basketball courts. At the same time, Denver and five surrounding counties spent $300 million of public money to build a stadium for the Denver Broncos. The stadium hosts 72,000 people, 9 times each year, at a minimum cost of $60 per seat, to watch football games. The youth sports complex is open seven days a week to everyone in the community for nominal fees. It is appropriate to ask which choice better serves the community, especially at a time of increasing concerns about physical activity and the consequences of obesity. It is also appropriate to imagine how many community facilities could have been built for $300 million.

A final, ongoing form of struggle is that between users of public spaces. These include struggles between cross country skiers and snowmobiles, between hikers and trail bikers, and between the use of public playing fields for sports introduced by immigrant communities such as cricket and kabbadi and traditional North American sports. However, these are struggles between users about the use of public space, and they are being resolved between users, often with demands for additional sports and recreational space to accommodate all of their needs. And the demands are being met, in some cases in creative ways. For example, some municipalities require that developers designate a certain percentage of space for the construction of sports fields or recreational facilities in exchange for zoning permission to construct housing subdivisions. It is important to remember that public parks, playgrounds, sports facilities, and access to wilderness areas did not just happen—it was won in the face of those who had private spaces in which to play and recreate and who resisted making public spaces and facilities that were open to all.

See also "At-Risk" Youth in Sports; Corporate Branding; Corporate Stadiums; Environmental Impacts of Sports; Government Sponsorship of Teams; Rights for Young Athletes; Sports for All and Fair Play Leagues; Urban Planning and Gentrification.

Further Reading: Donnelly, P. (1986). The Paradox of Parks: Politics of Recreational Land Use Before and After the Mass Trespasses. *Leisure Studies* 5 (2): 211–231; Hardy, S. (1982). *How Boston Played: Sport, Recreation, and Community, 1865–1915*. Boston, MA: Northeastern University Press; Olmstead, F. L. (1967). *Walks and Talks of an American Farmer in England*. Ann Arbor: University of Michigan Press, 1967.

Peter Donnelly

PSEUDOSPORTS

The course of the twentieth century involved the increased formalization and institutionalization of athletic practices into what we now regard as organized, competitive sports and the emergence of deliberately invented pseudosports designed to be commercially marketable to people. In the case of the latter, so-called invented sports tend to mock, exaggerate, and venture beyond the boundaries of mainstream sports in order to make the pastimes highly exciting for audiences. Other sports may be called pseudosports within a culture if they do not ostensibly possess several of the defining features of commonly accepted criteria attributed to mainstream sports. The analysis of invented, pseudosports illustrates how tastes and preferences for sports vary across cultures and how powerful interest groups in a society are able to define sports along "high" versus "low" cultural lines.

BACKGROUND

Where organized, competitive sports fit into a cultural world vision or belief system is often complex to locate; certainly when sports is located within debates about what constitutes "high" (the best) versus "popular" (the worst) forms of cultural expression within a society. High culture is typically regarded as the best or most progressive and enlightened of people's thoughts, expressions, institutions, or social practices. Dramatic literature, theater, art, and complex systems of law based on humanistic philosophic principles are each traditionally considered as high culture. By contrast, low or popular culture refers to thoughts, tastes, and expression of the "common" people. Popular culture is fleeting (think of fashion, television programs, or romance novels), easily accessed in the mainstream, and does not create, many cultural critics pejoratively argue, an indelible impression on the collective consciousness across history because it does little to elevate the intellectual, spiritual, or moral qualities of a society. Popular culture may be referred to as disposable culture in this regard. Sports has been traditionally, but not always, considered an aspect of popular culture within North America, especially in the period following World War II.

From roughly the 1940s onward, organized sports became a popular form of social interaction and entertainment, less directed toward the development of moral virtues within youth cultures (i.e., philosophies that had underpinned the institutionalization of youth sports in schools and community groups from the early 1900s onward) and more toward a commercial venture, even at the college and university levels. Elite amateur (i.e., Olympic) sports retained a place in the overall cultural hierarchy of sports in North America, but the burgeoning interest in mass spectator sports (facilitated in part by the advent and diffusion of television) radically recalibrated what North Americans conceptualized as mainstream sports practices. Ironically, Olympic sports that had been played for centuries around the world such as wrestling, archery, javelin/discus, equestrian sports, and running were viewed as somewhat highbrow cultural practices appropriate only for select groups of elites or stigmatized as definitively unsporting.

With regard to what counts as a sport in contemporary popular culture, Coakley's (2004) definition encapsulates the critical features. According to Coakley, sports are "institutionalized competitive activities that involve rigorous physical exertion or the use of relatively complex physical skills by participations, motivated by personal enjoyment and external rewards."

Several components of this definition warrant further highlight. First, sports are generally regarded as institutionalized activities with formal hierarchies, carefully defined roles and identities of participants, governing bodies, learning structures and techniques, codes of practice, and ethical standards. Thus, forms of disorganized "play" are immediately excluded as are sports organized on a haphazard, open, or local/organic basis. Second, sports are competitive in that they are undertaken for a rational purpose and defined quantitatively by time, distance, and scoring. Included in such a criterion is that sports is inherently social and represents interpersonal battles between two or more people.

Third, and perhaps most controversially within the definition, sports involves an intense level of physical exertion. Immediately, one might note, this criterion effectively eliminates many popular sports played in North America from the conceptual definition of sports. Equally, the exertion is complex and skilled in the sense that the athletic technique used in the sport has been learned and mastered over the course of long training periods. Stated differently, one is able to participate as an athlete in a *true* sport only when one has acquired sufficient physiological skill to do so. With regard to the last two criteria, sporting "snobs" regularly argue that globally popular pastimes such as bowling, sailing, golf, race car driving, table tennis, luge, curling, and others simply do not count. Even, then, in the world of popular culture, certain sports receive a short shrift. The question remains as to precisely why people either seek to include or exclude a physical cultural practice from a social group's hierarchy of legitimate sports.

Any review of the modern development of popular sports in North America reveals that their organization rested primarily in the hands of white, male, Christians from the middle and upper classes. Cultural traditions and preferences for sports have been embedded with this group's vision of the social utility/purpose of sports for well over a century. Masculinist (i.e., sports should be intense, skilled, and physically draining) and class-based (i.e., that sports should be commercial, with links between one's work within a sporting institution and one's eventual reward) ideologies have made particular impacts on what is considered to be a legitimate sport. These ruling groups have also been able to define the cultural athletic practices of others as nonsporting (i.e., not many people in North America consider kendo or kabaddi as mainstream sports) and have excluded and discriminated against women and gays and lesbians because their socially ascribed identities supposedly do not jibe well with the social purposes and uses of sports.

In thinking about the battle over commonly defined pseudosports, several conceptual categories become evident. The first category might be called socially contested sports. These sports meet each of Coakley's (2004) described categories but are normally excluded as legitimate sports in mainstream culture because the level and skill of the physical exertion in them is suspect. Sports practices such as darts (considered a working-class sport for nonathletes), rhythmic gymnastics (a feminized sport requiring flexibility more than strength), and NASCAR (a sport requiring one to sit for long periods) are prime examples. Other sports may not be recognized as legitimate if they are not traditional cultural pastimes in a society. Soccer, cricket, and rugby are perfect examples in North America. Even in lieu of the recent success of the National Soccer League (NSL) and the sport's status as one of, if not the, most played sports on the planet, North Americans' have yet to embrace the professional game as a cultural favorite.

The second category of contested sports or so-called fake sports is what we may refer to as simulated sports. Physical activities in this category generally fail to meet certain exertion standards but are mainly considered pseudosports within culture because they mimic or virtually simulate historically violent activities or sports in more passive or civilized ways. Clay pigeon shooting, rodeo, and archery, for example, symbolically represent social activities (hunting, farming exercises, and war) in competitively safe and sporting ways. Often included in this category are a wide range of animal sports such as greyhound and horse racing, fox hunting, and bullfighting, which are each social surrogates for, and representations of, physical warfare between people.

Finally, the last category of culturally defined pseudosports is sports entertainment. In this instance, the physical activity is what people often called acommercially invented sports, designed strategically to be mass marketed as an exaggerated example of a traditional sport. These sports are also less socially institutionalized or structured by traditional sports hierarchies, have few cultural codes or ethics of play, eschew any notion of the link between morality and sports, and may be described as solely orchestrated to be television phenomena. Prototypical examples of these sports include American Gladiators, professional wrestling, XFL football, and Spike television's Slamball. Sports in this category are among the most socially controversial because they often showcase violence, aggression, racism, homophobia, and (hetero)sexuality in flamboyant manners.

Even though many sports have been traditionally lumped into the category of popular or low culture, even within the world of sports there are divisions and separations between what is high and low sports culture. High cultural sports, such as elite amateur and Olympic Games, continue to be regarded as *pure* sporting forms that have been unblemished by commercialism and mass marketing. Others exist in the middle of the definitional continuum and tend to include the bulk of what North Americans normally consider mainstream sports. Finally, easily disposable and enduring pseudosports are treated with the least cultural regard but can be massively popular from time to time.

KEY EVENTS

The lack of public respect pseudosports tend to receive over time should not be conflated with a lack of mainstream popularity, historical significance, or their financial viability and diffusion within a culture. An ideal example in this regard is the National Association for Stock Car Auto Racing, or NASCAR.

In terms of the social events that would lead to the genesis of NASCAR, we must look to 1794, the year of the Whiskey Rebellion in the United States. The Whiskey Rebellion developed as a collective protest against the federal tax placed on whiskey and other spirits made by plains farmers. To avoid taxation, farmers brewed their products surreptitiously and covertly distributed it within towns. The illegal manufacturing and distribution of whiskey via covered wagons became a staple of early American frontier life, especially in the southern United States. During the Prohibition era of the 1920s and early 1930s, the underground "moonshine" economy skyrocketed because the public interest in spirits had never been greater but the supply never more restricted on the continent. Bootleggers transported alcohol illegally from hidden stills to hundreds of markets across the southeastern United States. Using early model automobiles to carry vast amounts of alcohol across state lines, bootleggers "raced" to avoid police apprehension and criminal prosecution. As time went on and a culture of bootlegging emerged, the drivers organized races among themselves to see who could drive the fastest between two specified places. Racing on Sunday afternoons, their "shine races" became among the first indigenous spectator sports in the South.

Nearly a decade and a half later, influenced by the "shine racing" traditions, Bill France, Sr. promoted racing events on the famous beach course at Daytona Beach, Florida. In 1947, France organized the separate automobile race circuits that had developed in the southern United States after World War II into NASCAR. Since its creation in 1947, NASCAR has been the fastest growing spectator sport in the United States.

While NASCAR is generally excluded from many discussions about *true* sports (perhaps due to its unsavory historical origins), consider the following relating to the impact of this pastime on the business of sports. The 1980s witnessed the increase of sponsorship of racing teams and events from Fortune 500 companies. Yearly, hundreds of millions of dollars are spent marketing corporations and their products on cars, tracks, and drivers. In the last 10 years, television coverage of NASCAR has expanded, series Cups and leagues have both increased and diversified, and attendance at the growing number of tracks in the United States has boomed such that stock car racing is now the number one (by attendance at events) spectator sport in the United States. By 1998, attendance at NASCAR's Winston Cup events alone rose to more than 6 million, up from 3.3 million in 1990 and 1.5 million in 1982. The sale of NASCAR-licensed products topped $950 million in 1998, from $80 million in 1990. By 1999, there

IS IT A SPORT? A FIRST-HAND ANALYSIS

In 1999, University of Wisconsin—Eau Claire Associate Professor of English David Shih played in The World Series of Poker in Las Vegas. Shih qualified for the world's most prestigious poker tournament by winning an online tournament. Shih described the experience as incredibly sports-like; he argued that the competitive aspect of the game is like no other sport, and the prize purses are larger than most mainstream sports. On his online blog about the game of poker, he admits the game doesn't require athleticism, but he argues that many players are at the table for 10 to 20 hours a day while competing. Shih stresses both the physical and mental stamina required to stay in the game. Do you think poker is a sport?

were 13 "NASCAR Thunder" (licensed retailers of NASCAR products) stores in 11 states selling NASCAR apparel and other licensed products. NASCAR almost single-handedly revolutionized the sports marketing and licensing industries.

The long-standing association between NASCAR racing and the working-class South is among the leading reasons as to why the sport of racing receives continued cultural stigmatization both outside of and within the world of sports. Despite consistent data that suggest its fans have diverse social backgrounds and interests, racing continues to be a socially contested sport because of its historical origins and perceived fan base. Its drivers are equally labeled as nonathletes because they do not visually measure up to hypermasculine corporeal standards established in popular mainstream sports such as football and basketball.

Among the most short-lived but widely publicly debated sports in the sports entertainment category in the recent past has been XFL football. Created as a joint venture between NBC and the World Wrestling Federation, the "XFL" or "X Football League" was established in 2001 by Titan sports owner and CEO Vince McMahon. McMahon is the venture capitalist who almost single-handedly spearheaded the professional wrestling revolution of the 1980s and 1990s through the World Wrestling Federation (now World Wrestling Entertainment). The XFL and its eight teams were the sole property of McMahon, and the league itself was founded on the idea that Americans would prefer to watch a more culturally radical (i.e., less rule-bound) version of NFL football, that is, a blend between football and professional wrestling. Competing with, or in some ways against, the legacies of the older Xtreme Football League and the Arena Football League (which merged in 1999), the XFL featured a more interactive, dramatic, violent, and audience-oriented brand of the game. The XFL had impressive television coverage for a new sports league, with three games televised each week on NBC, UPN, and TNN, but the league failed to excite fans for more than three weeks and was disbanded after merely one season. Many football fans argued that the games were untrustworthy due to who owned and operated the league. Another reason for the failure of the league to catch on, despite its financial solvency and massive visibility (perhaps infamy), was the lack of respect for the league in the sports media, who regularly called it a "fake sport" designed and carefully directed by script writers. The fact that the league was co-owned by NBC made ESPN (which was part of the same corporation as ABC) and Fox Sports Net (owned by Fox TV) disinclined to report on the XFL. Many local TV newscasts and newspapers (even in XFL cities) did not report league scores or show highlights as a form of social protest. This led to many football fans treating the XFL as a carnival act (like professional wrestling) rather than true sports competition to the NFL.

FUTURE PROSPECTS

The debate regarding which sports are legitimate versus which are mere replicas of authentic sports will continue to be waged. Definitions of sports contained within such debates are clearly laced with dominant and alternative cultural preferences for sports along with modern biases to view hypermasculine team sports as the ultimate sports standard. The ongoing corporate insurgence into sports should continue to influence the ways in which sports are presented to people and how collective tastes and preferences for even pseudo-sports develop.

See also Corporate Branding; Parkour (Free Running); Publicity in Sports; Skateboarding; Snowboarding; X Games; Yoga and Alternative Fitness.

Further Reading: Coakley, J. (2004). *Sport and Society: Issues and Controversies*. New York: McGraw-Hill; Gorn, E., and Goldstein, W. (2002). *A Brief History of American Sport*. Champaign: University of Illinois Press.

Michael Atkinson

PUBLICITY IN SPORTS

A publicity stunt is an event designed by one or more people as either a marketing gimmick or a statement of social protest. In the world of professional sports, publicity stunts can be organized by any number of groups to promote, generally, their own interests and agendas in athletics. Some stunts tend to be flamboyant and dramatic, while others take on a more ritual and subdued tone. Regardless of their form or content, publicity stunts in sports are normally intended to promote commercial investment. They are staged in public, are often heavily promoted by participants, and add to the spectacular or circus-like atmosphere in modern sports.

BACKGROUND

The rise of television media in the 1960s in North America dramatically changed the course of professional sports development. Or, as some historians of sports contend, television media served to amplify trends in sports' commercialization that had been developing since the early 1920s. While newspapers were a primary media platform for sports leagues and teams prior to the advent of television, the development of new, live visual media certainly changed the social purpose of sports' mass mediation. As television networks increasingly featured professional sports contests in their weekly complement

SHOW ME THE MONEY!

Consider the following, and think about the impact these figures have on the way in which sports is played, shown to audiences, and culturally understood as a commodity:

- Nearly 75 percent of NFL teams' annual revenues come from the sale of broadcasting rights to their games.
- The rights to televise NFL games from 1998 to 2006 were collectively sold to U.S. and international networks for $17.6 billion.
- In 1999, CBS agreed to pay the National Collegiate Athletic Association (NCAA) $6.2 billion over 11 years to broadcast the Division I men's basketball tournament.
- From 1996 to 2006, the rights to broadcast MLB baseball games in the United States were sold to Fox, ESPN, and NBC for $4.2 billion.
- NBC paid $705 million to broadcast the 2000 Sydney Games, $793 million for the 2004 Athens Games, and $894 million for the Beijing Games.

of programming, a "sports media complex" developed. Professional sports teams quickly learned that media corporations would pay leagues money for exclusive rights to broadcast their games, and corporate sponsors would pay huge sums of money to advertise during the televising of sports contests (i.e., as a way of marketing to thousands and then millions of viewers). A commercial holy trinity formed between sports leagues, media broadcasters, and commercial/production companies. Largely championed by ABC television in the United States and the CBC in Canada during the 1960s and 1970s, new allegiances between sports, media companies, and commodity production companies were systematically forged. Weekly sports programs were launched such as *Wide World of Sports, Hockey Night in Canada,* and later *Monday Night Football.* Not only would professional sports such as baseball, ice hockey, football, and basketball be aired on television to sell audiences the sports (to have them become loyal consumers of the sports as fans) but also as a means of selling a full range of commercial products to them.

The financial partnerships created through the sports media complex have altered sports in any number of ways. Included among these are simple and seemingly unproblematic forms of change to sports themselves. To sell more exciting games to audiences (read *consumers*), sports leagues have worked in conjunction with media and marketing experts to tinker with the very rules of the games. The introduction of the three-point line and the shot clock in the National Basketball Association (NBA) were structural tricks designed to produce faster-paced and higher-scoring games. The Canadian Football League (CFL) partly distinguishes itself from its National Football League (NFL) counterpart by its unique rules: such as the 3 instead of 4 down rule, the wider and longer field, and the single point award scheme for kicking "through" an end zone. Each of these rules is designed to sell a faster, more open, and higher scoring game. In the National Hockey League (NHL), the 1980s and 1990s saw the proliferation of the "television time out" in the sport. At designated points during televised games, natural stoppages in play are actually lengthened to 3 or 4 minutes to allow for a more commercial broadcasting time. When Fox Sports entered into the NHL broadcast market in 1996, they pioneered several media techniques to help American audiences understand, watch, and enjoy the game. Notable among these were their "FoxTrax Smart Puck" systems. Fox engineers designed an electronically enhanced puck that could be tracked by television cameras during play. A blue "halo" appeared around the puck on television during regular play, with the color changing to red when the puck was shot by a player at high speed.

Other changes to sports through its increased association with mass media and commercial production companies included the ownership of teams and leagues. Corporations realized that it would not only be lucrative to market through sports but also to invest in sports organizations. Media organizations as well realized that they could progressively brand sports with their images, logos, and icons even more directly by becoming majority shareholders on teams. Key global corporate media figures such as Rupert Murdoch, for example, were pioneers in this investment strategy and forged multibillion dollar corporate empires through sports investment. Other corporations such as Walt Disney (Anaheim Mighty Ducks, Anaheim Angels), Time Warner (Atlanta Braves, Atlanta Hawks, Atlanta Thrashers), Comcast (Philadelphia 76ers, Philadelphia Flyers), News Corp (Los Angeles Dodgers, New York Knicks, New York Rangers), and Roger's Media (Toronto Blue Jays) all entered into financial ownership alliances with sports teams in order to extend their control of the ongoing corporatization and commercialization of modern sports.

These trends and others laid the social foundation for sporting events to be regularly employed as a site for publicity stunts. Over the course of about 60 years, most professional (and now college) sports have been used as sites for selling an expanding number of commercial products and services. With their mass mediation to national and then international audiences, media corporate interests in sports have created a market battleground atmosphere in contemporary sports cultures. Each member of the sports media complex struggles for a bigger yearly share of sports consumers' dollars, and this may often be achieved by staging flamboyant or special events. At other times, because of the mass audiences that televised sports draw, they are poached by people who seek to disseminate political or ideological ideas to the world.

KEY EVENTS

From the establishment of mid-season all-star games in baseball, basketball, and ice hockey to the use of monkeys as jockeys in greyhound racing, sports organizers use a vast array of publicity gimmicks in order to sell their brands to consumers. In a competitive entertainment market and a flood of sports products from which to choose for present fans and consumers, individual athletes, teams, and leagues will go to great lengths to procure consumer loyalty and investment in their sports.

Called the "match race of the century," one of the earliest publicity stunts in American sports saw the horse Seabiscuit race against heavily favored War Admiral on November 1, 1938, at Pimlico Race Course in Baltimore, Maryland. Seabiscuit had been publicly heralded as the "horse of the (working-class) people" and a symbol of post–Depression era cultural resolve among the socially disadvantaged. Match racing in the sport dated back to the late 1800s, but this race featured a massive, triple-crown winning horse (War Admiral) against an atypically small horse in the sport. Organizers billed the match as a modern day "David and Goliath" contest, and their trick worked. An estimated 40,000 people attended the event, with 40 million more listening on the radio. The event stirred new consumer gambling interest in the sport of horse racing.

One of the first uses of a television stunt to promote fandom in Major League Baseball (MLB) was the 1959 *Home Run Derby* television series showcased on ABC. Staged at Wrigley Field in Chicago, the weekly show pitted two top hitters (including Hank Aaron, Mickey Mantle, Willie Mays, Ernie Banks, Frank Robinson, and others) of the era against one another in a mock 9-inning battle. Their goal was to hit as many home runs as possible in the 9 innings. The winner received $2,500 and was invited back in the next week to compete again. The show aired for three seasons and was the inspiration for the now massively popular home run derby first held at the MLB all-star game in 1985.

Other marketing and publicity stunts appeal to fans' desires to receive something for free at a sports event. Since the late 1970s, baseball teams have highlighted specific home days as promotional events on their calendar, giving a preset amount of fans a token gift when they enter the stadium. Beer mugs, foam hands with the team's logo on them, hats, replica bats, and hundreds of other gifts are given away each year to attract fans to games during periods of the year in which the team generally experiences low attendance (often midsummer during holiday season for North American families).

Failing or struggling sports organizations and leagues have also hired marquee talent as publicity stunts designed to stimulate fan interest in them. The 1975 signing of Brazilian soccer icon Pele to the New York Cosmos of the North American Soccer League (for $4.5 million) shocked the soccer world. In a desperate attempt to stimulate fan interest in the team and the sport, the Cosmos encouraged Pele to come out of retirement. Fast forward three decades, and soccer teams on the continent continue to use this publicity stunt. The 2006 signing of British player David Beckham of Manchester United and Real Madrid fame to the L.A. Galaxy soccer team made international headlines. Beckham signed a staggering five-year, $250 million deal with the Galaxy. Critics argue that Beckham had only been signed to raise the profile of the sport in the country, promote corporate investment in the Galaxy, and sell L.A. Galaxy merchandise worldwide.

Other sports have become even more aggressive in developing their links between teams, corporatism, and the media. The expansion of the NHL into Anaheim evolved into the first true "media team" in professional sports. The Mighty Ducks of Anaheim NHL team was founded in 1993 by the Walt Disney Corporation. The name for the stem linked directly back to the name of the Disney produced film *The Mighty Ducks*. Ducks' home games (played in an arena located a mere few blocks from Disneyland) were a mix between hockey, a Disney movie, and a circus with pyrotechnics, dancing, and music. Disney even launched a short-lived Saturday morning cartoon featuring the Ducks hockey team in 1995. Disney eventually sold the franchise in 2005 to Henry and Susan Samueli, who immediately changed the name of the team to Anaheim Ducks.

Athletes themselves may use mass-mediated publicity stunts to extend their own celebrity statuses. NBA player Dennis Rodman forged a mini career in publicity stunts in the 1990s, dressing in women's clothing, having high-profile sexual relationships with other popular cultural icons, heavily tattooing and piercing his body, and joining the World Championship Wrestling league. NFL football player Terrell Owens staged a number of publicity stunts in the early 2000s to extend his highly marketable "bad body" image in sports, including "public" workouts he performed in his own private driveway to which he invited reporters to attend and ask him questions about his career.

Rollen Frederick Stewart, also known as "Rock 'n' Rollen" and "Rainbow Man," was a fixture in U.S. sports culture best known for wearing a rainbow afro-wig and holding up signs reading "John 3:16" at stadium sporting events around the United States in the 1970s and 1980s. Stewart became a born-again Christian obsessed with "getting the message out" via television. His first major appearance was at the 1977 NBA Finals. By the time of the 1979 MLB All-Star Game, broadcasters actively tried to avoid showing him. He appeared behind NFL goal posts, near Olympic medal stands, and even at the Augusta National Golf Club strategically positioned for key shots of plays or athletes. Stewart's fame led to a Budweiser beer commercial, but he was arrested in 1992 after a standoff in a California hotel during which he entered a vacant room with two men he was attempting to kidnap and surprised a chambermaid who then locked herself in the bathroom. Reportedly, Stewart believed that the Rapture was due to arrive in six days. During the standoff, he threatened to shoot at airplanes taking off from nearby Los Angeles International Airport and covered the hotel room windows with "John 3:16" placards. Rollen is currently serving three consecutive life sentences in jail on kidnapping charges.

Businesses have used mass-mediated sports events such as the Olympics in the process of engaging in "guerrilla advertising." In addition to paying sports figures such as professional boxers to wear temporary tattoos with their corporate name, the online casino "goldenpalace.com" has been accused of many other infamous, and sometimes illegal, publicity stunts in sports. They hired Mark Roberts, a notorious sports streaker, to wear goldenpalace.com temporary tattoos for nude appearances at the Super Bowl and the UEFA cup final in 2003. They also publicly sponsored Mark Roberts and Dennis Rodman in the 2004 Running of the Bulls in Pamplona, Spain. The casino received heavy criticism for paying Ron Bensimhon (dressed in a tutu) to climb onto a diving platform during the synchronized diving competition at the 2004 Athens Games, but they repeated their stunt work at the Olympic 2006 Torino Games by paying a streaker to interrupt the men's bronze medal curling match between the United States and the United Kingdom.

The sheer number of different publicity stunts in sports suggests that the social field of sports is one of the most contested social spaces for marketing products, images, and ideologies to consumers. The competition for consumers' money in the world of sports has never been greater, and with the ongoing commercialization of games and their intersection with the media, we should expect to see newer and more dramatic publicity stunts in the future. In many ways, publicity stunts are no longer deviant or rare disruptions of games, they are rituals that fans expect to see as part of the spectacle that is modern professional sports.

FUTURE PROSPECTS

There is little dispute that mainstream professional sports will continue on the path toward hypermediation and their interlinking with corporate interests. It is difficult to conceive of a modern sports outside of its television format and without many displays of commercialization on and around playing fields. Few serious challenges have been made to transform mainstream sports into publicly owned leagues with the trappings of hyperconsumerism removed from fans' fields of vision. There are few reasons to believe that the sports media complex will be altered in the near future in any way other than increased privatization and commercialization.

See also Commercializing Ethnic Athletes; Corporate Branding; Corporate Stadiums; Field Invasions; Marketing Female Athlete Sexuality; Media Broadcasting Rights; Media Coverage of Women's Sports; Salaries of Professional Athletes.

Michael Atkinson

R

RACIAL PROFILING AND STACKING

Racial profiling and stacking is a process that identifies people as more or less "programmed" to excel at a particular sport because of supposed genetic abilities they possess and then slotting (stacking) them into particular positions or roles within the sport based on these believed capabilities. Profiling and stacking along racial lines is a pseudoscience used within sports and has evolved into a cultural tradition in mainstream youth sports. Data collected on the link between race and the sport one plays (or position within a sport) has consistently revealed the quasiscientific and enduring cultural beliefs within sports groups that continue to uphold that certain racial or ethnic background factors should be taken into consideration when encouraging athlete participation in sports. Critics have argued that profiling and stacking athletes along racial or ethnic lines is a form of social discrimination lacking any reliable empirical justification and thus serves to create or reinforce systems of social inequality between people.

BACKGROUND

The social justification of stacking (or overrepresenting) athletes into particular positions in sports because of supposed natural abilities determined by race has been justified historically along both eugenicist and cultural lines. In the first instance, the exclusion of "dark-skinned" athletes from sports stems from centuries-old "scientific" beliefs that nonwhites possess inferior cognitive reasoning capacities, the psychological traits and genetically determined muscular forms (somatotypes) that predispose them to either play sports that require brute strength and aggressiveness (such as boxing) or to play in power, strength, and speed positions within team sports (such as an outfielder in baseball or a running back in football). In rather Social Darwinistic terms, such beliefs emerged out of colonial perspectives that people from Africa and their global descendents suffered from arrested intellectual development. They were also supported by "innovative" body-typing sciences in the nineteenth century such as craniometry, physiognomy, and phrenology, which equally suggested that black men and women displayed outward physical characteristics that illustrated their lack of intellectual development, ability for moral reasoning, or capability for self-restraint. By contrast, whites were believed to be predominantly genetically suited to play in sports bound by intense codes of self-restraint sportsmanship and in athletic positions that require deep concentration, focus, reasoning, and leadership ability. These are identical cultural logics that have been deployed by whites for over four centuries in order to justify ethnic and racial discrimination in the workplace, educational institutions, legal systems, religious spheres, and the media.

The social history of professional sports in North America shows great evidence that athletes have been stereotyped by race, encouraged to participate in sports by racialization, excluded from sports due to their supposed natural abilities, or channeled into particular positions because of their race. The ostensible link between race and fitness for sports is now so culturally engrained that it appears more as a scientific fact than ever before. During the first decades of the twentieth century, blacks were first barred from competing against whites in boxing and later overrepresented in boxing due to beliefs in their genetically determined brutish nature. The stereotyping of young black males in North America as those best suited to participate in boxing has scarcely changed over time. Boxers including Joe Louis, Joe Frazier, Muhammad Ali, George Foreman, Mike Tyson, Evander Holyfield, and others have, at times, been linked to animals, savages, or "wildmen" in the popular press. On these grounds and others, black athletes were explicitly or implicitly excluded from participating in white-dominated professional sports such as baseball, basketball, tennis, golf, and others based on the stereotypical belief that their genes would either afford them an undue advantage in competition or that their lack of mental acumen would prevent them from appreciating complex codes of emotional restraint underpinning "civilized" sports. The National Association of Baseball Players, for example, banned black players from the game as early as 1868. As in the case of other sports, leagues were subsequently fashioned for black athletes, such as the National Negro League (est. 1920) and, arguably, the American Basketball Association to provide a "separate but (un)equal" terrain of play.

Perhaps the earliest, but rarely cited, black sports league on the continent developed in the city of Halifax, Nova Scotia, Canada: the Colored Hockey League of the Maritimes (ca. 1895). From 1895 to 1912, the league comprised mostly sons of runaway American slaves who fostered a community network of black players who would become recognized as among the most skilled in the country. At its peak, the league carried a dozen teams and almost 400 players. Black players had been excluded from participation in white leagues because racist cultural logic held that black players could not endure the cold, had ankle structures too weak for skating, and lacked the intelligence to appreciate complex team sports.

The league disbanded in 1912 after civil unrest between blacks and whites in the city of Halifax (particularly in the black neighborhood of Africville) threatened the safety of players. Exhibition games involving black teams were staged, however, well into the early 1920s.

As black athletes progressively breached the color line in mainstream white sports cultures through the 1940s and 1950s, their involvement was largely framed by stereotypically determined abilities. One theory explains the basis of such logic through its "centrality hypothesis." It can be argued that players on a team are best conceptualized as an "interactional group structure," wherein core position players need basic physical, leadership, and intellectual skills that allow them to control players on their team and therefore the flow of a game. Historical analyses reveal that players have been allocated to thinking/core positions by race. If we examine the content, by race, of most of the so-called thinking positions in sports, a startling trend emerges. Until the very recent past, almost all of the thinking/control positions in team sports were dominated by whites; such as quarterbacks in football, pitchers and catchers in baseball, or team captains in any sport. Consider some of the basic trends that have scarcely varied over the last 60 years. In professional baseball, blacks have historically dominated in outfield positions; in professional football, in running back and wide receiver positions; and in basketball, forward positions. Latin Americans (due to stereotyping beliefs that they are naturally nimble and blessed with fast reflexes) have been slotted into infield positions (shortstop and second base) in baseball.

Racial profiling and stacking does not end with the allocation of players to positions by their race. Despite the relative overrepresentation of black athletes in high-profile sports such as basketball, baseball, football, track and field, and boxing, the nearly 40 million members of the African American population in the United States are dramatically underrepresented in practically *every other sport* played in the country. Even a cursory review of high school, elite amateur, recreational, or Olympic sports cultures in the United States and Canada reveals that black males or females (and Latino or Native populations, for that matter) are rarely encouraged to enter into predominantly white-cultured sports.

EXPLAIN THESE STATISTICS?

Nearly 400 years of the scientific investigation on the link between race and sport has argued that black males are more suited for power and performance sports than whites. If this is the case, try to explain why black athletes tend to dominate (as a racial category) in certain sports but not in others. Following are the 2007 statistics detailing the percentage of black athletes in the top four professional sports in North America.

NBA: 81%
NFL: 70%
MLB: 9%
NHL: >1%

As a potential explanation to the trends mentioned in the sidebar, it is routinely suggested by sports insiders that when the historical belief that athletic abilities of dark-skinned people are genetically determined is combined with a history of racial segregation and discrimination and then added to the cultural encouragement of black athletes to enter into only a handful of sports, a cultural system is produced wherein young black males believe it is their physical and social destiny to enter those sports. Black males are socialized to believe that their bodies program them to excel at particular sports, that black identity is to be associated with involvement in particular sports (and/or as specifically positioned players in sports cultures), and that one's social worth is tied to success and failures on the sports field. Further still, over the course of many generations in North America, young black males come to emulate successful black athletes and come to believe that their best avenue toward success is through athletics; they may also believe that when playing a particular sport they should play the same position as their hero (this last point has also been used to explain why, in the context of a sport such as ice hockey, French Canadians have been statistically overrepresented in goaltender positions in the National Hockey League). Coakley (2004), like others, suggests that profiling and stacking, then, not only creates a sense of predestination for black, Latino, Native, and even Asian athletes (each group accorded to racial roles in sports) within sports, but it also serves to underline that racial minority groups' (in particular, African Americans) best opportunities for economic and social equality in the United States is through the use of one's body in sports.

KEY EVENTS

In a rather unintended way, the movement toward racial stacking in sports developed as a consequence of increased ethnic integration into predominantly white sports through the 1940s and 1950s. The most famous of the first black players to enter professional "whitewashed" sports was Jackie Robinson. Robinson broke the proverbial color line in baseball in 1947 when he became the first African American major league baseball player of the modern era when he suited up for the Brooklyn Dodgers. He was not the first black player to venture across the color line in professional baseball, but his signing with the Dodgers veritably saw the end of over 80 years of racial exclusions in the sport. Robinson nevertheless faced constant abuse and ridicule from baseball fans, players, and journalists, who each viewed black players as unwanted in the sport. Social historians of sports note that Robinson's involvement in professional baseball may have been on the one hand a symbol of changing racial ideologies, but on the other hand, the abuse he suffered as a player symbolized a general cultural backlash segments of white America waged against black America during the onset of the civil rights movement.

While Jackie Robinson's movement to mainstream white baseball was a watershed moment in the desegregation of sports, the movement of black players into the ranks of college and professional football at the position of quarterback is one of the stark challenges to stereotypical race logics in sports. The first mention of African Americans playing football was in a college football game played on November 23, 1892, between historically black colleges Biddle (later Johnson C. Smith) and Livingstone. Among the earliest quarterbacks in all of American college football was Frederick Pollard from Brown University (class of 1918). Pollard led his team to the Rose Bowl against Washington State, becoming the first African American to play in the Rose Bowl. He was later named the first African American head coach in the National Football League (NFL) and the first African American named to the College Football Hall of Fame. A sentiment of racial segregation and backlash, however, permeated college and professional football until the mid-1940s. Not until Kenny Washington's signing with the San Francisco Clippers and Willy Strode's signing with the Los Angeles Rams (both in 1946) would the black quarterback color line be truly broken in the sport. In 1953, seven years after Washington and Strode broke the modern color barrier in professional football, Willie Thrower became the first African American quarterback to solely play quarterback in an NFL game on October 18, 1953, for the Chicago Bears.

Between the years of 1950–1965, other notable African American quarterbacks to play in college, the NFL, or other professional leagues included Charlie Brackins, Sherman Lewis, Mel Myers, Wilbur Hollis, Jimmy Raye, and Sandy Stephens. By the late 1960s, however, it was increasingly evident that black quarterbacks were not highly sought after by the professional leagues. African American males were practically nonexistent in the position at the professional levels during this period as the nation struggled with second wave civil rights battles and a general cultural backlash against black men in the United States. By the end of the 1960s, two black quarterbacks were drafted out of college to professional teams, Eldridge Dickey (Oakland Raiders) and Marlin Briscoe (Denver Broncos). Their nationally recognized abilities on the field were a catalyst for an ideological change of the race logic in the sport.

BLACK QUARTERBACKS THROUGH THE 1970s–1980s

Black quarterbacks of the 1970s and 1980s helped to change the stereotypical race logic in sports that deemed people of color to be unfit for thinking positions such as quarterback. Among the frontrunners at the college and professional levels were: Donnie Little, Dennis Franklin, JC Watts, Thomas Lott, Condredge Holloway, Jimmy Jones, Gene Washington, Chuck Ealey, James Harris, Joe Gilliam, Warren Moon, John "JJ" Jones, Vince Evans, Dave Mays, Walter Lewis, Doug Williams, Reggie Collier, Walter Briggs, Homer Jordan, Ed Blount, Mark Stevens, Larry Miller, Willie Gillus, Tony Adams, Bernard Quarles, Tony Robinson, Greg Tipton, Willie Totten, Randall Cunningham, Rodney Peete, Walter Lewis, Danny Bradley, Steve Taylor, Turner Gill, Major Harris, Tracy Ham, Tory Crawford, Shawn Moore, Damon Allen, Stacey Robinson, Tony Rice, and Andre Ware.

The overrepresentation of black athletes in basketball and football perhaps masks larger and more obdurate historical patterns of exclusion from mainstream, white sports cultures for African Americans and other racial minority groups.

FUTURE PROSPECTS

There is little to suggest, at present, that the racial desegregation of sports and the stacking of particular races of people within particular sports will shift in the near future—quite to the contrary. North American culture seems to almost universally accept the idea that there are fundamental genetic differences between racialized groups that predetermine their athletic abilities. Widespread cultural proclamations about the changing face of race logics in North America aside, sports organizations, leagues, and teams continue to replicate centuries old ideologies that one's race should determine one's social roles and statuses. Rarely is the arbitrariness or discriminatory nature of such logic called into public question.

See also Commercializing Ethnic Athletes; Cool Pose; Ethnic Coaches, Managers, and Owners.

Further Reading: Coakley, J. (2004). *Sport and Society: Issues and Controversies*. New York: McGraw-Hill; Eitzen, S. (1999). *Fair and Foul: Beyond the Myths and Paradoxes of Sport*. Boulder, CO: Rowman and Littlefield; Evans, A. (1997). Blacks as Key Functionaries: A Study of Racial Stratification in Professional Sport. *Journal of Black Studies* 28: 43–59; Grusky, O. (1963). Managerial Succession. *American Journal of Sociology* 69: 72–76; Hoberman, J. (1997). *Darwin's Athletes: How Sport has Damaged Black Athletes and Preserved the Myth of Race*. Boston: Houghton Mifflin; Loy, J., and McElvogue, J. (1970). Racial Segregation in American Sport. *International Review for the Sociology of Sport* 5: 5–24; Margolis, B., and Pilivalin, J. (1999). Stacking in Major League Baseball: A Multivariate Analysis. *Sociology of Sport Journal* 16: 16–34.

Michael Atkinson

RAPE AND SEXUAL ASSAULT

> Let's face it, athletes are whores. We're paid to use our bodies. So sex becomes the same thing after the game. We become like dogs sometimes.
>
> *Eddie Johnson, NBA player (cited in Benedict, 1997, p. 61)*

Although perpetrators of rape and sexual assault cross all demographic groups, some groups are overrepresented as assailants. One overrepresented group is male athletes. It is, however, difficult to obtain accurate statistics on the incidence of rape because it is considered the most underreported violent crime. This is particularly true on college campuses, where it is estimated that less than 5 percent of attempted or actual rapes or sexual assaults are reported. It is estimated that one in four college-aged women will suffer a rape or rape attempt. Despite the difficulty in reporting, research has repeatedly demonstrated that male athletes at both the college and professional level are more likely to be accused of rape or sexual assault. Athletes self-report more sexually abusive behavior as well.

BACKGROUND

One study of 10 National Collegiate Athletic Association (NCAA) top-20 basketball and football programs found there were 69 cases of campus sexual assault between 1991–1993. Athletes were accused in 20 percent of them yet constituted less than 3 percent of the student body. Another study at a midwestern university found male athletes were 23 percent of those accused of sexual assault but only 2 percent of the student population. Surveys of 200 college police departments found that athletes are 40 percent more likely to be accused than other students. A three-year survey by the National Institute of Mental Health found athletes participated in approximately one-third of 862 campus sexual assaults. Another study found approximately 40 percent of campus gang rapes were perpetrated by male athletes. From June 1989 to June 1990, at least 15 alleged gang rapes involving about 50 athletes were reported. Peggy R. Sanday, Ph.D., University of Pennsylvania anthropologist and author of *Fraternity Gang Rape,* explained, "They get a high off doing it with their 'brothers.' "

Although they are more likely to be accused of and indicted for sexual crimes against women, male athletes are less likely to be convicted of these offenses than are others accused of the same offenses. The Justice Department has determined accusations against athletes result in conviction 31 percent of the time in contrast to a greater than 50 percent conviction rate against non-athletes. Of the 66 professional and college athletes tried for sexual assault between 1986 and 1995, 85 percent were acquitted. *USA Today's* research of 168 sexual assault allegations against athletes in the past dozen years also suggests sports figures fare better at trial than defendants from the general population. Of those 168 allegations, involving 164 athletes, only 22 saw their cases go to trial, and only 6 cases resulted in convictions. In another 46 cases, a plea agreement was reached. Combining the pleas with the six athletes convicted at trial and one who pleaded guilty as charged gives a 32 percent total conviction rate in the resolved cases involving athletes. That means more than two-thirds were either never charged, saw the charges dropped, or were acquitted. Jeff Benedict, author of *Out of Bounds: Inside the NBA's Culture of Rape, Violence, & Crime,* analyzed 22 formal police complaints involving felony rape by National Basketball Association (NBA) players. Of those, three cases were closed upon police investigation. Of the remaining 19 that were forwarded for prosecution, indictments were issued in only 5.

There are several explanations for the overrepresentation of athletes in arrests but underrepresentation in convictions. One argument is that women target athletes, thinking they will be able to make out financially or win fame through their accusations. B. Todd Jones, the Minneapolis attorney who won baseball Hall of Famer Kirby Puckett an acquittal on sexual assault charges, contends some district attorneys may be more inclined to file charges against a celebrity athlete because they fear that doing otherwise would make it appear they go easy on famous people. The charges are dropped or the cases are dismissed, according to this argument, because there is insufficient evidence to support them. Or it may be that athletes simply have the wealth, resources, and connections to obtain superior legal counsel, which leads to charges being dropped, pleas, and acquittals.

Part of the problem may be the many myths and misconceptions about rape. Rape myths are beliefs about rape or sexual assault that shape the ways we respond when we hear about a given situation. There are myths about victims as well as about who is likely to perpetrate a sexual assault and why. Common myths about victims include that they provoke rape through their looks, dress, and behavior; that sexual assaults are retribution for past misdeeds; and that they regularly lie about being sexually assaulted. A common myth about why rape occurs is that perpetrators are motivated by sexual desire or lust. Perpetrators are wrongly believed to be mentally ill and more frequently black or poor. Research has shown that athletes in revenue and team sports are more likely to believe in rape myths. These beliefs may help explain the high incidence of rape allegations against athletes. Over 20 percent of male athletes in one study believe women can prevent rape if they want to and believe women provoke rape; 50 percent believe women lie about rape. Another study involving 100 varsity football players at Cornell found 55 percent stated that physical touching and kissing were come-ons for sexual intercourse; 64 percent of the men's rowing team felt this way.

Without a doubt, media pays far more attention to rape allegations against athletes because they are nestled in the nexus of two areas of enormous coverage—sports and crime. Yet, the coverage frequently reinforces rape myths. In general, the popular media aggressively pursues accusers, often to attack their motive in filing charges. Further, because race is so integrally linked with the major sports in the United States, cases against athletes often bring forth issues regarding interracial rape—another tried and true media theme.

Many experts believe the root of the problem is that athletes feel they are entitled to special treatment. They are used to being aggressively wooed and promised and provided whatever they want. They may not be held to the same standards of conduct as are other people simply because the public idolizes them.

KEY EVENTS

A look at some of the higher profile cases involving athletes can provide some insight into how sexual assault allegations are treated. It is important to note that this is not an exhaustive list of complaints against athletes.

One of the most widely known cases is that of heavyweight champion Mike Tyson. In 1992, Tyson was convicted of raping Desiree Washington, an 18-year-old Miss Black America pageant contestant. Tyson was a judge of the pageant, and Ms. Washington had agreed to meet him in his room after hours. Because she willingly went to Tyson's room, and evidence was she did so wearing no panties under her skirt, Washington was widely vilified, both in trial and in the media. Yet, testimony from witnesses that she ran from his room clearly distraught, as well as physical evidence consistent with rape, convinced the jurors Tyson was guilty. He served 3 years of his 10-year sentence.

In the early 1990s, Victoria Alexander accepted a $30,000 settlement from 14 Cincinnati Bengals players. In exchange, she agreed to release them from liability for gang raping her in a hotel room and not to publicly disclose their names. Alexander was told she would make a terrible victim if the case went to trial, given that she purposely appeared at the hotel where the team was staying, dressed in provocative clothing, and willingly entered the players' rooms.

Between February 1991 and December 1994, 12 University of Arkansas football and basketball players were investigated for an array of felonies, mostly involving sexual assault of women. Yet, besides media attention, little came from the cases; the school's star and future NBA player Todd Day and three roommates were not charged with the rape of a 34-year-old woman who happened to be the daughter of the local prosecutor. During the same years, University of Nebraska football players were embroiled in sexual assault scandals. Most notable of these was the multiple allegations against superstar Christian Peter. Peter had a sordid past, having flunked out of one school and performed poorly at another. Despite his troubles, the University of Nebraska recruited him and offered him a scholarship. He had to sit out a year because he did not meet the NCAA's minimal standards, and he was red-shirted for his second year. In these two years, Peter was arrested six times. At the time he sexually assaulted Natalie Kuijvenhoven, there was a warrant for his arrest. Coach Tom Osborne defended Peter, and by most accounts, interfered in the investigation of the case. Peter was never held legally accountable for the attack on Kuijvenhoven. He also assaulted Kathy Redmond, who made a complaint to campus police two weeks before the team was to play in the Orange Bowl. The sex crimes unit of the Lincoln police received the report months later.

In 1997, a young lady accused Boston Celtics players Ron Mercer and Chauncey Billups of sexually assaulting her at a condominium owned by Celtics superstar Antoine Walker. On November 9, 1997, the victim and some other women met Walker, Billups, Mercer, and two of Walker's friends at a Boston comedy club. Once they got to Walker's home, she said that Mercer, Billups, and one of the other men performed a series of unwanted sexual acts on her. At one point she said she blacked out, only to come to and find used condoms all over. No criminal charges were filed, and the victim settled with the three athletes for an undisclosed sum. Only four years earlier, the same detective involved in this case had investigated claims against another Celtic, Marcus Webb, who was accused of anally raping a woman with whom he had a relationship. Webb eventually pleaded guilty to indecent assault and battery. Although he was sentenced to three to five years in prison, he served only 30 days in jail. He was, however, released by the Celtics.

In January 2000, 23-year-old Jenny Stevens agreed to take an interim nanny position working for Seattle Sonics player Ruben Patterson. According to Stevens, Patterson sexually assaulted her while she worked for him. He violated her both digitally as well as forced her to orally copulate him. Afterwards, Patterson warned her not to tell anyone. At the time, Patterson was on trial for different (nonsexual) assault. He had previously been charged with aggravated burglary against a former girlfriend. Patterson hired John Wolfe as his counsel, a private attorney with a reputation for defending athletes in sexual assault cases. Wolfe had previously defended Seattle Seahawks quarterback Gale Gilbert when, in 1987, he was charged with two different sexual assaults in a six-month period. In

1994, Wolfe succeeded in getting sexual assault charges on Gilbert dropped. The case against Patterson ended when he pleaded guilty to lesser charges. He was sentenced to one year in prison with all but 15 days of it suspended. Patterson was allowed to serve his time at his private off-season home in Ohio. In the civil case Stevens filed, Patterson was ordered to pay $400,000.

Mark Chmura, a 32-year-old, married, former all-pro tight end for the Green Bay Packers, was tried in 2000 for sexually assaulting a 17-year-old girl. He had been drinking and hot-tubbing with a bunch of teens after their senior prom. The young lady had babysat for Chmura's children. She was accused throughout the trial and media coverage of lying and of looking for fame, and she was painted as promiscuous and angry. Chmura was acquitted. Two days after his acquittal, Chmura acknowledged that his behavior was not appropriate for a married adult, chalking it up to the raucous craziness of the National Football League (NFL) lifestyle.

In 2002, the University of Colorado (UC) was mired in scandal and bad publicity when Lisa Simpson and two other women alleged that several UC football players and recruits had gang-raped them at Simpson's home during a December 2001 party. The women filed suits in federal court, but all were dismissed. At the same time, other allegations of sexual improprieties involving the football team emerged, including that they used women to recruit new players. In 2004, former kicker Katie Hnida told *Sports Illustrated* that she had been harassed and assaulted by members of the team when she was on it in 1999. Coach Gary Barnett responded by denouncing Hnida's ability and by saying he would fully support his players.

The rape allegation against Los Angeles Lakers star Kobe Bryant was one of the top stories in 2003. According to Katelyn Faber, Bryant forced her to have intercourse with him after she went to his room at the Lodge and Spa at Cordillero, a Vail, Colorado, resort where Faber worked. She consented to kissing him, Faber claimed, but she did not consent to sex. Faber was painted as a vamp in the media, with evidence of her prior sexual encounters and questions about her mental stability used to suggest she was lying. The criminal case was dismissed before the trial began, and Faber agreed to take an undisclosed amount in a civil settlement.

The Clery Act requires universities to report sexual assaults and other crimes that occur on campus. In 2006, La Salle University faced fines and other sanctions for violating the Act when they failed to report sexual assaults allegedly involving members of the men's basketball team in 2003 and 2004. One of the cases, alleging that stars Gary Neal and Michael Cleaves raped a woman working as a summer camp counselor on campus at a party, went to trial. Both Cleaves and Neal were acquitted, largely due to the fact that the prosecution claimed the woman was very intoxicated and had consented to sex with the men.

Although the FBI and other research has documented that false allegations of rape are uncommon, they do occasionally occur. When they do, they are devastating to the wrongly accused and their families. In 2006, three members of the Duke Lacrosse team were accused of raping a 27-year-old stripper who had been hired to perform at a party. On April 5th, the university chose to cancel the

Lacrosse season before DNA results came back. In spring of 2007, all charges were dropped against Colin Finnerty, Reade Seligmann, and David Evans. Durham County district attorney Mike Nifong was disbarred for violating rules of professional conduct.

FUTURE PROSPECTS

One program that schools have found useful to help athletes as well as the general population gain a better understanding of sexual violence is called Can I Kiss You? Presenter Mike Domitrz addresses dating, communication, respect, and sexual assault awareness. He has programs aimed at fifth to twelfth grade students as well as those at colleges and universities. At the College of Wooster, football and baseball players have been trained to present on their campuses about this topic. At Rutgers University, Sexual Assault Services and Crime Victim Assistance (SAS/CVA) and the Division of Intercollegiate Athletics have worked together to feature student-athletes in the performances and to disseminate the video's message to athletes on Rutgers' 27 teams. They have done so through an innovative theater program called SCREAM (Students Challenging Reality and Educating Against Myths) in which students address the many myths and misconceptions about rape. Men Can Stop Rape is a male-led movement that often uses athletes and athletic metaphors to educate and inspire men to end sexual violence. Their strength campaign and Men of Strength clubs help to demonstrate healthier ways for men to be masculine. Research has demonstrated that empathy-based prevention programs are the most successful, having the most and longest-lasting effects. In particular, males developed more sensitivity after watching a video of a male-on-male rape.

Jeff Benedict, author of several books about athletes and violence, has made three proposals. First, he argues that there should be a code of conduct for professional athletes that must be enforced at the league and team levels. Second, those who violate the code of conduct absolutely must face a penalty. And, rather than a fine, which means little to most wealthy athletes, the penalty should be a loss of playing time. Third, professional sports leagues must employ more stringent screening processes to minimize the number of players who have criminal convictions.

See also Academic Misconduct Among Athletes; Marketing Female Athlete Sexuality; Partner Abuse Among Athletes; Rights for Young Athletes; Sexual Abuse Among Athletes.

Further Reading: Benedict, J. (1997). *Public Heroes, Private Felons*. Boston, MA: Northeastern University Press; Benedict, J. (1998). *Athletes and Acquaintance Rape*. Thousand Oaks, CA: Sage; Benedict, J. (1998). *Pros and Cons: The Criminals Who Play in the NFL*. New York: Grand Central Press; Benedict, J. (2004). *Out of Bounds: Inside the NBA's Culture of Rape, Violence & Crime*. New York: HarperCollins; Finley, P., Fountain, J., and Finley, L. (2008, forthcoming). *Sport Scandals*. Westport, CT: Praeger; Humphrey, S., and Kahn, A. (2000). Fraternities, Athletic Teams, and Rape. *Journal of Interpersonal Violence* 15: 1313–1322; Sawyer, R., Thompson, E., and Chicorelli, A. (2002). Rape Myth

Acceptance Among Intercollegiate Athletes: A Preliminary Examination. *American Journal of Health Studies* 18: 19–26; Schwartz, M., and DeKeseredy, W. (1997). *Sexual Assault on the College Campus.* Thousand Oaks, CA: Sage.

Laura L. Finley

REFEREE ABUSE

Referee abuse is an intentional act of physical violence at or upon a referee by a player, coach, or spectator. Referee abuse, however, can also include verbal statements or physical acts not resulting in bodily contact, but which imply or threaten physical harm to a referee or the referees' property or equipment. There are no existing databases that document the historical prevalence of abuse against referees or the number of yearly cases that occur in sports. Nevertheless, the physical and verbal abuse of referees at the hands of players and coaches appears to be on the rise in many sports.

BACKGROUND

The National Association of Sports Officials (NASO) keeps information on over 100 yearly cases of reported referee abuse in youth/minor sports. They argue that the reported cases represent only the tip of the iceberg of assaults against referees in the United States. Instances where referees are punched, slapped, threatened, and even bludgeoned are increasing with a striking regularity. Scant public or criminal justice concern has been afforded to the abuse of referees until the past decade because dominant perspectives held that such abuse fell under a league or sports organization's policing territory. But of late, and as a result of the social lobbying of groups such as the NASO, sports insiders and social legislators are clamoring to determine the factors leading to referee abuse.

A report on the status of violence in Canadian youth ice hockey well documents current thinking regarding the main causes of referee abuse. The report discusses the role of both within-game situations that may lead to the abuse of an official and external cultural factors that make sports grounds dangerous places for referees. In the first case, when players, coaches, or spectators perceive a referee's decision making to be consistently poor or biased, there is a greater likelihood for violence to erupt. When other characteristics of a referee are added, such as if a referee is perceived to be inexperienced or incompetent (i.e., confusion about rules, poor management of players, etc.), they are at even greater risk of assault or abuse. The report also indicated that because so many referees in minor sports may be only a few years older than the players themselves, there is a tendency to see them as incompetent or unworthy of respect as authority figures because they are practically the peers of players. Troublingly, the data from ice hockey and other North American sports indicate that many minor leagues may lose up to one-third of their officials yearly because of their experiences with repeated abuse.

The report confirmed that outside factors such as parental overzealousness in sports were major contributors to referee abuse. Parents' over emphasis on the sporting successes of their children, and common beliefs that an official's decisions may be vehemently debated by them at every turn, has bred dangerous cultures of disrespect toward officials among fans. Referees in many instances become the symbolic targets of violence for frustrated parents whose child or children are not excelling in a sport. Additionally, coaches are symbolically likened to police by fan groups and thus treated with the same levels of condemnation and frustration that police frequently receive.

A popular explanation of referee abuse in minor leagues sports cultures stems from the common belief that young players who abuse referees are emulating the abusive behaviors toward referees that they have witnessed professional players undertake. The sport of baseball, for example, has long showcased the abusive or otherwise irreverent behaviors of players and coaches toward its umpires. Chest to chest tirades, kicking dirt on umpires, and throwing objects at umpires are common in both the minor and professional leagues of the sport. In 1996, Baltimore Orioles second baseman Roberto Alomar engaged in a heated exchange with home plate umpire John Hirschbeck about a third-strike call against him during a game against the Cleveland Indians. After a brief exchange between the two, Alomar spit in Hirschbeck's face. Alomar was immediately ejected from the game, showing more disrespect for the umpire when he said in a postgame interview that Hirschbeck had become "bitter" since the death of his 8-year-old son. League officials handed Alomar a five-game suspension for the abuse (which would begin the following season so that Alomar would be eligible to play in the postseason). Major league umpires were incensed with the light sentence and

SELECTED PARENTAL VIOLENCE CASES REPORTED TO THE NATIONAL ASSOCIATION OF SPORTS OFFICIALS IN THE UNITED STATES IN 2004

There was a noticed spike in reports of referee abuse in 2004, for reasons that still baffle sports insiders. Consider some of the more flagrant cases.

- Pennsylvania (Basketball): A parent body-slammed a high school referee after he ordered the man's wife out of the gym for allegedly yelling obscenities during a basketball game. The referee was treated at a hospital for a concussion and released.
- New Jersey (Soccer): Referee James Clay, a 50-year-old with seven years of officiating experience, was struck in the head and neck by a parent after ejecting a Clayton High School player in the game.
- Illinois (Football): James Camden, aged 43, was charged with two counts of aggravated battery and one count of battery after allegedly charging onto the field and attempting to choke game official Mike Byrne.
- Kentucky (Baseball): Roger Bratcher, the father of a T-ball player, was briefly jailed after an outburst against umpire Eddie Smith during a game involving 5 and 6 year olds.
- Illinois (Softball): A father head-butted softball umpire Tim Smith in a confrontation following a girls softball game.
- Oklahoma (Basketball): Five players and a spectator were charged with beating referee Eltonio Waylon Henry following a men's basketball league game.

HISTORICAL CASES OF UMPIRE ABUSE IN PROFESSIONAL BASEBALL

- On July 15, 1939, New York Giants shortstop Billy Jurges and umpire George Magerkurth brawled amid conflicting charges that each had spit in the other's face. Both were suspended for 10 days and fined $250.
- On May 29, 1943, Brooklyn Dodgers pitcher Johnny Allen grabbed umpire George Barr by the shoulders. He was fined $200 and suspended for 30 days.
- On September 16, 1978, San Francisco Giants coach Dave Bristol struck umpire Jerry Crawford in the face with a hat during an argument. Bristol was fined $500 and suspended for the remainder of the season (10 games).
- On May 1, 1980, Pittsburgh Pirates third baseman Bill Madlock fought with Jerry Crawford over a third-strike call. A few minutes later, Madlock hit Crawford with his glove three times. Madlock was suspended 15 days and fined $5,000. Umpires threatened to strike over the Madlock case if the suspension was not upheld in full.
- On July 17, 1982, Orioles manager Earl Weaver slapped umpire Terry Cooney. For his attack on Cooney, Weaver was suspended for one week and fined $2,000.
- On April 30, 1988, in a game between the New York Mets and Cincinnati Reds, Reds manager Pete Rose shoved umpire Dave Pallone during an argument. Rose was suspended for 30 days and fined an undisclosed amount.

threatened to strike. A Philadelphia judge, however, ordered the umpires could not strike because a strike would violate their labor contract. When Alomar stepped to home plate to bat in the first game of the playoffs against the Cleveland Indians that year, Baltimore fans gave him a raucous ovation. Baseball as a sport had inauspicious beginnings with regard to umpire assaults. Early twentieth-century baseball was plagued with violent confrontations between players and umpires. But in 1927, Commissioner Kennesaw Mountain Landis decreed that any assault on an umpire would result in a suspension ranging from 90 days to one year. The new rule managed the problem rather effectively, but the sport has always retained an air of disrespect for officials.

KEY EVENTS

Established in the 1980s, the NASO is the only national organization in the United States dedicated solely to the support of officials from grassroots local sports to professional sports; from the National Football League (NFL) to Pop Warner, to Major League Baseball (MLB), to Little League of America, to the National Basketball Association (NBA), and to youth and recreational programs across the United States. The NASO is an organization dedicated to consciousness-raising with regard to the critical role sports officials play as volunteers in the world of sports and the need to develop new initiatives to protect their physical and mental welfare. Among the primary functions NASO undertakes is that of watchdog (and statistics keeper) of reported cases of referee abuse and assault. Prior to the NASO's annual recording and dissemination of reported cases of abuse, there were no quasisystematically gathered databases to document the extent of the problem.

Approximately 17,000 officials worldwide now belong to the NASO, and collectively they campaign to improve working conditions for officials. A part of their collective work is to encourage those inside and outside of sports to see referees as workers within sports organizations with rights to protection and safety. In this regard, the NASO cooperates with state and local community associations to provide training seminars, books and manuals for educational purposes, and public relations programs designed to promote the need for positive and healthy working conditions for referees. The NASO developed over time into a legal reformer organization, acting as the public voice for referees in the context of national and state legislative review and change regarding referees' rights. As part of their legislative reform campaigns, the NASO brings to public light cases of official abuse and assault in order to expose the sheer prevalence and destructiveness of a relatively hidden social problem.

From time to time, flamboyantly violent cases of referee abuse do reach public discourse and are spotlighted as "tip of the iceberg" examples. A case that became mass mediated across North America involved university ice hockey players in Canada. On February 24, 1996, at the end of an overtime period in a championship game between the University of Moncton and the University of Prince Edward Island (UPEI), chief referee Brian Carragher was pinned to the boards and physically assaulted by eight players from the University of Moncton. The incident occurred after a controversial goal ended the hockey game in UPEI's favor. Moncton goaltender Pierre Gagnon initiated the assault by grabbing Carragher; his assistant coach, Patrick Daviault, and several other players joined in the attack by throwing punches at the referee. Carragher was repeatedly punched in the head and body by the Moncton players and speared in the groin with a stick. Eventually, Daviault removed a metal mooring from the net and threw it into a pane of glass in front of the goal judge, shattering the glass. Four players from the Moncton team were suspended from intercollegiate competition (suspensions ranged from 1–5 years) and assistant coach Daviault received a one-year suspension. Although police and Crown prosecutors in Charlottetown, Prince Edward Island, initially threatened criminal intervention into the sport in response to the event, none ever materialized. The case illustrates how difficult it is at times to convince court officials that the assault of referees is as grave of a social offense as common assault on the street.

To combat one of the primary causes of referee abuse, perceived poor or biased officiating in "big game" contexts, several professional and collegiate sports leagues have developed and implemented video review or instant replay policies in their sports. Essentially, new rules allowing coaches to challenge official's decisions (i.e., forcing them to review plays on video monitors) provide situations wherein disputed on-field calls may be challenged without aggression developing

AN EXAMPLE OF LEGISLATION TO PROTECT REFEREES IN NEVADA

Assembly Bill No. 474

A person convicted of an assault shall be punished:

(c) If paragraph (d) of this subsection does not apply to the circumstances of the crime and if the assault is committed upon an officer, a provider of health care, a school employee, a taxicab driver or a transit operator who is performing his duty *or upon a sports official based on the performance of his duties at a sporting event,* and the person charged knew or should have known that the victim was an officer, a provider of health care, a school employee, a taxicab driver, [or] a transit operator [,] *or a sports official,* for a gross misdemeanor, unless the assault is made with the use of a deadly weapon, or the present ability to use a deadly weapon, then for a category B felony by imprisonment in the state prison for a minimum term of not less than 1 year and a maximum term of not more than 6 years, or by a fine of not more than $5,000, or by both fine and imprisonment.

(d) If the assault is committed upon an officer, a provider of health care, a school employee, a taxicab driver or a transit operator who is performing his duty [,] *or upon a sports official based on the performance of his duties at a sporting event* by a probationer, a prisoner who is in lawful custody or confinement or a parolee, and the probationer, prisoner or parolee charged knew or should have known that the victim was an officer, a provider of health care, a school employee, a taxicab driver, [or] a transit operator [,] *or a sports official,* for a category D felony as provided in NRS 193.130, unless the assault is made with the use of a deadly weapon, or the present ability to use a deadly weapon, then for a category B felony by imprisonment in the state prison for a minimum term of not less than 1 year and a maximum term of not more than 6 years, or by a fine of not more than $5,000, or by both fine and imprisonment.

---

between players, coaches, and referees. Either the official in question, or a second (or even third) official, will, on the request of a coach (or even on an official's own request), be able to review a controversial play. The NFL first experimented with the instant replay system in 1986 and reformed its review practices, making them highly regimented and rule bound, in 1999. The use of video reviews emerged in National Collegiate Athletic Association (NCAA) football in 2004 and in the Canadian Football League in 2006. In each league, the system is now used widely.

The National Hockey League (NHL) started using video review in 1991 at the request of referees who had been repeatedly (verbally) assaulted for "poor calls." In the NHL, video review is used to determine whether a puck crosses a goal line, whether it crosses the goal line before the net is dislodged, whether it crosses the goal line before the time clock has expired, if a puck is directed into the net by a hand or a foot, or whether a puck is directed into the net by a high stick. Of note, in the 1998 season, the NHL also introduced a second referee onto the ice to help monitor penalty infractions and to provide a second assessment of decisions made by the primary referee. In NBA and NCAA basketball, video review is used sparingly, mainly to assess whether or not a player's shot is released before a time clock expires or to assess who was involved in an on-court flagrant foul. Other sports that include one or another form of video review are professional tennis, NASCAR, rodeo, cricket, and rugby. Major League Baseball refuses to use video review technology to this day. Their reluctance is rather curious, given the legacy of disputed umpire calls in the sport.

Within the U.S. legal system, states have progressively revisited, amended, or drafted new legislation to protect referees from harm within sports and to afford them legal recourse if or when they are abused. There is, at present, existing legislation in 22 U.S. states that defines the abuse or assault of officials as a criminal transgression. Common practice is to write the definition of referee abuse into existing legislation protecting workers in voluntary association roles.

Legislation initiatives and policy reform on the subject of referee abuse in the United States are path-breaking and have caught the attention of sports leagues and officials around the world. Organizers of professional soccer and rugby union in the United Kingdom have explored North American antiabuse practices to help combat rapidly developing cultures of referee disrespect and mistreatment in both of the sports. At all levels of play, soccer and rugby union referees have reported escalating incidents of abuse over the last eight years. The Football Association (FA), the UK's organizing body of soccer, announced plans in 2008 to invest a record £200 million into the problem of referee abuse in the sport. The FA canvassed 37,000 people on the subject, the largest public consultation on the problem in their history, to help generate its new "FA National Game Strategy 2008–2012." For well over a decade, the FA has been concerned by the high attrition levels of referees every season at the local levels. Key to the initiative is the recruitment and retention of referees and coaches. As part of the National Game Strategy, the FA is particularly keen to foster a new culture of respect for officials from both players and spectators.

FUTURE PROSPECTS

Because most referees act as volunteers within sports organizations in the United States, they hold a rather precarious and dangerous role therein as people with legal rights to safety. As a volunteer, a referee is generally viewed as only a temporary member of an organization and not a regular employee with organizational rights. Their status within sports organizations is often one, then, of limited liability as outlined in the Volunteer Protection Act of 1997. Leagues have used federal and state laws in the United States to argue that referees as volunteers cannot sue leagues for creating unsafe working conditions (i.e., their failure to adequately control spectators). Groups like the NASO argue that unless leagues begin to be held (partially) criminally responsible for the abuse of officials, the number of reported cases will only escalate.

See also Criminal Violence During Competition; Field Invasions; Hooliganism; Missile Throwing; Parent Misconduct; Taunting.

Further Reading: Dorsch, K., and Paskevich, D. (2007). Stressful Experiences Among Six Certification Levels of Ice Hockey Officials. *Psychology of Sport and Exercise* 8: 585–593;

Pascall, B. (2000). *Eliminating Violence in Hockey.* Special Report Commissioned by Ian Waddell, Minister Responsible for Sport, British Columbia, Canada; Rainey, D. (1999). Sources of Stress, Burnout and Intention to Terminate among Basketball Referees. *Journal of Sport Behavior* 22: 19–40; Staffo, D. (2001). Strategies for Reducing Criminal Violence Among Athletes. *The Journal of Physical Education, Recreation & Dance* 72: 239–255.

Michael Atkinson

RELIGIOUS EXPRESSION

There are few subjects in contemporary life that raise tensions and debates as much as sports or religion. Conversations about religious expression in sports are not nearly as common as they were 100 years ago, yet religious expressions around the playing field and controversies about them continue. Religious expressions vary but typically include forms of prayer by players or coaches, references to God in their speech, symbolic images of a particular faith such as a cross or Star of David in the sport, or conscientious objections to particular sports rituals (drinking, baring skin, or playing or practicing on a particular day) based on religious ideologies. North American sports presently wrestle with whether or not religious ideology or practice has any role in the performance of athletes and, if they do have such a role, how different religious ideologies may be accommodated appropriately.

BACKGROUND

By the mid-1800s, private education sports cultures in North America were saturated with middle-class, Protestant ideology. Athletics were increasingly inserted into educational curricula because educators felt that rigorous forms of physical activity had a role in developing personal character, fostered patriotism and community pride, and taught students to embody the central tenets of Christianity through competitive sports. Young boys' abilities to work, sacrifice, focus, be dedicated, and to respect a gentleman's code of moral conduct were deliberately nurtured through athletics.

In 1857, educators and social reformers in the United States and the United Kingdom started to speak of the need for creating a new generation of young, "muscular Christians." College sports in particular were to be the sites in which Christian values would be reinforced among athletes as a key component in their athletic training. British author Thomas Hughes published his novel *Tom Brown's Schooldays* in 1857, in which he praised the benefits of not only devoting one's heart and mind to God but the benefits of building a strong body through sports such as rugby, cricket, and soccer to do God's will. Hughes's book illustrates how the fictional character Tom Brown learns to be morally virtuous and socially responsible through sports.

The actual term *muscular Christianity*, which ideas in Hughes's book are based upon, appeared first in an 1857 review of a book by Charles Kingsley. Hughes argued across his collected works on youth and sports that the muscular Christian must train his body and discipline his habits so that he could protect the weak, advance righteous causes, and focus his energies toward obeying Christian life principles in general. The ideals of muscular Christianity entered America during the Civil War era through books such as Hughes's. At that time, recreation and athletics had become a fixture in public education systems and were driven by the muscular Christian ideals of such evangelical reformers as Lyman Beecher. Leading muscular Christian causes in sports cultures, and the need to link them in college, was the Young Men's Christian Association (YMCA). The YMCA was founded as a Christian outreach movement in industrial America that strived to ensure young Christians possessed the requisite skills to lead new generations at the turn of the twentieth century in America. George Williams was the driving force behind the YMCA, and historians have documented how he was influenced by American religious revivalist Charles G. Finney and religious theorist Luther Gulick. Williams and Gulick were strong proponents of muscular Christianity and added to its ideals the commitment to personal conversion through athletics. One of America's most notable muscular Christians was the Victorian-era evangelist D. L. Moody, who brought the YMCA's message to the nation. Interestingly, the sport of basketball has YMCA origins. Canadian-born James Naismith invented the sport at the International Training School of the YMCA in Springfield, Massachusetts. Naismith believed that basketball served as a perfect social ritual for teaching young men Christian values and encouraging young men to socialize and bond with others "like them."

Muscular Christianity survived as an ethos in the educational system in North America until the 1960s, during which ideologies of secular humanism (i.e., using sports to produce civic character in athletes without an overt religious link) and more scientifically dominant, kinesiological ways of understanding the need for physical training as a facilitator to health emerged. Nevertheless, education-based and recreational forms of sports continued to be rather exclusionary along religious lines. The entrenchment of muscular Christian ideologies in sports through the process of institutionalization at schools and its spread through popular culture may have simply normalized the idea that sports values are in line with Christian ideologies, even when the latter are not directly represented or considered as simply taken for granted. For example, references to the Christian God are found in anthems sung prior to the start of games in Canada (as part of the national anthem, "O, Canada," a lyric states, "God keep our land, glorious and free …") and the United States (songs such as "God Bless America" and "America the Beautiful," which contains the lyric, "America, America, God shed his grace on thee …"), players often kneel in the end zone and gesture in the sign of the Christian cross, and teams often lead Christian prayers before games without much public opposition or concern because most of them have been ritualized as standard sporting practices.

Two major debates arise about religion and sports in contemporary North American life. In the first instance, religious critics of modern sports at the scholastic, amateur, and professional levels lament the relative lack of moral boundaries of conscientious Christian practices in sports cultures. Sports to them is now like a secular religion itself, creating athletes as deities to be worshipped for their physical abilities and not their virtues. Sports' role in embodying the sacred on earth is also replaced with a profane commercialism and lack of ethical grounding. Games are played on the Christian Sabbath day, fans routinely pass over church to watch sports, and references to Christianity are even shunned or prohibited in certain sports leagues. In 2007, for example, head coach of the National Football League (NFL) Indianapolis Colts, Tony Dungy, spoke openly about his Christian beliefs during an interview related to an award he received from the Indiana Family Institute. The Colts organization immediately declared that while Dungy has the right to his own religious views, his beliefs did not represent those of the organization.

North Americans who do not subscribe to Christian practices have also suggested that either religious references should be stripped out of mainstream sports programs (such as in educational programs wherein all students attend gym class on a mandatory basis) or that room should be made for alternative religious ideologies in these sports settings. In both Canada and the United States, Muslim and Sikh parents have argued that dress codes in gym classes are in potential conflict with their religious beliefs. As part of these critiques, members of many faiths have decided to organize their own religiously themed sports leagues, classes, or community programs in order to promote alternative constructions of sports for their youth. Here, one of the most important cultural lessons learned is that not all religious groups understand how to socialize through sports, or define how identities should be represented in sports, in similar manners. Part of the task in planning North American sports in schools and elsewhere in the future is how to negotiate what sports means on religious grounds and whether or not any individual should be asked to deny or bend their own faith in order to play.

KEY EVENTS

One of the most poignant testimonials of how sports become a religion for a group of people is found in Bissinger's book *Friday Night Lights,* published in 1990. Bissinger followed the exploits of the Permian High School football team in Odessa, Texas, for a season and documented how local residents believed in the team like a congregation of idol worshipers. It is chilling in the book how teenage players are treated as sports deities and how the town's image is closely related to the victories and losses of their football gods. Bissinger's book has become an American classic and watershed text for critically interrogating how extensively the cult(ure) of sports helps to frame community ideologies and practice. In Canada, the children's story *The Hockey Sweater,* written in 1979 by Roch Carrier, reveals a similar theme. The story is about how a young Roch idolized, like the rest of his Francophone community in Quebec, players on the Montreal Canadiens such as Maurice Richard. In the book, Carrier states that there were two religions in Quebec, the Catholic faith and the ice hockey faith. Each shaped how the Quebecois practiced social life.

The past decade has witnessed a Christian resurgence in sports cultures. There has been a rise in Christian-based sports organizations across the country (such as the Fellowship of Christian Athletes, the Salvation Army Basketball League, and Christian Sports Productions), a Christian Sports Network television and radio channel, and more players, such as the NFL's Roland Williams, Antwaan Randle El, Troy Vincent, and Reggie White, are declaring that they have been "born again." Notwithstanding the regional acceptance of contemporary muscular Christians, there has been considerable opposition to overt expressions of Christian ideology made by players or promoted by teams.

The 2007 "miracle" run of the Colorado Rockies to the World Series was ascribed by their players to the Christian orientation of the team. A series of news articles in 2007 articulated how team owners, coaches, and players have purposely molded a Christian team that plays and prays together. Rockies General Manager Dan O'Dowd argued that they wanted a team with character and with Christian values; part of that means accepting Jesus as lord and savior. In fact, Christianity guides all aspects of the team and its representation. Players are not allowed to hang sexually suggestive pictures in their lockers, and profane music is prohibited from the locker room. Players are encouraged to attend chapel every Sunday and team-based Bible studies during the week. Rockies' CEO Charlie Monfort first encouraged the team to "go Christian" in 2004 after their pitcher Denny Neagle was charged with soliciting a prostitute. Monfort himself had been born again in the wake of his own legal trouble. Key sponsors such as Coors, whose name is branded on the Rockies' stadium, are staunch advocates of Christianity. Colorado Springs, the location of the Rockies minor league affiliate, is also home to "Focus on the Family," a hyperconservative political group, as well as evangelical publishers and several mega churches. Critics have decried the team's religious orientation as potentially alienating for nonbelievers on the team and a potentially discriminatory practice. Others have argued that implicit in the all-Christian team format (the club now openly speaks about recruiting Christian players) is a "whites only" policy as well (at the time of writing, there were only two black players on the Rockies).

IT'S OKAY TO BE DIFFERENT: AS LONG AS YOU WIN

One is hard-pressed to find symbols or expressions of non-Christian spirituality in professional or amateur sports. Sports such as basketball have been historically saturated with Christianity, and it is normative to be Christian in the sport, that is, unless you are coach Phil Jackson. Jackson has coached two National Basketball Association (NBA) teams (the Chicago Bulls and the Los Angeles Lakers) to a combined nine championships. Notably, Jackson is an avid promoter of Zen Buddhist and Native American spiritual philosophies as motivational tools. For this, he has been dubbed the "Zen Master" by players. Ask yourself whether or not Jackson is allowed to espouse alternative religious ideologies in mainstream sports culture only because of his winning record.

Other teams are following the Christian revivalism in baseball but not with the same veracity as the Rockies. Teams such as the Atlanta Braves, Arizona Diamondbacks, and Florida Marlins now sponsor "Faith Days" at their ballparks. These are religious-oriented promotional days held as the theme for specific games. As part of a Faith Day at a ballpark, local Christian churches receive discounted tickets to family-friendly evenings of sports and entertainment with a Christian theme. At one of the Faith Days in Atlanta, the team sells special vouchers to the game. After the game, the people with the Christian vouchers stay behind and are privy to several hours of live Christian music. Teams argue that one of the explicit motives of Faith Days like these is to promote a family environment at the ballpark, but critics claim that teams have simply found a new fan base to target.

The Colorado Rockies organization is but one of the new Christian fundamentalist groups in sports. The Promise Keepers is a Protestant social movement that cites and uses sports as a solution to contemporary problems among young males in the United States. The Promise Keepers believe that young Christian men need to reclaim their dominant leadership roles in sports, politics, government, and family life. Critics of their publications suggest that the Promise Keeper emphasis on restoring a patriarchal, Christian order through sports has no place in contemporary athletics.

Another overtly pro-Christian movement in North American sports is Athletes in Action (AIA), which was founded in 1966 by David Hannah who sought to spread Christian messages to vast, sports-loving audiences. Of late, Athletes in Action has become a global innovator and leader in what is now referred to as sports ministry. As a branch of the American organization Campus Crusade for Christ, Athletes in Action specifically targets college sports and their fans as potential supporters. In 2006, AIA had a ministry presence in 85 countries, on 100 U.S. college campuses, and in 35 U.S. professional sports teams. Every summer AIA sends teams of college athletes in multiple sports to compete overseas, grow their individual faith, and spread a Christian message.

In the Christian fundamentalist revival era in sports, alternative religious expressions and symbols on the playing field may be met with hostility. In 2000, Pardeep Nagra was told he could not box in, or for, Canada if he, a practicing Sikh, would not shave his beard. The Canadian Amateur Boxing Association (CABA) viewed his beard as a safety risk, believing particles of hair could damage an opponent's eye. The CABA also argued that a beard could potentially buffer the effects of a punch to the face and, thus, give its wearer an unfair advantage. Nagra countered that other types of body hair—from moustaches to eyebrows to forearm hair—are allowable and that, additionally, professional boxers can wear beards. Nagra filed official complaints against Boxing Ontario, protesting that he could not shave his beard due to his religious convictions. He obtained a court injunction to allow him to compete in the Canada 2000 Boxing Championships in Campbell River, Canada. The CABA agreed to drop amendments regarding mandatory shaving, acknowledging its potentially discriminatory basis. The CABA also agreed to ask the International Boxing Association to repeal their similar rules.

Players with non-Christian backgrounds or who are disinterested in sports opportunities provided to them in schools have come together to create their own religious-based leagues. Muslim sports leagues (especially in the wake of anti-Muslim sentiment in North America following September 11, 2001) have cropped up across the continent and are incredibly popular in cities such as New York, Los Angeles, and Toronto. Muslim leagues are created to allow players to participate in Western sports such as basketball and ice hockey without fear of religious discrimination or in traditional sports in their ancestral nations such as India or Pakistan (e.g., cricket and kabbadi) as a means of promoting religious and cultural bonding among them. Organizations such as Maccabi USA/Sports for Israel operate in the same capacity for members of the North American Jewish community. Established in 1977, the Orthodox Bungalow Baseball League (New York) also exists in North America as the largest sports league in the Jewish world. The league was initially developed to provide young Orthodox Jewish men with a pastime to engage in on Sundays while Christian America held its Sabbath day.

FUTURE PROSPECTS

Recent trends in North American sports pose a series of questions, and some might suggest contradictions, about the relationship between sports and religion. On the one hand, there is a noticeable upsurge in Christian fundamentalism in sports cultures on the continent and a simultaneous call to revive the muscular Christian ethos. Yet, even on teams and in leagues brimming with Christian values, the sports as a religion motif and ethos is still prevalent. Add to this the sheer, and crass, commercialization of the game, and it is difficult at times to see the overt links between Christian doctrines and actual sports practices. On the other hand, there is a movement toward segregation in sports where members of non-Christian faiths in North America find great benefit in establishing their own sports leagues, synced with their own religious ideologies. Such movements may be indicators, then, that the North American melting pot or cultural mosaic philosophies of social tolerance to diversity may be wearing thin in sports worlds.

See also Ethnic Coaches, Managers, and Owners; Yoga and Alternative Fitness.

Further Reading: Baker, W. (2007). *Playing with God: Religion and Modern Sport*. Cambridge, MA: Harvard University Press; Bissinger, H. (1990). *Friday Night Lights*. Cambridge, MA: Da Capo Press; Carrier, R. (1979). *The Hockey Sweater*. Toronto, ON: Tundra Books; Higgs, R., and Braswell, M. (2004). *Unholy Alliance: Sacred and Modern Sports*. Macon, GA: Mercer University Press; Prebish, C. (1992). *Religion and Sport: The Meeting of Sacred and Profane*. Westport, CT: Greenwood Press; Putney, C. (2001). *Muscular Christianity: Manhood and Sports in Protestant America*. Cambridge, MA: Harvard University Press; Williams, R. (2001). *Promise Keepers and the New Masculinity: Private Lives and Public Morality*. Lanham, MD: Lexington Books

Michael Atkinson

RIGHTS OF YOUNG ATHLETES

Over the course of the past 20 years, reports of young athlete abuse in a host of sports cultures have drawn attention to the need for establishing new codes and doctrines that protect young people from victimization in sports. A number of bills have been introduced by local, national, and now international sports and government groups to ensure that children are protected in cultural practice and by law within sports. Along with this, government and nongovernmental organizations have worked to use sports as a safe cultural space for the young who regularly encounter crime, violence, and other forms of risk in their everyday social lives.

BACKGROUND

What is referred to as the "Bill of Rights for Young Athletes" was first developed by Dr. Vern Seefeldt, professor emeritus at the Institute for the Study of Youth Sports in the United States, and Dr. Rainier Martens. In response to growing concerns regarding the abuse of young athletes, the two developed an idea that all athletes, regardless of age or background, have fundamental human rights that need to be protected and nourished in sports cultures. They believed a common doctrine or bill could be developed and upheld across youth sports federations in North America to ensure that young athletes would be protected from exploitation, sexual abuse, physical assault, and emotional abuse. Their bill has received global recognition as a first step in recognizing that young athletes are a special population in sports, and their bodies and minds require careful

---

THE SHELDON KENNEDY ABUSE CASE

Sheldon Kennedy was a young Canadian ice hockey player coached by Graham James, a highly respected and nationally famous coach. Kennedy had been a junior-level hockey player in Winnipeg and then, during the late 1980s, on the Swift Current Broncos of Canada's Western Hockey League. Between the ages of 14 and 19, Kennedy was sexually abused by James. Kennedy has said that James sexually assaulted him more than 350 times.

James told Kennedy that they were like husband and wife and that no matter where Kennedy would go, James would follow him. Emotional and psychological pressure in Kennedy built up over time, and the young player considered suicide on several occasions as his only escape from James. Eventually, Kennedy left the Broncos when he was drafted by the National Hockey League's (NHL) Calgary Flames. In 1995, Kennedy broke his silence about the abuse. Hockey insiders, including some of Kennedy's own teammates, knew of the abuse, but Kennedy finally pressed criminal charges against James. In January 1997, Graham James was sentenced to three years in prison for sexually assaulting Kennedy and another unidentified player. As a result, the Canadian Hockey Association instituted new coach screening and monitoring policies and developed a grass-roots program called "Speak Out," designed to encourage young players to speak out about acts of physical, emotional, or mental abuse they have suffered in the sport.

cultivation. As Seefeldt and Martens argued, the following are a child's basic human rights in sports:

1. Right to participate in sports.
2. Right to participate at a level commensurate with each child's maturity and ability.
3. Right to have qualified adult leadership.
4. Right to play as a child and not as an adult.
5. Right of children to share in the leadership and decision making of their sports participation.
6. Right to participate in safe and healthy environments.
7. Right to proper preparation for participation in sports.
8. Right to an equal opportunity to strive for success.
9. Right to be treated with dignity.
10. Right to have fun in sports.

KEY EVENTS

Following the introduction of the Bill of Rights for Young Athletes, sports federations, organizations, and teams; nongovernmental sports offices; and governmental sports agencies, as well as international sports advocates, have analyzed what best practices may be adopted to protect the rights of young athletes and to ensure that sports are youth-oriented everywhere. The 1989 UN globally ratified document *The Convention on the Rights of the Child,* for example, was a watershed statement on sports as a site of childhood development. It was shortly followed by the 1996 *Panathlon Charter on the Rights of the Child in Sport.* Emergent discourses across international organizations and subcommittees such as the United Nations Children's Fund (UNICEF) and the United Nations Educational, Scientific, and Cultural Organization (UNESCO) in the late 1990s described an ideal sports culture as a nondiscriminatory social environment that allows participants to develop as healthy and protected persons. The *Panathlon Charter* in particular stresses social mentorship and bonding through sports and the extensive benefits of providing children with voices to express their own desires for and interests in sports.

By the 2000 UN Millennium Summit and the 2002 UN Special Session on Children, a mantra of social development through youth sports had crystallized. The UN 2002 document *A World Fit for Children* and the related *Millennium Development Goals* (MDGs) were recognized by UNICEF and UNESCO as tools reframing the logic and practice of global sports. In July 2003, UN Secretary-General Kofi Annan formally addressed members of the international assembly, articulating how sports may be an ideal vehicle for achieving MDGs. The UN then established the Office of Sport for Development and Peace to broadcast Annan's message. Members of UNICEF agreed with the potential link between MDGs and sports and worked in conjunction with Adolf Ogi, the UN Special Adviser on Sport for Development and Peace, and the UN Inter-Agency Task Force on Sport for Development and Peace to produce *Sport for*

Development and Peace: Towards Achieving Millennium Development Goals in 2003. This document is the first global statement on sports as a basic human right for children and as a cultural site of international peace promotion. The UN continued the campaign by declaring 2005 the International Year of Sport and Physical Education. Politicians, health advocates, national governing bodies, and sports insiders around the globe discussed the effectiveness of youth sports programs in addressing health problems, educational opportunities, economic mobility, environmental protection, crime control, and social fragmentation.

Seeds of an international youth-sports-as-development social movement had been planted before the UN's half decade of mobilization around the issue. Canada, Norway, and The Netherlands led programs within their countries to examine the promise of sports in fostering social change for youths. The Canadian and Norwegian brainchild, the Right to Play organization (formerly Olympic Aid), had long operated outside of the international policy limelight. International sports organizations such as the International Olympic Committee (IOC), the Fédération Internationale de Football Association (FIFA), UK Sport, Sport Without Borders, the Union Européenne de Football Association (UEFA), and the Fédération Internationale de Basketball (FIBA), along with national sports organizing bodies in countries including Canada, Russia, Switzerland, The Netherlands, Egypt, Brazil, the United States, Italy, Hungary, Norway, and more than 70 others, also innovated either one-off sports events or long-term educational and participatory programs to promote sports as a site for achieving social and personal development for youths.

Proponents of a sports-as-safety-for-youths argument believe that sports programs work as preventive or reactive methods for confronting social problems. When sports is structured effectively, it offers education for children who may be alienated from mainstream school opportunities; shelters at-risk children within safely supervised spaces; provides children who have few or no family role models with positive socializing forces; teaches nonviolence, cultural diversity, and interpersonal tolerance; offers a healthy leisure-time option; and reduces child experimentation with drugs and firearms. To a degree, however, many of these claims are anecdotal, speculative, or simply naive. Inner-city sports programs designed to reduce youth crime in statistically problematic urban areas (such as midnight basketball leagues or road hockey leagues) meet with either temporary or uncertain results. Critics argue that sports may provide temporary relief for at-risk youths but does not alleviate problems such as poverty, poor educational opportunities, and racism that put them at risk in the first place.

In the future, policy makers in North America might find increased reason to test whether sports actually works in youth protection and development. Practically every academic theory of youth crime and deviance in the books argues that youths require structured and supervised activities and peaceful cultural spaces (such as those potentially provided by sports) to counteract biographical experiences such as family violence and fragmentation, peer rule-violating influences, discrimination, economic disparity, exploitation, and abuse that either push or pull children into patterns of unwanted deviance.

MIDNIGHT BASKETBALL LEAGUES

The National Midnight Basketball League was founded in Glenarden, Maryland, in 1986 by G. Van Standifer as a late-night summer basketball league for older teens in response to escalating crime rates and evidence of drug-related activities in the Glenarden Township. The program operated between 10 P.M. and 2 A.M. three nights weekly during the summer months. The season was divided into regular and championship tournament sessions. Young men between the ages of 17 and 25 are eligible, with proof of county residence, on a first-come, reserved basis. This program was started as an alternative for young adults to drugs, crime, and other deviant activities. The Midnight League also offered mandatory education, counseling, mentoring, and personal development workshops in a safe environment. On April 12, 1991, President George Bush visited Glenarden to celebrate National Community Point of Light Week. The president named the Midnight Basketball League the "124th Point of Light." In 1994, President Bill Clinton drew midnight basketball further into the media spotlight as he pushed for an anticrime bill that would lead to more police officers and more programs intended to deter crime, such as midnight basketball leagues, in American inner cities.

Realistically, however, for sports to combat the systematic problems that young people encounter, sports environments should first be cleaned up. One might call attention to the following conditions of Western youth sports cultures: the structural problems of access to sports for minority groups and youths with disability, the pervasive gender and sexual discrimination, the adult ideological domination, the high rates of dropout in competitive youth sports due to child anxiety and stress, the instrumentalization of young bodies and minds as part of physical education policies, the sexual and physical abuse of young athletes by coaches, the prevalence of drugs and violence in and around sports venues, and the disappearance of traditional youth games and free play in favor of competitive sports training programs. If sports is to be a safe haven for children, systematic rule violations in sports cultures that produce exploitation must be rectified. The Panathlon group of the United Kingdom clearly agrees with this statement and has produced six policy documents to be used when assessing problem structures and practices in youth sports: *Equal Opportunities Policy, Child Protection Policy, Mainstream Risk Assessment, Disability Risk Assessment, Fair Play Charter,* and *School, Officials and Organizers Responsibilities Charter* (www.panathlon.co.uk). Nevertheless, theorizing how sports may cure youth problems is partly premature when the sources of inequality, suffering, and exploitation *within* sports are yet to be fully understood.

FUTURE PROSPECTS

One of the most publicly significant lines of analysis in the youth-sports-rights protection field is research on the possible function of sports in fighting the spread of HIV and AIDS in countries with high rates of infection. Studies of sports in South Africa, Zambia, Nairobi, and Mumbai (Keim, 2003) uncover how local and national sports organizations use sports training and competition spaces as sites of education and collective mentoring. The rates of HIV infection are soaring among 15 to 24 year olds in these countries and cities, and researchers concur that transmission is amplified by youths' lack of knowledge about the disease, by silence about its causes, and by forced sexual activity (especially among young, poor females).

Research on multisite case studies of grassroots HIV and AIDS awareness programs in youth soccer cultures in Africa reveals how sports is used as an effective intervention. An overview of the Mathare Youth Sports Association, Go Sisters, and Youth Education Through Sports programs includes evidence of the effectiveness of peer mentorship about HIV and AIDS through youth soccer. The respective programs, akin to FIFA's Kicking AIDS Out! campaign, empower young athletes by linking physical, social, and moral development in sports with self-protectionist mentalities of health and safety. Research from South Africa demonstrates how sports involvement delays the onset of risky practices such as early initiation of sex, promiscuity, and unprotected sexual acts. The IOC, the UN, and various other international sports organizations have responded by publishing working documents and policy guides for teaching young athletes about social transmission of HIV and AIDS and other diseases. The collective reduction approach champions children's rights to play through opportunity and investment and emphasizes their right to know through education. The majority of educational programs are still in their infancy, however, and their effectiveness will be better assessed over the long term.

See also "At-Risk" Youth in Sports; Equipment Manufacturing in the Third World; Rape and Sexual Assault; Sports for All and Fair Play Leagues.

Further Reading: Keim, M. (2003). *Nation-Building at Play: Sport as a Tool for Re-Integration in a Post-Apartheid South Africa.* Oxford, UK: Meyer and Meyer; Martens, R., and Seefeldt, V. (1979). *Guidelines for Children's Sport.* Washington, D.C.: American Alliance for Health, Physical Education, Recreation and Dance; Paolo, D. (2004). *Human Rights in Youth Sport.* London: Routledge.

Michael Atkinson

SALARIES OF PROFESSIONAL ATHLETES

Few contemporary issues in sports raise as much public scorn as that of player salaries. In the "big four" North American professional sports leagues—the National Football League (NFL), the National Basketball Association (NBA), Major League Baseball (MLB), and the National Hockey League (NHL)—athlete salaries are at all-time highs, with most league average salaries in the millions. While fans and spectators often feel that athletes are overcompensated financially, the economics and historical battles over salary are rather complicated. Further still, the contemporary high-profile athlete often draws in more income from product endorsements and sponsors than teams or leagues.

BACKGROUND

In 2007, *Sports Illustrated* magazine published its "Fortune 50" highest paid North American athletes. The list's highest salary earner was pro golfer Tiger Woods at $112 million, and the 50th highest earner was NBA player Amare Stoudemire at $15 million. The earnings of the top 50 players are nothing short of staggering and reflect the massive contract signings and endorsement deals common in professional sports. In 2008, New York Yankees player Alex Rodriguez signed a 10-year $325 million contract, topping his own record-breaking contract of 2001. International soccer player David Beckham signed a reported $250 million 5-year deal with Major League Soccer (MLS) team the Los Angeles Galaxy. Beckham also owns the record for the largest endorsement deal in sports history, a $160 million contract with Adidas.

TOP 10 MONEY EARNERS IN NORTH AMERICAN SPORTS FOR 2007

Tiger Woods: $112 million
Oscar de La Hoya: $55 million
Phil Mickelson: $51 million
Shaquille O'Neal: $35 million
Kobe Bryant: $34 million

LeBron James: $31 million
Kevin Garnett: $29 million
Derek Jeter: $29 million
Alex Rodriguez: $28 million
Dale Earnhardt: $27 million

The salaries, contracts, and endorsement deals of professional athletes are the fodder of substantial public debate. Fans frequently attribute escalating player salaries with a range of problems in sports such as forced team relocations, bankruptcies, strikes and lockouts, and rising ticket prices. While on the surface player's salaries might appear causally related to such problems, a deeper analysis uncovers how the economics of sports are far more complicated and multidimensional.

An even more murky debate focuses on whether college or high school athletes should be paid for their involvement in post-secondary sports programs. Under National Collegiate Athletic Association (NCAA) rules, athletes are prevented from receiving gifts or direct income for their involvement in sports. Yet, a dozen scandals at U.S. colleges and universities—such as those at Southern Methodist University, University of Georgia, Tulane, Clemson, and others—revealed that athletes had received one or another forms of "special treatment" for their participation in sports. Political economists occasionally decry the NCAA rule, suggesting that programs (namely men's football and basketball) generate millions in revenue yearly off their players' backs. Countercritics cite how most college athletes actually receive scholarships or tuition reductions, and these should be considered a form of payment.

Gloria James, mother of St. Vincent-St. May High School basketball star LeBron James, created a national scandal when she received a bank loan from an Ohio bank of $80,000 to buy her son a Hummer H2 that he could drive to school. The bank apparently considered LeBron's future earning potential when considering his mother's application. The event prompted an investigation by the Ohio High School Athletic Association (OHSAA) because under their rules, no amateur may accept any gift valued over $100 as a reward for athletic performance. James landed in further trouble with OHSAA and NCAA when he accepted two sports jerseys from a retail shop as payment for pictures he posed for that were hung in the store. The NCAA had other issues with gifts James received as a high school player, including those given to him while attending a Nike camp. The NCAA announced James would be ineligible to play college basketball, and the OHSAA stripped him of his senior year of eligibility in high school. James appealed the OHSAA decision only, and a judge reduced the penalty to a two-game suspension (thus allowing him to play the remainder of his senior year).

The James case and others like it reveal the deep-seated economic atmosphere in high school, college, and professional sports. Historical analyses of player salaries and battles within sports about salary uncover entire cultures of player exploitation at the hands of team owners dating back to the turn of the twentieth century. As such, close inspection of player salary battles has exposed financial corruption or impropriety at all levels of professional sports. The issue of athlete salaries also raises important questions and battles about the cultural significance of high-profile sports. From a social institution historically designed to develop character and moral virtue among its participants, sports has morphed into a cultural milieu beset with greed, high finance, materialism, capitalist expansion, and self-interest.

KEY EVENTS

Sports first official million-dollar contract is believed to have been signed by NHL and World Hockey Association (WHA) player Bobby Hull. The Hull case represents an important market development in the modern sports business in the twentieth century that would play a colossal role in the escalation of player salaries: interleague competition for players. In 1972, the WHA was an upstart professional ice hockey league. As the first major competition for the NHL since the collapse of the Western Hockey League in 1926, the WHA struggled to find high-profile players for its fledgling teams. Without these players, fans would not invest in the WHA, and it would collapse. The WHA hoped to capitalize on the lack of hockey teams in a number of major North American cities, and it also hoped to attract the best players by paying more than the extant cartel of NHL owners would at the time. The owners of the WHA franchises recognized that the only way for the league to secure fan and player credibility would be to lure stars away from the NHL with huge salaries (i.e., for the players, compensation for going to a new and inferior league). One of the teams, the Winnipeg Jets, offered $1 million to NHL star Bobby Hull. Hull not only received $1 million ($2.65 million, actually, over five years) to play for the Jets, his contract was ground-breaking in that he received the amount as a one-off, upfront payment. As a result, Bobby Hull is regarded by sports historians as the first player in any professional sport to receive a $1 million contract. When adjusted for inflation, Hull's unthinkable contract at the time is less than impressive by contemporary standards; his $1 million equates to approximately $5,049,761 in 2008. According to the 2007–2008 salary figures in the NHL, 52 NHL players earned more than $5,049,760 in the regular season.

The WHA salary incentives (which they offered to players other than Hull) were partially grounded by the league's collective rejection of the reserve clause that was so often a part of player contracts in sports until that time. Even though the WHA disbanded in 1979, its outright challenge of the reserve clause system in player contracting changed the course of sports salaries. The reserve clause (common in all of the professional sports in the modern era) created a constraining employment situation for players. A reserve clause stated that, upon a player's contract expiration, the rights to the player were to be retained by the team. In essence, this meant that when a player's contract ran its course, he was not able to speak with or negotiate with other teams.

In the late nineteenth century, baseball teams were huge financial successes for their owners, and players increasingly demanded salary benefits and bonuses; in essence, they argued for greater revenue sharing. Team owners collided and instituted a standardized contract for the players containing the reserve clause. All player contracts would be for one year; and they would not be able to negotiate new contracts in an open market system with other teams. Basic economics illustrate why owners would devise the reserve clause: If players were released and allowed to search for the highest bidder in an open market system, team owners would eventually attempt to outbid one another for the best players. Salary standards and expectations among players, in general, would rise. The move by team owners curtailed the free agency system common in sports today. Players thus had a choice only of signing for what their team offered them or holding out (refusing to play and, therefore, not being paid). Today, none of the professional sports leagues have reserve clause practices because they have been progressively negotiated out of sports or deemed unconstitutional by federal courts. Free agency now reigns supreme in the world of professional sports and is often cited as a major contributor to escalating player salaries.

While Hull may have been the first athlete to sign a million dollar contract, Tiger Woods will, statisticians argue, become the first billion dollar athlete by 2010, a previously unimaginable feat, especially for an ethnic minority athlete. During his first 12 years on tour, Woods earned more than $100 million in tournament winnings and a reported $669 million through product endorsements. Woods, who is multiracial, is credited with prompting a major surge of interest in the game of golf and a revolution in sports sponsorship and endorsements within the game. Woods doubled attendance and TV ratings since 1996 and generated interest among a multicultural audience in a game that used to be considered insular and elitist. With booming public interest in golf, largely attributable to Woods, corporate sponsors have inundated the PGA with offers, driving up purses (and thus golfer's winnings) at nearly every major event. As such, Woods has been referred to as the world's most marketable athlete. Throughout his career he has signed multimillion dollar contracts with companies including General Motors, Titleist (who, at one time, paid Woods $1 million to simply use their ball in a tournament), General Mills, American Express, Accenture, Gillette, Gatorade (Woods developed his own drink brand with them called "Gatorade Tiger"), EA Sports, Rolex, Wheaties, Tag Heuer, and Nike. In 2000, Woods signed a 5-year, $105 million contract extension with Nike. It was the largest endorsement deal ever signed by an athlete at that time and reflected the fact that Nike Golf is one of the fastest growing brands in sport, with an estimated $600 million in annual sales.

The salary achievements of Hull, Woods, and the growing list of mega-rich sports stars, must be linked to the development of player unions in sports and their impact on players' abilities to be powerful economic agents. Each of the major professional sports in North America developed player unions (organized predominantly to protect players' financial interests) in the 1950s, and their early survival often depended on several core players.

For example, in 1957, Detroit Red Wings star Ted Lindsay helped organize ice hockey's first player association. The association demanded basic financial provisions in the sport such as a minimum salary and a properly funded pension plan. Hockey players of the 1950s typically earned less than $25,000 a year and had relatively no pension given to them following retirement. So, Lindsey and Doug Harvey of the Montreal Canadiens organized the first National Hockey League Players Association (NHLPA). NHL players were contacted in secret in fear that if word about their organization was leaked to the league owners before all players were "on side" they would be vulnerable to persecution in the league. They were right with the assumption that the association would raise the wrath of league officials and owners.

Players in the association were named and shamed by their teams as troublemakers, benched, fined, or sent to the minor league NHL affiliates. In response, Lindsay and others in the NHLPA argued that they needed to be certified as a union with legal rights and not merely an informal association. Lindsay, one of the league's top players, was subsequently stripped of his captaincy by Detroit and traded to the league's last-place team, the Chicago Black Hawks. Coach of the Red Wings, Jack Adams (whose name would be later used as a division title in the sport's Eastern Conference and as the title for the NHL Coach of the Year award) also made defamatory comments about Lindsay in an attempt to fracture player solidarity in the budding union movement by tarnishing Lindsay's character; publicly suggesting, for example, that Lindsay commanded a huge salary and received considerable financial benefits from the Red Wings. As a result, the players voted down the idea of union. Again, in response, Lindsay initiated an antitrust lawsuit against the league, alleging a monopoly since 1926. Fearing negative publicity and exposure of corrupt practices in the league, the NHL agreed to most of the players' demands regarding salary and pension. In 1968, the NHLPA crystallized into a permanent union. The struggle and need for a player's union in the sport well represents how players had to place their professional careers on the line to secure fair and equitable treatment in sports. Perceived financial injustices in sports (revolving largely around the issue of salary and pension) became so acute from time to time that players in professional sports would exercise their union rights and strike.

None of the major professional sports in North America have been immune to salary-driven strikes. The majority of strikes or owner lockouts have pertained to one subject: salary caps (an invention of 1940s and 1950s sports). In 1994, players in the MLB went on strike after team owners proposed the implementation of new salary caps. Major League Baseball teams pay players using what is called a luxury tax scheme, wherein any team can spend endless amounts on player

---

AVERAGE YEARLY PLAYER SALARIES IN THE BIG FOUR IN 2007

NBA: $5.2 million NHL: $1.8 million
MLB: $2.9 million NFL: $1.4 million

salaries, but after they reach the league mandated limit, they are required to pay a fine to the league. Players were irate with the owner's suggestion of a hard salary cap for all teams and the elimination of the luxury tax scheme. After rounds of negotiation with the league, the players walked out on August 12, 1994. Commissioner Bud Selig canceled the remainder of the season and the World Series, resulting in nearly $600 million in lost revenue and over $200 million in player salaries. Players returned on March 29, 1995, after governmental intervention and arbitration by U.S. District Court to play a shortened season. The District Court eventually ruled in favor of the players, but the results for the league were catastrophic and enduring. Baseball pundits report that television ratings, league revenue, merchandise sales, and sponsorships have never rebounded after the strike. Average player salaries, however, continue to rise.

NBA players were "locked out" for part of the 1989–1999 season over a salary cap dispute. In the summer of 1998, collective bargaining between the players and the owners broke down over the issue, and owners threatened to lock out the players. When the players refused to sign onto the new collective bargaining agreement (CBA) because they perceived its "hard cap" numbers to be too low, the owners declared a lockout. The two sides eventually reached an agreement, and the season was played with team schedules of only 50 games each. Even though the strike lasted just three months and did not impact the playoffs, NBA players collectively lost a fortune; $50 million a week and roughly $500 million in total salaries, not to mention the millions in potential earnings they lost after a salary cap was eventually instituted to contain team spending on salaries. Players also suffered a hit in terms of endorsement deals because a number of companies such as Nike suspended payments to NBA players under contract during the strike. With regard to fan support, when the NBA players returned to active play they did not receive the negative public backlash that their baseball counterparts received after their 1994 strike.

The 2004–2005 NHL lockout of players resulted in the only full-season cancellation in any professional league. It was the first time the Stanley Cup was not awarded since 1919 (due to a flu epidemic that year). Revolving around, once again, an NHL proposed salary cap, the lockout spanned 310 days. In the summer of 2004, team owners proposed to revise the CBA established after the player lockout of 1995. The negotiating teams reached an agreement on July 13, 2005, after both the NHL owners and players ratified the CBA. Players had deeply resisted the proposed hard cap of team salary spending at $39 million, with the team owners responding by suggesting that without new hard limits for all teams, smaller market franchises would be bankrupted. The NHL commissioner Gary Bettman often cited an economic feasibility study authored by U.S. Securities and Exchange Commission chairman Arthur Levitt, highlighting that NHL teams spent about 76 percent of gross revenues on players' salaries (higher than any other professional sport) and, as a result, collectively lost $273 million dollars during the 2002–2003 season alone. Despite player resistance, a lost season, millions in lost revenue and salary, and shaken public trust in an already fragile American sports market for ice hockey, the players acquiesced to league demands. The owners had successfully imposed a hard salary cap in the new CBA, linked player salary increases and decreases to league revenue, and players received a 24 percent "rollback" on all existing contracts.

FUTURE PROSPECTS

The subjects of salary caps, strikes, free agency, pension schemes, endorsement deals, and player economic futures often dominate public discourses about contemporary sports. The overemphasis on the financial aspects of leagues and teams creates an image of sports as a primarily economic enterprise. As such, where athletes, team owners, or league officials are cultural role models in any other capacity than income generators is in doubt. One must question, however, how long the ethos and practice of economic expansion and acquisition can survive in professional sports before the markets eventually collapse.

See also Academic Misconduct Among Athletes; Antitrust Violations in Professional Sports; Commercializing Ethnic Athletes; Corporate Branding; Corporate Stadiums; Drafting Amateur Athletes; Governments, Laws, and Gambling; Marketing Female Athlete Sexuality; Media Broadcasting Rights.

Further Reading: Knorr, C. (2005). *The End of Baseball as We Knew it: The Players Union.* Champaign: The University of Illinois Press; Lewis, M. (2006). *Moneyball: The Art of Winning and Unfair Game.* New York: W.W. Norton and Company; Miracle, A., and Rees, R. (1994). *Lessons of the Locker Room.* New York: Prometheus Books; Yost, M. (2006). *Tailgaiting, Sacks and Salary Caps: How the NFL Became the Most Successful Sports League in History.* New York: Kaplan Business.

Michael Atkinson

SEXUAL ABUSE AMONG ATHLETES

Relationships involving sexual interaction between people in sports cultures are complicated and vastly under-studied. Until quite recently, little has been publicly discussed about consensual and nonconsensual sexual practices occurring between players, coaches, and other sports insiders. What we do know is that most forms of sexual contact or relationships are strictly prohibited in a majority of sports cultures (such as those between coaches and athletes). Nevertheless, athletes, coaches, and others frequently violate social and institutional taboos regarding sex in sports through abusive and exploitative means. Stories emerging from sports in the past 10 years have called attention to particularly troubling cases of sexual abuse, exploitation, and domination involving coaches and athletes from a full range of sports settings and levels.

BACKGROUND

Celia Brackenridge suggests that there is a continuum of sexual discrimination and abuse athletes encounter (mainly women athletes) in sports. The types include: sex discrimination (i.e., a differential treatment regarding access, pay, and other structural aspects of sports), sexual harassment (i.e., sexually offensive and/or intimidating behavior), and sexual abuse (i.e., rape, assault, groping, and other forms of sexually coercive behavior). Aspects of sex discrimination have been well-debated in a post–Title IX North American sports world, but our social understanding of the patterns of sexual harassment and sexual abuse in sports remain critically fragmented and empirically disjointed. Particularly in the case of the latter, there is a dearth of systematic research on the processes involved, extent of, and possibilities for reducing the sexual abuse of young athletes at the hands of coaches and other sports insiders.

Logic and a working knowledge of sports would dictate that the increased number of reported cases of sexual abuse involving athletes and their coaches is neither a recent phenomenon nor accurately accounts for the full number of cases of sexual exploitation in sports. Still, it is estimated that roughly one in four female and one in nine male athletes have been sexually victimized. Athletes, however, are overwhelmingly reluctant to whistle-blow on a figure of power in the sporting community, partly because athletes are taught to be deferential to them as a component of elite sports development and partly in fear that no one will believe the allegations. This may be especially true as it pertains to male victims in sports.

The predominant explanation of why the sexual abuse of athletes occurs by coaches, administrators, or senior players pertains to how power and authority are established in sports. In brief, sexual abuse tends to occur between players and coaches when a series of critical factors related to motivation and power combine. When a powerful, authority-filled coach who is sexually motivated to offend is placed in a context of low social surveillance with easily exploitable targets, victimization will frequently occur. The typical sexual abuser is an older, senior, highly accredited, ostensibly trustworthy coach who is able to spend long periods of time alone with one or several athletes. Sports that involve close contact between players and coaches as part of instruction, involve frequent travel for competitions, and have weak or nonexistent codes of conduct or systems for monitoring coach behaviors are especially dangerous contexts for abuse. Victims of abuse tend to be young females, small in size or stature, and plagued with low self-esteem who exhibit intense commitment to their sport and their coach and have strained relationships at home. The work of crime theorists may help to explain these trends. The heart of their *routine activities theory* is that we can explain rates of victimization in a given social setting area by analyzing if three factors are present there: *motivated offenders, suitable targets,* and an *absence of guardianship* over the targets. The probability of sexual victimization in sports is, in this instance, high when these three factors converge or are consistently present over the course of time. In other words, the routine activities of sports—such as being trained by a coach in an insular sports environment—expose individuals to potential offenders. Simply put, the routine activities of social life provide motivated offenders (who are presumed to be everywhere) with opportunities to engage in crime.

Another important trend in the abuse of athletes at the hands of coaches and others is the pattern of grooming. *Grooming* refers to the systematic sexual targeting, nurturing, and long-term dominance over particular athletes. Over the course of months or even in some cases years, coaches become very close "friends" with their targets, developing a familial-like bond with them. Through this process, physical, psychological, and emotional boundaries separating them are broken down by the coach. This boundary crossing may seem to occur as an act of friendship or parental-like concern at first, but it turns into a process of social psychological control where the coach coercively demands that the athlete reciprocate the coach's physical (sexual) advances. A groomed athlete is one that fears her or his coach as a sexual abuser but feels a strong emotional loyalty to them, is constantly monitored and dominated by them, and feels shame for their involvement in the relationship (i.e., thinking it is their own fault).

Journalist and former Canadian national athlete Laura Robinson has conducted long-term research on another pathological form of sexual relationships in sports: the culture of gang/group sex involving athletes. A disturbing trend in high school, amateur, and university/college sports is the practice of male athletes engaging in group/public sex with one or more females, either with their consent or by force. Group sex becomes culturally practiced by the athletes over time as a rite of passage, form of hazing, display of hubris, or form of collective celebration in particular sports subcultures or on certain teams. The abuse of young female participants in group sex by athletes reflects a culture of privilege and sense of impunity they are socialized into accepting. Violent or publicly lewd and lascivious sexual relationships illustrate their desire to engage in a type of "sneaky thrill" or an excessively deviant practice they feel entitled to engage in because of their high social status (Katz, 1988). From a general perspective, however, while females who are asked or coerced into participating are sexually exploited and abused, one must ask whether or not the existing culture of group sex in certain sports coercively demands that young male players participate or risk facing ostracism, alienation, and outright discrimination on their teams (potentially interfering with their future aspirations in sports).

KEY EVENTS

The last five years of the twentieth century and the first five years of the twenty-first produced landmark cases of sexually inappropriate behaviors between athletes, coaches, and others involved in sports. Scandals were occurring at a time when youth and women's involvement in sports was increasing and at a time when the opening access of sports was lauded by physical fitness enthusiasts. Research conducted in the mid-1990s on young girls' involvement in sports produced impressively consistent evidence that they were at considerably lower risk of engaging in early sexual activity as teenagers, thereby at lower risk for contracting a sexually transmitted disease or becoming pregnant, if they played organized sports. Encouraged in part by such research, the Nike corporation produced a highly acclaimed "If You Let Me Play" television advertisement in 1995 highlighting the role of sports in combating sexual problems and victimization among teenage girls. In the commercial, young girls pleaded that if sports organizers simply "let them play," they would be less likely to be abused or face other unwanted sexual problems. While the campaign stirred national interest and faith in sports for young girls, the Nike claims would be placed under intense scrutiny as hundreds of sexual exploitation cases between athletes and their coaches came to public light in the early 2000s.

One case that underscored the massively concealed problem of athlete sexual exploitation at the hands of coaches was the case of Sheldon Kennedy. Kennedy was a young Canadian ice hockey player coached by Graham James, a highly respected and nationally famous coach. Kennedy had been first coached by James as a junior-level hockey player in Winnipeg and then during the late 1980s on the Swift Current Broncos of Canada's Western Hockey League. Between the ages of 14 and 19, Kennedy was sexually abused by James on a repeated basis. Kennedy has said that James sexually assaulted him more than 350 times, beginning when Kennedy was 14. The Kennedy case represents, in many ways, a classic case of grooming a young athlete. Every Tuesday and Thursday for six years Kennedy went to James's house and would be sexually assaulted by him. James told Kennedy that they were like husband and wife and that no matter where Kennedy would go, James would follow him. Emotional and psychological pressure in Kennedy built up over time, and the young player considered suicide on several occasions as his only escape from James. Eventually, Kennedy left the Broncos when he was drafted by the National Hockey League's (NHL) Calgary Flames.

In 1995, Kennedy broke his silence about the abuse, and the story became the most internationally mediated case of abuse in decades. Hockey insiders, including some of Kennedy's own teammates, knew of the abuse, but the story "broke" in Canada when Kennedy finally pressed criminal charges against James. In January 1997, Graham James was sentenced to three years in prison for sexually assaulting Kennedy and another unidentified player. As a result, the Canadian Hockey Association instituted new coach screening and monitoring policies and developed a grassroots program called "Speak Out," designed to encourage young players to speak out about acts of physical, emotional, or mental abuse they have suffered in the sport. The Kennedy case became a watershed moment in the reporting of abuse by athletes, encouraging athletes across North America to step forward. While many did, Mike Danton, an ice hockey player with the St. Louis Blues, did not, but his shocking story of sexual exploitation at the hands of a coach emerged nevertheless in 2004.

In the late spring of 2004, Mike Danton (born Michael Jefferson) was arrested and prosecuted for hiring a hitman to murder his agent, David Frost. Danton was found guilty and sentenced to seven and a half years in jail. The trial exposed, however, another tragic tale of coach-athlete abuse and control. Danton had known Frost since he was 12 years old. Frost had been Danton's coach and shepherded his career through Ontario minor and junior hockey leagues. Frost coached Danton on the Quinte Hawks Junior A team but was suspended for sexual misconduct with a player and for allowing his players to engage in sex acts with teenage girls while he watched. Stories started to surface about Frost's penchant for young boys, but their details were not pursued. Questions about his relationship with four young players he coached at Quinte (called by insiders as his "Brampton Boys") surrounded Frost, with claims suggesting they had been sexually assaulted and psychologically controlled by him for years.

In the case of Danton, however, a "special" relationship seemed to be in place. Danton spent most of his free time with Frost (who had actually relocated to Danton's Brampton, Ontario, neighborhood to be near him) and called him repeatedly during the day to profess how he "loved" him. Danton's parents were not allowed (by Frost) to speak to their son in and around the hockey arena, and he spent time with his younger brother Tom at Frost's cottage and even spent Christmases with Frost instead of his parents. Frost even helped to convince Mike Danton (who was legally named Mike Jefferson at the time) to change his name to distance himself from his family. When Danton was drafted by the New Jersey Devils in 2000, Frost actually became a legal player agent to maintain his contact with Danton. For the next four years, Frost retained his sexual and psychological control over Danton. But after years of abuse, control, and exploitation, Danton buckled under the pressure and attempted to hire the contract killer's services to finally terminate their relationship. A Canadian Broadcast Corporation's 2005 investigation exposed Frost's legacy of abuse and sexual control. To date, however, while Frost lost his agent's license, he has not been criminally charged for sexual assault because the boys he abused have refused to testify against him.

Following the Kennedy and Danton cases, the metaphorical lid blew off the culture of sexual abuse and exploitation in U.S. high school sports involving players and their coaches. Between 2004 and 2008, an almost exponential increase in cases of abuse and alleged abuse involving coaches and high school athletes has been tracked. A crime watch Web site Badjocks.com has collected data on filed or reported cases of coach–athlete sexual exploitation, reporting a mean number of cases of 213 per year. For example, girl's high school basketball coach Rick Lopez faced 55 felony counts of alleged sexual assault on a child in 2004. According to three of his female players, Lopez, who coached the elite Colorado Hoopsters, had a standard operating procedure: He would actually move into the basement of a girl's home on his team, groom them over time, and have sex with them on a regular basis. Lopez admitted that his first alleged victim was 13 when he initiated sexual contact with her.

Myths about perpetrators as exclusively male have been shaken considerably, if not challenged directly over the past five years. In 2004, 25-year-old gym teacher Kelsey Peterson at Lexington Middle School in Nebraska was caught having an affair with an eighth grader. After their affair came to public light, Peterson and the student, Fernando Rodriguez, a 13-year-old illegal immigrant, fled the country to Mexico where they were eventually apprehended by police. Peterson was sentenced on charges of kidnapping, child abuse, and contributing to the delinquency of a minor in Nebraska. Pamela Joan Turner, a 27-year-old physical education teacher and girls' basketball coach at Centertown Elementary School in Warren County, Tennessee, was charged in 2005 with 13 counts of statutory rape and 15 counts of sexual battery for encounters with a 13-year-old student. Later that same year, Jaymee Lane Wallace, a girls' basketball coach in Florida, was charged for an affair she initiated with a teenage student she coached at a Tampa high school.

Allegations of perhaps the most enduring subculture of athlete–coach abuse surfaced in 2005 in Merkel, Texas. Residents have long described the familiar or close relationship the high school athletes have with their coaches in Merkel. Commencing in 2005, of the 20 high school coaches in the community, 3 were fired for having sexual relations with their students. The Texas Child Protective Services were called in to investigate and reported allegations and rumors suggesting that coaches in Merkel had abused boys and girls athletics members for over 20 years. The case in Merkel is especially troubling but not entirely atypical of the growing social problem of athlete abuse at the hands of coaches. Other stories of coaches peeping into players changing rooms, paying them for sex, facilitating group sex sessions, masturbating or exposing themselves in front of players, or maintaining long-term relationships of exploitation with selected players continue to surface with a frightening regularity. Despite public disbelief and denial, there appears to be an entire subculture of predatory sexual activity in U.S. high school sports.

Beyond the level of high school sports, notorious cases of inappropriate sexual cultures in professional sports involving group or gang-based behaviors are increasing in number. Among the most infamous recent cases is the 2005 "Love Boat" scandal involving players from the National Football League's (NFL) Minnesota Vikings, namely, Daunte Culpepper, Fred Smoot (identified as the organizer of the Love Boat scandal), Mewelde Moore, Pat Williams, Bryant McKinnie, Nate Burleson, Ralph Brown, Troy Williamson, Travis Taylor, Kevin Williams, Jermaine Wiggins, Lance Johnstone, Moe Williams, Ken Irvin, and Willie Offord. According to an unnamed former player for the Vikings, the Love Boat ritual had been held on a regular basis, wherein several players would hire party boats and take paid female escorts for a cruise on Lake Minnetonka (at a reported cost of $5,000 per player). The 2005 version of the party featured escorts and exotic dancers flown in from Atlanta and Florida. The Love Boat evening started off with a dinner for team players at a Mall of America restaurant then continued at the Fahrenheit Night Club in Minneapolis, both of which were rented out by the players. Then, the players went to two rented boats, cruised the lake, and allegedly engaged in a wide range of group sex acts with the escorts. Several of the players denied involvement in the scandal, and four were eventually charged with felony misdemeanors (Culpepper, McKinnie, Smoot, and Williams). Charges were eventually dropped against Culpepper, with the others receiving small fines and community service. The Vikings instituted a new player code of conduct as a result of the scandal, and the NFL levied "one game" fines (1/17th of player salaries) on Smoot and McKinnie (who received a contract extension and salary raise only a day later). Each of the players were incredibly lucky to avoid federal prosecution and lengthy prison sentences for trafficking women for sexual purposes across state lines under the Mann Act.

Strangely enough, the 2005 Love Boat scandal had links to the Gold Club exotic dancer scandal of 2001. In an effort to make his Atlanta strip club a local hotspot, owner Steve Kaplan regularly invited high-profile athletes to his club and provided them with "complementary" sexual favors from dancers in the back rooms of the club; the sessions often involved several players and dancers. The police eventually stepped in and raided the Gold Club. National Basketball Association (NBA) stars Patrick Ewing, Reggie Miller, Dikembe Mutombo, Jerry Stackhouse, and John Starks were called to testify in the court trial, along with NFL players Jamal Anderson and Terrell Davis. Kaplan pleaded guilty to charges of racketeering in 2001 and forfeited his ownership of the Gold Club. Interestingly, the escorts participating in the Love Boat escapades of 2005 allegedly worked at the Gold Club in Atlanta.

FUTURE PROSPECTS

The sheer scope and extent of inappropriate sexual conduct that exists in the worlds of high school, college, elite amateur, and professional sports is arguably among the most pressing social problems in sports. Paled in the popular media by problems of drug abuse, game violence, and economic scandals, the sexual exploitation of athletes and the culture of public sex in sports raises important questions about the form and content of sports mentoring in North America. Although they are not regularly cast as such in mainstream thinking, athletes are especially vulnerable groups of people and are prone to being sexually exploited or exposed to morally questionable sexual cultures.

See also Academic Misconduct Among Athletes; Hazing; Partner Abuse Among Athletes; Rape and Sexual Assault; Rights for Young Athletes.

Further Reading: Brackenridge, C. (1997). He Owned Me Basically: Women's Experience of Sexual Abuse in Sport. *International Review for the Sociology of Sport* 32: 115–130; Brackenridge, C. (2001). *Spoilsports: Understanding and Preventing Sexual Exploitation in Sport.* London: Routledge; Cohen, L., and Felson, M. (1979). Social Change and Crime Rate Trends: A Routine Activity Approach. *American Sociological Review* 44: 588–608; Katz, J. (1988). *Seductions of Crime.* New York: Basic Books; Kennedy, S. (2006). *Why I Didn't Say Anything: The Sheldon Kennedy Story.* Toronto: Insomniac Press; Robinson, L. (1998). *Crossing the Line: Violence and Sexual Assault in Canada's National Sport.* Toronto: McClelland & Stewart; Sabo, D., Miller, K., Farrell, M., Melnick, M., and Barnes, G. (1999). High School Athletic Participation, Sexual Behavior and Adolescent Pregnancy: A Regional Study. *Journal of Adolescent Health* 25: 207–216.

Michael Atkinson

SKATEBOARDING

Skateboarding has been touted as a nontraditional sport. Unlike many other traditional youth sporting activities that are adult controlled and organized, skateboarding emphasizes the power of the participant to define the activity. For example, most skaters do not use coaches or join leagues. The activity has no conventional boundaries; there is no formal field of play, no sidelines, no rules, and no time limits. Skateboarding is, in fact, characterized by the participants' ability to continually develop new maneuvers or tricks in a variety of places. Although the sport is portrayed as a free realm for the participants to be creative, there are many other parties that have a stake in the activity including the industry advocates, media, local governments, and the youth cultural industry. Identifying who has the power to control the structure and meaning of skateboarding allows one to follow the social debates about the activity. The fight for control of the sport has been illustrated in the arguments over the legality of the sport, the authenticity of the participants, and the prolific commercialization of the sport. Depending on the social and political context, these stakeholders have at times worked together whereas other times they have been in conflict.

BACKGROUND

Through its 50-year history, skateboarding evolved from a hobby to a highly competitive sport. Significantly, the sport faced many challenges, and its popularity ebbed and flowed. It has survived by reinventing its technology, style, and cultural appeal. Skateboarding began in southern California in the 1950s, and its initial popularity occurred in the early 1960s when skateboards were first mass produced. At this point, the activity was primarily a youthful pastime that was frequently referred to as "sidewalk surfing." Most participants were teenagers who used sidewalks, streets, or playgrounds to practice their activity. Due primarily to bad publicity around injury rates, the first boom ended by 1966. In the 1970s, skateboarding experienced another surge in popularity because of improved equipment and a growing infrastructure of skateboard parks. The technological innovation of polyurethane wheels allowed for a smoother and, importantly, safer ride. By the end of the decade these parks were forced to shut down because of liability issues, which, in turn, drove skateboarding underground.

It re-emerged in the early 1980s by significantly revamping its style and image; this next iteration included not only the California beach and surf scene, but it also embraced an urban punk lifestyle as indicated by the anthem "skate and destroy." During this period, skateboarding had shifted to the street and, yet, was generally banned in public spaces. This struggle with the law became a central part of the skateboarding culture as exemplified by the very popular declaration, "Skateboarding is not a crime." The "ollie" was the crucial technical invention that allowed skateboarding to be infused in the urban landscape. This move enables the skateboarder to propel the board off the ground. With this technique skateboarders could jump on to a variety of everyday objects found in the street such as handrails or parking blocks. The urban environment and style along with this outlaw and streetwise image generated appeal, and the late 1980s saw the highest number of participants ever for skateboarding.

The ultimate boost to the sport's global popularity was the advent of the X Games, which was created in 1995 by ESPN, a major media corporation and a subsidiary of the Disney Corporation. These games are meant to be the "Olympics" of alternative sports. By the 2000s, participation rates in skateboarding were growing faster than in more traditional sports such as baseball. In addition, the sport evolved into a global, commercially vibrant phenomenon as exemplified by regular international competitions and widespread numbers of both private and public skateboard parks. Its general commercial appeal can be illustrated by the success of the spectacularized events such as Danny Way jumping the Great Wall of China in 2005 and Tony Hawk's traveling show of several nontraditional athletes called "boom boom huckjam." In addition, skateboarding's popularity can be illustrated by its widespread use to sell unrelated products such as soda, deodorant, and trucks.

The popularity of the sport is based, in part, on the control the participants have, which has translated into a subcultural identity that focuses on creativity, independence, and antiauthoritarianism. The more subversive practices have caused concern for the police, storekeepers, and much of the medical community. Yet, the avant-garde image has been accentuated by the youth cultural industry because it is a powerful tool to sell a variety of products to a youth market. These various stakeholders have vied for control over the structure and meaning of skateboarding.

KEY EVENTS

One of the clearest forms of control is having the power to determine legal boundaries of an activity. The debate has centered on the parameters of skaters' use of public space. Skateboarders see public space as embodying their independent ethos: unsupervised and dynamic space where participants take risks in their creative maneuvers. Often their activities disrupt conventional practices prompting some negative responses. Medical bodies and proprietors have wanted to restrict skateboarding, although for different reasons, while the alternative sports industry and other youth cultural industries have tried to secure more opportunities for people to skate.

Those who want to restrict skating in urban spaces do for two main reasons: to prevent injury and to reduce costs. Medical associations have long commented on the inherent danger and the injuries that result from skateboarding. The rates of injury are highest in urban spaces that are unsupervised and where protective gear is not required. This fact played a significant role in the decline of skateboarding in the late 1970s when private skate parks were unable to afford liability insurance, forcing them to close. Since then, various groups have lobbied to try to change the legal status of skateboarding, one that would be similar to bicycling in which liability would shift more to the participants than to property owners. The International Association of Skateboard Companies, which was founded to promote the sport globally, successfully lobbied the California legislature to change the legal status of skateboarding, which thereby relieved the liability burden. This set a precedent and opened up opportunities for skate parks to be re-established, which occurred at a great rate during the 1990s.

In many communities throughout the United States, young skateboarders organized campaigns to have local recreation departments fund and manage public skateboard parks. They argued that they should have the same support and funding as baseball and football. A confluence of interests made these publicly funded skate parks popular. First, business and medical communities wanted kids off the street and in a safer, more supervised, location. Second, the liability laws had changed to make this more feasible. Finally, parents also advocated for the legitimacy of skateboarding and a safe place for their children to practice the sport.

While clearly defined skate parks were established, skateboarding in urban spaces was clamped down. As noted previously, participants value their ability to move freely about public spaces, but their use of these spaces can cause damage to property and disrupt normal commercial practices. In particular, a group of skaters using a storefront as their playground can put off shoppers. In addition, any liability for injury that may occur is another monetary concern. The presence of skaters, then, is likely to negatively impact the storekeeper's finances. The business and medical fields' disapproval prompted many city councils to ban skateboarding. Ironically, the laws only fueled the rebellious image of skaters, and not surprisingly, many skaters continued to use urban spaces, openly defying these laws as a means of proving their antiauthoritarian identity. In response, businesses owners developed devices to deter skaters, especially objects that disrupted smooth surfaces. This, in turn, only prompted skaters to invent new techniques to skate around these.

Love Park is one example of the conflicting positions on skateboarders using public space. This park is located across from the city hall in Philadelphia, and until the mid-1980s, the park was used by a wide variety of people. But in the late 1980s and 1990s, the park became a popular skate spot and ultimately a skateboarding cultural icon as it was featured prominently in skate magazines and videos. It was a major factor in drawing the X Games to Philadelphia in 2002 and 2003. Nonetheless, city officials banned skateboarding and spent large amounts of money to beautify and alter the landscape to make it inaccessible to skateboarders. Importantly, this disagreement was not simply skaters on one side and business elite on the other. The business community was actually split. Those focusing on the cultural industries like entertainment, such as ESPN, found skateboarding in the city as positive for economic development. Whereas more traditional business elite thought skaters in city centers were disruptive to commercial flow. As in many other cases, one compromise was to build a separate skate park outside of the city center. This provides a safe place, but it also serves to segregate and contain "noncompliant" youth. Importantly, skateboarders' main source of legitimacy comes from independence, thus, participating in supervised skate parks has less status than being in the street.

Among skateboarders there is a hierarchy based on the degree to which each participant embodies the core values. Whoever is considered authentic reaps the benefits of that status. "Real" skaters garner the credibility that lands them opportunities to compete professionally and to receive endorsements and media coverage. In other words, they get money and a voice. Thus, whoever controls the boundaries of what is considered the core values has significant power because they act as a gatekeeper.

Many in the skateboarding community do not agree that there are gatekeepers. They point to the core value orientations of do-it-yourself (DIY) and creativity as countering the assumption that there is some formal and official procedure that determines who can participate. In fact, the core values support the claims that skateboarding is a meritocracy and that the only thing keeping people from participating is their lack of desire or skill. Others suggest that, especially with the advent of urban skating, the core values favor a "streetwise masculinity," which leads to differential treatment. The degree and ways in which gatekeeping may occur is a contentious issue because the vast majority of skaters are white, young adult males, and if their claims to legitimate status are true, that suggests that others simply can't make the grade. This dynamic is exemplified in the conversation about the dearth of female skateboarders.

When males discuss the lack of female participation they have three main explanations. First, they say skateboarding entails a lot of physical pain and injury, and girls don't want to take physical risks in which they could scar their bodies. Second, they claim females are not as athletically gifted as males. Finally, they claim that females prefer to do more traditionally feminine activities such as talking on the phone or shopping with their friends. In addition, males commonly assume that females who want to skateboard are solely using that as a means to mingle with them or be associated with the "cool" crowd. This position assumes that females are not as committed to "core" or "true" values of skateboarding and, instead, are only visiting the culture. This explains why females who align themselves with skateboarding are frequently labeled as skate Betties or posers.

Many female skaters use the masculine attributes of skating to position themselves differently from what they consider typical girls. In doing so, they distance themselves from normative femininity and, thus, tend to take on similar explanations as males for lack of female participation. In this way, female skateboarders claim that they are the exception and thus create a distinctive gender identity. Nonetheless, females acknowledge that they have an additional barrier and that is the lack of support from males, especially where status is greatest, in the unsupervised street spaces.

The power to control the boundaries of the authentic skater not only happens in the everyday practices but in the industry and especially in the control of media coverage. It is important to note that skaters gain most of their reputation not by winning formal competitions but through photographic documentation of one's skills, which are distributed primarily through skate-specific media. Research has documented that solo males performing high-risk tricks in desolate urban settings is the most prevalent mediated image, reinforcing the core values of street skating, independence, and risk-taking. Whereas the skateboarding industry has largely ignored female participants as is evidenced in the lack of media coverage and professional sponsorship, women have responded by creating their own companies and media outlets and by organizing advocacy groups.

FUTURE PROSPECTS

Skateboarding is a global multibillion dollar industry. One of the main debates within skateboarding has been about the costs and benefits of its commercial success. Frequently, the debate over commercialization is framed as if there are mutually exclusive positions of the authentic skater who "keeps it real" by doing it for the love of the sport and not the money. This is in contrast to the outside commercial interest who is "selling out" the soul of skateboarding. It is a false dichotomy to suggest that there are purely outside commercial interests or purely skateboarders' interests because both want skateboarding to thrive.

Skateboarding's popularity is due to two main things: mainstream availability, which is predicated on commercial success, and delivering an "authentic" product, which is predicated on representing the urban skateboarding lifestyle. Corporations provide the necessary capital, whereas participants provide the authentic storyline. This is a tenuous relationship because the corporate capital has more power to produce and distribute the story that goes with the products. This power dynamic can be represented by Nike's presence in the market. In the late 1990s, Nike tried to enter the skate footwear market. They had a clever advertising pitch in which they acknowledged the absurdity of the illegal status of skateboarding in public spaces. The ad showed traditional sports athletes being chased and harassed by police and then shifted by saying, what if every athlete was treated like a skater? Although the advert was well received, skaters rejected their shoes. There was still enough of a desire to maintain an alternative image that skaters did not want to support the icon of mainstream sports. Nike responded by investing heavily in the sport, and eventually the tide shifted; Nike is now a successful producer of skate shoes and sponsor of a skate team.

The industry is concerned with promoting the sport and has done so by creating quality equipment and by establishing governing bodies and formal competitions. But more profoundly, the industry is concerned with a youth market. Skateboarding has had a long history of a mutually beneficial relationship with other youth-oriented products. For example, in the 1960s, the surfing industry made the strongest impact on creating and promoting the sport. Surf industry leader Hobie Alter worked with a surf shop and a roller skate company to sell skateboards. Alter then promoted skateboarding by linking exhibitions with the tour of the legendary classic surf film *The Endless Summer*. Currently, skateboarding is integrated with a variety of teenage products and activities such as music, movies, fashion, video games, and sports. For example, corporations that produce video games purposefully create a holistic lifestyle in their representation of skateboarding by incorporating music and fashion. MTV has used skaters to create the series *Jackass,* which has been developed into two successful feature-length films. And corporations that originally focused on building and selling skateboard products have expanded into media and music. Some companies have branded everything from perfume to bed sheets. By incorporating various products under a lifestyle brand, corporations are able to sell more products to a broader audience. Skateboarding provides a primary means for synergistically conveying a "cool" brand image.

Obviously, some skaters benefit more from this commercialization than others. Skaters such as Tony Hawk are among the most popular sports figures. He has capitalized on his popularity and created a variety of entertainment packages including video games, movies, books, and live sports or music events. But even skaters entrenched in the industry have expressed concern about the degree to which most skaters are benefiting from this commercialization. The X Games participants have threatened to strike if their purse and working conditions weren't improved; ESPN ultimately settled with the skaters. Female skateboarders have created on-going advocacy groups and made alliances with others to fight for equitable treatment within the industry. Some editors of skate magazines have quit when a major media corporation bought them out because they did not want to be associated with a magazine that did not connect with skaters and their social worlds and would, ultimately, misrepresent them.

Most amateur skaters are generally glad that their sport has gained cultural legitimacy and that global corporations provide substantial support to professional skaters and the sport. Yet, many remain cautious about the long-term effects of commercial success. They doubt whether anyone can experience the skateboarding lifestyle by purchasing auxiliary products such as designer t-shirts. Most skaters suggest that one needs to be committed to skate on a regular basis and to embrace the "do-it-yourself" ethos to truly experience the skateboarding lifestyle. Thus, commercialization doesn't fit neatly into skaters' core values, and, some claim, could negatively alter them. Some amateur skaters are adamantly against corporate involvement. For those who resist global corporate presence, numerous media venues, such as local magazines and Web sites, have been created to voice opposition.

Even as skateboarding becomes more mainstream, which clearly has some benefits, many skaters continue to develop an identity and lifestyle that differs from the status quo. This represents the history of skateboarding, a struggle with the mainstream that drives change and innovation. And that innovation, in turn, is picked up by corporations and sold as the latest "authentic" expression of youth culture. As has been noted, various stakeholders have differing degrees of power to control the structure and meaning of skateboarding. In each historical time period, the stakeholders have been forced to negotiate their divergent interests in skateboarding.

Further Reading: Beal, B., and Wilson, C. (2004). "Chicks Dig Scars": Commercialisation and the Transformations of Skateboarders' Identities. In *Understanding Lifestyle Sports: Consumption, Identity and Difference,* edited by B. Wheaton. Routledge: London; Borden, I. (2001). *Skateboarding, Space & the City: Architecture and the Body.* Oxford: Berg; Brooke, M. (1999). *The Concrete Wave: The History of Skateboarding.* Toronto: Warwick Publishing; Rinehart, R. (2005). "Babes" & Boards: Opportunities in New Millennium Sport? *Journal of Sport & Social Issues* 29: 232–255; Thorpe, H. (2006). Beyond "Decorative Sociology": Contextualizing Female Surf, Skate, and Snow Boarding. *Sociology of Sport Journal* 23, 205–228; Willard, M. N. (1998). Séance, Tricknowlogy, Skateboarding, and the Space of Youth. In *Generations of Youth: Youth Cultures and History in Twentieth-Century America,* edited by J. Austin and M. N. Willard, 327–346. New York: New York University Press.

Becky Beal

SNOWBOARDING

Snowboarding—the act of standing sideways on a board and sliding down a snow-covered slope—has gone from a marginal activity for a few diehard participants to an Olympic sport with mass appeal in the past three decades. The much-debated question is, "Did snowboarding sell-out?" Also, consider the subsequent question: "If snowboarding sold-out, who sold it and to whom?" Various agents, both external (e.g., major corporate sponsors, mass media, international sporting bodies) and internal (e.g., snowboarding companies, snowboarding media, athletes), have contributed to its commercialization and institutionalization. Some of the costs and benefits of these changes are perceived by snowboarders from different generations.

BACKGROUND

Dating the precise birth of snowboarding is impossible. People have been standing on sleds and trying to slide on snow for hundreds of years; recent "discoveries" include a board dating back to the 1920s and a 1939 film of a man riding a snowboard-type sled sideways down a small hill in Chicago. But snowboarding, as we understand the activity today, arguably emerged in the late 1960s and 1970s in North America with a new piece of equipment that appealed to the hedonistic desires of a new generation of youth.

The Pioneering Years

In 1964, Sherman Poppen (Michigan) invented the Snurfer when he bolted two skis together and added a rope to help stabilize the equipment. Jake Burton Carpenter (Vermont) experimented with foam, fiberglass, steam-bent solid wood, and vertically laminated wood with the goal of making a board that was more maneuverable and faster than the Snurfer. In 1978, he established Burton boards. The early Burton boards had a rubber water-ski binding for the front foot, which allowed greater control and maneuverability; turns became easier and more stable. Thus, Burton modified the board and the action.

Burton was not the only one to experiment with board designs. Other pioneers included Dimitrije Milovick (Utah), who established Winterstick; Tom Sims and Chuck Barefoot (California), who established Sims Snowboards; Chris

---

JAKE BURTON CARPENTER: AN INDUSTRY PIONEER

Twenty-three-year-old Jake Burton Carpenter established Burton Snowboards in 1977 in Londonderry, Vermont. An avid Snurfer in his teenage years, Burton saw the activity as an untapped opportunity for capital accumulation. Indeed, he confessed that his primary drive was to "create a successful business" and "make a good living … like 100 grand a year or something."

Within the first year, the fledgling company had sold 300 boards for $88 each. In 1984, sales of Burton Snowboards reached $1 million. The sport and the industry continued to grow during the 1980s and into the mid-1990s. During this period, Burton Snowboards grew on average about 100 percent per year, and by 1995, it employed 250 workers and was worth well over $100 million. Burton Snowboards remains privately owned by Jake and his wife. While they do not release financial information, estimates suggest that Burton Snowboards currently controls approximately 40 percent of the multibillion dollar global market.

and Bev Sanders (California), who established Avalanche Snowboards; and Mike Olsen (Washington), who established GNU Snowboards. Olsen's motivation was "just fun," and according to one pioneer, all these early board makers wanted "an alternative" to the elitist culture associated with skiing.

In 1983, Stratton Mountain in Vermont became the first major ski field to open its downhill ski trails to snowboarders. Others quickly followed. This newly found access was the result of two major factors. First, a number of snowboarders actively campaigned for access. Second, skiing had reached a growth plateau, and snowboarding offered ski-fields a new youth market and ongoing economic prosperity. Snowboarding was soon described as the biggest boost to the ski industry since chairlifts. But even after gaining access to the ski fields, snowboarders continued to see themselves as different than skiers, and tensions between skiers and snowboarders remained throughout the 1980s. Physical confrontations and fights between skiers and snowboarders were not unusual as the two groups vied for territory and eminence.

Snowboarding continued to develop in opposition to the dominant ski culture. Skiing was an expensive sport with participants mostly white and middle to upper class. Snowboarders were typically younger, less educated, single, male, earning lower incomes, or students. Summarizing the cultural differences during this period, Duncan Humphreys (1996) explains that whereas "skiing embodied technical discipline and control," snowboarding "embodied freedom, hedonism and irresponsibility" (9).

In 1985, only 7 percent of American resorts allowed snowboarders, and in 1988, snowboarders only made up 6 percent of the ski resort population. Negative media coverage influenced the mainstream's opinion of snowboarding and its followers during this period. For example, in January 1988, *Time Magazine* declared snowboarding "the worst new sport." By the early 1990s, snowboarding still remained a minority activity. While there were undoubtedly geographical variations in approach, commentators in the early years frequently refer to a pervasive community spirit based on "a fun, non-judgmental scene that valued personal style" (Howe, 1998, 23).

Early Competitions

Modern competitive snowboarding began in 1981 with the first U.S. national titles held at Suicide Six (Vermont). Early snowboard competitions were poorly organized and, in keeping with countercultural traditions, privileged fun over serious competition and individualism. The Japanese held their first national snowboarding contest in 1982, and in 1986, the Europeans organized regional events such as the Swiss Championships in St. Moritz. More than 100 competitors from 17 nations competed in the World Championships at Livigno (Italy) and St. Moritz (Switzerland) in January 1987. At the end of the 1980s, however, the organization of snowboarding competitions lay in chaos. For example, two World Championships were simultaneously held in 1987, one in Livigno (Italy) and St. Moritz (Switzerland), the other in Breckenridge (Colorado). Recognizing the commercial opportunities in developing the sporting side of snowboarding, groups of sporting-inclined snowboarders and manufacturers formed the North American Snowboard Association (NASBA) and the Snowboard European

Association (SEA) later that year. Their goal was to work together to create a unified World Cup tour, similar to that of skiing. In 1988, devotees formed the United States of America Snowboarding Association (USASA) to standardize rules and organize events. Similar organizations emerged in snowboarding countries worldwide. The wheels of the institutionalization and commercialization process were in motion, and concerns about the "selling out" of snowboarding loomed large on the horizon.

KEY EVENTS

Significant change occurred in the late 1980s and early 1990s. The convergence of several factors contributed to the escalating number of snowboarders. More ski resorts opened their pistes (trails) to snowboarders, the mainstream media started reporting favorably on snowboarding culture, and snowboarding magazines (e.g., *International Snowboarder Magazine, Transworld Snowboarding*) and films (e.g., *Totally Board* [1989], *Snowboarders in Exile* [1990]) communicated images, attitudes, and styles to local snowboarding cultures across North America and around the world. Technological advances and an increasingly competitive market also provided participants with a cheaper and wider variety of equipment. Economic growth and further institutionalization accompanied higher levels of participation. Television and corporate sponsors also started to identify the huge potential in so-called extreme sports as a way to tap into young-male consumer markets, and mainstream companies began appropriating the alternative, hedonistic, and youthful image of the snowboarder to sell products ranging from chewing gum to automobiles.

Commercialization of the sport angered many snowboarders, and some overtly resisted the process. Jeff Galbriath, senior editor of *Snowboarder Magazine,* recalls one Professional Snowboard Tour of America (PSTA) event sponsored by Body Glove (clothing) where Shaun Palmer (a top snowboarder) "hit the main sponsor guy in the face … with a hot dog." Body Glove subsequently pulled out: "culturally, none of the riders were prepared to deal with contest structure" (Howe, 1998, 56). For some, competitive boarding stood in symbolic juxtaposition to "soul" boarding. For example, in 1990, world champion U.S. snowboarder Craig Kelly retired at the peak of his career from the competitive circuit, which he likened to "prostitution" (Howe, 1998, 82).

Snowboarding and the Olympics

The inclusion of snowboarding into the Olympics was a defining moment in the sport's short history and divided boarders. The loudest voice of opposition came from Terje Haakonsen who criticized the International Olympic Committee's (IOC) lack of understanding of snowboarding culture or consideration of snowboarders' needs. "The fact is that the big wigs ride in limousines and stay in fancy hotels while the athletes live in barracks in the woods," he argued (Humphreys, 2003, 421). Not surprisingly, Haakonsen refused to enter the Games because he believed that the IOC comprised a group of Mafia-like officials and that the event was tantamount to joining the army. He refused to be turned into a "uniform-wearing, flag-bearing, walking logo."

While many snowboarders resisted snowboarding's inclusion in the Olympics, it is important to note that some embraced these changes: Snowboarder Jimi Scott said, "I want to go to the Olympics ... be the first snowboarder to win a gold medal and be written into the history books" (Howe, 1998, 151). Debates among snowboarders over the commercialization process and the 1998 Winter Olympics more specifically are illustrative of the growing divisions and cultural fragmentation within the broader snowboarding culture during this period.

Snowboarding Goes Mainstream

Inevitably, incorporation and commercialization continued regardless of boarders' contrasting viewpoints, and snowboarding culture increasingly became controlled and defined by transnational media corporations such as ESPN and NBC via events such as the X Games and Gravity Games. In 1998, ESPN's different sports channels beamed the X Games to 198 countries in 21 languages (Rinehart, 2000). According to a Leisure Trends survey, 32 percent (nearly 92 million people) of the U.S. population watched the 2002 Olympic Snowboarding Half-Pipe competition in which Americans won gold (Ross Powers), silver (Danny Kass) and bronze (J. J. Thomas) in the men's event (note that this was the first U.S. Winter Olympic medal sweep since 1956) and gold (Kelly Clark) in the women's event. Of that percentage, 18.6 million Americans said they wanted to try snowboarding after viewing the event. The incorporation of snowboarding into the X Games and the Winter Olympics, video games including *Playstation's Cool Boarders* and *Shaun Palmer Pro-Snowboarder,* and blockbuster movies such as *First Descent* (2005) helped further expose the mainstream to snowboarding and contributed to the creation of the star system. For example, after winning gold in the 2006 Olympic half-pipe, Shaun White was featured on the cover of *Rolling Stone* and declared "the coolest *kid* in America."

The mainstream exposure of snowboarding had a significant influence on cultural demographics in the sport. Snowboarding attracted an influx of participants from around the world and from different social classes and age groups. Snowboarding has seen a 385 percent increase in participation between 1988 and 2003, and during the late 1990s and early 2000s it was one of America's fastest growing sports. While the snowboarding cultural demographics have changed considerably over the past two decades, it should be noted that more than 75 percent of snowboarders are 24 or younger, approximately 70 percent are male, and only 11 percent of American snowboarders are members of racial or ethnic minority groups.

The Snowboarding Industry: An Agent of Commercialization

During the late 1980s and 1990s, snowboarding developed a cohesive industry complete with its own media, international events and competitions, trade shows, fashions, and professional and amateur athletes. By 1995, the North

SNOWBOARDING TIMELINE

1964—Sherman Poppen invents the Snurfer.

1978—Jake Burton Carpenter establishes Burton Boards; Toms Sims establishes Sims Snowboards.

1981—First American snowboard nationals held at Suicide Six in Vermont.

1983—Stratton Mountain in Vermont becomes first major U.S. ski field to allow snowboarders.

1985—Less than 7 percent, that is 39 of approximately 600, ski areas in the United States allow snowboarding.

1985—First snowboarding magazine, *Absolutely Radical,* is released (renamed *International Snowboarder Magazine* six months later).

1987—Two World Championships held simultaneously, one in Livigno, Italy and St. Moritz, Switzerland, the other in Breckenridge, Colorado.

1987—Wrigley's chewing gum uses snowboarding in a national commercial.

1987—North American Snowboard Association (NASBA) established with the goal of working with the Snowboard European Association (SEA) to create a unified World Cup tour.

1987–1988—The first World Cup is held during the winter season with two events in Europe and two in the United States. The circuit also introduces major corporate sponsorship (O'Neill, Suzuki, and Swatch) into the competitive arena.

1994—Ride Snowboards becomes the first snowboard company to go public on the NASDAQ stock exchange; all 500,000 shares are sold in the first two weeks.

1996—Snowboarders constitute approximately 19 percent of all U.S. ski resort visits.

1997—Snowboarding features in first ESPN Winter X Games held at Snow Summit Mountain Resort at Big Bear Lake, California.

1998—Snowboarding makes its debut as an official medal sport at the Nagano Olympics.

1999—Nike begins marketing snowboards, boots, and bindings.

2002—Americans Ross Powers (gold), Danny Kass (silver), and J. J. Thomas (bronze) sweep the men's Olympic half-pipe in Salt Lake City.

2005—6.6 million snowboarders in the United States.

2006—Snowboarders compete in three events (half-pipe, snowboardcross, and giant slalom) at the Winter Olympics in Torino, Italy.

2006—U.S. Olympic half-pipe gold medalist Shaun White is featured on the cover of *Rolling Stone Magazine* March issue. The headline reads "Attack of the Flying Tomato: Meet the Coolest Kid in America."

2006—Overall sales for the winter sports market was $2.24 billion.

American snowboard retail industry was worth $750 million (Randall, 1995). That same year more than 300 companies peddled snowboard equipment, apparel, and accessories at the industry trade show, compared with just 90 companies in 1993. Industry sources predicted that snowboard market sales would double to $1.5 billion at retail by the end of the 1990s. When Ride Snowboards became the first snowboard company to go public on the NASDAQ stock exchange in 1994, it sold all 500,000 shares in the first two weeks: It then released another 75,000. Within a month the shares had reached $28 each, six times the release price.

The growth of the sport and industry attracted an influx of new companies, many of which had their roots elsewhere in surfing (e.g., Billabong, Ripcurl), skateboarding (e.g., DC, Etnies, Airwalk), skiing (e.g., Rossignol, Soloman, Voikal), and general athletics (e.g., Nike, K2, Adidas-Saloman). These companies were very well-financed and invested significant amounts of money in their marketing programs. They sponsored groups of elite boarders and invested heavily in advertising, product design, and packaging. However, with the influx of new companies from outside the culture, perceptions of cultural authenticity became a central concern among core boarders. As the president of one mainstream company stated, "it's a difficult category. It's highly technical, and core snowboarders are loyal to core snowboard brands. They are not really open to mainstream brands" (Dick Baker, cited in Deemer, 2000). To core boarders—the most savvy of consumers—the authenticity of a snowboarding company is central to their consumption choices. Moreover, they shy from companies that appear too commercially successful. According to one cultural commentator, core snowboarders base their consumption decisions on:

> values such as loyalty and commitment: Is the company committed to snowboarding? Does the company truly understand snowboarding? Companies that are seen to have ulterior motives or as not part of the snowboarding culture will generally be boycotted. Such companies cannot be trusted. (The Principles, 2002)

In a highly competitive industry, it is not simply products but the corporate image itself that is essential. Snowboarding companies thus employ various strategies to create and re-create a culturally authentic corporate image (e.g., advertising in snowboarding magazines, sponsoring athletes and events, and funding snowboarding videos).

Today, hundreds of companies provide snowboarding-specific equipment and clothing in an abundance of styles. While most products have functional purposes, they also serve as important symbolic cultural markers, distinguishing insiders from outsiders and professionals from poseurs. Snowboard equipment and clothing carries status based on understanding the nuances of the culture. To the initiated member, decoding a combination of snowboard graphics, clothing labels, and other visual signifiers is an automatic process. Moreover, with the increasing number of participants, turnover rates in fashion trends have accelerated. Having worked in the snowboarding industry for many years, American snowboarder Moriah is acutely aware of the importance of the latest fashions among core boarders, "if you're not wearing the coolest gear, or what the top riders are, or rocking the newest bindings and board, then you're wack [uncool]" (personal communication, November 2005). According to Ford and Brown (2006), concern with authenticity of various boarding clothing brands may be viewed as a response not only to the increasing levels of participation in the board sports but, more importantly, to the global appropriation of boarding fashion by mass youth culture.

The Snowboarding Media: An Agent of Commercialization

The snowboarding media, especially films and magazines, play a decisive role in the lives of snowboarders by confirming, spreading, and consolidating cultural perceptions. Snowboarding companies use these mediums extensively to advertise their products and, more importantly, for corporate image work. Doug Palladini, publisher of *Snowboarder* magazine, observes that

> Snowboarders are passionate consumers.... magazines are not just something you pick up at the airport. To the core, it is the bible. Companies are spending up to 50% of their budgets on advertising. Snowboarding is a completely image-based sport and the most direct line to kids is through our magazines. (Howe, 1998, 104)

Snowboarding historian Susanna Howe identifies photographers and filmmakers as "the real image makers" because their work "creates the dream that is snowboarding" and "sells lifestyle."

Though the niche media resides closest to culture, various social and economic factors limit and complicate their intimate relations. For example, *Blunt* magazine, established in 1993 by snowboarders Ken Block and Damon Way, had more cultural authenticity among core snowboarders than any other magazine because it was seen as providing a truthful representation of snowboarding culture. Richards (2003) describes the *Blunt* formula as "alcohol, party, party, party, oh, and snowboarding," and adds, "it was really popular among snowboarders and really unpopular among ski resorts, parents, and snowboarding companies because of its blatant disregard for authority. It also covered the most progressive snowboarders and turned down advertising from big companies like Burton and Morrow" (162). But in 1998, due to political and economic reasons, *Blunt* magazine folded. "Distributors and advertisers wanted mainstream readers, while mainstream readers' parents wanted a more subdued, politically correct publication," explained one industry insider (Blehm, 2003, 33). Simply put, *Blunt* was subjected to the major forces and constraints of the commercialization process.

Commercial processes also complicate the production of contemporary snowboarding magazines. For example, although snowboarders work as journalists and editors for *Transworld Snowboarding*, it is owned by Time4Media and is a subsidiary of Time Warner Inc. In 2004, *Transworld Snowboarding* had a circulation of 207,000, featured a total of 1,333 pages of advertisements, and generated $21.9 million in revenue, up from $14.9 million in 2000. Responding to concerns about the amount and type of advertising featured in the magazine, Cody Dresser, associate editor of *Transworld Snowboarding*, acknowledged that "editorial and advertising are two separate departments—we're often bitching about the corporate ads diluting our magazine." Ste'en Webster, editor of *New Zealand Snowboarder,* admits to similar tensions, but as a smaller, snowboarder-owned and -operated company with a circulation of 10,000, he retains more control over the final product:

> Our goal is to represent what's happening within New Zealand snowboarding. I think that is an important goal, a lot of magazines get distracted and rather than portray what's going on [in the culture] they tend to dictate [based on] what they think the advertiser wants them to say. (personal communication, October 2005)

Simply put, there are numerous forms of snowboarding niche media; some target a trasnsnational audience, while others cater to smaller national and local niche markets. The limitations and complications of the commercialization process vary between the different forms of snowboarding niche media.

The Virtues and Vices of the Commercialization Process

As snowboarding became popularized and incorporated into the mainstream, it adopted many of the trappings of traditional modern sports: corporate sponsorships, large prize monies, rationalized systems of rules, hierarchical and individualistic star systems, win-at-all costs values, and the creation of heroes, heroines, and in the words of Michael Messner, "rebel athletes who look like walking corporate billboards" (2002, 178). Professional U.S. snowboarders such as Shaun White, Danny Kass, Todd Richards, Tara Dakides, Gretchen Bleiler, Lindsey Jacobellis, Kelly Clark, and Hannah Tetter have benefited from the recently commercialized form of snowboarding. They have achieved superstar status within the culture, attracting American corporate sponsors including Target, Play Station, Visa, Nike, Mountain Dew, Campbell's Soup, and Boost Mobile. Some earn seven-figure salaries.

FUTURE PROSPECTS

Snowboarding has experienced rapid growth and considerable changes over the past three decades. But it is important to note that commercialization is not solely a co-opting force. Residues of the countercultural philosophies remain, and the snowboarding culture will continue to adapt and change, contesting cultural meanings, spaces, and identities. Snowboarders are not simply victims of commercialization but active agents who continue to resist and negotiate the images and meanings circulated in and by global consumer culture. While it is difficult to predict how much longer corporate sponsors will persist in using snowboarding to tap into the youth market, it seems inevitable that the sport, culture, and industry of snowboarding will continue to grow and change for many years to come.

See also Adventure Racing; Cool Pose; Media Broadcasting Rights; Skateboarding; Surfing and New Water Sports; Video Games; X Games; Yoga and Alternative Fitness.

Further Reading: Blehm, E. (2003). *Agents of Change: The Story of DC Shoes and its Athletes.* New York: Regan Books; Deemer, S. (2000). Snow Business is Booming in Sunny Orange County. *Los Angeles Business Journal* (January 24). http://www.allbusiness.com/north-america/united-states-california-metro-areas/442072-1.html (accessed December 12, 2005); Ford, N., and Brown, D. (2006). *Surfing and Social Theory.* London: Routledge; Howe, S. (1998). *(SICK) A Cultural History of Snowboarding.* New York: St. Martins Griffin; Humphreys, D. (1996). Snowboarders: Bodies Out of Control and In Conflict. *Sporting Traditions* 13 (1): 3–23; Humphreys, D. (2003). Selling Out Snowboarding. In *To the Extreme: Alternative Sports, Inside and Out,* edited by R. E. Rinehart and S. Sydnor, 407–428. New York: State University Press; Messner, M. (2002). *Taking the Field: Women, Men and Sports.* London: Minnesota Press; *National Sporting Goods Association: Research and Statistics.* (2005). NGSA: Women's Participation Ranked by Percent Change 2003. http://www.nsga.org/public/pages/index.cfm?pageid=155 (accessed January 12, 2005); The Principles of Snowboarding (August 2002). http://www.boardtheworld.com (accessed January 18, 2004); Randall, L. (1995, March 27). The Culture that Jake Built. *Forbes* 155 (7): 45–46; Richards, T., with Blehm, E. (2003). *P3: Pipes, Parks, and Powder.* New York: Harper Collins; Rinehart, R. Emerging/Arriving Sport: Alternatives to Formal Sports. In *Handbook of sports studies,* edited by J. Coakley and E. Dunning, 504–519. London: Sage; Snowboarding and the Olympics. http://www.burton.com/company/default.asp (accessed July 17, 2004).

Holly Thorpe

SOCCER TRAGEDIES

Since the 1980s and 1990s, the world of professional soccer has been increasingly plagued by a number of catastrophic tragedies involving mass fan deaths within stadiums. While North American sports has been largely immune to mass deaths or injuries among fans while they attended sports games, the continent is relatively unique in this respect. Tragedies at soccer stadiums, rightly or wrongly, have most often been attributed to acts of hooliganism and hooligan cultures, especially in the context of England.

BACKGROUND

There have been countless attempts to explain soccer hooliganism and understand its outcomes. Many cite what is seen as the inherent violence of the English working class. Others argue that somehow fighting is in the gene pool—a nation that has sent almost every generation of its men folk to war throughout antiquity has produced a social stratum naturally predisposed to violent disorder. It could simply be that if 40,000 people are crammed into one place and given even the slightest reason to confront each other, there will be a small proportion that will do so and a greater proportion that will allow themselves to be drawn into a crowd contagion.

Whatever the reasons, by the mid-1980s, violence was endemic in and around soccer grounds throughout England. With little closed-circuit television and largely indifferent policing, hooligan firms had a relative carte blanche to fight across the country. Leeds United fans were particularly notorious for their violent outbursts, as were Newcastle United, Cardiff City, Swansea City, and the

Sheffield and Manchester City club fans. However, it would be Liverpool Football Club (LFC) hooligan supporters who would eventually draw international attention to the culture in British football. Despite a prevailing rough terrace culture, Liverpool supporters had no particular reputation for violence; perhaps outside of an intense rivalry with Manchester United fans (during the 1985 Football Association Cup semifinal between the teams supporters had hurled golf balls with eight-inch nails driven through them at each other). Yet, in a 1985 European Final Cup match pitting Liverpool against the Italian side Juventus at Heysel stadium in Brussels, everything changed.

    The game was due to be the last match ever played at the ground because it had been condemned many years previously for failing to meet modern standards of safety and design. As a result, little money had been spent upon it, and large parts of the stadium were crumbling. There was little segregation of supporters, a factor exacerbated by the indiscriminate selling of black market tickets by scalpers, and many fans found that it was possible to enter the ground by simply lifting a section of the makeshift fencing surrounding the terraces. There had been skirmishes around Brussels all day, and local police responded by getting fans into the stadium as quickly as possible rather than arresting and detaining offenders. This haphazard stewarding of rival fans proved to be crucial as the tragedy unfolded: Because there was no way of knowing who was in the ground and where they were, it was impossible for police to weed out known troublemakers and easy for pockets of hard-core hooligans to assemble wherever they wished. As a result, two hours before kick off, perhaps the most malevolent assembly of soccer supporters ever seen in one place had gathered, and as far as they were concerned, it was payback time. It should be understood that not just Liverpool hooligans were present. There were contingents from a great many hooligan firms all over the country, from Luton MIGS to Millwall Bushwackers, West Ham ICF, and Newcastle Toon Army. After the events in Rome, club rivalries had been put aside: Juventus was to catch the full fury of the English hooligan elite.

    Italian fascists, who were present in force among the Juventus contingent, goaded supporters into making incursions into the main body of Liverpool fans at the western end of an enormous shared terrace. What were initially scuffles quickly escalated into a series of serious terrace battles. At 8:45 P.M. local time, the Liverpool fans charged into a solid mass of Juventus support, which was hemmed in on three sides by crumbling concrete walls. The Juventus supporters attempted to fall back. However, with no avenue of retreat, they simply piled on top of each other. Panic set in among the Italians, some of whom were now getting crushed at the rear of the terrace as the Liverpool supporters continued to charge against the front. At this moment, with police and stewards too stunned to react, a wall at the eastern end of the terrace gave way. Dozens of Juventus supporters were now trapped against what remained of the wall and were trampled underfoot as thousands of people stampeded over them. Thirty-nine people, mostly Juventus fans, lost their lives in the scuffle.

    Meanwhile, there was mayhem in the ground itself. Italian supporters invaded the pitch in an effort to get at the English. It appeared that one Italian fan was firing a gun into the Liverpool fans; this later turned out to be a starting pistol.

In desperation, several Liverpool players spoke across the public address system in an attempt to calm the supporters. Eventually, with the arrival of police reinforcements and elements of the Belgian army, enough order was restored for the match to commence. Official reaction to the event was swift, and English teams were banned from European competition for six years. This damaged the English game because top players, deprived of competing at European level, chose to play on the Continent instead. Also, several smaller clubs, whose domestic performances would otherwise have qualified them for the various European tournaments, missed their chance. Prime Minister Margaret Thatcher and the Queen of England issued formal apologies to the people of Belgium and Italy.

The tragic events of Heysel were nearly mirrored only four years later on April 15, 1989. Liverpool FC played the FA-Cup semifinal against Nottingham Forest at Hillsborough in Sheffield. The interest for the match was enormous, and many Liverpool supporters could not get a ticket. In the hours before the match the streets outside the stadium were overcrowded. The turnstiles were few, and it took a very long time to get the crowd through the doors. People became impatient when they realized that they would not get in before the match started. Ten minutes prior to the kick-off, an order was issued by stadium officials to open the gates in the hope of avoiding a catastrophe. Large numbers of spectators now poured into the stands, and people were crushed against a fence located inside the stadium's front doors. Those who tried to climb over to escape onto the field were driven back by the police and the guards. In the continued press of the crowd forward into the stadium, people were crushed and trampled to death. In the end, 96 people were killed.

While global soccer has been victim to ongoing mass deaths at stadiums around the world, a clear and perplexing pattern of tragedies developed on the African continent in the 2000s. In July 2000, 13 people were killed in a stampede when police deliberately fired tear gas into the near-capacity 60,000 crowd in Harare stadium during the World Cup qualifier between Zimbabwe and South Africa. Zimbabwean and South African players had to lay face down on the pitch and were treated by medical personnel, while a cloud of tear gas hung over one stand in the bowl-shaped stadium. An inquest into the tragedy found the police action to blame for the 13 deaths, but there have been no prosecutions of suspended police officers.

In 2001, more than 100 people died in Ghana in the fourth major soccer tragedy to strike Africa that year. On April 11, 43 soccer fans died and 250 were injured at the Ellis Park Stadium in Johannesburg during a local league derby between rivals Kaizer Chiefs and Orlando Pirates. People were crushed to death when crowds continued to pour into the stadium, which was already packed to capacity. A couple of weeks later, 14 people died and 51 were injured on April 29 during a match at Lubumbashi in the southeast region of the Democratic Republic of Congo when violence broke out in the league game between TP Mazembe and Lupopo. Again police fired off tear gas as a method of crowd control, causing spectators to rush onto the pitch. Both gates of the stadium, which contained at least 30,000 people, were barred shut, causing delays in evacuation. Then, on May 6 in the Ivory Coast, incidents between supporters and police led to 1 death and 39 injuries at the Houphouet-Boigny stadium in Abidjan. Supporters of the

SOCCER STADIUM TRAGEDIES

1946—Bolton, England; 33 people were killed and over 400 injured when a wall collapsed at Burden Park before an English FA Cup match. The collapse crushed fans and sparked a stampede.

1964—Lima, Peru; 318 people were killed and another 500 injured in riots at National Stadium. The pandemonium broke out when the referee disallowed a Peruvian goal in the final two minutes.

1968—Buenos Aires, Argentina; 74 people were killed and over 150 injured following a game when fans trying to leave the stadium mistakenly headed toward a closed exit and were crushed against the doors by other fans unaware of the closed passageway.

1971—Glasgow, Scotland; 66 people were killed and 140 injured when barriers in the stands collapsed near the end of a match. The incident occurred when fans met a group trying to return after hearing that the Rangers had scored an equalizer.

1982—Moscow; 340 were reportedly killed at a European Cup match between Soviet club Spartak Moscow and Haarlem of The Netherlands. Police were blamed for pushing fans down a narrow, icy staircase before the end of the match. Moscow officials disputed the claims made in the publication of the Soviet Sports Committee, saying only 61 died and police did not push fans.

1988—Katmandu, Nepal; 93 people were killed and more than 100 injured when fans fleeing a hailstorm stampeded into locked stadium exits.

1989—Sheffield, England; 95 people were crushed to death at an English FA Cup semifinal game between Liverpool and Nottingham Forest when police opened gates to alleviate crowding outside Hillsborough Stadium. The resulting rush of people onto the already filled terrace sections trapped fans against riot control fences ringing the field.

1991—Orkney, South Africa; 40 people were killed, most of them trampled or crushed along riot-control fences that surrounded the field, when fans panicked and tried to escape brawls that broke out in the grandstand.

1992—Bastia, Corsica; 17 people were killed and 1,900 injured when a temporary grandstand, erected to increase the capacity of the stadium from 8,500 to 18,000, collapsed before a French Cup semifinal match between four-time defending league champion Olympique Marseille and second-division Bastia.

1996—Guatemala City; At least 78 people died and about 180 others were injured during a stampede at a stadium before a World Cup qualifying match between Guatemala and Costa Rica.

2001—Johannesburg, South Africa; 43 people were killed when a stampede began as the crowd tried to get into the Ellis Park stadium to watch the match between the Kaizer Chiefs and Orlando Pirates.

2001—Ghana; A stampede killed at least 100 people at a match between Accra's Hearts of Oak and Assante Kotoko. With five minutes left in the game Assante supporters began throwing bottles and chairs onto the field. Police then fired tear gas, creating panic and a stampede toward the exits.

top two clubs in the Ivory Coast, Asec Mimosa and Africa Sports, both based in the main commercial capital, Abidjan, clashed violently during a local league derby. On top of these incidents, there have also been serious riots at soccer stadiums in Algeria, Ghana, Nigeria and South Africa since 2006, where deaths have only been narrowly averted.

Much of the African media have said that stadium disasters resulted from the rapid increase in soccer's popularity in Africa, which has grown much faster than the development of secure modern facilities. It is certainly true that most of the stadiums in Africa lack proper facilities and fully trained staff. But it is also common practice for police to indiscriminately fire tear gas to quell rioting supporters under conditions where stewarding and safety measures are almost nonexistent and exits from the grounds are often blocked. Such aggressive methods of crowd control perhaps reflect the policing approach to working-class people taken by most African regimes. Moreover, the provision of sports facilities is hardly a priority in countries that are amongst the most heavily indebted in the world. The role of the soccer clubs has also been a factor in most of the disasters. Top league matches attract record numbers of fans, but even so, tickets are usually sold on the day of the game. This encourages overselling and, in some cases, sales of fake tickets, which leads to the problem of overcapacity.

FUTURE PROSPECTS

Stadium tragedies are among the least noted or debated forms of patterned death in the world. Clearly, new and multi-institutional measures are required in order to protect fans (especially in economically developing nations) from unsafe sports facilities. There is some evidence to suggest that the Western European, Interpol-led crackdown on soccer hooliganism has played a great role in combating stadium tragedies in countries such as England, but the problem needs to be addressed with far greater attention around the world. At a minimum, security at stadiums should be enhanced by: more stringent ticket procedures and monitoring of illegal ticketing industries; increased fines for fans entering onto the field of play; zero tolerance of fans abusing one another verbally within the stadium; increased surveillance efforts and technologies at stadiums; modification of alcohol sales practices; detailed police profiling of suspected hooligans; closure of problematic bleacher sections in stadiums when needed; and increased criminal prosecution of anyone harming another fan on a stadium's grounds.

See also Criminal Violence During Competition; Field Invasions; Hooliganism; Missile Throwing; Player–Fan Fighting.

Further Reading: Dunning, E., Murphy, P., Waddington, I., and Astrinakis, A. (2002). *Fighting Fans: Football Hooliganism as a World Problem*. Dublin: University College Dublin Press; Perryman, M. (2001). *Hooligan Wars*. London: Mainstream; Scraton, P. (1999). *Hillsborough: The Truth*. London: Mainstream; Ward, C. (1997). *All Quiet on the Hooligan Front: Eight Years that Changed the Face of Football*. London: Headline Books.

Michael Atkinson

SPORTS DOCTORS, TRAINERS, AND DRUGS

As a field of practice consisting of a variety of health care professions, *sports medicine* is a broad term that in many ways eludes exact definition. Health care practitioners in sports medicine traditionally include physicians, orthopedic surgeons, and physical therapists such as sports physiotherapists, athletic therapists (sometimes referred to as sports or athletic trainers), and massage therapists. However, other health care practitioners also practice sports medicine, including chiropractors, dentists, osteopaths, nutritionists, and even clinical psychologists. While policies and legislation around the regulation of health care professions vary from country to country, at this point in time, many health care professions identify and market their sports-specific subdisciplines as sports medicine because the title is not restricted to one single profession. In other words, no one profession can identify themselves as the sole practitioner of sports medicine, and thus, different health care professions compete and negotiate with one another for authority and legitimacy in the sports medicine system. Furthermore, contemporary sports medicine is closely related to the sports sciences such as exercise physiology and biomechanics. Whereas sports medicine practitioners tend to focus on the prevention and treatment of sports- or exercise-related injury, sports scientists often focus their research and interventions on performance enhancement. This is not to suggest that a focus on health care and a focus on performance enhancement are mutually exclusive or independent of one another. Rather, sports medicine and sports sciences do overlap in terms of their sociohistorical development and in terms of their scopes of practice.

BACKGROUND

Medical and scientific interest in exercise and the sporting body, including interest in diet and hygiene, can be traced back to the time of the Ancient Greeks, such as Hippocrates and Galen. However, sports medicine, as we know of it today, emerged chiefly in Germany in the early 1900s. At that point in time, many physicians and scientists saw the athletic body as a tool with which to better understand biology and anatomy and with which to expand their knowledge of physiology. By the early twentieth century, the situation was reversed and advances in science and medicine were utilized to help athletes better train for and

---

ATHLETIC TRAINER OR ATHLETIC THERAPIST?

In the United States, the term *athletic trainer* is used, whereas in Canada, *athletic therapist* is the appropriate terminology. Why the two different names? Although athletic trainers/athletic therapists have a history as long as sports medicine physicians, they have often not been accorded similar levels of prestige or recognition, in part because of their name. In Canada, in the early 1970s, the governing body regulating athletic training decided to change the name to athletic therapy in order to disassociate their discipline from personal training or coaching and to enhance their status as professional health care practitioners.

perform in sports competitions. It is important to reiterate that the development of sports medicine dovetailed with the growth and development of such sports sciences as physiology or biomechanics in the nineteenth and twentieth centuries. However, the focus on the prevention, treatment, and rehabilitation of sports- and exercise-related injury—the primary focus of contemporary sports medicine—took shape chiefly from the mid-twentieth century onward.

KEY EVENTS

The production of international high performance sports following World War II has played a major role in the development of contemporary sports medicine. Currently, for many countries competing in the international high-performance sports arena, clinical/therapeutic support for athletes is naturalized and institutionalized as part of the nation's high-performance sports system. Countries competing in sporting events provide their athletes with sports medicine services before, during, and after the competitions, and the various sports medicine professions are seen, to varying degrees, as experts on the health of the sporting body. A number of scholars acknowledge the connections that exist between high-performance, particularly Olympic, sports and the development of sports medicine. Following World War II, and as a result of a number of social, political, and economic factors within and outside of sports, high-performance sports in many countries became especially focused on success and medal counts rather than participation or education. High-performance sports became more professionalized and commercialized, and the production of high-performance sports—that is, the training and development of athletes—became more disciplined, methodical, and rationalized. The production of high-performance sports now focused primarily on the pursuit of excellence and, as Hoberman puts it, the "promise of limitless performances." However, the promise of limitless performance does have its limits. Athletes, in pushing themselves to excel, regularly train and compete at the borders of physical breakdown, and this implicates sports medicine and the various sports medicine professions. There is a cyclical relationship here in that as the need for sports medicine is stimulated (i.e., the need for "expert" knowledge to manage the negative consequences of sports participation), the institutionalization of sports medicine is legitimated. In other words, sports medicine stimulates a need for its services, provides the means with which to meet the needs of athletes who seek sports medicine professions' expertise, and this, in turn, further secures its authoritative position on the health of the sporting body.

As the nature of international high-performance sports changed following World War II—as competitions became more intense, as training techniques became more rigorous, and as knowledge of performance enhancement became more sophisticated—athletes were pushed harder to prepare for competitions and, in turn, experienced more injuries and health concerns. In many countries around the world, this rise in injuries and health problems was not met with critique but rather with support for the professional development of sports medicine and its various disciplines. For example, the Canadian government created and funded the Sport Medicine Council of Canada (later known as the

Sport Medicine and Science Council of Canada) in the late 1970s in response to these changing dynamics. It is important to point out that sports medicine developed, in large part, out of concern for the health and well-being of athletes. However, critical researchers are also quick to point out that the provision of health care to athletes, particularly high-performance athletes, was often limited to their preparation for and participation in major games and often in order to maintain their peak performance rather than to prevent injury. If success in high-performance sports was seen as a way in which to bolster national prestige and social status in the international arena, government support for sports medicine was a way in which to ensure that success by minimizing the risks to the athletes' "limitless performances."

Participation in sports is often believed to be healthy, but there is growing evidence among researchers that the health benefits of intense participation in sports are questionable and that intense sports participation may in fact contribute to increased rates of morbidity and mortality. Nowhere is this more evident than for athletes participating at the extreme end of vigorous competitive physical activity—high-performance sports.

The focus on excellence within high-performance sports demands, on the part of the athlete, the development of disregard for the body's physical limits. Given the intense, rigorous training and competition regimens involved in high-performance sports, it is somewhat ironic that while athletes are often seen as symbols of strength and vitality, they often sacrifice their health and well-being in the pursuit of success and idealized athleticism. Simply put, as athletes move up the competitive ladder, they often wear down their bodies through a variety of health-compromising behaviors such as the uncritical tolerance of pain or injury, dangerous dieting practices, or the use and abuse of drugs—performance-enhancing or otherwise. A grossly underresearched topic in the critical study of sports medicine revolves around the use and abuse of painkillers in sports. Performance-enhancing drugs, such as steroids, erythropoietin (EPO), or beta-blockers, are widely recognized as illegal in high-performance sports. Athletes caught using such substances are heavily penalized through suspensions or outright bans from participating in their sport. Yet, there is very little attention paid to athletes who use and abuse legal drugs such as painkillers. In other words, sports governing bodies often turn a blind eye to athletes who regularly risk their health and well-being by "playing through pain." If sports is supposedly good for one's health, why

SPORTS MEDICINE BEYOND HIGH-PERFORMANCE SPORTS

Sports medicine is more than just the provision of health care in high-performance sports. There is a significant, and significantly underresearched, sports medicine industry (including clinics, medications, and orthopedic products) that generates hundreds of millions of dollars in income annually in North America alone. As more and more people engage in physical activity as a way to achieve and maintain health, they risk sports- or exercise-related injury. Given such potential for profit, it is not far-fetched to suggest that the lucrative economic aspect of sports medicine supports injury treatment and rehabilitation but not necessarily prevention.

is it acceptable for athletes to dope themselves on painkillers in order to be able to perform? Furthermore, could the use and abuse of painkillers be interpreted as a type of performance enhancement? If so, what are the consequences of this for high-performance sports?

Athletes' immersion in what is referred to as sports' "culture of risk" sees their often-unquestioned acceptance and re/production of norms and behaviors that endanger health. Many athletes come to understand pain and injury as physical and symbolic cues of identity, such that pain tolerance and the disregard of bodily limits are often seen as reflections of strength of character. The pervasiveness of this ideology extends into the lives of male and female athletes and becomes part of the construction of athletic identity for many of these individuals. Not all athletes identify as athletes through such disregard for the body, but these health-compromising norms often make up the mindset and culture of many athletes in competitive sports. It is in this framework that athletes learn to expect, accept, minimize, or ignore pain and injury as a normal part of the game and even take pride in their pain threshold as proof of their character as athletes and their dedication to the team. This discussion leads us back to the paradox of competitive sports. Many people see sports as building, enhancing, and improving the body, but it also hurts and damages the body. This destructive process implicates other participants in the sports system such as sports medicine practitioners. As much as the "culture of risk" frames how athletes understand pain and injury, the "culture of risk" also frames how sports medicine clinicians negotiate treatment with athletes. Research has shown that, under certain circumstances, sports medicine clinicians reproduce the "culture of risk" in their negotiations with athletes, but the "culture of risk" is also tempered by a "culture of precaution" that works to resist the acceptance and tolerance of pain and injury in sports.

DOPE DEALERS?

Despite a few high-profile cases, there has been very little critical scholarly attention paid to the involvement of physicians and therapists in the use and abuse of performance-enhancing drugs by athletes. Such high-profile cases include Dr. Jamie Astaphan's involvement with Canadian sprinter Ben Johnson in the 1988 Seoul Olympic Games and Italian physician Dr. Michele Ferrari's involvement with a number of national and international cyclists, including Lance Armstrong. Athletes are often publicly punished for their decision to use performance-enhancing drugs; less often punished are those individuals who have access to and who supply them with the drugs. Why is this the case? Furthermore, what motivates a health care practitioner—someone committed by legislation and oath to do no harm or to do no further harm to their patient—to help an athlete dope? One reason could be quite altruistic, that is, health care practitioners know that an athlete is going to dope and would rather try to ensure—as best as possible—the health and safety of the athlete while they are doping rather than try to police or discipline them. Much more critical research is needed in this area in order to flush out the relationship between sports medicine and drugs in sports.

FUTURE PROSPECTS

It would be wrong to suggest that there are no health benefits to sports—participation in sports can and does have a positive impact on the health of many people. However, the structure of sports—particularly high-performance sports, its "culture of risk," and its commitment to an ideology of excellence—often makes positive health effects the exception and not the rule. The structure and production of competitive sports promotes the production and tolerance of a certain threshold of pain and injury, and this implicates the provision of health care to athletes. Sports medicine and various professions that make up the field of sports medicine have come to assume expertise and authority on the sporting body and have created a niche for themselves in the sports and health care systems of many countries. However, we must question how much of a role they have played in the prevention and reduction of sports injury and the implications of their more curative role in the treatment and care of sports injury.

See also Antidoping Rules and Policies; Ergogenics; Illness; Steroid Use by Athletes; Whistle-Blowers and Drugs.

Further Reading: Berryman, J., and Park, R. (1992). *Sport and Exercise Science: Essays in the History of Sports Medicine.* Urbana: University of Illinois Press; Hoberman, J. (1992). *Mortal Engines: The Science of Performance and the Dehumanization of Sport.* New York: Free Press; Waddington, I. (2000). *Sport, Health and Drugs: A Critical Sociological Perspective.* London: E & FN Spon; Young, K. (Ed.). (2004). *Sporting Bodies, Damaged Selves: Sociological Studies of Sport-Related Injury.* Oxford: Elsevier.

Parissa Safai

SPORTS FOR ALL

In the phrase "sports for all," sports is understood in its broadest sense to include various levels of competitive sports, exercise, and a wide range of recreational physical activities. The sports for all movement is grounded in the idea that, because moderate participation in sports and recreational physical activity is beneficial—particularly in terms of physical, mental, and community health—opportunities to participate should be available to all people. The term *sports for all* is not widely known in North America. Recreation, active leisure, exercise, grassroots sports, and community sports are all terms that are captured in the idea of sports for all. However, when the idea is expressed as sports for all it raises questions about who should fund and provide those opportunities to participate. Sports for all also finds itself in a continuing struggle with high-performance / elite sports, which has an insatiable appetite for money and facilities that fund and provide opportunities to participate only for those who are the best athletes.

BACKGROUND

The original idea for "sports for all" was a European worker's response to the middle-class nature of sports in the early part of the twentieth century.

The Labour Sports Confederation (Confédération sportive internationale du travail, CSIT) was founded in Belgium in 1913 "to secure sporting rights for working people and their families—especially women and children." This evolved into the workers' sports movement in Europe and Canada during the 1920s and 1930s, but the modern idea of sports for all emerged following World War II. The climate of postwar reform saw the establishment of public pensions and unemployment insurance, increased access to higher education, and the creation of public health care systems in many countries. It also saw the emergence of human rights—the Universal Declaration of Human Rights was proclaimed in 1948—and democratizing movements such as attempts to combat poverty, the civil rights movement for racial equality in the United States and other countries, the women's rights movement, disability rights, and so on.

The CSIT was re-established after World War II (1946), and by the 1960s, movements such as Jedermann-Sport in Germany had begun to appear. In a parallel movement, concerns about physical fitness and access to fitness opportunities were also being expressed, and a series of biannual conferences began in 1969. The initial conference brought together representatives from more than 60 countries, representing the European-oriented "trim" movement and the North American–oriented "fitness" movement. Various national sports for all/physical activity associations organized, and many of these came together in 1990 (including Canada's ParticipAction) to form the Trim and Fitness International Sports for all Association (TAFISA).

Given this background, the formal start of the sports for all movement in Europe can be traced to the Council of Europe's Sports for all Charter (1975), which brought the movement widespread public attention. The Charter is grounded in the idea that, given the positive consequences of participation in sports and recreational physical activity (e.g., enhanced citizenship and community development, health, social and mental development), such benefits should be available to all. The Charter affirmed that all citizens had the *right* to participate in sports, and it outlined the terms by which that right might be realized.

KEY EVENTS

Since the 1970s, there has been growing recognition in wealthy nations that health care costs are continuing to increase and that physical activity represents an extremely effective form of preventive health care. The emergence of the sports for all movement represented an ideal opportunity for governments, especially in Europe, to develop programs and facilities in order to promote increased participation in physical activity. These were most successful in Northern Europe, particularly in Scandinavia. However, the idea that people had a right to participate in sports and physical recreation began, in some cases, to be reinterpreted as a responsibility to participate in physical activity. Where the requirements to participate were overly prescriptive—for example, 30 or 60 minutes of vigorous physical activity daily, with specific heart rate increases—physical activity became less fun, and there were measurable declines in participation.

MAJOR AFFIRMATIONS OF THE RIGHT TO PARTICIPATE IN SPORTS

1975: European Sports for all Charter

- Every individual shall have the right to participate in sport.

1978: United Nations Educational, Scientific and Cultural Organization (UNESCO) International Charter of Physical Education and Sport

- The practice of sport and physical education is a fundamental right for all.

1979: UN Convention on the Elimination of All Forms of Discrimination Against Women (CEDAW):

Article 10   States Parties shall take all appropriate measures to eliminate discrimination against women in order to ensure to them equal rights with men in the field of education and in particular to ensure, on a basis of equality of men and women:
   (g) The same Opportunities to participate actively in sports and physical education;

1980: Sports for the People (USA):

- The right to sports for everyone of every age, every nationality, every race and both sexes.
- The right to sports whether rich or poor.
- The right to programs funded by the government and organized by the community.
- The right to sports facilities—pools, playgrounds, gyms, beaches, parks, rings, rinks, courts, fields and diamonds—open in every community, every day, all day long.

1989: UN Convention on the Rights of the Child (CRC):

Article 31   1. States Parties recognize the right of the child to rest and leisure, to engage in play and recreational activities appropriate to the age of the child and to participate freely in cultural life and the arts.

1994: International Olympic Committee—Olympic Charter, Fundamental Principles:

- The practice of sport is a human right. Every individual must have the possibility of practising sport in accordance with his or her needs.

2001: European Sports Charter:

1. to enable every individual to participate in sport and notably:
    a. to ensure that all young people should have the opportunity to receive physical education instruction and the opportunity to acquire basic sports skill
    b. to ensure that everyone should have the opportunity to take part in sport and physical recreation in a safe and healthy environment; and in cooperation with the appropriate sports organisations;
    c. to ensure that everyone with the interest and ability should have the opportunity to improve their standard of performance in sport and reach levels of personal achievement and/or publicly recognised levels of excellence.

2007: UN Convention on the Rights of Persons with Disabilities (CRPD):

Article 30   5. With a view to enabling persons with disabilities to participate on an equal basis with others in recreational, leisure and sporting activities, States Parties shall take appropriate measures:

a) To encourage and promote the participation, to the fullest extent possible, of persons with disabilities in mainstream sporting activities at all levels;

b) To ensure that persons with disabilities have an opportunity to organize, develop and participate in disability-specific sporting and recreational activities and, to this end, encourage the provision, on an equal basis with others, of appropriate instruction, training and resources;

c) To ensure that persons with disabilities have access to sporting, recreational and tourism venues;

d) To ensure that children with disabilities have equal access with other children to participation in play, recreation and leisure and sporting activities, including those activities in the school system;

Since the 1980s, in contrast to many European countries, North America has been characterized by significant budget cuts to the public sector, resulting in the increasing privatization of opportunities to participate in sports and physical activity. Thus, at the same time that physicians and exercise physiologists were offering their exercise prescriptions, the opportunities to participate in publicly funded municipal recreation programs, and in schools, were declining, as was participation in physical activity. Therefore, despite widespread concerns about the low levels of physical activity of North American children, the obesity epidemic, and related chronic diseases, 'ports for all opportunities were decreasing—especially for low-income families.

Surprisingly, public sector spending on sports in wealthy countries (private sector spending in the United States) was increasing during this same period of time. That funding was going to elite sports and to the pursuit of Olympic medals and international success in sports. Medals are far more attractive politically; they represent short-term tangible benefits (despite the calculation that each gold medal won by Australians at the 2000 Sydney Olympics cost the government/Australian taxpayers US$35 million); they provide photo opportunities; and they provide a great deal of media coverage. Publicly funded sports for all opportunities are far less attractive. They represent long-term investments, and the benefits are somewhat less tangible—for example, is a reduction in juvenile delinquency in a neighborhood a result of the government-funded sports programs, or is it something else?—and a long-term improvement in the health and quality of life for the Smith family provides a much less attractive photo opportunity than one with an Olympic gold medalist pretending to take a bite out of the medal they have just won.

While such spending may seem irresponsible in terms of government responsibility to all citizens, the International Olympic Committee (IOC) has provided a welcome justification. The organizations of the sports for all movement were never very strong (in comparison to the international sports organizations), and the movement was effectively taken over by the IOC in the mid-1990s. While this may seem paradoxical because the IOC is so strongly associated with elite international sports, it proved to be an important public relations exercise for the IOC who could claim that they represented sports in general, rather than just elite sports. When the Olympic Charter was amended in 1994 to include the "right" to participate (see sidebar), the IOC also developed the double-pyramid theory. The IOC: "encourages the development of sports for all, which is part of the foundation of high-level sports, which in turn contributes to the development of sports for all" (Olympic Charter, 1994). In other words, "thousands of people practising sport at the base [of the pyramid] lead to a few Olympic champions and, at the same time, the existence of champion role models encourages thousands of people to take up some form of sport" (IOC Sports for All Commission, 2000).

The first pyramid, a seamless sports system from grassroots sports to national teams, does not exist anywhere. Most wealthy countries have an underfunded and fragmented system of grassroots and development sports from which talented athletes are identified and recruited into a separate system of elite sports. With regard to the second pyramid, governments and sports organizations frequently claim that gold medals inspire increased participation in sports, thus justifying their spending and demands for funding for elite sports. There is no evidence to support this claim, although the Australian government did find that there were increases in sports spectating and viewing sports on television following the 2000 Sydney Olympics.

However, although the IOC proposed a double pyramid with the assumption that each pyramid is dependent on the other, governments have tended to pretend that there is a seamless sports system (the first pyramid), and they use the second pyramid as a justification for increased spending on elite sports. Such spending is identified as an investment in sports for all because the investment in success is supposed to have a trickle-down effect by inspiring increased participation.

FUTURE PROSPECTS

Aging populations, concerns about obesity and inactivity, and increasing health care costs all suggest that there is a bright future for sports for all. However, it is likely that governments and corporations will continue to provide far more funding for elite sports and sporting mega events until citizens demand their *right* to participate in sports and physical activity.

See also Athlete Unions; Funding Equality Legislation; Government Sponsorship of Teams; Private vs. Public Sports Spaces; Rights for Young Athletes; Urban Planning and Gentrification.

Further Reading: International Olympic Committee. (2000). Sport for All Commission, http://www.olympic.org/uk/organisation/commissions/sportforall/index_uk.asp; International Olympic Committee. (2004). Olympic Charter. Lausanne, Switzerland: DidWeDo Press.

Peter Donnelly

STEROID USE BY ATHLETES

The World Anti-Doping Agency's (WADA) "2008 Prohibited List" states clearly: "Anabolic agents are prohibited." The list prohibits 47 *exogenous* anabolic androgenic steroids (AAS), 21 *endogenous* AAS, and five *other anabolic agents*. Steroid use in any sport governed by WADA's Code is subject to a two-year suspension the first time and lifetime suspension the second time. According to WADA, the Code preserves "what is intrinsically valuable about sport ... The intrinsic value is often referred to as 'the spirit of sport': it is the essence of Olympism: it is how we play true ... Doping is fundamentally contrary to the spirit of sport."

Following the Canadian government's inquiry into the use of drugs in sports, Chief Justice Charles Dubin articulated similar reasons for banning AAS. The use of banned drugs is cheating, Dubin maintained. Drugs threaten "the essential integrity of sport" and destroy "its very objectives." Drugs "erode the ethical and moral values of the athletes who use them, endangering their mental and physical welfare while demoralizing the entire sport community."

Although the primary objection to AAS in sports is ethical, concerns over their physiological impact have also influenced the ban. First synthesized in 1935, it was then noted that despite the initial, positive response by some scientists, the conservative medical establishment was wary of a synthetic hormone that might "turn sexual weaklings into wolves and octogenarians into sexual athletes." The concern today is the negative side effects from AAS, even though almost all are reversible in postpuberty males (and knowingly accepted by females). Nevertheless, sports leaders have used the potential negative side effects as a deterrent to AAS use and grounds for their ban.

Two further sentiments underlie the AAS ban in sports although they are rarely noted. The first concerns the symbolic power and significance of sports and the association of steroids with certain reprehensible events in sports or social history. The second is a fear of the unrestricted, scientifically assisted pursuit of the outer limits of athletic performance. Increased musculature and steroids' performance-enhancing attributes cause concern about where the use of unrestricted science, technology, and pharmacology might ultimately lead.

BACKGROUND

The moral arguments against AAS and sports' symbolic importance stem from Baron Pierre de Coubertin's efforts to create the Modern Olympic Games as a unique moral and educational program. Feeling that late nineteenth-century Europe was falling into spiritual decline, Coubertin wanted to re-establish its traditional values through a far-reaching, innovative, educational project. His plan grew out of the philosophy of the "muscular Christian" and the spirituality of the Ancient Games. Character, Coubertin maintained, "is not formed by the mind, it is formed above all by the body." Sports, as it was practiced in the British public schools, could revitalize the moral and spiritual fiber of Europe's youth.

Coubertin's image was inspiring. "The athlete enjoys his effort," Coubertin wrote (2000, p. 552) . "He likes the constraint that he imposes on his muscles and nerves, through which he comes close to victory even if he does not manage to achieve it. This enjoyment remains internal … Imagine if it were to expand outward, becoming intertwined with the joy of nature and the flights of art. Picture it radiant with sunlight, exalted by music, framed in the architecture of porticoes." This was "the glittering dream of ancient Olympism" that "dominated ancient Greece for centuries."

Coubertin's project would create "an aristocracy, an elite"—"a knighthood" of "brothers-in-arms." Chivalry would characterize the Games—"the idea of competition, of effort opposing effort for the love of effort itself, of courteous yet violent struggle, is superimposed on the notion of mutual assistance" (Coubertin, 2000, p. 581). Chivalrous brothers-in-arms, bonding in the cauldron of competition, would forge Europe's new moral elite.

Winning was irrelevant to Coubertin; character development in the struggle to win a fair, man-to-man contest (the gender is intentional) against a respected opponent, within a chivalric code of conduct was everything. Performance enhancement of any type—even physical training—was completely foreign to the ethos of Olympism. The true "essence of sport" was far loftier than crass, competitive sports; it centered on the character development upper-class youths gained on the playing fields of Rugby, Eton, and elsewhere in civilized Europe.

One cannot emphasize enough how this idealized image serves as the key reference point for AAS policies at the present time.

Symbolism was central to the Modern Games from their inception. To achieve the appropriate solemnity, Coubertin launched his project "under the venerable roof of the Sorbonne [where] the words 'Olympic Games' would resound more impressively and persuasively" (cited in Beamish and Ritchie, 2006, p. 32). It was, however, the 1936 Games in Nazi Germany and the long shadow of World War II that demonstrated the Games' symbolic power.

Nazi Propaganda Minister Joseph Goebbels was a master at manipulating information and emotions for political gain. The Nazis frequently used imposing, emotive, Wagnerian-styled *gesamtkunstwerke*—total works of art—in enormous venues such as sports stadiums, to blend music, choreography, costume, and neoclassical architecture into captivating, exhilarating, and emotionally draining experiences. Knowing the power that well-crafted propaganda had on the hearts and minds of the masses, the 1936 Games let Goebbels use the Promethean symbolic power of the Olympics to project the commanding presence of Nazi Germany across Europe.

The Games' marquee icon—the chiseled, muscular, racially pure Aryan, crowned with a victor's olive wreath, rising above the goddess of victory atop the Brandenburg Gate—embodied the Nazi's quest for world domination. The image soon included the cold-blooded brutality of German troops as they conquered Europe and marched on to Moscow.

In the post–World War II period, amid the ashes of destruction and defeat, rumors that Hitler's Secret Service had taken steroids while perpetrating the Holocaust and destroying Eastern Europe were added to the image of Nazi barbarism. The 1936 Games linked steroids, ruthless aggression, moral depravity, and totalitarianism into one stark, chilling entity.

Admiring the Nazis' use of the Games to project their power, the Soviet Union joined the Olympic Movement for similar ends. At the 1952 Games—the first post–World War II confrontation between the super powers—Soviet success quickly dispelled any notion of America superiority.

Confirming at the 1954 world weightlifting championships that the Soviets had used testosterone to enhance performance in world competitions, U.S. physician John Ziegler developed methandieone, or Dianabol, to level the playing field. Dianabol quickly spread from weightlifters to the throwers in track and field and on to other strength-based sports. By the early 1960s, steroids were commonplace in world-class sports, and the unfettered use of science to win Olympic gold would increasingly dominate nations' and athletes' approach to sports after 1954.

KEY EVENTS

From the outset—and enshrined in the Olympic Charter in 1962—the Modern Games were restricted to amateur athletes. The type of competitor that Coubertin and the International Olympic Committee (IOC) wanted was the turn of the twentieth-century British amateur. Only the well-educated, cultured, physically active, male aristocrat had the appropriate appreciation of sports to realize Coubertin's goals. Well before 1952, however, the IOC had little control over the athletes who competed, and it failed miserably in achieving Coubertin's educational objectives. Nevertheless, the IOC—especially Avery Brundage (president from 1952 to 1972)—struggled to maintain the Games' integrity. The Olympics, Brundage claimed, "coming to us from antiquity, contributed to and strengthened by the noblest aspirations of great men of each generation, embrace the highest moral laws … No philosophy, no religion," he maintained, "preaches loftier sentiments." But the social pressures outside the Movement quickly overwhelmed those lofty claims.

Throughout the 1950s and 1960s, Cold War politics, expanding consumerism, and the growth of television with its vast commercial resources and thirst for targeted audiences increasingly pressured the IOC to open the Games to the world's best athletes. Furthermore, developments in sports science encouraged athletes to devote longer periods of their lives to the pursuit of Olympic gold and financial reward—Olympic athletes became increasingly professional. By 1970, pressure grew to replace the amateur rule with a new eligibility code. The 1971 code remained restrictive, but a 1974 revision opened the Games to the best athletes money could buy and governments and sports scientists could produce.

Danish cyclist Knud Jensen's death at the 1960 Olympics, allegedly from amphetamine use, symbolized the value athletes placed on victory. The IOC established its Medical Committee in 1961 to recommend how to prevent or control drug use by athletes. The 1964 recommendations included athlete testing, signed athlete statements confirming they were drug-free, and heavy sanctions. Rule 28, added to the Charter in 1967, prohibited any "alien or unnatural substances" that created an unfair advantage; although banned in 1967, the IOC did not test for AAS until 1976.

The Nazis and Soviets had used the Games to occupy center stage internationally and symbolically project their importance to the world. The German Democratic Republic (GDR) developed similar aspirations—especially after Munich was awarded the 1972 Games. The decision to hold the Olympics on the soil of the GDR's most bitter rival—the Federal Republic of Germany—was pivotal in the history of AAS use by world-class athletes. The GDR initiated "State-Plan 14.25"—an extensive, high-level, classified, laboratory research program involving substantial state resources—to develop a scientifically based program of steroid use. By the 1976 Olympics, AAS were fully integrated into GDR's high-performance sports system as a matter of state policy.

Throughout the 1970s and 1980s, the Games increasingly centered on the all-out pursuit of victory. For nations, Olympic gold signified strength, power, and international supremacy; for athletes, it meant wealth and celebrity.

Ben Johnson crushed Carl Lewis and shattered the 100-meter world record in the 1988 Games' premier event, but his positive test for stanozolol created a major crisis. In short order, *Sports Illustrated* ran articles on steroids in sports, and the Canadian government and the U.S. House of Representatives began investigations into AAS use in sports. The entire credibility of the Olympic Movement was at stake—was the IOC serious about steroids and the purity of the Games? Steroid use, it was clearly evident, was widespread.

In March 1998, French customs officials found erythropoietin (EPO) in the TVM cycling team's van, and criminal charges followed. Then in July, mere days before the Tour de France began, the Festina team was implicated in the EPO scandal. But it was IOC President Juan Antonio Samaranch's comments that shocked the world. Drugs could damage an athlete's health as well as artificially improve performance, Samaranch observed. If it only improves performance, he continued, it did not matter: "Anything that doesn't adversely affect the health of the athlete, isn't doping." Potentially implicating the IOC in white-washing AAS use, Samaranch's comments forced the IOC to establish an independent body to oversee drug testing from then on.

Created in 1999, WADA hosted a world conference on drug use that led to its June 2002 draft of the World Anti-Doping Code. A subsequent draft in October led to unanimous adoption of version 3.0 in March 2003 at the second world conference. Despite WADA's efforts, steroid use did not stop; AAS users simply found ways to avoid detection. In July 2003, track coach Trevor Graham gave the American Anti-Doping Agency a syringe containing the designer anabolic steroid tetrahydrogestrinone (THG). Graham alleged that Victor Conte, through the Bay Area Laboratory Co-Operative (BALCO), was giving THG to world-class American athletes at their request. BALCO was just beginning.

President Bush's 2004 State of the Union Address focused on education reform, Medicare, the Patriot Act, the war on terrorism, and military engagements in Afghanistan and Iraq. The President turned next to family values and the war on drugs. "One of the worst decisions our children can make is to gamble their lives and futures on drugs," Bush warned (Associated Press, 2004). To make the right choices children need good role models, but, Bush maintained, "some athletes are not setting much of an example … The use of performance-enhancing

KEY EVENTS

1896—The first Olympic Games are held.
1935—Synthetic steroids produced.
1952—Steroids used by Soviet athletes at the Olympic Games.
1954—John Ziegler makes Dianabol available to U.S. athletes.
1960—Knud Jensen dies of alleged drug use in Rome Olympics.

Cold War and Professionalization of Games

1961—IOC Medical Commission formed.
1967—Rule 28 bans performance-enhancing substances.
1974—Rule 26, The Eligibility Code, liberalized to open the Games.
1972—GDR initiates State-Plan 14.25 and seeks to upstage FRG at Munich Games.
1976—GDR ranks second behind USSR in unofficial rankings.
1988—Ben Johnson tests positive for steroids.
1989—*Sports Illustrated* publishes high-profile series on steroids in sports.
1990—U.S. House of Representatives investigates steroids; Federal inquiry in Canada.
1998—Samaranch suggests doping concerns athletes' health and not improved performance.
1998—Baseball revels in Mark McGuire's andro-assisted home-run record.
1999—WADA formed.
2003—World Anti-Doping Code adopted.
2003—Graham exposes BALCO and THG.
2004—President Bush addresses steroid use in State of the Union Address; Kelli White is first BALCO athlete to fall;
2005—U.S. House of Representatives' Oversight and Government Reform Committee investigates steroids in sports; Montgomery suspended for THG use.
2006—Mitchell investigates steroid use in baseball; Graham indicted for false statements in BALCO probe.
2007—Jones stripped of medals and records for THG use.
2008—Knoblauch, Pettitte, Clemens, and McNamee testify before U.S. House of Representatives' Oversight and Government Reform Committee.

---

drugs like steroids in baseball, football and other sports is dangerous, and it sends the wrong message—that there are short cuts to accomplishment, and that performance is more important than character." Bush challenged professional sports "to get rid of steroids now."

Within days, the *San Francisco Chronicle* published allegations that Greg Anderson, homerun king Barry Bonds' personal trainer, had ties to BALCO and gave Bonds THG. The *Chronicle* alleged that Anderson supplied Jason Giambi, Gary Sheffield, and others with AAS. Steroids and BALCO were now linked within America's national pastime.

In May 2004, U.S. sprinter Kelli White admitted to taking THG supplied through BALCO. In December 2005, the Lausanne-based Court of Arbitration for Sport suspended 100-meter world record holder Tim Montgomery for THG use, stripping him of his 2002 record. In November 2006, a federal grand jury indicted Graham for three counts of making false statements to the Internal Revenue Service Criminal Investigation Division officials around the BALCO investigations. And in October 2007, sprinter Marion Jones was stripped of her medals and records for taking BALCO-supplied THG.

From a trailer-like office operation (BALCO), run by a self-aggrandizing schemer-entrepreneur (Conte) assisted by his "steroid guru" (Patrick Arnold), BALCO now symbolized the sleaziest aspects of athletes' greed and lust for record performances and celebrity.

On March 17, 2005, Denise Garabaldi and Don Hooton told the House of Representatives' Oversight and Government Reform Committee that steroids had killed their sons. Subpoenaed to testify, Mark McGuire evaded questions, Rafael Palmeiro denied he had used AAS, and Jose Conseco said his book *Juiced* told the full story. The event forced Bud Selig to appoint former Senate Majority Leader George Mitchell to conduct an independent investigation into steroid use in baseball. Mitchell's report identified 86 players as users and led to Chuck Knoblauch, Andy Pettitte, Roger Clemens, and personal trainer Brian McNamee testifying before the Committee in February 2008. The reality of AAS use by athletes had never been so clear, although its full extent is still shrouded in secret.

FUTURE PROSPECTS

The future of steroid use by athletes depends upon how four fundamental sets of questions are answered:

It is clear that the Olympic Games do not embody Coubertin's principles and goals; they are a commercial extravaganza that nations exploit for international status, while athletes use them for fame and money. One must ask whether the principles that really underlie contemporary, world-class, high-performance sports justify the exclusion of performance-enhancing substances such as AAS. On what grounds should officials try to restrict scientific performance enhancement in commercial, entertainment spectacles where the ultimate attraction is athletic performance at the outer limits of human potential? What principles apply?

What are the long-term health implications of AAS use by athletes (and people in the general population)? How safe or dangerous are steroids—unmonitored or monitored by physicians? What are the emotional and cognitive effects that lead to, and may result from, AAS use? Do existing laws on AAS possession and use protect or endanger users?

AAS are not confined to enhancing athletic performance. Athletes are just one source of "ideal body images" that saturate commercial and entertainment media. "Megarexia"—muscular dysmorphia—has become a serious issue among a growing percentage of young males (and some females). Does the sports ban on AAS help limit the spread of muscular dysmorphia among contemporary youth, or are there more significant factors? Does the WADA ban on steroids limit AAS use among young athletes and nonathletes? If not, what would?

Finally, one must consider the widespread use of drugs in people's lives today. What are the fundamental concerns and issues related to the increasing use of over-the-counter, prescription, and black market drugs? Where do steroids fit into those concerns? To reduce steroid use, what changes have to occur in the broader culture?

See also Antidoping Rules and Policies; Biology and Athlete Performance; Ergogenics; Erythropoietin (EPO); Marijuana, Alcohol, and Illicit Drugs; Sports Doctors, Trainers, and Drugs; Whistle-Blowers and Drugs.

Further Reading: Associated Press. (2004). Text of President Bush's State of the Union Address. Retrieved October 22, 2006 (http://www.post-gazette.com/pg/04021/263842.stm#drugs); Beamish, R., and Ritchie, I. (2006). *Fastest, Highest, Strongest: A Critique of High-Performance Sport.* London: Routledge; Coubertin, B. P. (2000). *Olympism: Selected Writings.* Lausanne: International Olympic Committee; Todd, J., and Todd, T. (2001). Significant Events in the History of Drug Testing and the Olympic Movement: 1960–1999. In *Doping in Elite Sport: The Politics of Drugs in the Olympic Movement,* edited by W. Wilson and E. Derse. Champaign, IL: Human Kinetics Press; Yesalis, C., and Bahrke, M. (2002). History of Doping in Sport. *International Sports Studies* 24: 42–76.

Rob Beamish

SURFING AND "NEW" WATER SPORTS

In the 1940s and 1950s, one of the first alternative sports cultures emerged on the California coast. Surfing, the art and sport of riding waves on a specially designed board, ascended to popularity at a historical point when young generations of Americans sought out new modes of athleticism and athletic experiences than those offered in the cultural mainstream. The esoteric youth practice of surfing developed into an entire surfing culture, scene, and lifestyle crystallized in California during the 1960s. Surfing culture had an immediate impact on popular culture, and the "surf style" became almost synonymous with West Coast popular culture for nearly two decades.

BACKGROUND

Throughout the course of the early 1900s, North Americans rediscovered the ancient art of wave riding. As documented in the journals of explorers such as Captain James Cook while he traveled to Polynesia in the late eighteenth century, wave riding had roots in various parts of the world for centuries before Californians produced a global "surfing" renaissance in the 1940s and 1950s. Surfing emerged in North America has perhaps the first authentic lifestyle sport in the country (Wheaton, 2004). A lifestyle sport is something that practitioners do not merely participate on weekends or as a leisure pursuit; the sport itself represents the person's overall worldview, beliefs, relationships, and sense of place in the world. Until the rise of surfing lifestyles in the 1950s and 1960s, one might argue that aside from professional athletes, there were no (and certainly no "outsider") lifestyle sports practitioners in North America.

A central feature of lifestyle sports is that they fit into the participants' daily lives like a religion. Athletes in lifestyle sports also stress the importance of communing with nature through sports and encountering forms of spirituality not found in mainstream religions. Again, few had approached sports practices in the cultural mainstream in America in these ways. From the turn of the twentieth century, sports have been modeled by adults as a tool for teaching young boys the requisite skills they would need to flourish as young men in conventional society. Organized team and league sports, in conjunction with sports in the education system, were neither viewed by participants as defining features of their identity nor were they vehicles for pursuing socially alternative spiritualities. Until surfing, few sports if any had originated from a grassroots youth level or extolled the virtues of pleasure-seeking through unsupervised athleticism with others.

The somewhat antisports surfing ethos that developed in California surf cultures cannot be disassociated from social circumstances and cultural moods germinating in southern California at the time. Two subcultural movements in particular seem to have impacted youth cultural attitudes in the area in particular, gearing them toward an interest in hedonistic, exploratory, free, creative, and socially avant-garde lifestyles.

Surfing subcultures in California came together at a time when "Beat Generation" poets, artists, and social radicals had moved from New York to various parts of California, bringing with them rather non-mainstream cultural philosophies. The poetic, confrontation, spiritual, and antiauthoritarian "beatniks" like writers Jack Kerouac, Allen Ginsberg, William Burroughs, and Gregory Corso encouraged young Californians to expand their minds toward social radicalism. The beatniks ended up together in San Francisco in the mid-1950s, where they met and became friends with figures associated with their original counterparts on the West Coast, the "San Francisco Renaissance." The surf culture in California during the 1950s and 1960s had clear links with another group of self-professed social outsiders, the California bohemians. *Bohemian* was a term first used in the nineteenth century to describe the untraditional lifestyles of marginalized and impoverished artists, writers, musicians, and actors in major European cities. Bohemians in California in the 1950s and 1960s were associated with unorthodox or antiestablishment political or social viewpoints, which were often expressed through extramarital sexual relations, frugality, or voluntary poverty.

Through the 1950s and 1960s, surfers came to represent a diverse culture based on riding the naturally occurring process of ocean waves. Some practiced surfing as a recreational activity or serious competitive sport, while others demonstrated extreme devotion to the activity by making it the central focus of their lives. Surfing lifestyles were devoted to freedom and self-expression, something incredibly unique on the North American continent at the time (Booth, 2001). Surfing culture in California promoted a type of spirituality associated with being one with nature and releasing one's desires to be a mainstream, middle-class American. Indeed, social critics of the upstart surfing culture often decried it as wasteful, self-indulgent, and nomadic. Nevertheless, at the height of surfing's popularity in California during the era, it created a series of indelible marks on U.S. popular culture, evidenced through the production of surf movies, surf music, surfing language, and lifestyle sports ideologies.

The growing popularity of surfing in the 1950s and the 1960s had its own series of negative consequences for its lifestyle participants. The commercial exportation of its culture to the rest of the United States and the world through popular films such as *Gidget* (1959), *Ride the Wild Surf* (1964), and *Endless Summer* (1964), or its representation through the music of the Beach Boys, Jan and Dean, and the Chantays, transformed a predominantly local and contained lifestyle sport into a cultural phenomenon, ready for insertion into and eventual caricature by the mainstream. During this period, many of the long-term soul surfers in southern California emigrated from the area to a more pristine Hawai'i surfing culture.

History indicates that surfing is the sports world's contribution to youth countercultures in the 1950s. Bleached-blonde, board short–wearing, and argot-speaking surfers poached the California beaches as a battleground for exploring a surf-based way of alternative life in the hyperconservative and disciplined McCarthyist America. Their sport and culture led to the development of dozens of other beach-based sports cultures (wakeboarders, windsurfers, jet skiers, and others) and outsider social scenes. Surf lifestyles played their part in transforming the western coast of the United Stated into a playground for social rebels and soul seekers during the era.

KEY EVENTS

The genesis of the California surf culture is multifaceted and complex, but most historians agree that several key events helped to solidify the surf movement. In 1907, author Jack London traveled to Hawai'i. There were a few surfers on the beach at Waikiki at that time, comprising a loose clique of Hawai'ians and part-Hawai'ians who formed a surfing club called the Waikiki Swimming Club. London met that crew and was introduced to surfing by Alexander Hume Ford, an eccentric journalist and wanderer. Ford took London surfing, and there London met the most celebrated Waikiki surfer of the time, a 23-year-old Irish/Hawai'ian named George Freeth. London wrote a story about surfing that year called *A Royal Sport: Surfing in Waikiki,* which included descriptions of surf culture in Waikiki. London's story was so compelling that Freeth was invited in 1907 to California by railroad and real estate magnate Henry Huntington. Huntington requested that Freeth put on a demonstration of "wave-riding" in southern California to promote the Redondo to Los Angeles Railway.

A few years later, a Hawai'ian surfer named Duke Paoa Kahanamoku (three-time world record holder in the 100-meter freestyle) passed through southern California en route to the 1912 Summer Olympics in Stockholm, Sweden. His surfing demonstrations at Corona del Mar and Santa Monica caused a public sensation and interest in the sport much greater than Freeth's. Kahanamoku continued to surf in California through the 1920s, and the population of surfers there grew slowly around him as a tightly knit cluster of enthusiasts.

Between the 1930s and 1940s, surfing remained largely the practice of a small group of devotees who embraced the spirit and philosophy of the wave riding lifestyle. Events leading to the eventual development of professional and popular surf cultures occurred at the end of the period, however. These seemingly minor events helped lead to the creation of a California surf counterculture but also facilitated the dismantling of the activity's pure lifestyle sports essence on the continent.

Surfing remained virtually hidden from the world during the Great Depression, World War II, and the Korean War. During this period, the world's surfers numbered only in the hundreds, and the California surfers only in the dozens. A handful of these men, lobstermen and fishermen of Dana Cove, California, transformed the face of surfer culture. Lorrin "Whitey" Harrison, Art Pobar, and their associates surfed Dana Cove when off work. Other California surfers joined them from time to time, including Phil Edwards, Hobie Alter, Walter Hoffman, Bruce Brown, Grubby Clark, and John Severson. These men each played roles in the development of surfing as a commercial industry in California. Each enthralled with the surf lifestyle, they developed a scheme to earn a modest living doing what they loved.

Hobie Alter began making surfboards in his family's garage in 1950, learning the process from Walter Hoffman. Alter made light balsa and fiberglass boards at a studio on the Pacific Coast Highway, and refined his board-making skills in the early 1950s and experimented with chemicals to make lighter and more buoyant boards. Grubby Clark helped Hobie further refine his technique to produce lightweight and sturdy surfboards that were easily transportable. The modern industry of board making was born through their efforts.

From the same group of surfers, John Severson developed his skills in surf writing, art, and filming in the early 1950s. Severson made the first surfing film, *Surf,* and devoted a part of his surfing lifestyle at Dana Point to make even more of them. These films would later become the main media platform for surf culture in the United States, *Surfer* magazine. Another member, Walter Hoffman, and his brother Phillip "Flippy" Hoffman became the first "big wave" riders. Walter and Flippy Hoffman lived on Beach Road in Capistrano Beach, California, and developed the first surfing lifestyle clothing and fabrics. Bruce Brown started filming surfer culture in Dana Point and other places and chronicled the rapid rise of surfing as a new sport and culture. He showed and narrated his films across California. He eventually produced the legendary surf film *Endless Summer.* This group of men became known in U.S. surfing history as the "Dana Point Mafia." Their separate and collective appreciation for the lifestyle sport and the ideologies of personal freedom and creativity underpinning it led them to scratch out livings by producing goods for the pastime they adored. However, by transforming Dana Point into the hub of the surfing industry, they perhaps unintentionally started the mass commercialization and popular cultural co-option of the sport.

Another key event in the commercialization and mass proliferation of surfing culture occurred in 1953 with the construction of Malibu Canyon Road in Malibu, which linked Malibu to the San Fernando Valley. The road's construction fit into a multicounty and even State plan to reconstruct and economically revitalize a decaying Malibu business district. A slate of new businesses and services appeared quickly, as did beach clubs such as The Malibu Beach Sports Club and Malibu Rendezvous. With increased commercial interest in the area, public traffic along the pier, and public visits to the beach clubs, exposure to surfers grew. Malibu's reputation as a surfing nexus, once esoteric and little known, expanded, and the name *Malibu* became emblematic of sun, fun, and the Californian "in-crowd." Surfers migrated to Malibu beaches from across California. By the late 1950s and into the 1960s, surfing established a new culture on the beach based on youth, sex, drugs, and music that would catch on further in the 1960s youth rebellion era.

Further amplifying the scene was the novel *Gidget* by Malibu resident Frederick Kohner. The book is a fictionalized version of the beach lifestyle of his daughter, Kathy Kohner. In 1959, the movie version of *Gidget* opened, and the national "surf craze" commenced. Popular beach movies followed *Gidget*'s lead (each prominently featuring Malibu), and Malibu was dubbed "Surf City, USA."

The connection between surfing and its commercialization was especially strong with the explosion of surf music in Malibu. Surf music of the 1960s lyrically and melodically represented beach life as an idyllic counterculture of self-definition and freedom, of parties, sexuality, and hedonism. A typical night's entertainment by bands at Malibu featured not only surf music but cover versions of popular hits of the day. The popularity of the surf music genre led groups from other places in the country to emulate its guitar styles and drum beats. The Astronauts (Boulder, Colorado) and the Trashmen (Minneapolis, Minnesota) emulated the surf music and mythologized the California beach lifestyle. Their Billboard hits "Baja" (Astronauts in 1963) and "Surfin Bird" (Trashmen in 1964) showed that the popularity of the genre was spreading widely. The Rivieras from South Bend, Indiana, also created a hit in 1964 with "California Sun." The Malibu scene, through its movie and music representations, attracted countercultural nomads to the area who lived on its beaches in shacks and studied eastern religions such as Buddhism. Motorcycle gangs also swarmed to the beach to sell drugs to the experimental surf crowds. Malibu surfing even stimulated copycat beach cultures and scenes in California in the late 1960s such as Venice Beach, a beach (in)famous for not only its surf culture but also its bodybuilding culture (the "Muscle Beach" section), the emerging California cocaine culture (led by dealer George Jung), and the development of the California psychedelic music culture (led by bands such as the Doors).

Surfing purists, historians, and self-described surfing outsiders lament that by the early 1960s, "Surfrider Beach" in Malibu was no longer a nirvana for non-mainstream sports enthusiasts. The activity had been transformed into a hobby, spectacle, competitive sport, fitness tool, conduit for drugs and sex, and

SURFING AS A GLOBAL COMMERCIAL EXPORT

The number of surfers in the United States is estimated to be between 2.3 and 2.5 million, and the surf industry generates nearly $1 billion annually. It has also been exported as a culture and an industry across the globe to countries such as the Republic of South Africa (RSA). In the RSA city Durban alone, the surfing industry contributes (RSA)$1 billion to the Ethekweni economy; approximately 40,000 surfers have learned to surf at legendary Vetch's beach; almost 200 new surfers per month emerge from the surf schools at Vetch's beach; Roxy Surf School in Durban has produced over 7,000 women surfers since 2000; and RSA economists predict a 15–25 percent growth in the culture over the next 10 years.

overall U.S. (and indeed global) popular cultural commodity. The esoteric surfing lifestyle transformed into a soulless form of leisure or business where few people actually appreciated the "Zen" of surfing. The Californian beach scene continued to grow during the 1970s and 1980s through to the 1990s, with people from the United States and across the world traveling there to tap the West Coast beach vibe. Additionally, surfing developed into a full-fledged competitive sports culture spanning the globe as a commercial enterprise. Other sports cultures stemmed from the California and Florida beach scenes during the era, including windsurfing, kite surfing, jet skiing, wakeboarding, and others. None emerged as a countercultural lifestyle sport such as surfing in the 1940s and early 1950s because each was, from their inception, predominantly contrived, expensive, middle-class, and technologically oriented style cultures. Few of the new water sports cultures profess a spiritual meaning to their practice or stress the importance of connecting with nature through one's (lifestyle) sport.

FUTURE PROSPECTS

There is an argument to be made that the original surfing lifestyle cultures of the 1930s and 1940s in southern California were intended to be battlegrounds but only in a private and not public sense. For first- and second-generation surf riders in California, the sport fit into their collective quest to find personal meaning and spirituality through communion with the water. They did not intend to change the world but simply find a space to be themselves in somewhat of a rebel fashion. Flash forward several decades and surfing has been commodified and mass mediated into not only a lucrative global business but part of U.S. mythology. Those who still pursue lifestyle sports such as surfing claim that only for a very brief moment can they be pure lifestyles unaffected by commercialism and co-option by others. In the future, it will be interesting to see whether or not a lifestyle sport such as surfing can exist as relatively unspoiled for any significant period of time.

See also Environmental Impacts of Sports; Marijuana, Alcohol, and Illicit Drugs; Skateboarding; Snowboarding; X Games; Yoga and Alternative Fitness.

Further Reading: Booth, D. (2001). Australian Beach Cultures: The History of Sun, Sand and Surf. London: Frank Cass; Kampion, D. (2003). Stoked: A History of Surf Culture. Salt Lake City, UT: Gibbs Smith Inc; Wheaton, B. *Understanding Lifestyle Sports*. London: Routledge, 2004; Wright, A. (1973). Surfing California. Redondo, CA: Mountain and Sea; Young, N. (2008). The Complete History of Surfing. Salt Lake City, UT: Gibbs Smith Inc.

Michael Atkinson

T

TAUNTING

Taunting in sports typically refers to the act of physically (through symbolic gestures) or verbally intimidating a player or coach. Players, coaches, and fans conduct taunting behaviors, and in most professional, collegiate, and amateur sports organizations taunting is either banned outright or strongly controlled through specific rules. The goal of taunting is normally to disrupt players' focus through the use of either annoying or irritating verbal and physical gestures or profane insults directed at the player. Certain forms of taunting are viewed by sports insiders as commonplace and simply "part of the game" as a legitimate tactic, while others are viewed as emotionally cruel and inappropriate in sports.

BACKGROUND

Taunting is often described and defended by sports insiders as a harmless form of banter or teasing. Take for example the eight-decade-long teasing of Red Sox fans by rival New York Yankee fans. Yankee fans argued that the Red Sox had not won a World Series as sort of a mythic punishment for the 1920 trading of icon Babe Ruth to the Yankees. "The Curse of the Bambino," teased Yankee fans, would forever prohibit the Red Sox from winning. In 1920, Red Sox owner Harry Frazee sold Ruth to the New York Yankees. In his next 15 seasons in New York, Ruth led the majors in a range of categories, championed them to victories, and set a number of league records. By contrast, the Red Sox franchise of the post-Ruth era floundered for decades after having been previously the most successful Major League Baseball (MLB) team prior to the trade. At times in their history, such as their 1986 improbable loss to the New York Mets in the

World Series, the Red Sox openly appeared as psychologically cursed. The curse may have effectively ended in 2004 when the Red Sox won their first World Series title in 86 years.

At its core, taunting is a form of mild aggression in sports. The act of taunting is designed to have a psychological effect on its targets; it intimidates, frightens, destabilizes, and angers players to the point where they either lose their concentration or their composure. Viewed from this perspective, taunting has a strategic role in individual and team sports. Pumping a fist at an opponent in tennis or doing a celebratory dance in front of them is a tactic intended to humiliate and display power over another player. Part of athletic training in elite sports cultures is the necessary development, then, of mindsets where taunting can be blocked out to the best of one's abilities.

Taunting has links with hypermasculinity in sports and is therefore a means by which some male players exert a male superiority over other players. Taunting a "weaker" or lesser opponent is intended to ritually degrade him and call public attention to his masculine deficiencies. Calling a player "soft" in these ways can deeply wound the self-image and self-confidence of (particularly) young athletes, whose gender images matter greatly to them. In sports cultures such as basketball and football, taunting has become a part of subcultural logics of practice and a form of style. "Trash talking" in basketball is considered by some as simply part of the game, as evidenced in movies such as *Blue Chips*, *White Men Can't Jump*, *Hoop Dreams*, and *He Got Game*.

For others, taunting is not merely an innocent masculine or subcultural tradition in sports but rather a form of systematic bullying. Certain social problems in sports, such as anorexia and early dropout, have been linked to the experience of ritual taunting at the hands of players, parents, and coaches. Because verbal forms of taunting often attack one's personal characteristics (such as masculinity, height, weight, ethnicity, sexuality, religion, etc.), its form can be especially insidious and emotionally consequential. Racist and homophobic forms of taunting are especially prevalent in clusters of North American sports cultures and have been targeted by concerned parents and rights advocates as inexcusable.

KEY EVENTS

There is a veritable shopping list of ways players, fans, and coaches can taunt. Among the most popular methods of taunting in sports are simple phrases and gestures that are designed to throw players off their games. One of the earliest and certainly most storied taunts of all time is Babe Ruth's "called shot" in the 1932 World Series. While at bat in the 5th inning of the game against the Chicago Cubs, the New York Yankee made a pointing gesture with his finger to the centerfield bleachers. He hit a homerun on the next pitch. In later years, Ruth explained the called shot was a retaliation or taunt back to the Cubs' players heckles of him throughout the Series. Taunting in this manner had been considered somewhat taboo in sports, but Ruth's seemingly "innocent" taunt encouraged others to follow in kind.

Ruth's called shot taunt, for example, played a minor role in the historical evolution of the "walk away" home run. A tradition developed after Ruth's era (ca. early 1950s) of a batter walking slowly down the first base line while admiring his home run ball leaving the field (thus, in baseball lingo, "showing up" the pitcher). It is no coincidence that this taunt led to a proliferation of bean balls (pitches thrown directly at a batter's body) being thrown at the next batter of a game who followed the "walk away" home run hitter. By 1956, MLB had to adopt the protective helmet to help protect batters against bean ball pitches. To critics of the helmet, by placing a hard plastic shell on batter's heads pitchers were inadvertently given a license to aim for them. Seven players were killed in the minor leagues and amateur baseball from 1956–1964 as a result of being hit in the head from bean balls following the helmet era.

The most infamous beaning of the 1950s took place at Shibe Park on August 27, 1954, in a game between the Chicago White Sox and the Philadelphia Athletics. Chicago third baseman Cass Michaels was hit in the head by a fastball from Marion Fricano and had to be carried from the field. Michaels was actually given last rites while in the hospital in critical condition. He recovered, but the 27-year-old never played baseball again.

Other pitchers used a more civilized variant on the bean ball called the "brushback." Sal Maglie is one of the most notorious brushbackers in baseball history. Maglie played for several teams and was referred to as "Sal the Barber" for his tendency to deliberately throw balls so close to players' heads that he could provide them with a "shave." Maglie used his brushback pitch to create success throughout his career. Power hitters Roy Campanella, Stan Musial, Pee Wee Reese, and Jackie Robinson were four of Maglie's favorite brushback targets. The logic behind the brushback is that a player will be more hesitant, anxious, and less focused when they worry about the potential of a bean ball hitting them. Remarkably, Maglie actually only made contact with the heads of 2 players in 13 years.

One of the most prolific taunters of all time was boxer Muhammad Ali. Ali's ability to taunt is something of a sports legend. He possessed a rare ability to get inside the mind of practically every boxer he faced in his professional career. Ali's taunts were largely verbal, especially during press coverage of his training or other interviews in which he would routinely berate his opponents with critical remarks such as, "I'll beat him so bad, he'll need a shoehorn to put his hat on," or "If you even dream of beating me you'd better wake up and apologize." During his "Rumble in the Jungle" match in 1974 against George Foreman, for example, Ali taunted his opponent continuously by asking him to hit harder (a tactic that ultimately worked, as Foreman "punched himself tired" by the middle rounds of the fight). Ali's uncanny taunting abilities were immortalized in a still photograph of him standing over fallen Sonny Liston (Ali looking down on Liston with his hand cocked) after knocking him unconscious during the first round of their 1965 heavyweight title match. Ali's taunting style method and purpose became the norm rather than the deviation in boxing culture.

In the sport of professional football, National Football League (NFL) player Billy Johnson was to end zone celebrations what Babe Ruth was to the home run or Ali to the knockout. Johnson was better known as "White Shoes" during his playing days and made the post-touchdown end zone dance a ritual with his "Funky Chicken" routine in 1974 as a rookie with the Houston Oilers. Elmo Wright of the Kansas City Chiefs had actually pioneered the end zone celebration on November 18, 1973, after catching a touchdown pass thrown by Len Dawson in a 38–14 win over the Houston Oilers. Wright spiked the ball and danced in the end zone. But it was Johnson who transformed the ritual into a taunting exercise. In years to come, other players would custom tailor off-beat and taunting celebrations, such as Gerald Wilhite of the Denver Broncos, who gymnastically flipped after scoring; Houston Oilers receiver Ernest Givins, who orchestrated the "electric slide"; or Ickey Woods of the Cincinnati Bengals, who choreographed the "Ickey Shuffle." In 1984, largely because of the choreographed routines of the Washington Redskins, the NFL rules committee wrote an "excessive celebration" amendment into their rule book to prevent these taunts.

In 1991, NFL commissioner Paul Tagliabue changed the celebration rule to allow end zone celebrations that were not engaged in the spirit of taunting. Complications again arose in the late 1990s, when players such as Brett Favre of the Green Bay Packers, Warren Sapp of the Tampa Bay Buccaneers, Keyshawn Johnson of the New York Jets, and Willie Whitehead of New Orleans Saints would intimidate other players by gesturing a "throat slash" motion to them. The NFL banned the throat slash in 1999 and sent a warning to players that such gestures would lead to future fines and suspensions if continued. During the 2002 season, Terrell Owens' varied end zone celebrations caused concern among NFL officials and forced the league to once again crack down on player taunts. After a touchdown drive during a "Monday Night Football" contest against the Seattle Seahawks, for example, Owens mockingly pulled a Sharpie pen out of his sock and signed the game ball, which he then gave to his financial adviser who was sitting in a seat close to the end zone. Critics of the ban on player celebrations argue that the predominantly white team owners and league executives are unfairly targeting black, masculine forms of player expression in the sport.

Even coaches may, from time to time, perform taunting. Unlike instances of player taunting, however, a coach will almost always receive strong punishment for taunting because coaches are explicitly prohibited from conducting any sort of taunting in minor, amateur, or professional sports. Prior to the zero-tolerance atmosphere in sports, several notorious examples of coaching taunting occurred. Many of the taunts were directed at officials for poor or biased officiating. Among the most infamous was National Hockey League (NHL) coach Roger Nielson's (Vancouver Canucks) taunting of the referees during a Stanley Cup playoff game in 1982 against the Chicago Blackhawks. Nielson became outraged when the referee called four successive penalties against the Canucks. Neilson grabbed a white towel from the bench and dangled it on the end of a hockey stick, waving it back and forth as a mock gesture of surrender. When the Canucks returned to Vancouver for their next home game in the playoffs against Chicago, 5,000 replica white towels were distributed to fans as they entered the arena before the game. Fans waved

MIKE TYSON QUOTES

When reading the following infamous quotes from boxer Mike Tyson, who routinely used aggressive speech as an intimidation or taunting technique, consider whether they can be simply ascribed to player taunting and psychological warfare or if they are offensive and inappropriate in a sports culture such as boxing:

> "You're sweet. I'm going to make sure you kiss me good with those big lips. I'm gonna make you my girlfriend."
>
> "I want to rip out his heart and feed it to him. I want to kill people. I want to rip their stomachs out and eat their children."
>
> "I try to catch him right on the tip of the nose [with a punch], because I try to push the bone into the brain."
>
> "My power is discombobulatingly devastating. I could feel his muscle tissues collapse under my force. It's ludicrous these mortals even attempt to enter my realm."
>
> "I just want them to keep bringing guys on, and I'm going to strip them of their health. I bring pain, a lot of pain."
>
> "I'm on the Zoloft to keep from killing y'all."
>
> "I'm just a dark guy from a den of iniquity. A dark shadowy figure from the bowels of iniquity. I wish I could be Mike who gets an endorsement deal. But you can't make a lie and a truth go together. This country wasn't built on moral fiber. This country was built on rape, slavery, murder, degradation and affiliation with crime."

them constantly throughout the game as a "rally towel." The playoff taunting tradition of towel waving at referees continues to this day in Vancouver.

Less frequently policed in the world of sports is the fan taunting of players. Unless missile-throwing, physical interference or attacking, or profane language is involved, players are generally allowed to engage in taunting. Jeering and booing is a historically pervasive form of taunting. Notable recent cases include the continent-wide booing of baseball player Barry Bonds of the San Francisco Giants. Amidst a sea of doping allegations, anti-Bonds fans sing songs, hold up signs, and yell phrases at him to articulate their disgust. Perhaps more consequentially, the jeers are intended to throw him off his game. Throughout the early 1990s, one of the best goaltenders in ice hockey, Patrick Roy of the Montreal Canadiens, faced jeers from U.S. and Canadian fans. Fans mocked the French Canadian pronunciation of his name, chanting "Ru-ah, Ru-ah" at him as a psych out tactic.

Fan taunts at players can take on a more sinister and culturally insensitive tone. In the United Kingdom, for example, crowd chants sung at English soccer songs are not only aggressive but often profane and violent. Legendary chants among Manchester United fans take aim at Liverpool team players by calling them the derogatory term "scousers." A popular crowd chant states, "he's only a poor little scouser, his face is all tattered and torn. He made me feel sick, so I hit him with a brick, and now he don't sing anymore." Another one directed at

Manchester City players simply states, "With a knick-knack paddy-wack, give a dog a bone, why don't City fuck off home." Debates about soccer chanting and taunting came to a head in the 1980s when allegations of racism in chants or other taunts toward black players were common. Fans in the lower leagues of English soccer were known to shout monkey noises at black players whenever they touched the ball. In the sport of ice hockey, former NHL coach Ted Nolan was humiliated while coaching in the Quebec Major Junior League in 2005. Racial slurs were leveled at Nolan during a match between his Moncton Wildcats and the Chicoutimi Sagueneens. Chicoutimi fans barraged him with racial slurs, negatively referring to his Ojibwa descent. Fans shrieked out war cries, performed the "tomahawk chop" with their hands and arms, and pretended to shoot bows and arrows at him.

FUTURE PROSPECTS

As further evidence surfaces about the psychologically and emotionally problematic nature of taunting, minor leagues and amateur organizations throughout North America have placed strict caps on what will be tolerated as spirited taunting in and around the field. But unless professionals, after whom many amateur players model their behaviors, shift their practices and are not consistently prevented from taunting, there is little reason to believe that it will be eradicated from sports. Further, because taunting is heavily tied to cultures and codes of masculinity in sports, with coaches frequently supporting its use as a vital in-game strategy, we should not expect to see it disappear from the social landscape of sports. Teams and leagues may crackdown on socially offensive (i.e., racist) forms of taunting, but others should remain alive and well in the foreseeable future.

See also Cheating During Competition; Cool Pose; Player–Fan Fighting; Referee Abuse.

Further Reading: Brackenridge, C. (2004). Women and Children First? Child Abuse and Child Protection in Sport. *Sport in Society* 7: 322–337; Kerr, J. (2004). *Rethinking Violence and Aggression in Sport.* London: Routledge.

Michael Atkinson

TERRORISM AND THE OLYMPICS

Terrorism is relatively hard to define because what it means and entails varies considerably throughout the world. The U.S. Department of Defense defines *terrorism* as the calculated use of unlawful violence or threat of unlawful violence to stimulate fear in people; intended to coerce or to intimidate governments or societies in the pursuit of goals that are generally political, religious, or ideological. Within this definition, there are three key elements: violence, fear, and intimidation. Definitions of terrorism generally include the idea that terrorist acts are premeditated forms of violence perpetrated against noncombatant targets by groups, usually intended to strike fear into the hearts of audiences. The United Nations produced a definition of terrorism in 1992 that states that it is an "anxiety-inspiring method of repeated violent action" employed by a (semi-) clandestine individual, group, or state actors, for idiosyncratic, criminal, or political reasons, whereby the direct targets of violence are not the main targets. Terrorism is, in most countries, a criminal act that influences an audience beyond the immediate victim. The strategy of terrorists is to commit acts of violence that draw the attention of the local populace, the government, and the world to their cause. The terrorists plan their attack to obtain the greatest publicity, choosing targets that symbolize what they oppose. For this reason, sports events such as the Olympics have become increasingly inserted to the global politics of terrorism.

BACKGROUND

Although sports has not been a principal locus of terrorist activity to date, sports organizers, athletes, political leaders, corporations, and military agents around the globe have certainly been impacted by growing concerns about terrorism in sports. Stadiums have been reconstructed for security purposes in a post–September 11, 2001 (9/11), world; international events have been canceled or relocated; and mini-armies have been employed to protect participants and spectators at high-profile events such as the FIFA World Cup or the Olympic Games. Given the global popularity of sports and the sheer size of modern sports gatherings, games and matches have become high-risk terrorism settings. This is partly due to the fact that sports is a central social context for showcasing differences in religions, political systems, traditions, and ideologies between communities of various sizes (towns, cities, countries, continents, hemispheres). Competitions and tensions on the field get acted out off the field as well between ethnic groups that are positioned on opposite sides (real or imaginary) of the early twenty-first-century U.S.-led "global war on terror." For example, on August 7, 2006, former Australian cricketer Dean Jones (then an analyst for South African television's Ten Sports) was fired for referring to South African player Hashim Amla as a "terrorist" during a live broadcast. On April 23, 2004, former Manchester United manager Ron Atkinson resigned from his analyst's job with ITV after a racist/terrorist comment he made about Chelsea's black French international defender Marcel Desailly was inadvertently broadcast.

Since the modern inception of the Games in 1896, they have been staged as the premier global sporting event on earth. As such, each summer and winter event has been highly mediated and experienced threats of terrorism and, in some cases, concrete acts of political violence. The "father" of the modern Games, Pierre de Coubertin, envisioned that international sports events might actually help to pacify conflict between nation-states. Yet, the modern Olympic competitions undeniably represent a platform upon which political struggle, military posturing, and ideological warfare may be staged.

The Olympic Games typically become linked with matters of political violence and terrorism along one of two axes. In the first instance, the Games may be targeted as a site for direct terrorist action or violence. Politically or religiously motivated individuals or organizations might find suitable targets in athletes participating in the Games, spectators attending the events, or selected corporate sponsors of the contests. Equally, the Olympics might become a "spill-over" context for violence where local military, political, religious, or other conflicts between nations become manifest. Especially in those situations where athletic contests draw sizeable international audiences in geographical settings already embroiled in warfare or other forms of political violence, the Olympics may be utilized as a vehicle for waging politically charged violence against others or further engaging conflict between nations.

The Games may also be used by political opportunists as a forum for ideologically underlining differences between their constituencies and those of others. In this context, terrorist activities may be juxtaposed against the explicit and tacit philosophies underpinning sports contests—whether it be "innocent" philosophies such as civil liberties and human freedoms or more contrived goals such as nation-building, commercialism, and the rule of those with power.

KEY EVENTS

While threats of terrorism have been present at the Olympics since the London Games of 1908, the 1972 Summer Games in Munich were the first to experience terrorism firsthand and experienced the most dramatic instance of terrorism at the Olympics to date. On September 5, 1972, a politically outsider Palestinian group known as "Black September" stormed an Olympic village in Munich, fatally shooting Israeli wrestling coach Moshe Weinberg and, later, weightlifter Yossi Romano and holding others hostage. They demanded the release of approximately 200 Palestinian prisoners held in Israel. Following a 20-hour standoff at a nearby German airfield, and during a failed rescue attempt by the German authorities, nine further Israeli athletes were killed, along with one German police officer and five of the terrorists. The event, commonly referred to as the "Munich Massacre," led to the withdrawal of several Arab countries from the Games, including Egypt, Kuwait, and Syria, all fearing retaliation, and the early departure of Jewish American and seven-gold-medal winner, Mark Spitz. The Munich tragedy sent shockwaves across international sports communities and seriously undermined the likelihood of peaceful future Games. The events of Munich and the political hostilities between nations following the Games were highlighted in the 2005 movie *Munich*.

The 1996 Summer Games in Atlanta highlighted the constantly changing face of violence and terrorism at the Olympics. On July 27, 1996, a pipe bomb exploded near a bandstand in Atlanta's Centennial Olympic Park. Two people were killed and over 100 others injured. Police in Atlanta held in custody 33-year-old security guard Richard Jewell in connection with the bombing, but they subsequently cleared him as a suspect. Unlike the earlier Munich incident, little further information on the Atlanta case has reached the public, and it remains unclear as to whether the incident may accurately be defined as terrorism at all. Following the Atlanta bombing, news stories about thwarted attacks at other Olympic

Games surfaced. Unnamed terrorists attempted an attack on the 1998 Olympics in Nagano and the 1988 Games in Seoul (on at least two occasions). Former Police Chief and consultant to the U.S. State Department during the 1984 Los Angeles Games, Bill Rathburn, suggested that the "Weather Underground," a U.S.-based political extremist group, also planned an unsuccessful attack on the Los Angeles Olympics using plastic explosives.

In light of such real, threatened, and alleged terrorist activities linked to the Olympics, the issue of securing the Games is now paramount in Olympic-bid processes. The mere suggestion or implication that a host city might be politically or militarily vulnerable to a terrorist attack is enough to quash a bid. For example, during the 1997 bid process for the 2004 Summer Games, the Swedish Olympic Committee's proposal suffered a fatal blow following a bomb explosion in Stockholm's main Olympic stadium. The explosion, to this date unsolved but widely thought to be an act of terrorism, contributed to the failure of Sweden's bid. In Sweden, the 2004 Games subsequently became referred to as the "Lost Games." By contrast, bids for the Olympic Games from Sydney (2000), Salt Lake City (2002), and Athens (2004) were all partially successful because of the intensive security programs promised by the respective organizing committees and the degree to which their members carefully incorporated the need to secure all aspects of the events from terrorist outsiders as an integral component of their Olympic bid (Atkinson and Young, 2003).

As the first major international sports event held following 9/11, the 2002 Winter Games in Salt Lake City pushed security measures to unprecedented levels. Fearing that an Olympic Games held on U.S. ground would be a Taliban target, the Salt Lake City Olympics were the most heavily secured to date. The committee spent in excess of $310 million on security for the event; approximately one-quarter of the overall event budget and the highest amount ever for an Olympic Games. The post–9/11 context of the Salt Lake City Games also provided a unique opportunity for the relationship between terror(ism), political ideologies, and sports to be played out in the eyes of the world via the mass media at this time. Segments of the Western media opportunistically framed the 2002 Winter Games as an international summit wherein political relationships in the "new war on terrorism" became plainly evident. The process of securing the Games became a symbolic metaphor for the struggle to secure the United States and the rest of the "free" world.

Interestingly, few people in and around the Salt Lakes City Games opposed the "militarization" of the Olympics on U.S. soil. One of the only dissenting voices of the Games came from Gerhard Heiberg, a Norwegian IOC member, who commented that "a country at war cannot organize the Olympic Games" (Atkinson and Young, 2003). Heiberg's comments instantly appeared in media around the world, but such was the emerging weight of critical media responses that he later felt forced to apologize for his comments and rescind them. With Afghanistan's exclusion from the Winter Olympic Games—on the basis of Taliban's prohibition against female participation in sports—there would be no main opposing viewpoint about terrorism offered by those described as the main enemies of the United States at the Games.

THE PRICE OF FREEDOM

Consider the sheer resources devoted to securing the Salt Lake City Games. Just over 16,000 security personnel were employed during the Games. There was continuous surveillance by F-16 fighter jets and Blackhawk helicopters during the Games, a 45-mile "no fly zone" encircling the city, integrated efforts of U.S. military/intelligence ground personnel (Federal Bureau of Investigation; Central Intelligence Agency; Bureau of Alcohol, Tobacco and Firearms; U.S. Marshals; Center for Disease Control; National Guard; Army; and Marines) with advanced antiterrorism training, and an expansive list of detection technologies utilized to monitor every person's move during the Games (e.g., biometric scanners, portable X-ray equipment, metal detectors, surveillance cameras, computer monitoring systems, and other identification technologies). In total, security accounted for over one-third of the total budget for the Games.

From one point of view, the 2002 Salt Lake City Winter Games may have lulled Olympic officials into a false sense of security; they were situated in an isolated area within the United States, a region of the world relatively free from intense political turmoil and terrorist violence. Securing the Games proved to be achievable in this context. The 2004 Athens Games, by contrast, were positioned within a world region beset by political conflict. The budget for securing the 2004 Games was over three times the size of Salt Lake City's budget and for good reason. Concerns about the terrorist organization "November 17"—alleged to have committed in excess of 23 political assassinations since 1975, including U.S. military official Stephen Saunders in 2003—abounded in pre-Olympic discourses. "November 17" has been blamed for the 2002 and 2003 bombings of Olympic sponsor offices in Greece.

In February 2004, a terrorist group known as "Phevos and Athena" (the names of the Olympic mascots for the Athens Games) claimed responsibility for the firebombing of two Greek environment ministry vehicles in Athens. Only one month later, the Athens-based terrorist group "Revolutionary Struggle" claimed responsibility for a bomb disarmed outside a Citibank outlet situated blocks away from Olympic facilities. Stories about the 1988 Abu Nidal killing and wounding of 108 passengers on a ferry in the Athens port of Piraeus, the potential presence of Hamas, Hezbollah, and the Afghani PKK were circulated in the media, alongside stories of rabid anti-American sentiment in Greece since the initiation of "Operation Enduring Freedom." Equally, warnings about violent anti-World Trade Organization protests in Athens during the Games were being touted as yet another security headache, and local concerns about protesters' behaviors were partially fueled by memories of the violent, anti–world trade, environmentalist demonstrations in Sydney prior to the 2000 Summer Games.

The problem of securing the Athens (and indeed future) Games was complicated by the geographic and physical infrastructure of the city (and future cities). Global critics of the Athens Games pointed to the notoriously poor security reputation of the Athens international airport, the heavy traffic congestion in the city, the floating population of illegal Muslim immigrants in Greece, the relatively porous borders, and the degree to which the country had been an access point for terrorists seeking entry into Europe. Such criticisms were amplified by the tardy construction of Olympic facilities, limited and haphazardly successful security tests at Olympic facilities, and the U.S. State Department's "Patterns of Global Terrorism Report" of 2002, which pointed to cities such as Athens as ripe terrorism targets. However, despite these problems, the Games were a security success—save for the disruption of a men's platform diving contest when a Canadian spectator (Ron Bensimhon) wearing a blue tutu jumped into the Olympic Aquatic Centre pool as a publicity stunt for the online casino "www.goldenpalace.com"; and when an Irish protestor (Cornelius Horan) calling himself the "Grand Prix Priest" tackled and dragged Brazilian runner Venderlei de Lima into the crowd during the final stages of the men's marathon. These were hardly significant events in a security sense, but, predictably, the media cashed in on their newsworthiness given the broader sensitivities to matters of security at the Games.

The spike in concern about security in Athens and at the Olympics in general, however, became counterbalanced by the relatively placid 2006 Winter Games in Torino. Several events leading up to the Games, however, reminded organizers not to become complacent with security efforts. Only four weeks prior to the Games, new threats of terrorism surfaced after Muslim rioting broke out in several European cities. Muslims in cities such as London, Paris, Rome, and Istanbul became enraged after several European newspapers published satirical cartoons depicting the Prophet Muhammed. The controversial cartoons first appeared in Denmark. In days leading up to the Olympics, mobs attacked Danish, Norwegian, and Swedish embassies in six European countries. As a result, Danish athletes and five Danish officials in Torino received extra personal security during the Games. The Italian organizing committee had previously spent $170 million securing the Games and had anticipated civil disturbances by local extremist groups such as the Red Brigades. Italian protestors, disgruntled with everything from the Games' presence in the country to Coca-Cola's corporate involvement in sports, regularly disrupted pre-Olympic events including the torch relay into Torino.

The actual Torino Games were not without incident, either. In the closing ceremonies, during a final speech by Valentino Castellani (Chairman of the Torino Olympic Organizing Committee), a Spanish man sponsored by "www.goldenpalace.com" (their logo emblazoned across his t-shirt) invaded the stage. He shouted to the audience, "Passion lives in Torino"—the slogan of the Torino Olympics—just before security tackled him and dragged him offstage. A 20-year-old Polish adult film actress then attempted a similar stage invasion, holding an Italian flag bearing the handwritten inscription "Mi consenta" and with a drawing by Roman artist Ettore Wallemberg on her skin. Security officials managed to stop her before she reached the stage.

In terms of the role played by the media in constructing Athens and Torino as security concerns, the 2004 and 2006 Games clearly became co-opted into the discourses regarding terrorism in sports established in Salt Lake City. Much as in 2002, security at the 2004 Games (and the assessment of its effectiveness) was framed by established U.S. military experts, NATO members, and other globally recognized politicians. The security effort in Athens, for example, was decisively led by U.S. political–military agents, backed by NATO at the request of the United States, and aligned with framings of the war in Iraq promoted in Western media.

FUTURE PROSPECTS

The problems of political violence, security, and terrorism are not anomalies of the recent past but, rather, contemporary global realities that the IOC and other international sports organizations must anticipate and manage. With increasing numbers of nations included in the Olympic Games and the massive international audience the Games bring together, political groups and nation-states might seek to further exploit the Olympics as a context of military or political struggle. Consequently, staging the Games will become a military exercise as much as it is a global celebration of athlete excellence, with sites taking on the appearance of occupied camps policed by highly trained officials from powerful nations.

See also International Olympic Committee (IOC); Militarism and the Olympics; Collective Protests and Social Movements.

Further Reading: Atkinson, M., and Young, K. (2003). Terror Games: Media Treatment of Security Issues at the 2002 Winter Olympic Games. *OLYMPIKA* 11: 53–78; Lenskyj, H. (2002). *Best Games Ever? The Social Impacts of Sydney 2000.* New York: SUNY Press; Roche, M. (2002). The Olympics and Global Citizenship. *Citizenship Studies* 6: 165–181; Senn, A. (1999). *Power, Politics and the Olympic Games.* Champaign, IL: Human Kinetics.

Michael Atkinson

TICKET DISTRIBUTION AND SCALPING

Ticket scalping, also known as ticket resales, secondary ticket sales, or ticket remarketing, is the practice of buying tickets to an event and reselling them for more than their face value. In the United States alone, economists estimate that the business of reselling tickets generates over $125 million yearly. Ticket scalping started as an illegal street business in the late nineteenth century in North America and has grown steadily into a multimillion dollar underground economy. There are both illegal scalping trades and legal trades in the form of ticket brokers. Ticket scalping is illegal in Canada and 27 states in the United States and is most commonly found at sporting and musical events.

BACKGROUND

The criminal nature and legal enforcement of ticket scalping continues to be hotly debated in North America today. While some people view the activity as a surreptitious and profane feature of the modern sports industry, others view ticket scalpers as providing a useful service. The trade has continually been linked to debates about free-market enterprise in North America and whether any individual in a "free" economy has the right to sell a ticket for more than its face value. The issue of ticket scalping has also helped to shed light on the sometimes borderline legal practices of the legitimate ticket distribution system in sports, which involves teams and hired distribution agents such as Ticketmaster.

A main question raised in debates about scalping is, invariably, whether the act of scalping is a victimless crime or a form of tolerable deviance. Defenders of ticket scalping in North America argue that the average person does not have access to the best seats at a sporting event and that a scalper can help them in this regard. Equally, no one forces a person to use a scalper's service, and the price a scalper will eventually charge for a ticket is only what the consumer market is willing to pay. On both pragmatic and moral grounds, it is also argued that the police have a far longer and more serious list of crimes to police within a metropolitan area. The allocation of vast resources to police a crime that the North American public scarcely complains about seems unwarranted.

An overemphasis on the victimless crime argument obscures the critical analysis of how the act of scalping is tied to a series of other political and economic debates and battles within the sports economy that have been presented since the criminalization of scalping in the early twentieth century.

Beginning as early as the mid-1800s, scalpers, known then as "sidewalk men," were charging what the street economy would bear for event tickets. Although these speculators were generally viewed as street thugs and vagabonds, and thus public opinion was against the practice, legal attempts to limit their activities were far from successful. Boston enacted minor laws as early as 1873 to combat street selling, and Pennsylvania followed suit in 1884. Still, such measures did little good because some laws were declared unconstitutional and in many cases repealed.

The first serious legislation in the United States that focused specifically on ticket scalping appeared in 1918 in response to limited-access stage shows and college sports games. Today, the regulation of ticket scalping is a matter of state legislation in the United States and provincial legislation in Canada. The first generation of antiscalping statutes in the United States attempted to curb the activities of on-site scalpers. At both the state and local level, laws were passed to prohibit the resale of tickets above face value (with perhaps a nominal service fee) and outlaw scalping on public property or within a certain distance of the event site. A sizable number of statutes appear to have been passed to try to limit "nuisance effects" (i.e., the public disruption caused by scalpers at events). All the early statutes made scalping a misdemeanor with fines, possible jail sentences, and confiscation of the tickets (Seagrave, 2005).

Following World War II, the improved economy of the nation allowed many individuals an increase in leisure time and a more expendable income. With additional attention and money being spent on sports, there was an increase in season ticket sales, which resulted in fewer seats being available for single pregame sales. This demand also contributed to ticket scalping as well as fraudulent practices by many box office employees; some would buy tickets and then resell them on their own for a large personal profit. In an effort to curb such practices, cities and states began passing different types of antiscalping legislation. This first strong wave of antiscalping legislation included various levels of restrictions for reselling tickets, such as limiting resale price to $1 above the printed ticket price, adding a maximum $3 service charge to the original ticket price, or putting percentage limitations on the amount for which a ticket could be scalped (Happel and Jennings, 1989). Most states still utilize these types of antiscalping laws. For example, the 2004 Florida statute on ticket scalping states:

817.36 Resale of tickets of common carriers, places of amusement, etc.—

(2)(a) Whoever shall offer for sale or sell any ticket good for admission to any sporting exhibition, athletic contest, theater, or any exhibition where an admission price is charged and request or receive a price in excess of $1 above the retail admission price charged therefore by the original seller of said ticket shall be guilty of a misdemeanor of the second degree, punishable as provided in s.775.082 or s.775.083.

Other restrictions in the early wave of antiscalping laws included requiring owner/promoter authorization for resale above the printed ticket price, restrictions on scalping locations (e.g., no sales at event, on site property), ticket sales and resales limited to printed price, scalping deemed illegal for specific types of events (e.g., athletics), broker licensing, and charity/nonprofit exceptions for resale (Happel and Jennings, 1989). Many jurisdictions have laws that prohibit scalping within a certain distance from the sports venue. Attempting to curb scalping in this manner is often weak, however, because scalpers can simply, and legally, sell tickets 200 hundred feet away from the premises rather than illegally at 199 feet.

These early laws made ticket scalping a misdemeanor offense and punishable by fines, possible jail sentences, and/or the confiscation of tickets and simply aimed to control the location, price, and nuisance effects. These laws held through the 1970s and 1980s, however, enforcement of them was typically infrequent (Happel and Jennings, 1989). Within the past 20 years, scalping laws have differentiated ticket scalpers on the street from ticket brokers or agents (basically, scalpers with state licenses to sell tickets at a premium) operating on behalf of the event producer.

Twenty-seven U.S. states and all Canadian provinces presently have some form of antiscalping legislation. The present content of the laws, the degree to which they are enforced, and their effectiveness in controlling scalping varies considerably. The variance in legal codes is often cited as an indicator of North Americans' general ambivalence toward scalping. Rarely are any of the laws enforced, unless a group of citizens complains about them, or carry a significant punishment (normally, a fine of around $500). Ticket resale on the premises of the event (including adjacent parking lots that are officially part of the facility) is mostly prohibited by law, but ticket resellers may simply conduct business on nearby sidewalks or advertise through newspaper advertisements. Some states and venues even encourage a designated area for resellers to stand in, on, or near the premises, while other states and venues prohibit ticket resale altogether. In the United States, many ticket resellers use a loophole and sell their tickets outside of the state of an event. Therefore, a ticket reseller who is reselling tickets to an event in California is not subject to that state's antiscalping laws as long as the sale takes place outside of California.

Of course, the pivotal question of "why criminalize scalping" still looms large. Even though the public are willing users of scalpers' services, critics of their trade point out that they seize seats from the open market that consumers would have access to and could purchase at cheaper rates. Owners of sports teams, who are often key state lobbyists in either the reformation or enforcement of antiscalping laws, castigate the business of scalping as a form of tax law violation. In the early 2000s, Phoenix Sun's owner Jerry Colangelo became an outspoken critic of scalping. Economists are critical of owners such as Colangelo, however, arguing that he has hidden political and economic interests in being a "moral crusader" against scalping: by keeping ticket prices somewhat low and not inflated by the secondary sales market, fans are more likely to increase their spending on concessions and souvenirs once inside the arena or stadium, thereby creating more revenue for teams (Criscuolo, 1995). Finally, scalping laws are routinely described as needed because scalpers themselves are part of a criminal organization that also

COMMON METHODS BY WHICH SCALPERS ACQUIRE TICKETS

- Sending "diggers" (normally youth) to stand in line at the box office.
- Using high-speed dialing equipment and other methods to increase their chance of getting through quickly to an operator on the telephone.
- Buying tickets, for a legal premium, from fans that have been able to buy tickets.
- Sending in numerous mail orders for Broadway shows, generally in the individual names of employees or of surrogates, such as family and friends.
- Obtaining seats from promoters, performers, and representatives of venues (including box office treasurers and ticket sellers). In some instances, box office personnel have ownership interests in ticket brokers or have family members who are ticket brokers.
- Obtaining tickets from computer ticketing companies such as Ticketmaster, whose employees are skimming tickets for themselves and selling them to brokers.
- Obtaining tickets from the box office "house seats" that are not used by those persons entitled to use the house seats or that are held for performances at which such seats are released.
- Buying from each other, or they may have a "hook" (a contact) at one venue. Thus, there is a constant stream of tickets flowing between them.

dabbles in prostitution, drug dealing, and other vice-related activities; these men are clearly not wanted in and around the sports world.

KEY EVENTS

The sporadic public and police attention granted toward the crime of ticket scalping has not produced a set of discernable battleground events in its history. A series of events in the 1980s and 1990s did, however, change the course of the secondary market industry and has caused the act of scalping to become even more socially grey as a criminal activity.

A subculture of generationally interconnected street vendors carved out scalping's history in the majority of the twentieth century. But in the 1980s, a new occupation developed that altered the face of the business: ticket brokers. Brokers are, in essence, ticket scalpers with a state license to sell in the secondary market. In an effort to regulate the illegal industry and collect tax revenue from scalpers, states that license brokers tightly regulate the amount that can be charged for their services.

Ticket brokers often run into legal trouble when their means of acquiring tickets are illegal, such as bribing the person in control of the tickets at the original point of sale. Ticket brokers have received much criticism because they often control a large percentage of the tickets made available to the public by sports teams, thereby making it difficult for fans to obtain tickets through the box office.

Difficulty arises, though, when police try to enforce antiscalping laws when it is concluded that a broker is in violation of them. For example, a travel agent may sell tickets to a sports event to someone as part of a holiday package for far more than the face value of the ticket or the over-value allowed by law. But when tickets are sold in travel packages, they are exempt from antiscalping legislation. The ticket broker industry has also illustrated the sometimes comical ways in which antiscalping laws may be beaten. New York City, one of the biggest commercial zones for ticket sales to sports event in the country, has strong antiscalping legislation in place. Undeterred by antiscalping laws, however, ticket brokers set up business just outside of the "no scalping" geographic zone within New York City and could legally mail or deliver scalped tickets to citizens in the city. The first generations of ticket brokers were often arrested and fined in the United States for violating antiscalping legislation at times, but as the sheer number of them grew through the 1990s, and with a lack of public outcry against them, the industry presently operates as a predominantly free market.

Far more critical attention and concern has been devoted to another group of legal scalpers. Authorized ticket agencies, such as Ticketmaster or Ticketron in North America, are given permission to resell tickets by sports teams and leagues. These agencies receive tickets directly from sports teams and are permitted to add any number of surcharges above the original ticket price without violating the antiscalping laws. Ticketmaster came under heavy scrutiny in the 1990s in the sports and entertainment industries for alleged monopolization and antitrust violations, but the legal cases against Ticketmaster failed, and

HAS SCALPING GONE PROFESSIONAL?

In 1994, the National Association of Ticket Brokers was formed to help create a better public image of their profession. They even participate in an annual conference titled "Ticket Summit," which brings together guest speakers, educators, and marketing experts and ticket printing and verification experts. A list of conference attendees includes:

- Ticket brokers
- Ticket wholesalers
- Software vendors
- Venture capitalist firms
- Search engine marketing firms
- Concert and event promoters
- Advertising agencies
- Sports management firms
- Media relations experts
- Venue/performer agents

---

rivals such as StubHub, TicketLiquidator, and TicketWeb emerged. The biggest competitors to Ticketmaster have arrived through the Internet, one of the least regulated or controlled social spaces for selling tickets. The global exchange network eBay.com virtually redrew the secondary sales industry by creating a space where individuals (scalpers and brokers alike) could create public auctions for their tickets. Web sites such as Yoonew.com and TicketReserve.com took this initiative even further by selling the *prospect of buying a ticket* to people; people bid to buy tickets to sports events that the companies have not secured from sports teams yet.

Ticketmaster quickly innovated by upping their corporate ante and venturing more deeply into the online secondary sales industry. In 2007, Ticketmaster announced plans for its own auction-format Web site and purchased the UK-based Getmein.com. The company also pioneered "Ticket Forwarding," which allows season ticket holders (traditional sources of high-market tickets for street scalpers and brokers) for several sports teams (including the New York Knicks, Rangers, and Giants) to e-mail extra "virtual tickets" to other users. Ticketmaster charges the sender $1.95 per transaction. They also innovated "TicketExchange," which provides a forum for season ticket holders to auction tickets online. The seller and buyer pay Ticketmaster 5 to 10 percent of the resale price. Critics say Ticketmaster's virtual monopoly share of the resale industry, and now movement into "outlaw" Internet space, will drive prices in the industry even higher.

Economists who have studied the secondary sales industry argue that the teams themselves avoid public and legal reprimand by facilitating scalping. Teams and their venues, in the first instance, provide tickets to brokers and legal scalpers such as Ticketmaster with full awareness about where the tickets are headed and that they will be sold at high premiums. Second, by "holding

TICKETMASTER SURCHARGE FEES

Surcharge fees are regulated in the United States and Canada but are very confusing to deconstruct and difficult to police. The typical fees charged by a company such as Ticketmaster include:

- Service Charge (basic surcharge for their service)
- Building Facility Charge (determined by the venue/team)
- Processing Charge (for processing an order and making the tickets available)
- Shipping, E-Ticket Convenience, or Will Call Charge (for issuing the tickets and/or delivering them)

A ticket to a sports event, if ordered through Ticketmaster and delivered to the person via e-mail, can be double the price of the original ticket after all of these surcharges are accounted for.

---

back" blocks of tickets from sales and distribution and releasing them only after demand reaches its height, teams deliberately drive up prices to generate high profits. From this perspective, teams are complicit in creating an intense supply and demand atmosphere in the sports ticketing world, wherein people will pay incredible prices to acquire tickets.

With all this in mind, the media campaigns (led by ticket agents such as Ticketmaster or sports teams) and police actions against them seem somewhat misplaced and ironic. The street vendors may be the veritable scapegoats of the entire industry and unfairly targeted as the major source of problems in the secondary sales industry.

FUTURE PROSPECTS

If the recent past is any indicator, the merger between teams, legal brokers, and outsider ticket scalpers should draw tighter and along a greater number of social lines. In the future, there may be little analytical difference between the primary and secondary sales avenues. With the mass proliferation of online sales and distribution techniques and the lax enforcement of antiscalping laws, all parties involved (expect for the majority of sports fans) are jumping on the Internet bandwagon to pursue the free-market ticket sales industry to its fullest. With ever-escalating demand for sports tickets in most metropolitan areas, it appears as if the primary and secondary sales markets will continue to thrive separately and together for years to come.

See also Antitrust Violations in Sports; Athlete Unions; Equipment Manufacturing in the Third World; Governments, Laws, and Gambling.

Further Reading: Criscuolo, P. (1995). Reassessing the Ticket Scalping Dispute: The Application, Effects, and Criticisms of Current Anti-Scalping Legislation. *Seton Hall Journal of Sport Law* 5: 189–192; Florida Statute §817.36. (2004). Resale of Tickets of Common

Carriers, Places of Amusement; Happel, S., and Jennings, M. (1989). Assessing the Economic Rationale and Legal Remedies for Ticket Scalping. *Journal of Legislation* 16: 1–14; Seagrave, K. (2005). *Ticket Scalping: An American History.* McFarland and Co.

Michael Atkinson

TRANSSEXUAL ATHLETES

Transsexual athletes are individuals who claim they belong in a gender other than the gender that they were born into and strive to participate in sports. The term *transsexual* refers to a specific population of individuals who have typically undergone surgery and hormonal therapies to transition to the gender that they identify with. These surgeries and hormonal therapies are seen as necessary to reconcile the differences between the external sexed body that individuals are born into with their gender identity, or their internal sense of themselves as male or female. Because sports is currently organized using the rigid structure of the gender binary, the participation of transsexual athletes has become a contested issue. The *gender binary* is the organization of gender using only the categories of female and male and an assumption that these categories are fixed. When the gender binary is used as an organizing principle in sports it can lead to the exclusion of many people, including transsexuals, transgender individuals, intersex individuals, and others whose chromosomal and hormonal profiles, or gender identity, are not clearly male or female.

BACKGROUND

When considering transsexual athletes, some contend that these athletes may have an unfair advantage. Concerns are raised regarding the equity of those who are born as male competing against those born as female. However, generally, transsexual individuals born as female are likely to use testosterone, which could arguably also provide an advantage in their athletic competitions against those born as male. Many scholars believe that transsexual athletes should be allowed to compete as the gender that they identify with. Support for this is found in the belief that with hormonal therapy transsexual individuals have the same physiological advantages and disadvantages associated with their reassigned sex. Other advocates of transsexual athletes adhere to theoretical perspectives that disrupt the gender binary. They may look to Queer Theory as the basis for their contention that sex and gender are neither natural nor purely biologically based and that these concepts are socially constructed. If sex and gender are socially constructed, then the strict organization of sports into categories of male and female becomes arbitrary and perhaps even absurd. While the implications of this perspective may seem quite disruptive to traditional understandings of sports, it has the potential for sports to be more inclusive of all individuals and for sports to be organized around more salient determinants of ability rather than a strict reliance on gender.

Discussions of transsexual athletes are complex because definitions of transsexuality can be difficult to pin down. While some transsexual athletes feel that they are completely identified with their reassigned gender, other individuals might identify as transgender or resist the idea that there are only two genders. Indeed, a significant component of the deliberations related to transsexual athletes rests in the assumption that there are only two distinct categories of sex and gender: male and female. Biologically and theoretically this contention can be debated. There are individuals who do not fit clearly into these categories biologically: individuals who are intersex, hermaphrodites, and individuals who are not born with XX or XY chromosomes, but rather XXY or XYY. Additionally, gender is usually seen as having two distinct categories. Individuals might identify as feminine or masculine, female or male. However, some individuals question these categories and feel that neither category adequately describes their sense of gender. *Transgender* is typically used as an umbrella term that encompasses transsexual individuals but also includes those for whom their gender assigned at birth does not accurately describe their gender identity. Thus, even defining the terms *transsexual* or *transgender* athlete can be difficult.

Despite the difficulties of defining terms, it is clear that transsexual and transgender athletes have competed and will continue to compete in sports. The central issue of debate surrounding the participation of transsexual athletes is whether or not they can compete as their reassigned gender and whether such participation would be fair to competitors. This concern is primarily raised about the participation of male-to-female athletes, that is, individuals born as male who currently identify as female. A related aspect of the debate is under what conditions transsexual athletes can and should be allowed to compete, who should set the standards, and under what criteria transsexual athletes will be allowed to participate.

Curiously, sporting federations and organizing bodies rarely explicitly consider that female-to-male transsexual athletes might compete in athletic competitions against other males and that they may have an unfair advantage. This is true despite the International Olympic Committee (IOC) rules that require female-to-male (FTM) athletes to take testosterone (ordinarily regarded as a banned performance-enhancing substance) to qualify. Theorists suggest that because of the assumption that male athletes will always exhibit

ALYN LIBMAN

Alyn Libman participated in figure skating from an early age and reached high levels of competition as a young girl. His coaches often chastised him for skating too much like a boy and paralleled his performances to top-level male skaters. As he grew up, Libman always felt like a boy, and when he was 18, he began the transition from female to male. He has continued to skate competitively, and in 2004, he was given permission by U.S. Figure Skating to compete with other males.

superior performances as compared to female athletes, there are rarely concerns voiced that biologically female-born athletes may attempt to covertly compete against men, whether they are female identified or transsexual men. Lack of media attention given to female-to-male competitors may lead the public to believe that these athletes simply do not exist at high levels of competition, which is not the case.

KEY EVENTS

One of the earliest and widely publicized reports of a transsexual athlete participating in sports in the United States was Renee Richards. Richards was born Richard Raskin and played competitive tennis as a male. In 1976, she played in a local women's tennis tournament and was identified by a reporter who recognized her as the former Raskin. Soon after the story broke, and she was outed as transsexual, she announced her intention to participate in the 1976 U.S. Open. In response, the U.S. Tennis Association announced that it would require that all female competitors submit to a sex chromatin test, essentially adopting a policy that would dictate that only women biologically born with XX chromosomes would be allowed to participate. Richards, claiming that this was a discriminatory policy, took her case to the New York Supreme Court and was ruled eligible to play in the 1977 U.S. Open. Her career in women's tennis was relatively short-lived, but the incident garnered significant media attention at the time. The focus on transsexual athletes, however, soon faded, and most sporting bodies instituted policies that only allowed "women-born-women" to play and relied upon chromosomal testing to verify athletes' status as females.

While the issue of transsexual athletes was certainly a concern for transgender advocates, little attention was given to the subject in the mainstream media after Renee Richards retired from tennis. In 2004, however, the issue was brought back into the public's awareness when the IOC made a surprising announcement regarding their policy allowing transgender athletes to participate in the Olympics. The policy, generally referred to as the Stockholm Consensus, states that individuals who had undergone complete sex reassignment surgery and hormone therapy at least two years prior would be eligible to participate in the Olympics and to be recognized as their identified gender. The policy was a significant departure from the IOC's previous policy that required women to demonstrate their gender, initially through visual inspections and, beginning in 1968, through chromosomal testing. The intent of these tests was allegedly to prevent male athletes from passing as female in order to have an unfair advantage during competition, however, through chromosomal testing there have been no such schemes uncovered. Prior to the commencement of gender verification testing in the Olympics, the only known case of a male athlete competing as a female athlete was when Hermann Ratjen of Germany was pressured by the Nazi party to compete as a woman in the Berlin Olympics of 1936. Chromosomal testing has, however, resulted in the disqualification of several female athletes from IOC events. These have all resulted from so-called chromosomal abnormalities varying from XX, which medically defines the category "female."

MIANNE BAGGER

In 2004, Mianne Bagger made history by becoming the first transsexual athlete to compete in a women's professional golf tournament and to qualify for the Ladies European Tour. While she has continued to compete in the Ladies European Tour, she has yet to compete in a United States Golf Association (USGA) sanctioned tournament. Although the USGA rules have changed from allowing only "female at birth" competitors and has adopted the same policy outlined in the Stockholm Consensus, Bagger has stated that the rules are too restrictive and invasive. The USGA policy requires that athletes provide complete medical, psychiatric, surgical, and postsurgical treatment records, which would include documentation of hormone therapy. Athletes must also sign a waiver allowing officials to contact their physicians. These requirements create an environment where transsexual athletes are treated as suspect individuals who must prove that they are indeed "real" transsexuals. Thus, although Bagger could compete in USGA sanctioned events, she has refused to comply with the requirements they have set forth because of the invasive nature of the policy that dictates athletes give up much of the privacy "female at birth" athletes are allowed to retain.

The practice of gender verification was abandoned by the IOC in 1999, largely because the only individuals disqualified from the games were individuals who had always identified as female and had been socialized and trained as women throughout their athletic careers.

Since the IOC announced its policy several other sporting bodies have adopted similar policies, including the National Collegiate Athletic Association (NCAA) and the Ladies Professional Golf Association (LPGA). Although the policy has been lauded by some for allowing transsexual athletes to participate in sporting events, others see the policy as restrictive. Additionally, the policy was not developed in consideration of any apparent medical or scientific research or significant understanding of the physiological implication of hormone therapy or sex reassignment surgery.

The Gay Games is another sports venue that has grappled with the issue of transgender and transsexual athletes. Although it was promoted as an inclusive and welcoming event for gay, lesbian, bisexual, transgender, and straight athletes, it had adopted a policy requiring transgender athletes to prove that they had undergone sex reassignment surgery in order to compete as their self-identified gender. This policy inspired protests by transgender and transsexual rights groups. By 2002, the Games adopted a more generous policy that allowed athletes to compete as the gender they identified with if they had legal documentation that could confirm their gender, medical documentation that they were undergoing hormone therapy, personal letters, or testimonials. This policy allows athletes to participate who would not be accepted in the policy laid out by the Stockholm Consensus and similar policies. While some argue that the IOC policy requires that transsexual athletes have to give up too much of their privacy and allow individuals who may not be medically qualified to review their psychiatric and medical records, others believe that this is important to maintain a fair playing field.

FUTURE PROSPECTS

As the ability to transition genders becomes more socially acceptable, legally sanctioned, and medically available, it is likely that more individuals who identify as transgender will have the option to transition fully into the gender they identify with. With increased legal and public support for transsexuals, it is likely that there will also be an increasing number of transsexual athletes who desire to compete at all levels of sports.

While the debate surrounding transsexual athletes' participation in sports typically is based on issues of fairness, there are other aspects of the discussion. As discussed earlier, a fundamental issue is the categorization of sports along the lines of the strict gender binary. Without this organizational strategy the participation of transsexual athletes would be significantly less contentious. For example, if all levels of sports were open to participation by all, then gender would be irrelevant. Some have suggested that rather than gender being the central organizing principle athletes should be categorized based on weight or height or other measurable aspects related to each sport. Alternatively, athletes could be categorized based on ability. Any type of reorganization of sports would require a radical rethinking of how sports competitions are organized and the meanings given to them, particularly at the elite level. Certainly at the recreational level, the existence of coed teams indicates that men and women can compete together, and within recreational leagues there are often divisions based on ability indicating level of competition. Thus, while initially this type of reorganization may seem radical at the elite level, it could also be seen as extending existing structures at the recreational level up to the elite level.

While some have seen the new IOC policies as a sign of progress for inclusion of transsexual athletes, others see the policy as overly intrusive. The requirement that psychological and medical records must be disclosed to the IOC is seen as unnecessary and a violation of athletes' privacy, creating an environment of mistrust of transsexuals and assuming that they are attempting to deceive in order to gain fair advantage. While most media and academic discussions have focused on transsexual athletes competing at elite levels, it is also critical to be aware that transsexual and transgender individuals participate in sports, play, and exercise

MICHELLE DUMARESQUE

Canadian downhill mountain biker Michelle Dumaresque, a male-to-female transsexual, has been competing in internationally sanctioned downhill mountain biking events since 2000 and has been named to the Canadian national team. She has encountered teammates and opponents accusing her of having an unfair advantage because she was born male. While she has endured a lack of support from some teammates, others have been quite supportive, and she has been supported by the governing bodies of her sport. Other downhill mountain bikers, such as Missy Giove from the United States, have spoken out in support of Dumaresque and welcomed her as a competitor.

at all levels. Gender segregated locker rooms, showers, and restrooms can become battlegrounds for those who support or oppose the rights of transgender individuals to participate in sports and exercise. Additionally school systems need to develop policies for how they will instruct transgender students in physical education programs that separate students based on gender, whether on the sporting field or in the locker room. Some researchers have explored the issue of transgender individuals in the context of recreational sports and exercise. The future debates and dialogues regarding transgender and transsexual athletes will doubtless begin to address issues broader than elite level competition. They will also begin to acknowledge that transgender individuals participate in sports and exercise at all levels and that public discourse and sports administrators can adopt a variety of perspectives. These perspectives can range dramatically from a complete acceptance of transgender athletes with no restrictions on participation to those who believe that transsexual and transgender individuals are unnatural intruders into the sports and exercise setting. Although discrimination on the basis of gender identity is legally prohibited in Europe and in some states in the United States, the majority of U.S. states and many countries internationally do not protect against discrimination on the basis of gender identity. Additionally, while the European Union has adopted a policy of nondiscrimination on the basis of gender identity, sporting bodies have been granted exemptions to these laws. Thus, while it is certain that transgender and transsexual participants will continue to participate in sports and exercise, how welcoming those sporting environments will be and the debates that will ensue from their participation and presence have yet to be determined.

See also Gay Games; Gender and Game Rules; International Olympic Committee (IOC); Men in Women's Sports; Women in Men's Sports.

Further Reading: Birrell, S., and Cole, C. (1990). Double Fault: Renee Richards and the Construction and Naturalization of Difference. *Sociology of Sport Journal 7* (1990): 1–21; Califia, P. (1997). *Sex Changes: The Politics of Transgenderism.* San Francisco: Cleis Press; Cameron, L. (1996). *Body Alchemy: Transsexual Portraits.* San Francisco: Cleis Press; Carlson, A. (2005). Suspect Sex. Lancet 366: S39–S40; Cromwell, J. (1999). *Transmen and FTMs.* Chicago: University of Illinois Press; Duthie, K. (Producer/Director), and Duthie, K. and Wilson, D. (Writers). (2004). *100% woman.* (Motion picture). Canada: Artemis Pictures; Green, J. (2004). *Becoming a Visible Man.* Nashville: Vanderbilt University Press; Halberstam, J. (2005). *In a Queer Time and Place: Transgender Bodies, Subcultural Lives.* New York: New York University Press; Namaste, V. K. (2000). *Invisible Lives: The Erasure of Transsexual and Transgendered People.* Chicago: The University of Chicago Press; Stryker, S. and Whittle, S. (Eds.). (2006). *The Transgender Studies Reader.* New York: Routledge; Sykes, H. (2006). Transsexual and Transgender Policies in Sport. *Women in Sport and Physical Activity Journal* 15: 3–13.

Tamar Z. Semerjian

U

UBERSEXUALITY

Ubersexuality is an ascribed social status given to (usually) men. The prefix *uber* derives from the German *über* meaning "greatest." A man is deemed to be an ubersexual when he is seen to possess both the traditional characteristics of the hegemonic (dominant, strong, authoritarian) man and characteristics of contemporary, sensitive, fashion-concerned, artistic, and peaceful (stereotypically *feminized*) men. The ubersexual is a hybrid man in many respects; he is socially and sexually attractive because he retains elements of the strong, silent, intellectual male, but he also embraces (but is not over-preoccupied with) sensitivity and emotionality. While sports worlds have been veritable social factories in the production of hegemonic/dominant males, more athletes are being regarded as quintessential ubersexuals. The rise of sports ubersexuals not only illustrates how gender ideals may be changing in sports but how sports play a fundamental role in shaping cultural sensibilities about masculinity.

BACKGROUND

The rise of ubersexuality in general, and certainly its rise in sports worlds, can be linked to Darwin-like debates about masculinity and masculinity crises in North America. Masculinity is increasingly studied as a complex cultural and institutional problem in countries such as the United States and Canada and something that needs reworking. Scholars in sociology, gender studies, psychology, history, cultural studies, media studies, and a range of other disciplines have devoted volumes to the link between traditional forms of rugged, hegemonic masculinity and a range of social problems such as inequality, exploitation, violence, interpersonal abuse, and trauma. In a new generation of cultural life in North America, where men do not have a proverbial "license to be men," critics argue that young generations of males will either need to evolve socially or die off. While people inside and outside of academics continue to argue about the causal relationship between masculinity and social problems, few have acknowledged that our social constructions of men and masculinity are far more diverse than ever before. This could not be illustrated any more directly than in the case of sports.

Changing ideas about what it means to be a man in sports and elsewhere are related to bigger shifts in sociocultural conditions. Alterations in the structure and cultural philosophies of work life, families, educational systems, and other social institutions toward equality and tolerance have brought about tremendous change in social practice and public debate regarding the performance of masculinity over the past 20 years. While hegemonic masculinity remains explicitly or implicitly dominant in a full spate of social cultural settings (such as sports), there are far more masculinities coloring the current social landscape than in any other era. As the cultural status and practice of masculinity has been placed on the social table for dissection and revision, some men feel a deep sense of doubt, anxiety, confusion, and anger about their socially ascribed and achieved masculine identities. They argue that there are many ambiguities, inconsistencies, and contradictions in what we describe as appropriately masculine in the current era. They describe feeling as if men and masculinity are unjustly targeted as the primary cause of most social problems. Men often exist, they articulate, in a greyed gender space, feeling as if they are unable or not allowed to adopt the traditional forms of practices of hegemonic masculinity but are equally unable to be a so-called renaissance man.

A collection of important analyses of men and masculinity in the past 20 years suggests that, indeed, men's statuses, roles, and identities have shifted in most late modern Western nations and that traditional forms of masculinity are problematic cultural ideals for contemporary men (and women). As a result, we cannot nor should not see masculinity as a single or easily understood gender category

WHAT MAKES THE MODERN (SPORTS)MAN?

Although ubersexuality has been defined in a number of ways, think about the following central constructions of what it means to be ubersexual. How many athletes do you know fit this description?

- Ubersexuals are passionate about business, politics, and global affairs.
- Ubersexuals respect and like women but prefer the company of male friends.
- Ubersexuals follow their experience and reason.
- Ubersexuals are concerned with the world around them.
- Ubersexuals are emotionally available.
- Ubersexuals invest their money in sound business strategies.
- Ubersexuals are obsessed with quality and integrity.

underpinned by simplistic binary oppositions: male/female, strong/weak, powerful/powerless, straight/gay, authority/subject, or active/passive. Some contend that with the symbolic fracturing of family, economic, political, educational, sports–leisure, technological–scientific, and media power bases, masculinity codes have been challenged within most social settings. As such, men no longer possess exclusive ownership over the social roles once held as bastions for establishing and performing hegemony. Others suggest that with an increased presence of femininities in (especially middle-class) social institutions, a resulting masculine anxiety has followed. When such masculine anxiety is coupled with the proliferation of gender equity movements, ideologies of political correctness, and the spread of misandry (male-bashing) in popular media, some men selectively perceive a cultural war against men and masculinity in North America. In the midst of the perceived crisis, certain men discover innovative ways to reframe their bodies/selves as socially powerful in newly masculine, or even what we may call "male feminine" (or ubersexual), manners.

Feminist and profeminist gender scholars often suggest that most men are still predominantly hegemonic in their orientation and not ubersexually inclined at all. Analyses of the rise of ubersexuality are either theoretically lazy, then, or part of a cultural backlash against feminism(s), unreflective of social–structural conditions largely underpinned by a masculine hegemony, a product of media amplification, and generally unreflective of men's experiences with gender and the micropolitics of everyday life.

Ubersexuals are a hybrid social identity, then, retaining the so-called best of old versions of masculinity and blending them with contemporary variants. Ubersexuals in sports are the most attractive (not just physically) men, most dynamic, and most compelling athletes of their generations. Thus, they are traditionally hegemonic role models and powerful leaders who develop entire lifestyles geared toward excellence. But they are also quietly sensitive and intelligent, reflexive, stylish, and committed to quality in all areas of their lives. The ubersexual athlete is ultimately one who shows an extreme confidence about his identity and purpose in his life.

Given the high-profile nature of sports and the degree to which male athletes are revered as role models by young boys, athletes who play around with their genders and present particular images of gender through sports have a considerable power in changing what it means to be a man. Sometimes purposefully and sometimes unintentionally, ubersexual athletes become iconic characters in a society not for their spectacular achievements on a sports field but through the impressions they make on cultural constructions of gender identity.

KEY EVENTS

Historically speaking, not all ubersexual men were created equal. The first few generations of what may now be described as ubersexual athletes did not embody all of the characteristics of the contemporary ubersexual. Their collective efforts, however, established a social benchmark for understanding what it takes to be lauded as a special, progressive male within sports and within broader society. Each of the following men were social rebels, dominant male figures, paragons of sporting excellence, and sexually objectified athletes. None of them perfectly fit into traditional molds of masculinity, and each one's variation in masculine performance had deep links to social–political struggles during their careers.

Muhammad Ali is regarded as one of the most accomplished boxers in U.S. history. Ali's status as an ubersexual in the sport of boxing is firmly grounded in his ring prowess as an amateur and Olympic champion and as a four-time heavyweight champion of the world. Ali's ubersexuality also relates to his commitment to black political activism in the United States. Ali risked his personal safety and his athletic career in the 1960s by participating in civil rights movement struggles. At the time, athletes were neither expected, nor in many cases allowed, to be so politically critical of U.S. social and cultural race ideologies. He stood out as an ubersexual through his conscientious objection to the war in Vietnam and conviction in a U.S. court for his refusal to accept his conscription to the U.S. Armed Forces (for which Ali was stripped of his World Boxing Association and World Boxing Council heavyweight titles in 1967) and for his joining and championing of the Nation of Islam (wherein he officially changed his name from Cassius Clay to Muhammad Ali). Ali's ubersexuality also stems from his poetic style of speech and rhythmic/dance/shuffle style of boxing. Ali was a master psychologist and intellect in a sport not historically replete with them, pioneering techniques such as the infamous "rope-a-dope" style he used to beat George Foreman in the 1974 legendary "Rumble in the Jungle" in Kinshasa, Zaire. Because of Ali's strength, prowess, style, and physical attractiveness (he repeatedly referred to himself as too "pretty" to be hit), female fans loved him, and male fans envied him. After his career ended in 1981, Ali enhanced his ubersexual status by becoming more politically involved in international affairs. In 2002, Muhammad Ali traveled to Kabul, Afghanistan, as a U.N. Messenger of Peace. In 2005, he received the Presidential Medal of Freedom at a White House ceremony. In the same year, he also received the Otto Hahn Peace Medal of the United Nations Association of Germany for his work with the U.S. civil rights movement and the United Nations.

The National Football League's (NFL) bad boy quarterback Joe Namath was among the first true sporting sex symbols in a post–sexual liberation era North America. Namath achieved notoriety as a professional athlete by captaining his New York Jets to a massive upset over the heavily favored Baltimore Colts in the 1969 Super Bowl. He created a national stir when, only a few days before the game, he "guaranteed" a Jets victory in the press. Namath also became a media favorite for his flamboyant personal style and fashion sense; indeed, he achieved infamy in popular culture as one of the first athletes to be a fashion icon. He grew his hair and sideburns long, sported an outrageous moustache (which he later shaved publicly to raise money), and wore floor-length fur coats to games. While images of and physical styles practiced by men in popular culture had changed in the 1960s, they had not done so in sports, where "squeaky clean" masculinity still predominated. Namath thus represented a somewhat liberated male in sports cultures. He also stood out from the rest of his Jets teammates by wearing potentially feminine-looking white shoes on the field rather than the traditional black. His nickname became "Broadway Joe," and male sports fans appreciated his strong and confident (borderline cocky) style of play, while female fans adored him for his overtly stylish and sexual image. Namath lived a blatantly hedonistic lifestyle in some respects during the late 1960s and early 1970s, and he set a new mold for men in the sport to follow. He later appeared in television advertisements both during and after his playing career where is ubersexual status was cemented—most notably in a shaving cream ad wherein his face was shaved by a young Farrah Fawcett and then a highly suggestive and controversial advertisement for pantyhose in which Namath actually donned the product.

British soccer player David Beckham is one of the most globally recognized male sporting celebrities of all time. Beckham's soccer career has included stints in England (Manchester United), Spain (Real Madrid), and the United States (L.A. Galaxy), including three World Cup appearances with England. A highly skilled player in his own right (ranked on separate occasions by FIFA as the second-ranked player in the world), Beckham has come to symbolize a new generation of sports men for his polymorphic masculinity. On the one hand, Beckham displays many of the markers of traditional masculinity: his sports talents, financial success, chiseled body, and glamorous/successful partner (Spice Girls singer Victoria "Posh" Adams). But Beckham is also a self-indulging fashionista; he allows himself to be objectified and commodified as a pin-up boy for both

---

CONSIDER BECKHAM'S POPULARITY

Soccer superstar and popular icon David Beckham's global popularity is such that international fans have devoted entire Web pages to his tattoos. They post photographs of each tattoo on their Web site, discuss their meanings, and celebrate their beauty. In particular, fans suggest that athletes such as David Beckham have dramatically altered the social stigmas surrounding tattoos. Their documented chronology of Beckham's tattoos include:

   1999—His son Brooklyn's name on his back.
   1999—An angel on his back.
   2000—Hindi design for "Victoria" on his left arm.
   2002—Roman numeral VII on his right forearm.
   2003—Latin phrase "Perfectio In Spiritu" on his right arm.
   2003—Latin phrase "Ut Amem Et Foveam" on his left arm.
   2003—His son Romeo's name on his back.
   2003—Classical art design on his right shoulder.
   2004—Winged cross on his neck.
   2004—Angel with motto "In The Face of Adversity" on his right arm.
   2005—His son Cruz's name on his back.
   2006—Second angel and clouds added to right arm and shoulder.
   2008—Portrait of Victoria on his left arm.

straight women and gay men, and he openly speaks about the love he has for his children. While Beckham is an overtly straight man, his cross-gender and sexual orientation charm has transformed him into a personality whose diversely constructed social masculinity has brought to the fore what both *male* and *straight* mean in sports. Befitting of a true ubersexual, Beckham is active as a global humanitarian by supporting UNICEF's Sports for Development program in Africa and "Malaria No More," a New York–based nongovernmental organization (NGO) launched in 2006 to help prevent malaria among African peoples.

The ubersexual male is controversial inside and outside of sports because he violates standardized images and expectations of men inside sports. The ubersexual is at once a nostalgic male icon of perfectionism that most people laud but yet a progressive, political, and quasifeminine persona that can be disquieting for certain conservative audiences. Only a few men in sports are able to lay claim to a recognized ubersexual status, and ubersexual men often come under criticism for either being too concerned with being superman themselves or for promoting unrealistic, ideal-type masculine identities to other men. Not every man has the ability to engage in the sorts of rule-breaking masculine behaviors that men such as Nameth, Ali, and Beckham did without incredible social stigma or ridicule.

FUTURE PROSPECTS

Because of their celebrity, and a certain sin license that male athletes are given in North America, athletes are able to test the boundaries of ubersexuality. Nearly every generation of athletes offers a small selection of ubersexual men that push back not only the boundaries of acceptable, or ideal, masculinity, but they also press the limits of what an athlete's social and political role entails. Despite claims that young boys no longer have ideal-type masculine role models to valorize, the staggering popularity of ubersexual athletes among young men suggests that they embody something deviantly special that youth admire.

See also Cool Pose; Gay Games; Men in Women's Sports.

Further Reading: Hise, R. (2004). *The War Against Men*. Oakland, CA: Elderberry Press; Horrocks, R. (1994). *Masculinity in Crisis: Myths, Fantasies and Realities*. Basingstoke, UK: St Martin's Press; Nathanson, P., and Young, K. (2000). *Spreading Misandry*. Montreal: McGill-Queen's; Whitehead, S. (2002). *Men and Masculinities: Key Themes and New Directions*. Cambridge, UK: Polity Press.

Michael Atkinson

ULTRAENDURANCE RUNNING

Rising in prominence within global sports and leisure cultures over the last 10 years, ultraendurance sports are those that exceed, through either time or distance measures, standard running or cycling races. A running race, for example, is considered an ultraendurance event when it exceeds marathon distance

(26.2 mile) or when the race is stretched out over the course of several days. Ultramarathons, as they are called, vary from 50–1,000 miles and may take days to complete. Ultraendurance events in cycling typically last for several days or weeks and normally involve riding 100–200 miles per day, such as the now famous "Race Across America," which stretches over 3,000 miles.

BACKGROUND

The booming interest in ultramarathon and cycling races is perhaps attributable to the spread of extreme sports cultures in North America and around the world. From the 1990s onward, serious, recreational, amateur, and elite athletes have explored high-risk sports such as bungee jumping, skydiving, tunnel snowboarding, kite surfing, BASE jumping, and helicopter skiing as extreme thrill-seeking in sports. Risk or extreme sports subcultures challenge traditional cultural understandings of sports as safe leisure and principles of strict self-care and health safety in recreational pursuits. Extreme sports culture is underpinned by a credo of pushing and testing the body's limitations and often places one in physically hazardous or emotionally draining contexts.

A sport such as the ultramarathon well-qualifies as a nascent extreme sport, and it has deep cultural roots. The global cultural ascendance of extreme sports is interlaced with the blossoming popularity of its older extreme sports sibling, the marathon. The modern marathon commemorates the historical run of the Greek soldier Pheidippides from a battlefield at the site of the town of Marathon, Greece, to Athens in 490 B.C.E. Legend has it that Pheidippides delivered a momentous military message of "Niki!" (victory) to the Athenians, then collapsed and died, thereby setting a precedent for dramatic conclusions to the marathon.

When the modern Olympic Games were inaugurated in 1896 in Greece, the legend of Pheidippides was revived by a 24.85-mile run from Marathon Bridge to Olympic stadium in Athens. Traditionally the final event in the Greek Olympics, the first organized marathon on April 10, 1896, was especially important to all Greeks. At the 1908 Olympic Games in London, the marathon distance was changed to 26.2 miles to cover the ground from Windsor Castle to White City stadium, with the 2.2 miles added on so the race could finish in front of the royal family's viewing box. The 26.2-mile distance was established at the 1924 Olympics in Paris as the official international marathon distance. Today, marathons have become a running tradition throughout the world. Over 800 marathons are hosted each year across 126 host nations, with a majority sponsored by the Association of International Marathons and Distance Races. The Boston, New York City, Rome, Chicago, Paris, Berlin, London, and Athens marathons are among the most globally revered races. Since the 1980s, marathon racing has developed a more extreme and exotic edge. Races are held, for instance, across tundra in Antarctica and Greenland, along the Great Wall of China, across the Tibetan Himalayas, and on inhospitable African savannahs.

Prior to the 1970s, marathon running was once a sport for an exclusive cadre of elite athletes. However, amid a surge in health concerns among the baby boomer populations in the United States, training for and running marathons "caught on" in the late 1970s. Although the precise cause of the peak in interest is debated, other notable influences included the generational popularity in aerobic exercise among men and women in the middle class, the national broadcast of the New York City marathon in 1970 and the establishment of major marathons across the United States, American Frank Shorter's gold medal victory in the marathon at the 1972 Olympic Games in Munich, and the publication of health guru Jim Fixx's, *The Complete Book of Running* (1977). According to noted running expert Tim Noakes, the 1970s witnessed a renaissance in (marathon) running in the United States and elsewhere. A second renaissance occurred in the 1990s, with new generational interest in running spawned (at least) by new public concerns and fears about health among "out of shape" or obese populations in the West and the spread of running and marathon cultures in major cities.

At the same time that world marathons were including more and more members of the global population, ultramarathons were increasingly sought out by men and women seeking to push the sporting envelope. As marathon culture became more socially inclusive and evolved into a sport less concerned with records than participation and fun, some of the more serious runners became engrossed with ritually punishing races covering, at a bare minimum, 30 miles. In quintessential sporting form, as marathon running was no longer the benchmark of athletic excellence for endurance athletes, human competitiveness drove athletes to fabricate races that would challenge even the most conditioned of runners; the global culture of running once again had a club for its elite. Not surprisingly, during the late 1970s and early 1980s, when ultramarathon blossomed, other sports such as the Ironman triathlon (1978) in Kona, Hawai'i (a 2.4-mile swim, 112-mile bike, and 26.2-mile run) and cycling's Race Across America (1982) emerged as more people experimented with distance sports. For critics and outsiders, however, running ultramarathons (or *ultras*, as they are often referred) poses too many health risks for participants and represents an extreme sports culture that needs to be more strictly policed and discouraged among running enthusiasts.

TRAINING VOLUME AND CONDITIONS

Did you know that the average ultramarathoner trains year-round just to compete in one race? For most runners, this will include one, if not two, running sessions per day over the course of 10 months, requiring a daily caloric intake during that time between 3,000–5,000. During a 6- or 7-hour "short" ultramarathon, an average runner expends 800 to 1,000 calories per hour, while only being able to replenish around 85 percent of that energy loss through food. Ultra runners often come dangerously close to death, losing up to 8 to 10 percent body weight through fluid loss, especially in humid running conditions. With these considerations in mind, many will not even consider entering an ultra until they have successfully (i.e., comfortably) raced a marathon in under 2 hours and 45 minutes or have been involved in distance running for a decade or more.

The two most popular, or certainly most renowned, ultramarathons are the 34-mile Two Oceans Marathon in Cape Town, South Africa, and the 60.2-mile Comrades Marathon in KwaZulu-Natal, Africa. The two events, in conjunction with the 6-day, 151-mile Des Sables Marathon in Morocco, well-represent the grueling tone and flavor of ultramarathon running. First and foremost, the sheer distance of an ultramarathon challenges the mind, body, and spirit. Races endorsed by the International Association of Ultra Runners are typically run over incredibly rugged terrain, involving many elevation changes, course obstacles, and exposure to extreme weather conditions.

While the cultural home of ultramarathoning is ostensibly southern Africa, the sport is growing in global popularity as more people seek to push their personal limits beyond the marathon. Estimates suggest that nearly 70,000 people race in ultramarathons yearly (although the Comrades Marathon alone accounts for approximately 20,000 of registered participants). The sport is popular in Australia and New Zealand, with running time and distance records recently smashed at the Australian Cliff Young Ultra by Yiannis Kouros of Greece in 2005. Kouros ran 644.2 miles (1,036.85 km) in 6 days. Over 200 ultras are held in Europe each year, including the small but historic 152-mile Spartahlon run between Athens and Sparta. Nearly 400 ultras are held yearly in the United States, with a majority raced through wilderness trail terrain. Four popular U.S. races are collectively called the "Grand Slam of Ultras": the Western States (established in 1974, it is the world's oldest 100-mile trail ultra), Leadville, Vermont, and Wasatch ultras.

Long-term members of ultrarunning culture find the increased interest in ultrarunning similar to what "happened to" marathoning in the 1970s. They are

THE WESTERN STATES ENDURANCE RUN

Established in 1974 by Gordy Ainsleigh, "Western States" begins yearly in Squaw Valley, California. Covering 100 miles, the course is arguably the most grueling ultra in the United States. The following factors show why competing in the Western States race is not to be taken lightly:

- extreme heat (it is not unusual for temperatures in the canyons to exceed 110 degrees),
- the possibility of snow in the mountain section
- altitude and elevation changes (18,000 feet of elevation gain and 22,000 feet of elevation loss during the 30+-hour race),
- falling rocks on the trails,
- river crossings,
- nighttime running where temperatures drop below freezing,
- rattlesnakes, mountain lions, and bears,
- dehydration, hyperthermia, hypothermia, kidney shutdown, and frequent bee stings (to name only a few).

especially concerned with the sport's global popularity and mass participation in storied races such as Comrades and Two Oceans (which were historically approached as hallowed terrain for only the elite in the sport). Critics charge that the sport has become overly commercialized like the marathoning culture and has therefore lost a considerable amount of its sporting integrity. For example, ultra clothing lines, periodicals, and Internet discussion groups all serve as vehicles for promoting economic investment in the sport globally. Nevertheless, participation rates continue to skyrocket on most continents.

KEY EVENT: THE COMRADES MARATHON

Arguably the greatest ultramarathon in the world, the Comrades Marathon in South Africa, run between the cities of Pietermaritzburg and Durban, owes its beginnings to the vision of Vic Clapham. Clapham was born in London on November 16, 1886, and later immigrated to Cape Colony in South Africa with his parents. At the outbreak of the South African War (Anglo-Boer War, 1899–1902) he enrolled as a paramedic and ambulance driver. With the outbreak of World War I, Clapham signed up with the 8th South African Infantry and fought and marched 1,700 miles of the eastern savannahs of Africa.

The hardships he and his comrades faced during those awful days, and the resolve that they embodied during the war, left a lasting impression on him. When peace was declared in 1918, Clapham felt that all those who had fallen in the war should be remembered and honored in a unique way. Remembering the searing heat and punishing terrain through which the soldiers had campaigned, he settled on the idea of a marathon, and he approached the athletic authorities of the day to sound their views. His inquiry led him to the doors of the League of Comrades of the Great War, a company of South African ex-soldiers who had formed an association to foster the interests of their companions who had survived the war. Clapham asked for permission to stage a 56-mile race between Pietermaritzburg and Durban under the name of the Comrades Marathon and for it to become a living memorial to the spirit of the soldiers of the war.

The first Comrades Marathon took place on May 24, 1921, South Africa's Empire Day, starting outside the City Hall in Pietermaritzburg with 34 runners. It has continued since then every year with the exception of the war years of 1941–1945, with the direction alternating each year between Pietermaritzburg and Durban. The Comrades Marathon is a cherished national treasure in South Africa and attracts thousands of runners, spectators, and television viewers every year. It is the veritable "World Cup" of ultramarathon culture and symbolizes the pain, suffering, and ritual torture runners put themselves through as part of this rather unusual sport.

FUTURE PROSPECTS

Ultramarathon running appears to have become a staple in the global endurance sports calendar. Indeed, it seems that as every year passes, the desire shared among elite runners to do battle with their bodies through endurance events encourages them to seek out longer races on even more incomprehensive terrain. Partly fueled by an inner resolve to test the self through sporting performances and a social competitiveness to distance themselves from more everyday marathon culture, the sport of running appears to have fallen into a very familiar cultural trap. In short, many ultrarunners seem to uphold the rather standard, Western mantra of "anything you can do, I can do better."

See also Adventure Racing; Biology and Athlete Performance; Yoga and Alternative Fitness.

Further Reading: Bale, J. (2003). *Running Cultures.* London: Frank Cass; Fixx J. (1977). *The Complete Book of Running.* New York: Random House; Noakes, T. (2003). *The Lore of Running.* Champaign, IL: Human Kinetics.

Michael Atkinson

URBAN PLANNING AND GENTRIFICATION

Sports facilities have increasingly become key components of broader urban development projects designed to revitalize communities, especially in blighted downtown cores. As a result of this process, debates are waged related to the degree of public involvement and the impacts development has on existing communities. Issues of gentrification often emerge because building sites are often chosen in rundown or brownfield areas, and facilities are surrounded by more upscale residential development.

BACKGROUND

Many cities throughout the world—particularly in established U.S. cities that were the centers of industry—have seen serious economic declines in the past decades due to shifts in the global economy away from traditional industries. As a result, industrial cities have declined in population and wealth as traditional manufacturing has moved overseas to emerging economies. At the same time, concerns over safety led many middle-class families to move to suburban locations. Thus, while the overall populations of the metropolitan areas grew, the populations of many industrial cities declined. This led to several problems, including high unemployment, crime, and safety issues. To remain economically viable, cities have moved more toward service-based economies, where downtowns are repositioned as exciting places to visit and shop. Here cities develop entertainment zones or "tourist bubbles" that attract new spending in economies.

As a result, substantive sports facility–anchored urban development projects have been completed in a number of cities, including Cleveland, Ohio (which has built three new sports facilities); Baltimore, Maryland; and Columbus, Ohio. These projects are an attempt to make downtowns safer and more vibrant and exciting places to live, work, and visit.

DID YOU KNOW?

Proponents of stadium construction have often touted the number of jobs that will be created and the positive economic impacts on the city that will be generated as a result of the construction of a new facility. However, over the past 15 years or so, independent research has virtually unanimously shown that sports arenas and stadiums have negligible economic impacts. There are several reasons why impact studies tend to overestimate the actual financial benefits of sports facilities. First, studies often measure economic activity, not the increased welfare gains. For example, the total amount spent at a sporting event does not represent new spending; people would likely spend their money elsewhere in the economy if they did not attend the gain (this is known as a substitution effect). Second, where money is new to an economy (such as where someone comes in from another city to attend a game), this may represent time-switching, where the spectator simply changes their schedule to coincide with a game. In other words, they were going to come to the city anyway and adjusted their travel schedule in order to attend the game. Thus, you cannot credit the team or game with generating the new impact because the spectator was going to be in the city anyway.

Another issue occurs where a team moves into a new facility in the same city, and the use of the old facility is not taken into account. If people are attending the same number of games but in a new location, there is no new economic impact. A final issue that is not often considered when conducting economic impact studies relates to export functions. This occurs when a team or facility actually discourages other spending. This happens when people avoid going put and spending money because they want to avoid traffic or noise associated with people going to a game; they may even spend their money elsewhere outside of the local economy. An example of this might be when someone decides to take a trip to another city on a weekend when there is going to be a big sporting event in their home city.

KEY EVENTS

From the 1950s through the 1970s, the construction of sports facilities followed the exodus of middle-class residents from urban cores to the suburbs. Large, multiuse facilities were built with convenience to local highways an important consideration. As a result, suburban fans could access events easily and return home by car relatively quickly. The result was a series of "cookie cutter"-style stadiums that often served host to more than one professional sports team and were not easily discernable from one another. In addition, because facilities were designed to accommodate more than one sport (such as professional baseball and football), facilities were not always ideal places to watch certain sports because fans had to sit too far from the field of play or sightlines were restricted.

In the meantime, many cities that once were centers of industry witnessed significant declines, and downtown cores became sites of higher crime, boarded up buildings, and the ongoing flight of residents and businesses. City leaders recognized that a key to stopping decline was to develop ways to encourage both residents and visitors alike back to downtowns. As a result, cities such as

Baltimore began substantial redevelopment projects that often included new shopping areas, residential developments, convention centers, and other arts, cultural, and entertainment amenities. These projects began to include major sports facilities, which were viewed as anchors that could guarantee a certain number of visits per year. For example, a baseball team might average 2 million fans per year in attendance, which certainly could boost activity in a city's downtown core.

A turning point for this process occurred in Baltimore in the early 1990s. Already well into its Inner Harbor redevelopment project, it was decided that a new ballpark for the local Major League Baseball (MLB) team, the Orioles, would be built nearby. While other new facilities had already started to be placed in downtown cores, the new Oriole Park at Camden Yards (OPCY) was designed to be integrated into the existing urban landscape. In addition, it was considered the first "retro" ballpark, with design elements that included an asymmetrical playing field (which recalled older facilities that were often crowded into urban space), open-beam steel construction, and brick work that blended with the warehouses in the surrounding district. In addition, the facility incorporated into its design a huge brick railway warehouse that was already on-site. In the next 15 years, OPCY inspired another dozen baseball-only facilities in major U.S. cities.

There are a number of different arguments regarding the benefits and drawbacks to placing a large sports facility in an urban core. As mentioned previously, a major reason is to encourage more activity and spending in a city's downtown. This is especially important when cities have witnessed the outward migration of residents and business alike. While new sports facilities generate negligible new jobs and economic impacts, many cities are concerned about *where* money is being spent. The idea here is to create a facility-anchored urban entertainment district that will get visitors and residents alike excited about being downtown again.

Thus, sports facilities have been used as jumping off points for integrated entertainment development that will encourage downtown employees to stay longer or even consider living downtown. This can facilitate a movement away from the car cultures that have encouraged urban sprawl and develop an increased emphasis on other forms of transportation, where proximity makes it easy for those downtown to access shopping and other amenities.

Another key argument for the development of urban entertainment districts relates to the overall image that the city can project. A vibrant downtown is thought to be an important asset for cities that seek to attract new business investment and tourism dollars. In addition, the provision of civic amenities such as arenas, stadiums, performing arts centers, and other entertainment options are considered points of differentiation for cities competing for global flows of capital.

In most cases, the areas that are seen in need of renewal are also those areas where there is likely to be low-income residents with a smaller proportion of property ownership by residents. This is because land is generally less expensive, and some suggest land acquisition requires fewer administrative hurdles or opposition. Unfortunately, residents in these same areas are those that cannot afford to pay the increased rents that result from rising land values as the development project progresses, and they are unable to benefit from the increased property values because they typically do not own the properties they live in. Instead they are "squeezed out" to other less desirable areas of a city, where rents are cheaper, but many of the same urban problems (crime, unemployment, etc.) remain.

Another compelling argument against the construction of downtown urban sports facilities relates to the subsidies these facilities receive. Because there is a limit on the number of franchises leagues are willing to grant, teams can leverage the threat of relocation to exact substantial public subsidies from local communities. As a result, it has been estimated that the average public subsidy for all major league facilities in North America is around $175 million. Taxpayers are concerned that their hard-earned dollars are going to pad the pockets of millionaire team owners and players, and this is even more pronounced when it is clear that there is very little use for a facility outside of the sport that serves as the major tenant. The biggest culprits are National Football League (NFL) stadiums, which are now mainly designed for single use (with baseball teams demanding their own facilities). As a result, these massive facilities are unused for all but a handful of game days per year. It becomes very difficult to justify how the teams and their stadiums benefit those who are not sports fans and do not attend the events held in the facility, and the facility often sits empty and disconnected from the surrounding community.

Another concern relates to the characteristics of tourism bubbles, which cater to visitors and try to capture spending. This is good for cities because tourism dollars represent an injection of new money into an economy. However, a major drawback is that the amenities designed to attract tourists are not meant for locals. In other words, in most cases the people who are displaced in order to develop shopping and entertainment districts designed to attract and service a "visitor class" will never use or access these amenities.

Finally, a criticism relates to the opportunity costs of the facility development. What could have been built instead? What other services, such as road improvements or education, could have been better served by any public money invested? Because cities operate with finite resources available and multiple needs, it is critical to determine the best use of public funds when examining sports facility development.

FUTURE PROSPECTS

Cities continue to use public funds and displace lower-income residents in order to create comprehensive sports facility–anchored urban development projects. In response, interests groups are becoming more effective at demanding additional concessions in order to help offset the impacts that facility development might have on the local community. One demand relates to the inclusion of local companies and businesses into the construction process. As a result, recent developments have included community benefit agreements that guarantee that a certain percentage of construction contracts be granted to local minority and women-owned businesses. Others have ensured commitments for a certain number of event tickets to be made available for free or at reduced rates. Another possibility relates to what are called linkage policies, where developers are responsible for bearing the cost of increased taxes to local residents. For example, if property taxes increase as a result of new development surrounding a facility, the developer must help to offset the increased costs to the existing residents or businesses through subsidies. This technique then allows the existing community to be able to continue functioning and reduces the likelihood of gentrification driving out the existing community members.

See also Corporate Stadiums; Government Sponsorship of Teams.

Further Reading: Cagan, J., and deMause, N. (1998). *Field of Schemes: How the Great Stadium Swindle Turns Public Money into Private Profit.* Monroe, ME: Common Courage Press; Euchner, C. (1993). *Playing the Field: Why Sports Teams Move and Cities Fight to Keep Them.* Baltimore: The Johns Hopkins University Press; Long, J. (2005). Full Count: The Real Cost of Public Funding for Major League Sports. *Journal of Sports Economics* 6: 119–143; Rosentraub, M. S. (1997). *Major League Losers: The Real Cost of Sports and Who's Paying for It.* New York: Basic Books.

Daniel S. Mason

V

VIDEO GAMES

Sports video games have become almost synonymous with the term *home entertainment* for youth. Today, there are dozens of sports games on the commercial market, featuring a diversity of sports such as the Olympics, BMX, football, golf, hockey, sailing, rugby, baseball, cricket, darts, boxing, horseracing, and many others. Sports games have become a common feature in the everyday lives of many youth and a central part of popular culture. The staging of professional sports in the contemporary era almost universally involves its mass mediation and brand extension through video games.

BACKGROUND

In 2006, North Americans spent nearly $13 billion on home video game systems. Among all of the categories of games played by people, sports games account for nearly 50 percent of all games sold.

The history of modern home video gaming has been written through the development of systems primarily designed to play simulated sports games. However, the first video games to be commercially sold in North America had little to do with sports. In 1971, Nolan Bushnell and Ted Dabney created the game "Computer Space" for U.S. consumers as the first commercially sold, coin-operated video game. The home version was connected to a standard television and game-generated video signal for display. After the initial success of the game, what is recognized as the first home entertainment game unit, the Magnavox Odyssey, was developed by Ralph Baer and released in 1972.

Led by Nolan Bushnell, the young electronics company Atari, however, changed the face of home entertainment in 1975 when it released a version of a coin operated arcade game called "Pong." Bushnell struck a deal with Sears to sell his ping pong / table tennis style game. In 1975, Sears began selling PONG under their branded "Tele-Games" label, and Pong landed on the market 150,000 strong, just prior to the Christmas shopping season. Amazingly, just a year after Pong's release and its global success, Magnavox, Wonder Wizard, Telstar, Coleco, Fairchild, and RCA all developed similar home video game systems. In practically every case, the systems that were designed to play multiple games all featured sports games (i.e., mostly ice hockey and tennis) as the alternatives to Pong. By 1977, Atari further exploited the burgeoning interest in more interactive sports video games among a new generation of youth gamers, developing games such as Basketball and Stunt Cycle. The release of the Atari 2600 in 1977 was another watershed moment because it became the first game unit that used game cartridges that could be inserted into the machine. Magnavox followed suit with new systems of their own, with each iteration offering a greater range of sports games.

The home gaming market shifted considerably through the early 1980s. With the development of more complex systems and the design and marketing of space, action, and role-playing games, sports games no longer owned a veritable monopoly of home play. Gamers, while tolerant of primitive graphics in games during the 1970s, were no longer appreciative of the primitive-style of sports simulation in extant gaming systems in the early 1980s. Space and other action games, while equally primitive, were more easily designed and palatable to gamers. As new and innovative home electronic products flooded the industry in the early 1980s (VHS systems, home computers, and others), the new generation of sports gamers were unimpressed. Additionally, the Japanese company Nintendo Entertainment Systems entered the gaming marketing in 1985 with its highly popular "Mario Brothers" game, and sports game sales continued to decrease.

Through the late 1980s and early 1990s, new game systems emerged such as Sega Genesis and Saturn, Panasonic's 3DO, SNK's Neo Geo, and Sony's Playstation, and the sports video game made a decisive comeback. Each of the new systems was equipped to handle more complex graphics and worked at greater computer processing speeds. These systems allowed for a new type of realism within games that appealed to sports enthusiasts. Since the early 1990s, sports gaming has accounted for a lion's share of retail sales across subgenres. The latest gaming systems, such as X-Box, Playstation 4, and Wii, all contain massive lines of sports games.

The social and cultural significance of sports video gaming is, indeed, a more complex matter to decipher. For the first and second generations of gamers (ca. 1975–1985), one can easily understand the allure of novel games and the collective interest in innovative (and relatively affordable) electronic systems at a time when there was a veritable boom in the home entertainment market. While many of the games had been launched in video arcades or amusement parks in North America, home versions (and not a pay-per-play variety) were obviously appealing. But these gamers, who were a part of what Douglas Coupland would

TYPES OF SPORTS VIDEO GAMES

Arcade

Sports games have traditionally been very popular coin-operated arcade games. The main objective of an arcade sports game is usually to obtain a high score within a sport. The arcade style of play is generally an unrealistic and modified game simulation style and focuses on fast gameplay experience.

Simulation

In comparison to arcade sports games, the simulation style of play is usually a more realistic, emulative rendition of real-life sports.

Management

Sports management games situate players into the role of sports team manager. Management games normally place the player against computer-controlled teams. Players are expected to handle strategy, tactics, transfers, and financial issues.

Fantasy

A fantasy sport is a game where players, as owners, build a team that competes against other fantasy owners based on the statistics generated by individual players or teams of a professional sport.

---

go on to describe as "Generation X," became a driving force in the mass fetishization of personal entertainment systems and modalities of leisure. The ability to own these new games signaled not only one's social status in the consumeristic United States, but it also appealed to the desires of increasing numbers of kids who preferred to stay home and play within their basement or room rather than in the park. In other words, these home entertainment systems appeal to what is now known as the slacker culture in North America: a generation that felt alienation and boredom and was privileged financially to be able to idly play video games for significant amounts of time per day. Ironically, these youths were frequently simulating play through sports games.

The boom in sports games and other video games occurred also during a historical period in which the civic participation declined, threats of crime and violence encouraged parents to keep their children inside of the house, and technological products designed to better our lives increasingly crept into the home. The late 1970s and early 1980s might be historically regarded as a critical time period when the home became a veritable battleground of electronic market expansion. Basements, kitchens, living rooms, recreation rooms, bedrooms, and dining rooms have all become places were electronic gadgets may find residence, each of which play a "critical" role in the operation of daily life. In the case of sports games, they were increasingly used for a variety of fundamental household tasks: entertainment, emotional withdrawal and relaxation, babysitting and child-minding, the illustration of social status, diversion, socialization and peer bonding, and the expression of loyalty to particular sports teams and players.

The long-term effects of sports gaming are only now being debated with either seriousness or consistency. Here, three important debates surround sports video games and their play (especially by youth). First, and perhaps most common in recent dialogues, is the role of video sports (and other games) in promoting obesity among youths. Video games encourage sedentary lifestyles and have been linked to poor physical education and nutritional practices among youths. Argument follows that rather than encouraging youths to play virtual sports, they should be encouraged to play "real world" sports. Second, sports video games have been critiqued for the simulated violence they contain and the type of real world violence they may encourage. In particular, football, ice hockey, and professional wrestling video games were attacked repeatedly in the late 1990s as chief contributors to violent outbursts by their players. Third, and somewhat more conceptually abstract, critics note that by encouraging a detachment from the reality of everyday life, sports video games encourage people to disengage from healthy social interaction. The playing of sports games by youths further encourages a brand of individualism and self-identification that inhibits the development of basic social skills and appreciation for others necessary in everyday life.

KEY EVENTS

The success of sports video games over both the short and long term in North America has been largely secured by the mass popularity of several marquee games. Among the most influential companies to produce, market, and sell sports video games has been Electronic Arts Tiburon (EA). The company's "EA SPORTS" line of games continues to reign supreme in the field. One game in their commercial arsenal, "Madden NFL Football," has been the flagship sports game for nearly two decades, selling nearly 62 million units worldwide.

No video game in history has endured the test of time, economics, and a fickle public better than Electronic Arts' "Madden NFL Football." The game is named after John Madden, a well-known football commentator and formerly a successful Super Bowl–winning professional football coach during the 1970s with the Oakland Raiders. Madden insisted that he would only give his endorsement to a game that was as close to real-life football as possible. From the very beginning, "Madden NFL Football" has been at the top of the charts because of its unique approach to bringing a video game "to life," offering gamers unparalleled qualities that no other sports video game can. The original version of the game was commissioned by EA founder Trip Hawkins in 1984 and ran on an Apple II computer. Electronic Arts had just shipped the hit "Dr. J and Larry Bird Go One on One" and would soon begin work on "Earl Weaver Baseball" and "World Tour Golf," which together were the foundation for the EA SPORTS line of video games. The Apple II was not fast enough to show all the players running in real formations on the field, and Madden personally rejected the initial proposed build because there were only seven players on each team. After several years of unsuccessful experiments, the game finally shipped in the late 1980s and did not sell well. In 1989, EA producer Richard Hilleman hired Gamestar's Scott Orr to redesign "Madden NFL Football" for the new Sega Genesis computer. Since the 1991 edition of the game, it has been the most popular selling sports game on the market.

The video game has been, and continues to be, a pioneer in the field due to the ways in which it progressively simulates more life-like interactive gaming contexts. The contemporary success or failure of games appears to be anchored in their ability to simulate real life in complex ways. Equally, sports games such as "Madden NFL Football" provide users with an increased element of control in the game; for example, there are multiple modes of game play, from a quick head-to-head game to running a team for a whole season or even multiple seasons. Each iteration of the game has offered improved three-dimension graphics and sound and given users more control over the game environment (i.e., allowing them to control all aspects of play on the field, customize teams, and even control the facial expressions and speech of players).

EA SPORTS used the success of "Madden NFL Football" as a springboard for launching an entire range of sports games and extended its hegemony in the video gaming industry. EA sports has also been a leading group in the ongoing cross promotion of video games with sports franchises. In 2004, EA secured a series of deals that granted them exclusive rights to several prominent sports organizations, such as the National Football League (NFL), the National Basketball Association (NBA), the National Hockey League (NHL), and the National Collegiate Athletic Association (NCAA). They also secured a lucrative long-term deal with cable station ESPN. From rather humble beginnings, the company has gained an immense market share of the video game industry and secured millions in branding revenue from the development of one simple game.

Of course, controversies surround a game such as "Madden NFL Football" and others in the genre for creating hyperreal, detached zones of leisure activity for youth. As the games become progressively life-like and encourage players to live in simulated worlds of sports, they encourage people to become detached from the reality of physical sports cultures. Further still, the interlacing of gaming with sports corporations exacerbates the mass commodification and commercialization of contemporary sports and leisure. With these two factors combined, players of games become passive consumers of mediated sports realities, watching football as consumers on television and then living in a pay-for-play world of simulated football through gaming.

The corporatization and commercialization of sport through video gaming has also been facilitated by the ways in which popular games have hyperbolized violence and aggression. Through the 1990s, incredibly popular arcade and home console games such as "Blades of Steel" (ice hockey), "NFL Blitz," and "NBA Jam" each allowed players to engage in flamboyant forms of virtual violence in the games. In a few cases, players can score extra points in the games by winning fist-fights, administering particularly vicious hits, or completing

THE "MADDEN CURSE"

One of the most interesting controversies surrounding sports video games has been called the "Madden curse." Prior to 2000, all of the "Madden NFL Football" game box covers prominently featured John Madden only. When EA started to have NFL players on the cover of the games, some later (half-jokingly) speculated that there was a "Madden curse" because of a coincidental series of misfortunes that befell the product's cover-athletes after they appeared on the video game. In the 2002 edition of the game, quarterback Daunte Culpepper appeared on the cover and then suffered an injury-plagued season. St. Louis Rams' running back Marshall Faulk appeared on the 2003 cover of the game after a Super Bowl winning season, and the following year his stats dropped sharply compared to his prior season. The next year, Atlanta Falcons' star quarterback Michael Vick was injured during the 2003 preseason after posing for the cover of "Madden 2004." Vick suffered a broken fibula in a preseason game against Baltimore, the day after "Madden 2004" was released to retailers. Ray Lewis was able to evade the curse until the 2005 season after being featured on the cover of "Madden 2005." He suffered a hamstring injury that sidelined him for the rest of the season after only six games. Cover player of the 2006 game version, Donovan McNabb, injured his chest in week one of the season and played in only nine games before being sidelined for the season after undergoing surgery for a hernia.

---

aggressive moves. Many of the showcased forms of violence are, of course, either nonconventional (illegal) in the sports or absurdly unrealistic with regard to their contextual tolerance in games. Proponents of the thesis that states "violent video game play is causally related to violent real life behavior" have argued that with the proliferation of excessively violent sports games, new generations of emotionally or aggressively charged youth have been nurtured who exhibit so-called unhealthy preoccupations with sports games.

Recent developments in sports gaming ushered in by the Internet age have also caused concern among North American parents. Since the early 2000s, which saw the development of faster and more powerful home computers linked to high-speed Internet networks, online fantasy games have mushroomed. Fantasy sports games allow a player, normally for a fee, to participate with others in virtual game space in a competitive league. Each player takes ownership of a team as a general manager and coach. One picks one's favorite sport, joins an online virtual league with a dozen or so others, drafts players from that sport, and makes one's own fantasy team. Normally, the team is selected from a list of real world players in the sport. All of the play is facilitated by an Internet host, such as Yahoo!, ESPN, or Fantasy Online Sports; each of the professional leagues offers its own fantasy leagues as well. In every week of the virtual season, your fantasy sports team "plays" against others in your league in simulated games. The player is able to manage and direct the team over the course of the virtual season and playoffs in lieu of the team's weekly performance. Critics of fantasy leagues point out that not only are they thinly veiled fronts for gambling in many instances (problematic because of the volume of young players involved), but they are also merely another site for the mass marketing and commodification of professional sports. Online fantasy games received international press and notoriety in this regard during 2006 when the FBI filed reports that New York Giants' professional football player Jeremy Shockey deliberately dropped passes during games that year in order to win a fantasy league football pool in which he was entered.

Finally, since as early as 1977, video game developers have strived to produce real-world experiences for players by engineering more interactive modes of play, specifically through the advent of technological apparatuses that are connected to game consoles and resemble real-life sporting apparatuses. Faux steering wheels used to drive racing cars, golf clubs, baseball bats, and guns and fishing reels for sport hunting and fishing have all been developed to provide gamers with more life-like sports experiences. The latest development is the Nintendo Wii system. The Wii sports games are fully interactive styles of gaming whereby players must emulate the actions of an athlete on the virtual field. A small, hand-held device tracks the player's movements and such movements are represented on the screen through game play. One can bowl, swing a baseball bat, run, jump, shoot a basketball, and perform other athletic movements in real-world time, and one's player moves accordingly. Developments such as the Wii system illustrate the ongoing "cyborgification" of modern home entertainment systems and the degree to which virtual forms of simulated play/athletics have become more common, in many households, than actual sporting competitions.

FUTURE PROSPECTS

The surging global interest in, and market for, sports video games has been cited as an empirical indicator of a vast array of pressing social problems; from social alienation, to the cyborgification of youth, to obesity and sedentary lifestyles, to teen violence, and to the detachment of "Generation D" from the real, physical world of reality. Sports gaming may be an easy and convenient target, however, and a scapegoat for deeper cultural and structural problems in North America that may more directly cause these issues. Nevertheless, the sports gaming market continues to thrive, and there is every reason to believe that the interconnection between sports, corporatism, and gaming will only extend and intensify in the foreseeable future.

See also Corporate Branding; Virtual Sports.

Further Reading: Anderson, C., and Bushman, B. J. (2001). Effects of Violent Games on Aggressive Behavior, Aggressive Cognition, Aggressive Affect, Physiological Arousal, and Prosocial Behavior: A Meta-Analytical Review of the Scientific Literature. *Psychological Science* 12: 353–359; Graves, L., Stratten, G., Ridgers, N., and Cable, N. (2007). Comparison of Energy Expenditure in Adolescents when Playing New Generation and Sedentary Computer Games: A Cross Sectional Study. *British Medical Journal* 335: 1282–1284; Kutner, L., and Olson, C. (2008). *Grand Theft Childhood.* New York: Simon & Schuster Adult Publishing Group; Putnam, R. (2000). *Bowling Alone: The Collapse and Revival of American Community.* New York: Simon and Schuster; Wiegman, O., and

Schie, E. (1998). Video Game Playing and Its Relations With Aggressive and Prosocial Behavior. *British Journal of Social Psychology* 37: 367–378.

Michael Atkinson

VIRTUAL SPORTS

Virtual sports are symbolic representations of embodied, expressive, and real-world athletic experiences. These sports can involve complete "out of body" practices wherein participants play a sport without exerting their bodies in a traditionally athletic way (i.e., a sports video game) or more embodied performances involving physical activity in a simulated sports environment (i.e., athletic movement in a modified sports setting such as a cyclists' wind tunnel). Centrally, virtual sports involve human beings as either real or represented athletes in a technologically enhanced setting. Although certain play and leisure activities might be considered representations of sports (e.g., touch football, "pick up" ice hockey, or go-kart racing), virtual sports are those that place either embodied or computer-generated athletes in simulated sports spaces.

BACKGROUND

Virtual sports have, by and large, escaped debate as a battleground in sports. Nevertheless, three types of virtual sports are ripe for investigation. First, and perhaps most commonly, virtual sports abound in home and arcade video games. Through the advent of home entertainment systems in the 1970s and 1980s, such as Atari, Intellivison, Collecovision, and Vectrex, sports video games became a staple of both popular and youth cultures in North America. From the 1980s onward, game players have competed in virtual sports ranging from hockey to basketball to hunting to skateboarding. Indeed, one of the very first video games commercially marketed in the United States, "Pong," resembled a crude form of table tennis. Since then, digitally refined and interactively dynamic computer systems such as Sega, Nintendo, Odyssey, PlayStation, and X-Box have enabled consumers to play practically every mainstream Western sport. Sports games presently account for approximately 20 percent of video game sales in North America, the world's largest gaming market, grossing $8 billion yearly.

Second, virtual sports enthusiasts now have access to physically interactive video games. For example, players may literally "step into" virtual golf courses. A person stands on an Astroturf tee box holding an electronically sensored golf club and swings at a virtual ball. A simulated ball instantaneously appears on a large video screen situated several feet in front of the tee box and flies down the virtual course according to the celerity and spin at which it had been virtually struck. Individuals may play an entire round of golf on the machine, selecting from any number of professional courses. For a cost of $10 to $100, people may also use similar machines to drive virtual race cars, bat against virtual Major League Baseball (MLB) pitchers, shoot virtual basketballs, ride virtual race horses, or even paddle virtual kayaks.

Third, simulated sports environments may be utilized as training tools for elite athletes. Virtual training machines carefully monitor and strictly control the effort levels of athletes in order to study and help improve their physical abilities. For example, swimmers are often placed in "current tanks" to scientifically evaluate the efficiency of their strokes and pinpoint $VO_2(max)$ rates. Elite-level ice hockey players' skating strides are technically studied in laboratories by using treadmills with simulated ice surfaces. Professional cyclists straddle stationary racing bikes in wind rooms and peddle through virtual rides that appear on video screens in front of them, twisting and turning when they go through turns and exerting effort when tackling hills.

KEY EVENTS

The ascendance of virtual sports over the past 30 years points to how a host of social and cultural shifts within Western societies have altered our understandings of embodied athleticism. First, virtual sports are of increasing importance at a time in which both amateur and professional sports are intensely commercialized; that is, sports are viewed as moneymaking practices. Critics of sports suggest that, particularly in Western nations with state-sponsored, rigidly institutionalized and professional sports cultures, the entire sporting experience is fragmented into market commodities (such as pay-per-view television programs, jerseys, video games, and magazines), including sports simulations that allow users to become more actively involved fans. As sports is consumed as a common cultural commodity, sports organizations profit by aggressively tapping home entertainment and gaming markets. Global and national sports organizations such as the International Olympic Committee (IOC), the National Football League (NFL), and the National Basketball Association (NBA), among others, package virtual game experiences for consumers, allowing them to create fantasy leagues and manipulate player performance at the push of a button or thrust of a joystick.

Second, athletic contests are globally promoted as contexts of what some people call social mimesis. Audiences are sold virtual sports as symbols of emotionally charged and risky, yet rule-bound, scenarios of physically intense competition. Because of the openness of the aggression, struggle, and toughness in sports, they provide a type of excitement for audiences that we are not allowed to experience in everyday life at work, home, or in school. Virtual sports games highlight and exaggerate the taken-for-granted physicality and excitement inherent in both mainstream and alternative sports. Extreme hitting, bloodletting, brutal tackling, and flamboyant injuries, for example, are common in virtual sports games. Rules are broken without penalty, virtual players do not experience the catastrophic effects of rough play, and users receive reward incentives within games for the number of on-field hits levied or styles of aggressive play mastered.

Third, the booming popularity of virtual sports games should be contextualized against what we might refer to as the simulation of social reality and experience. Virtual sports games, for instance, create unreal representations of athleticism and transform social constructions of real sports for users. Basketball players are seen in games jumping dozens of feet through the air, skateboarders do impossible tricks, and boxers receive beatings that no athlete could withstand in the real world of sports. Problematically, some argue, the games not only mimic what actually occurs in a sport, they now partially define what audiences expect from embodied sports. A normal sports game is rather boring compared to the incredible action seen and directed by the player of a video game.

Virtual sports games may also be more accessible forms of sports for many users because one can play dozens of sports regardless of one's physical fitness level. Furthermore, one is granted an unprecedented freedom to direct the events and change parameters of an athletic contest at whim (i.e., players involved, physical settings, length of competitions, speed of games, and rule structures). One can play with a team from a historical era, create their own super-players, and square off against legendary opponents. This distorts our nature of reality and what we come to expect from real-time games. Comparatively, for athletes who are plugged into virtual sports machines, simulated sports fields allow for incredible physical exertion without many of the physical dangers inherent in competition. Therefore, performance evaluating or rehabilitating sports machines generate simulated contexts of performance so that athletes may become "swifter, higher, and stronger" during competition.

Fourth, virtual sports underscore how machines and bodies "cybernetically" (the blending of humans and machines) intersect in Western cultures. The social critic Donna Haraway noted, some time ago, that the current historical era is one in which our bodies are increasingly taken over by technology. For Haraway and others, it is difficult to conceive of any social activity, including a full range of sports performances and athletics, that has evaded technological improvement, innovation, control, and monitoring. When individuals are able to kick a soccer ball, catch a baseball, throw a javelin, or perform a ski jump by tapping a computer button or moving the body expressively in a sports-like motion in front of video sensors, one cannot overlook how modern-day forms of athleticism are deeply tied to computer technology.

Fifth, the prominence of virtual sports reflects our widespread cultural preference for stationary, home-based digital entertainment. Virtual sports participation through video game play fits nicely with our inactive North American lifestyles. Virtual sports are a part of the social "sit down" lifestyles widely attributed to long school or work days, poor dietary practices, and exposure to computers as everyday tools. Troublingly, at a time when physical passivity in the leisure sphere and overall obesity rates are on the rise in North America, and as physical education programs are disappearing from educational curricula at all institutional levels, virtual games are a primary form of sports participation for "growing" populations of North Americans.

FUTURE PROSPECTS

The topic of virtual sports has not entirely escaped public concern and debate. In fact, one of the most heated controversies in all of popular culture is the degree to which violent video games, including sports games, promote violence and aggression among youth in North America. Psychologists, sociologists, and anthropologists have all studied the potential link between video game play and aggressive social behavior. This line of research gained tremendous attention after the Columbine High School shooting because the shooters, Eric Harris and Dylan Klebold, were reportedly avid video game players. The bulk of the limited empirical research on virtual sports addresses how exposure to aggressive sports games is correlated with aggressive interpersonal behaviors. Virtual sports are especially targeted in the contemporary moral panic about youth deviance and the consumption of violent video games.

Critics of virtual sports argue that they alienate users from actually enjoying free, embodied athletic experiences and eliminate the socially interactive aspects of competitive sports. Even though people can play video games online with others in virtual space, one might never actually see or occupy the same physical space with someone you play with socially. As critics of virtual sports, the people contend that the companies who develop them only use video games and other virtual sports products as ways of securing fan investment in athletics; that is, video game companies or innovators of training systems that simulate real-world movement do not care if athletes move, they just care if people buy video game products. Furthermore, they argue, virtual sports such as video games discourage the first-hand experience of athleticism in sports and motivate individuals to participate passively via video interface.

Finally, critics of high-performance sports at the Olympics and elsewhere examine the negative impacts of computer technology on athlete training, performance, and rehabilitation. Debra Shogan, for instance, has studied athletes' bodies as things that have been technologically invaded and subjected to penetration/improvement at the hands of therapists, doctors, and trainers. Shogan points out that the relatively new research and academic field of kinesiology in the United States and elsewhere emphasizes the biomechanics and physiology of human performance over the human and spiritual joys of athleticism. Athletes, as the subjects and targets of medical experts and knowledge bases, are strategically crafted into cybernetic entities that resemble carefully engineered machines rather than people. Virtual sports machines used in athletic training or in recreational leisure pursuits blur the boundaries between natural human performance and artificially engineered, biomechanical athletes. We must question why the contemporary athlete is one whose performance is carefully mapped, dissected, analyzed, predicted, and monitored by a full spectrum of computer systems and what this might do to the future of natural human sports.

See also Biology and Athlete Performance; Video Games.

Further Reading: Haraway, D. (1991). *Simians, Cyborgs, and Women: The Reinvention of Nature*. London, UK: Free Association Books; Shogan, D. (1999). *The Making of High Performance Athletes: Discipline, Diversity, and Ethics*. Toronto, ON: University of Toronto Press.

Michael Atkinson

W

WHISTLE-BLOWERS AND DRUGS

Whistle-blowing is the process of drawing public attention to an illegal, contranormative, or surreptitious practice within a group. The person or people doing the whistle-blowing provide(s) inside evidence or allege(s) that something untoward is occurring, normally within an organization. Testimony is typically given to authority figures that have a particular mandate to punish offenders or introduce a new set of policies to curb their behaviors. Whistle-blowing in sports is particularly rare because sports cultures tend to be very tightly knit and socially policed. However, a series of important whistle-blowers regarding the use of illegal drugs in sports have broken the diffuse code of silence in the recent past.

BACKGROUND

Among the many truisms in sport is that one should never, in any circumstance, violate the trust of one's fellow players or coaches. Social scientific research on the nature of sports cultures has consistently documented that sports teams and leagues, especially male, can be likened to esoteric Greek fraternities on college campuses, with the inner workings and cultures of the groups guarded strictly by past and present players. Particularly in team sports, athletes develop deep bonds with one another and often describe their fellow teammates as brothers in arms. It comes as no surprise, then, that athletes who blow the whistle on the surreptitious, lascivious, salacious, or potentially illegal activities are treated as social pariahs within their sports culture.

Two sports most historically plagued by whistle-blowing are college basketball and college football. One of the most recurring reasons for whistle-blowing pertains to the illegal recruitment of high school athletes by universities and colleges. The process of illegally recruiting athletes gained international attention through critical films produced in the 1980s and 1990s such as *Blue Chips, He Got Game, Unnecessary Roughness,* and *The Program*. According to the National Collegiate Athletic Association (NCAA) bylaws, any athlete (their friends, families, or acquaintances included) is ineligible to receive any financial incentive for either considering enrollment in a university/college or for joining a team while at a university/college. This does not mean, however, that top universities adhere to these regulations or fail to exploit loopholes in them. Winning seasons by a high-profile sports team can mean thousands if not millions of increased revenue for an educational institution (not to mention the social accolades and national profile gleaned from winning a national championship in a given sport), so the incentive to violate the no recruitment rule is significant. In 1989, Bruce Pearl, then assistant coach at the University of Iowa, blew the whistle on the University of Illinois. Pearl claimed Illinois illegally recruited star high school basketball player Deon Thomas. Pearl provided the NCAA with audio tapes of a conversation he had with Thomas, detailing the automobile and money Illinois gave Thomas in order to play for their school. The NCAA's investigation did not find any violation with Thomas's recruitment by Illinois, but they did uncover other violations that resulted in a one-year postseason ban from competitive play for Illinois's basketball team. For his whistle-blowing and violation of the code of silence in sports, Pearl was ostracized by other coaches and their players.

In 1999, Janice Gangelhoff similarly blew the whistle on the University of Minnesota's athletics department for the questionable "special treatment" of their athletes. Gangelhoff, who had worked as a basketball office manager at Minnesota, allegedly wrote over 400 term papers or other assignments for Gophers' basketball players from 1993 to 1998. During an internal investigation prompted by Gangelhoff's claims, Minnesota uncovered what its university president called "'the most serious case of academic fraud ever reported to the NCAA." Basketball head coach Clem Haskins "voluntarily" resigned, along with several members of the athletics department's executive team. In one of the harshest punishments levied by the NCAA to date, the school's basketball records (from 1993 to 1998) were expunged from the national records.

In a similar instance of whistle-blowing in college sports, James Gundlach, a professor at Auburn university, blew the whistle on his university athletics department in a 2004 story printed in the *New York Times*. Gundlach exposed the university's secret system of developing reading courses (one-on-one) for star athletes. This was a long-term practice in universities and colleges wherein courses were designed especially for athletes so that they would pass them without substantial effort. Among the most legendary of such courses are so-called rocks for jocks modules offered in Geology departments. Gundlach's claims prompted an internal school investigation, and Auburn eventually altered the manners by which directed reading courses (most notably in its sociology and education departments) could be offered and administered.

While cases of whistle-blowing in colleges and universities have steadily risen since the 1980s, only very recently have whistle-blowers come forward and exposed cases of performance-enhancing drug abuse in sports. Arguably, those stepping forward to expose drug cheats have done so in an era preoccupied with catching drug abusers in sports. The mass mediation and critique of many sports as forever tainted by drug cheating (and the considerable social rewards now offered to whistle-blowers who "name names") has stirred global initiatives in sports to find and punish illegal substance users. At the same time, the burgeoning culture of whistle-blowing in college/university sports may have very well inspired whistle-blowers in other sports settings, showcasing that "snitching" may not be as taboo in contemporary sports cultures.

KEY EVENTS

In the past 10 years, several notorious cases of whistle-blowing on drug cheats have altered the course of elite amateur professional sports training, funding, and sponsorship. They have also shaken public trust in athletic federations or leagues and perhaps forever destroyed the cultural notion that athletes are especially moral people. Published in 2005, former baseball homerun king Jose Canseco's book *Juiced: Wild Times, Rampant 'Roids, Smash Hits and How Baseball Got Big* detailed not only his own prolific career with steroid use but also the extensive culture of drug cheating in the sport. It is, to date, the single most damning set of allegations regarding the manners in which antidoping rules are flagrantly violated by professional athletes. In the book, Canseco claims credit for introducing steroids to baseball (referring to himself as the "Godfather of steroids") and believes he was blackballed and exiled from professional baseball when Major League Baseball (MLB) commissioner Bud Selig decided to cleanse the league of its cheats. Even though Canseco blew the whistle on the culture of drug cheating and named at least a dozen high-profile players as patterned cheats, he still argues that steroid use could improve the entertainment value of the sport. Canseco "names and shames" players such as Mark McGwire, Juan González, Rafael Palmeiro, Iván Rodríguez, Dave Martinez, Tony Saunders, Wilson Alvarez, Jason Giambi, Barry Bonds, Sammy Sosa, Bret Boone, Brady Anderson, Roger Clemens, and Miguel Tejada. He claims that he personally injected McGwire, Palmeiro, González, and Rodríguez with anabolic steroids when they were teammates and that he gave instructional information about steroids to dozens of other players in baseball. Canseco claimed that all levels of the MLB organization had extensive knowledge of steroid use in the mid-1990s but chose not to act in fear of damaging the sport's financial position. In particular, he argued that the rekindling of public interest in the sport following the McGwire–Sosa 1998 home run race could not be jeopardized by a drug scandal.

During the 1998 season, in a popular cultural story that caught the world's attention, Sammy Sosa and Mark McGwire competed to break the home run mark previously set by Roger Maris. By the season's end, Sosa had eclipsed the record with 66 home runs, while McGwire set the single season record by hitting 70 home runs. They continued to battle for home run supremacy in the next season with Barry Bonds entering into the mix two years later. Each was hitting home runs at an incredible pace, and Canseco's book explained why. At the age of 37, Canseco pointed out, how else could Barry Bonds break a home run record?

Following Canseco's startling revelations, confessions, and allegations, professional baseball could no longer ignore the burgeoning problem of steroid abuse. The same year his book reached publication, a specially appointed Congressional panel sought to explore the veracity of Canseco's claims and subsequent revelations about the nutrition center BALCO's role in the steroid distribution industry. In a modern-day McCarthyist investigation into the sport, on March 17, 2005, suspected players including Palmeiro, McGwire, Sosa, Canseco, and Curt Schilling were summoned to testify in front of Congress about their knowledge of illegal substance abuse in the sport. As a result of pressure from Congress, MLB and the Major League Baseball Players Association (MLBPA) began applying stricter regulations and established a zero-tolerance policy regarding performance-enhancing drugs. By 2006, another controversial book *Game of Shadows* was published offering researched claims that Barry Bonds' trainer was providing illegal performance enhancers to Bonds and other athletes. Canseco's revelations and the Congress inquest added evidence to a doping scandal that unearthed the most extensive conspiracy to promote steroid use in sports.

In 2003, owner of the Bay Area Laboratory CoOperative (BALCO) in San Francisco, Victor Conte, was advising top athletes in the United States about their nutritional requirements. His stable of loyal clients had grown considerably and included the star of the 2000 Sydney Olympics, Marion Jones, and the 100-meter world record–holder Tim Montgomery. Rival coach Trevor Graham shepherded a cadre of ultra-elite athletes at the Sprint Capitol Club in North Carolina and believed Conte's BALCO organization was merely a front to supply performance-enhancing drugs to athletes. On June 5, 2003, Graham managed to obtain a sample supplement Conte administered to his athletes (called "The Clear") and mailed a syringe filled with the substance to a personal contact of his (Rich Wanninger) in the U.S. Anti-Doping Agency (USADA). The sample contained a BALCO-designed steroid undetectable by conventional testing procedures. Authorities eventually called the new steroid tetrahydrogestrinone (THG). Amazingly, and in some ways only believable in the world of sports, on the same day that Graham had sent the drug to the USADA, Conte had corresponded with the International Association of Athletics Federations (IAAF) and accused Graham of doping his athletes with anabolic drugs from Mexico.

Federal investigators raided BALCO labs in 2004 and arrested Conte, who was later sentenced to four months in prison for his role in steroid distribution. But neither the drug scandal nor whistle-blowing ended with Conte. Suspicious of Graham, Federal investigators struck a deal with track and field coach Angel Heredia in exchange for his inside information about Trevor Graham's doping activities. In exchange for immunity from prosecution, Heredia told investigators about how he helped to smuggle and distribute steroids into the United States from Mexico at the request of Trevor Graham (to be given to high-profile athletes under Graham's tutelage). By 1997, Heredia had worked with marquee athletes including Tim Montgomery, Marion Jones, Antonio

Pettigrew, CJ Hunter, Jerome Young, and others. Armed with considerable material evidence that Heredia kept and documented about the steroid ring, Federal agents arrested Graham for his pivotal role in one of the most consequential doping schemes in U.S. sports history. Heredia, quite predictably, expressed remorse over his snitching, suggesting that, "I felt I was betraying my oath, the underground oath among athletes."

The BALCO case illustrates how self-protectionist cultural codes of silence in sports have shifted, however slightly. Leagues, federations, and teams do not unanimously operate under a "don't ask, don't tell" social policy regarding drugs. The BALCO scandal also highlights how, given the sheer number of people involved in steroid abuse, cracks in the chain of silence will now inevitably manifest. While whistle-blowing regarding drugs has become a modern reality in sports worlds, whistle-blowers tend to be treated with continued social contempt and alienation.

Jorg Jaksche's whistle-blowing in 2007 in the world of professional cycling underscores how a chilly climate is still present in sports for those who name names. In an interview with the German magazine *SPIEGEL*, he broke the code of silence regarding drug abuse in the sport and publicly admitted to his own patterned use of performance-enhancing drugs. He also revealed that his former team, T-Mobile, fostered a culture of cheating among its athletes. Professional cycling teams have long been accused of facilitating performance-enhancing drug use among their athletes, but rarely has a rider or team trainer substantiated allegations publicly. As a result of the whistle-blowing, Deutsche Telekom (the parent company of T-Mobile) withdrew its funding from professional cycling after 16 years of involvement in the sport.

For his admission, Jaksche received a one-year ban from participation in international cycling. Even more consequential for Jaksche, however, is that when his one-year ban from cycling expires in late 2008, few if any professional teams will seek his services. T-Mobile expressed no interest in rehiring Jaksche despite Deutsche Telekom's public declarations that they should respect him for bravely confronting the issue of doping on the team. Critics of T-Mobile's position argue that their exclusion and ostracism of him only further illustrates how those involved in whistle-blowing effectively terminate their careers.

FUTURE PROSPECTS

Whistle-blowing has the potential to be one of, if not the most, effective techniques of social control in the world of sports in the quest to combat illegal performance-enhancing drug use. Crime control officials in the United States have used criminal insiders (known often as "rats" or "moles") for years in the process of breaking extensive criminal enterprises, and there is every reason to believe that the technique would prove fruitful in sports over the long term. Still, unless more leagues and teams are willing to protect whistle-blowers by developing structures and cultures designed to secure their careers, the process of whistle-blowing should continue to meet with condemnation and threat in sports worlds.

See also Academic Misconduct Among Athletes; Antidoping Rules and Policies; Biology and Athlete Performance; Cheating During Competition; Ergogenics; Marijuana, Alcohol, and Illicit Drugs; Sports Doctors, Trainers, and Drugs; Steroid Use by Athletes.

Further Reading: Asinof, E., and Gould, J. (2000). *Eight Men Out.* New York: Holt; Canseco, J. (2005). *Juiced: Wild Times, Rampant 'Roids, Smash Hits, and How Baseball Got Big.* New York: Harper Entertainment; Canseco, J. (2008). *Vindicated: Big Names, Big Liars, and the Battle to Save Baseball.* New York: Simon Spotlight Entertainment; Fainaru, M., and Williams, L. (2006). *Game of Shadows.* New York: Gotham.

Michael Atkinson

WOMEN AND THE APOLOGETIC

The female apologetic in sports refers to the ways in which women athletes often feel pressured to emphasize their femininity to others. Because sports has been historically defined as masculine territory, women are asked by coaches, corporate sponsors, and others to look, move, and act feminine in order to apologize for participating in this masculine field. In other terms, because of their participation in a masculine activity, women should at least symbolically illustrate how they are not trying to be men or adopt the social roles and power statuses assigned to men. The apologetic can be accomplished, for example, by wearing "girly" clothing in sports, by appearing to be overly heterosexual, and by allowing one's body to be objectified as aesthetically pleasing to audiences.

BACKGROUND

The prevalence of the apologetic in women's sports brings to the forefront the question about whether or not a genderless social interaction is possible. Sports has been certainly cleaved along gender lines since the turn of the twentieth century and continues to be in many respects to this day. However, sports has been increasingly used as a gender battleground where men and women seek to disrupt cultural stereotypes, role expectations, and social power chances assigned to them by their gender status. Critics have suggested that sports might very well be a place where androgyny can be prevalent, and thus, people will no longer be treated therein as different, special, or lesser because of their gender status. By focusing on one's characteristics as an androgynous athlete, rather than a male or female in the social sphere of sports, athletes may be able to transgress one of the chief markers of power and identity in North America.

Androgyny refers to two basic concepts. The first is the mixing of masculine and feminine characteristics and self-representational practices such as fashion. Second, it describes something that is culturally considered as neither inherently masculine nor feminine; for instance, a job as a restaurant cook may be considered a socially androgynous role. Androgynous traits are those that either have no immediate gender value or power in a society, then, or have some aspects generally attributed to the opposite gender. Physiological androgyny is distinct from *behavioral* androgyny, which deals with personal and social anomalies in gender, and from *psychological* androgyny, which is a matter of one's perceived self and socially recognized gender identity.

Still, androgyny is seen as a relatively unique gender role identity that consists of a balance of positive feminine and positive male traits. It is thought to be a balanced social identity that combines the virtues of both genders. However, gender stereotypes do not include only desirable aspects of femininity and masculinity. Socially undesirable feminine and masculine traits are also important to gender stereotypes and may even be dominant. Logically then, an androgynous gender role identity may also consist of a balance of negative genders and thus creates the possibility of an undesirable or negatively androgynous gender role identity.

To say that a culture or social institution is one that values androgyny is to say that it lacks rigid gender roles and that the people involved display characteristics or partake in activities traditionally associated with the other gender. The term *androgynous* in this vein is often used to refer to a person whose look or build make determining their gender difficult. Importantly, when people of a particular culture are difficult to read as gendered beings, it becomes difficult to discriminate against them within a culture along gender (and sex) lines. One might argue that only by moving toward a degendered, androgynous culture can power differences and inequality between people ever be achieved.

During the counterculture revolution in North America during the 1960s, music and fashion industries inspired an androgynous trend toward self-exploration, sexual experimentation and self-definition, individual freedom, and self-realization. The first North American women's liberation movement of the 1970s refuted the idea that women were naturally passive, emotional, and weaker than men and should be assigned to appropriate social roles as a result. The gay liberation movements of the 1970s and 1980s also embraced the idea of androgyny because it allowed lesbians and gay men to show their often mixed gender characteristics openly in society. The spread of the North American androgyny movement has been, arguably, fueled by the economic transformation of the workforce in developed countries. As nations became more affluent, a greater amount of energy was required for production, thus businesses demanded a larger number of workers (men and women) in the workforce. The economic situations of wealthy nations enabled women to work with men as equals due to the current elevated women's status in male-oriented societies. Similarly, the restructuring of families in North America from the 1960s onward to accommodate women's entrance into workforces also impacted what is viewed as a male or female social role.

Evidence of androgyny being embraced by North American society appears everywhere, including in institutionalized entertainment and fashion cultures and, more explicitly, in expanding gay and lesbian communities. As trendsetters, entertainment and fashion industries have played an influential role in advancing a challenging perspective on human gender and sexuality for modern times. The fashion industry promoted the meteoric rises of fashion designers—Helmut Lang, Giorgio Armani, Pierre Cardin, to name a few—for their unisex-styled clothes. To this day, glamorous male and female models sporting androgynous garments have often been found on catwalks or posing for the covers of fashion magazines. Recently, the cosmetic companies have joined in to lure *metrosexuals* (aesthetically conscientious straight men) to the lucrative markets of beauty products, which once were considered exclusively for women.

Because sports can underline the supposed natural physiological differences between men and women, and has been historically a social institution where power between men and women is symbolically played out, it makes sense that North Americans typically view sports and athleticism as masculine and dominant rather than feminine. Yet, as women participated in sports in increasing numbers over the course of the twentieth century, notions about what constitutes male and female roles and identities were challenged. Women athletes of the 1970s and 1980s, such as tennis player Martina Navratilova, eschewed simplistic dichotomies between male and female; Navratilova displayed her own brand of androgynous female-masculinity in the sport. Questions were raised that asked if a woman could excel in sports as physically strong and dominant, why couldn't a woman excel in other masculine social roles and institutions?

Sports and sports fans often responded to the encroachment of women into sports and the blurring of gender boundaries and roles therein with a backlash. In certain sports, women were expressly told to be less androgynous and to engage in a sort of "emphasized femininity" (Connell, 2005) or to practice the apologetic. If they did not, they would be released from teams and dropped by sponsors, or the very rules of their sports would be altered to make their games less rigorous and demanding than men's. Ask yourself why, for example, women tennis players at Wimbledon only play the best two out of three sets during a match, while men's matches are the best three of five sets. Ask yourself why, in the sport of professional volleyball, women are regulated to wear revealing two-piece bathing suits, while the men wear tank tops and baggy shorts.

KEY EVENTS

There is practically no better example in the world of sports that illustrates the battle about gender, androgyny, and the deployment of the apologetic than women's professional bodybuilding. Physique contests for women in North America date back to at least the 1960s, with contests such as the Miss Physique and Miss Americana. However, these early bodybuilding contests were little more than bikini contests. The first American Women's National Physique Championship in 1978 is generally regarded as the first "pure" female bodybuilding contest, that is, the first contest where the entrants were judged solely on muscularity like their male counterparts in the sport. More of these contests appeared as early as 1979 and drew much public interest and concern about the gendered messages being sent to young men and women about how a female body should look.

While the early events were regarded as authentic bodybuilding contests, the women were asked to appear on competitive stages wearing high-heeled shoes and bikinis, and they were told not to flex their muscles. Additionally, they were

A COINCIDENCE?

A 2007 poll conducted among college students in the United States produced a list of the most popular/favorite female athletes. Eighteen women on the list were also featured that same year in *Maxim* magazine as the "hottest women in sport."

25. Anna Rawson (LPGA)
24. Swin Cash (WNBA)
23. Tanith Belbin (Figure Skating)
22. Jennifer Barretta (Billiards)
21. Malia Jones (Surfing)
20. Michelle Wie (LPGA)
19. Ashley Force (Drag Racing)
18. Sasha Cohen (Figure Skating)
17. Niki Gudex (Mountain Biking)
16. Lokelani McMichael (Triathlete)
15. Lindsey Kildow (Skiing)
14. Maria Kirilenko (Tennis)
13. Amy Acuff (Track and Field)
12. Natalie Gulbis (LPGA)
11. Anna Kournikova (Tennis)
10. Heather Mitts (Soccer)
9. Maria Sharapova (Tennis)
8. Sophie Sandolo (LPGA)
7. Ana Paula Mancino (Beach Volleyball)
6. Milene Domingues (Soccer)
5. Allison Stokke (Pole Vaulting)
4. Ashley Constantini (Softball)
3. Amanda Beard (Swimming)
2. Gretchen Bleiler (Snowboarding)
1. Kristi Leskinen (Skiing)

not allowed to use the majority of men's poses that would highlight their size, such as the front double biceps flex, crab flex, and lateral spread.

The first Ms. Olympia (initially known as the "Miss Olympia") was established in 1980 as the most prestigious contest for women professionals. Initially, potential entrants were asked to send in resumes and pictures that the organizing committee would scrutinize for their audience appeal. The first winner of Ms. Olympia was Rachel McLish. McLish turned out to be a very marketable figure in the sport because of her overt femininity. But as the sport grew, the competitors' level of training gradually increased (most of the competitors in the earliest shows had very little weight training experience), and the sport slowly evolved toward more muscular, masculine-looking physiques. During this period more of the competitors experimented with anabolic steroids. The

1985 movie *Pumping Iron II: The Women* (a variation of a documentary about male bodybuilding culture in California starring a young Arnold Schwarzenegger) was released. This film documented the preparation of several women for the 1983 Caesars Palace World Cup Championship. Competitors prominently featured in the film were Kris Alexander, Lori Bowen, Lydia Cheng, Carla Dunlap, Bev Francis, and Rachel McLish. Mainstream sports media interest grew, and television company ABC often featured highlights from professional contests on their weekly "Wide World of Sports" program.

The 1992 Ms. International contest proved to be a pivotal battleground event in the sport's history. Somewhat dismayed by growing public criticism of the sport as grotesque (meaning unfeminine) and allegations that the women appeared to be more masculine than feminine, the International Federation of Body Builders (IFBB) made an attempt to feminize the sport and used the Ms. International competition as a watershed event in that regard. The IFBB, led by bodybuilding icon Ben Weider, created and instituted a series of femininity rules to be enforced during judging; one line in the judging rules said that competitors should not be too muscular, while other lines focused on sex appeal and overall appearance. The judges' guide to the competitors stated that they were looking for a feminine but not emaciated physique. The contest winner was Germany's Anja Schreiner, a blue-eyed blonde with a symmetrical physique who weighed only 130 pounds at 5′7″. Observers felt that the IFBB had instructed the judges to select the most marketable contestant, not the best bodybuilding physique.

Following events in 1992, the judging rules were once again rewritten. The new rules retained central provisions for aesthetics but allowed the contests to be judged as physique contests, not beauty pageants. Nevertheless, the IFBB had altered the course of the sport and clearly emphasized a tone of the apologetic in the sport. By 2000, the IFBB introduced several new changes to female bodybuilding, including amended judging guidelines for athlete presentation. Women would, once again, be judged increasingly on feminine attributes such as healthy appearance, face, make-up, and skin tone. No such criteria have ever been instituted in men's bodybuilding. Also indicated in the new rules was that women would be negatively assessed for atypical or extreme muscularity, characteristics revered in the men's sport. An even more aggressive feminine rule change occurred in 2005 when IFBB Chairman Jim Manion introduced the 20 percent rule, which stated that athletes in women's bodybuilding under the control of IFBB were to decrease the amount of their muscularity by a factor of 20 percent. Additionally, they would be dismantling the weight-class system in the sport, effectively sending out the message that larger women would no longer be able to win major competitions.

Through the late 1990s and early 2000s, two other categories of more feminine forms of body competition developed under the IFBB, fitness competitions (where athletes are judged as part bodybuilders, part gymnasts, part models, and part rhythmic dancers) and figure competitions (where athletes are mainly judged as toned models. Contemporary critics have argued that these iterations of the sport are merely sexist, male-oriented "skin shows."

One of the most notable mainstream battles over gender, androgyny, and the apologetic pitted tennis player Martina Navratilova against others in her sport. Navratilova, a muscular and powerful player who openly talked about her intense physical training regimen (and as of 1980, an openly gay athlete in the sport), symbolically played out the battle between femininity and androgyny with, among other players, long-time rival and American "sweetheart" Chris Evert. For more than 10 years, beginning in 1973, the two met more than 80 times and were often pitted against one another in the media as the female hero (Evert) and antihero (Navratilova). In this instance, Navratilova's irreverence to the apologetic and drift toward androgyny cost her financially. Despite her winning record, Navratilova had more difficulty receiving endorsement and sponsorship contracts in comparison to Evert.

FUTURE PROSPECTS

One might argue that the existence of the apologetic in sports owes more to media construction, academic interpretation, and myth than reality. Others might suggest that the pressure some women feel to engage in the apologetic comes down to a personal matter or is very isolated to certain individuals rather than entire sports cultures. Nevertheless, it is difficult to ignore how a series of women's sports, as they move toward more androgynous or gender "deviant" cultures, are reacted to negatively by insiders and outsiders. Few people would argue that traditional, sexualized images of women in sports do not sell more than androgynous images and that sports continues to be a social institution where clear boundaries between genders are created and reinforced. As long as North American society chooses to value gender as a chief marker of identity and as a source of social power, women (and men) athletes who become more androgynous in sports will most likely continue to engage in apologetic practices for some time to come.

See also Biology and Athlete Performance; Gay Games; Gender and Educational Opportunities; Gender and Game Rules; Homophobia; LGBT Sports Leagues; Marketing Female Athlete Sexuality; Openly Gay Athletes; Transsexual Athletes; Ubersexuality; Women in Men's Sports; Women Sportscasters.

Further Reading: Bem, S. (1974). The Measurement of Psychological Androgyny. *Journal of Consulting and Clinical Psychology* 42: 155–162; Birrel S., and Theberge, N. (1994). Ideological Control of Women in Sport. In *Women and Sport. Interdisciplinary Perspectives,* edited by D. Costa and S. Guthrie, 341–360. Champaign, IL: Human Kinetics; Connell, R. (2005). *Gender.* Oxford: Polity Press; Griffin. P. (1998). *Strong Women, Deep Closets: Lesbians and Homophobia in Sport.* Champaign, IL: Human Kinetics; Lowe, M. (1998). *Women of Steel: Female Bodybuilding and the Struggle for Self-Definition.* New York: New York University Press; Wughalter, E. (1978). Ruffles and Flounces: The Apologetic in Women's Sports. *Frontiers: A Journal of Women Studies* 3 (1): 11–13.

Michael Atkinson

WOMEN COACHES AND OWNERS

Sports has been widely recognized as a gendered arena. Certain sports, including synchronized swimming, figure skating, and field hockey, have historically been associated with women, while other sports, including football, baseball, and wrestling, have been associated with men. Aesthetic sports, for example gymnastics and figure skating, emphasize grace and form and are considered to be feminine, in contrast to those sports that stress strength and power, for example rugby, and are considered masculine. It would therefore seem natural that women become the coaches or administrators of aesthetic sports activities and men of masculine sports. Yet, with help from gender equity initiatives in sports, such as Title IX, more girls and women are participating in traditionally perceived masculine sports at all levels. This has led to more women gaining experience competing at the international level, which theoretically should lead to more women becoming involved in coaching, sports administration, and even ownership of teams. However, historically this has not been the case.

Athletic coaches and team owners are expected to prepare athletes for competition and provide them with the guidance and tools necessary to succeed. Due to the inherent nature of these professions, they have traditionally been perceived as male occupations because men have been considered the logical choice to take the lead, make decisions, and be instrumental in a team's success. Both coaching and ownership require superior knowledge of the skills, techniques, and tactics associated with the specific sport. Because men have traditionally been considered superior athletes, they are therefore considered more naturally associated with coaching and team ownership. An underlying ideology exists that the images of the ideal coach and team owner are associated with masculinity, and thus, men have dominated the realm of coaching and team ownership.

BACKGROUND

Sports has traditionally been an arena reserved for men to display their masculinity. It has widely been considered an ideal venue to create men out of boys. Even dating back to ancient Greece, at the Crown Games at Olympia male athletes battled against one another, sometimes to the death, to honor their families and cities and to publicly display their physical prowess. Women, on the other hand, were largely barred from the sacred site, except the High Priestess of

---

DID YOU KNOW?

Athletes at the Ancient Olympic Games did not wear clothing. Instead, competitors rubbed olive oil over their bodies and then sprinkled themselves with fine-grained sand. Some have suggested that the rubbing of the oil helped warm up and limber the muscles, prevented the loss of body fluids during exercise, and protected the skin from the sun and elements. The oil also produced a glistening body that was aesthetically pleasing and desirable.

Demiter and female virgin spectators. So strict were the rules regarding female spectators that violators faced potential execution, "On the road to Olympia … there is a precipitous mountain with lofty cliffs … the mountain is called Typaeum. It is a law of Elis that any woman who is discovered at the Olympic Games will be pitched headlong from this mountain."

It was here at Olympia that we learn of the first female "coach." Pherenike, daughter of Diagoros the famous boxer from Rhodes, disguised herself as a trainer to attend the Games at Olympia to watch her son Pisidorus compete in the boxing event. When he won, Pherenike was exhilarated and rushed forward to celebrate with her son. However, during her excitement Pherenike's cloak fell off and revealed that she was indeed a woman. While the penalty should have been death, the judges forgave her because her father, her brothers, and now her son were all Olympic victors. To prevent future embarrassment, all trainers were then required to appear naked, the same as the athletes.

It is also in ancient Greece that the first recorded female owners existed. While women were not permitted to compete at the Olympic Games, they could, however, own horses and were allowed to enter their teams in the chariot events. The first and most famous owner was Kyniska, the daughter of King Archidamos of Sparta. Kyniska's horses won at the Games in Olympia and some have claimed that she was a feminist, a woman who proved that women could perform the same tasks as men given the opportunity. Others, however, have argued that in fact it was her brother who used her name to prove that winning at the Olympic Games in the chariot events was done solely with money, not skill.

There have been other women throughout history who have been involved in sports other than as athletes. During the Renaissance, socially elite women commonly owned hawks for the sport of hunting. However, women's involvement in sports prior to the turn of the twentieth century was largely designed to develop their bodies to become wives and mothers. As such, female coaches, or physical educators, refrained from instructing women on the finer skills of competitive sports. One woman in particular, Swedish-born Martina Bergman-Osterberg, was instrumental in the development of young girls and women for their inevitable domestic responsibilities. Bergman-Osterberg arrived in 1881 in England and soon became the director of physical education in which she established an education system to instruct young women on the strategies and tactics involved in physical fitness and training.

KEY EVENTS

It was not until after the turn of the twentieth century that more women became involved in competitive coaching and athletic team ownership. However, the increased professionalization of women's sports has led to fewer women being involved in competitive coaching. For example, prior to Title IX, women coached more than 90 percent of women's college teams, but in 2008, women held less than 43 percent of these positions.

There have been notable female coaches and sports team owners during the later half of the twentieth century and beginning of the twenty-first. One of the most famous professional coaches is Ashley Reneé McElhiney. A former college basketball player at Vanderbilt University in Nashville, Tennessee, McElhiney won numerous awards for her athletic excellence, including Most Outstanding Defensive Player from 2001–2003, and she was named Tennessee State Amateur Athlete of the Year for 2002. At the end of her college career she was drafted in the third round of the 2003 Women's National Basketball Association (WNBA) Draft by the Indiana Fever, but she never played and was released before the season began. She was then hired to coach the Nashville Rhythm of the American Basketball Association (ABA) for the 2004–2005 season; this made her the first female coach of a male professional basketball team. Her career with the Rhythm was short lived, however; at the end of the season, McElhiney quit to take a position at the University of Alabama as the director of women's basketball operations.

Another notable female coach who has worked with men's athletic programs is Penny Chuter. Penelope Ann Chuter was an international rower during the early 1960s; her best performance came at the 1962 European championships where she won a silver medal in the single sculls event. In 1973, she was hired by the Amateur Rowing Association to be the head coach for the British women's crews. They were so impressed with her coaching abilities that, in 1978, she was promoted to work with the British men's program to serve as the head coach of the junior men's international team and then to coach the senior men's eight in 1979. Chuter became the first British woman to coach international men's crews.

One of the earliest female sports team owners was Effa Manley. With her husband, Abe, Manley was co-owner of the Negro League baseball team the Newark Eagles during the 1930s and 1940s. Known as a players' advocate, she negotiated for better schedules, travel, and salaries. As a testament to her fight for better working conditions for athletes, Manley was said to have provided the Eagles with an air-conditioned bus for travel, a first for the Negro Leagues.

Another famous female owner was Marge Schott, who purchased the Major League Baseball (MLB) team the Cincinnati Reds in December 1984. While Schott was passionate about the team she owned and loved, she had a tumultuous tenure with the Reds. In 1993, Schott was fined $25,000 and suspended from operating the team for one year after she was quoted in the *New York Times* using racial slurs and indicating that Adolf Hitler was initially good for Germany. After her return to baseball a year later, her relationship with the Reds was fraught with controversy. In 1999, she was convinced to sell her shares of the team.

In April 1979, Georgia Frontiere became the primary shareholder of the Los Angeles Rams after her husband, Carroll Rosenbloom, drowned while swimming near his Florida home. In 1995, Frontiere moved the team to St. Louis, and they won the Super Bowl five years later.

FUTURE PROSPECTS

Despite the introduction of gender equity legislation throughout a large percentage of the world, women remain underrepresented in the roles of coaching and sports administration. There are significant barriers that women face if they choose to become coaches or sports team owners, including social, institutional, organizational, and family responsibilities. Additionally, sports management scholars have also suggested obstacles including perceptions of the success of the old boys' network and a lack of support systems for women; administrators' perceptions of the lack of qualified female coaches; burnout; athletes' preferences for a male coach; and male coaches becoming increasingly interested in coaching women's teams. Arguably, all of these reasons have resulted in women avoiding careers in coaching.

Although female owners still face the challenge of negotiating their time between family and work, team ownership has a different set of obstacles for women. Historically, access to influential positions has been gendered and frequently favors men, while women have had difficulty gaining access to power networks. Additionally, many people believe that women should not act like men. Men are expected to be aggressive, assertive, and able to take control; these are considered paramount to success in sports administration. Women, by contrast, are to be nurturing, caring, and understanding. If women do act like men and display these traits, they risk not being taken seriously by their male colleagues, the media, or their employees. However, if a woman does display stereotypical feminine characteristics in her job as a team owner, she also faces the same risk of not being taken seriously by her male colleagues, the media, or her employees.

See also Funding Equality Legislation; Gender and Educational Opportunities; Gender and Game Rules; Sport for All and Fair Play Leagues; Women and the Apologetic; Women Sportscasters.

Further Reading: Acker, J. (October 1998). The Future of "Gender and Organizations": Connections and Boundaries. *Gender, Work and Organization* 5 (4): 195–206; Carpenter, L. J., and Vivian Acosta, R. Women in Intercollegiate Sport: A Longitudinal, National Study Thirty One Year Update 1977–2008. http://webpages.charter.net/womeninsport/2008%20Summary%20Final.pdf; Guttmann, A. (1991). *Women's Sports: A History.* New York: Columbia University Press; Shaw, S. (2000). The Construction of Gender Relations in Sport Organisations. Ph.D Dissertation. De Montfort University, England; Staurowsky, E. J. (1990). Women Coaching Male Athletes. In *Sport, Men, and the Gender Order: Critical Feminist Perspectives,* edited by M. Messner and D. Sabo, 163–170. Champaign, IL: Human Kinetics; Theberge, N. (August 1993). The Construction of Gender in Sport: Women, Coaching, and the Naturalization of Difference. *Social Problems* 40: 301–313; West, A., and Brackenridge, C. (1990). *A Report on the Issues Relating to Women's Lives as Sports Coaches in the United Kingdom, 1989/90.* Sheffield: Sheffield City Polytechnic and PAVIC Publications.

Amanda N. Schweinbenz

WOMEN IN MEN'S SPORTS

Along with the military, sports remain one of the last social institutions that is almost exclusively underpinned by and socially performed through hypermasculinity codes and ideologies. Increased participation by women in the socially protected male terrain of sports over the course of the twentieth century has led to debates about dominant cultural constructions of masculinity and femininity and the role of sports in reaffirming a traditional, hegemonic masculinity in young men. We might consider that women's "encroachment" into sports may be considered a social and gender boundary crossing in two main ways. First, by their very participation in hypermale sports such as boxing, football, rugby, and ice hockey, women have tacitly and explicitly resisted dominant constructions of docile femininity. Second, through girls' and women's participation alongside men in situated contexts of competitive sports, key questions about so-called essentialist differences between men and women have been raised.

BACKGROUND

Until rather recently, dominant social/male constructions of women in sports have mirrored the sentiments expressed by Baron Pierre de Coubertin (founder of the modern Olympic Games). In 1898, de Coubertin argued:

> I am opposed to the indecency, ugliness, and impropriety of women in sports because women engaging in strenuous activities are destroying their feminine charm and leading to the downfall and degradation of sport. Would sports practices by women constitute an edifying sight before crowds assembled for an Olympiad? Such is not the IOC's [International Olympic Committee] idea of the Olympic Games in which we have tried to achieve the solemn and periodic exaltation of male athleticism with internationalism as a base, loyalty as a means, art for its setting, and female applause as its reward.

De Coubertin's words smack with historically pervasive essentialist or biologically determinist views about gender and sexuality that have served to exclude women from sports. *Biological determinism* is a worldview that believes one's genetics determine not only one's physical form but also one's moral and ethical capabilities and the social roles one is predestined to perform. Biological determinism leads to the belief in *essentialism,* which posits that humans are, in essence, differently capable of social tasks and behaviors as a result of their genetics. Of course, patriarchal cultures in the West have long used *scientific essentialism* to justify men's roles as leaders, aggressors, workers, and intellectuals, and in other powerful roles. Stated differently, essentialism places men at the top of the social hierarchy by arguing that they possess the requisite genetic materials. Men are thus given the mandate to rule economically, politically, and domestically. A common corollary belief is that while men are physically and rationally superior, women are morally superior or emotionally more nurturing than men. Such a belief has often been used to give women a sense of power in the role of morality enforcer (family steward) and emotional caregiver, qualities not needed, one might argue, in power and performance sports.

Masculine and feminine traits have thus been culturally placed in opposition to each other and claimed to complement each other and result in harmony when men and women are constrained within the accepted sex roles. Masculine roles differ across societies but are nearly always portrayed as not only different from but also superior to the feminine. Women and men who transgress the social boundaries of the accepted sex roles are considered "not real" men or women, and they are usually denigrated and sometimes abused and punished by outraged defenders of normative sex roles. Such has been the case, historically, in the masculine defined and defended world of sports.

From the turn of the nineteenth century until the late 1980s, women's sports has been culturally defined and socially performed in dramatically different ways than men's. Very few women competed in sports until the late nineteenth and early twentieth century, when social changes in North America favored increased female participation in society as "equals" with men. However, women's participation in an overtly male terrain would be discouraged along largely essentialist lines. Donald Walker's 1837 book, *Exercise for Ladies,* warned women against horseback riding and other sports because it deforms the lower part of the body (i.e., a woman's reproductive abilities). Catherine Beecher's book *Physiology and Calisthenics for Schools and Families* (1856) is regarded as the first fitness manual for women, but it similarly contains cautionary tones about "too much" physical exertion by women. In 1865, Matthew Vassar helped to found Vassar College, which had a special School of Physical Training with classes in riding, gardening, swimming, boating, and skating for women, each designed to enhance the "physical accomplishments suitable for ladies to acquire … bodily strength and grace." A year later, Vassar College fielded the first two women's amateur baseball teams. Between 1866 and the early 1970s, women participated in predominantly amateur, club, or scholastic sports, with few opportunities to compete as professional athletes. Separate governing bodies, leagues, and rule structures served to define women's sports as "lesser" quality and seriousness than men's games. For example, in 1917, the American Physical Education Association formed a Committee on Women's Athletics to draft standardized, separate rules for women's collegiate field hockey, swimming, track and field, and soccer.

Until the late 1970s and early 1980s, women's (mass) involvement in sports remained localized to a few traditionally feminine (or, at least, not overtly masculine) groups. Sports such as gymnastics, swimming, equestrian, tennis, golf, and running have been historically popular. Even though women have participated in boxing, ice hockey, lacrosse, rugby, and other symbolically masculine sports since the nineteenth century, the number of women involved was statistically rather small until the last two decades. Certainly, the participation of women in men's sports (and thus participation in men's social roles) has been limited or constrained considerably; even more limited have been opportunities for women to play alongside men in an amateur or professional sports contest.

Consider a recent example of how enduring essentialist/determinist ideologies play out in the world of college sports. In mid-July of 2000 a U.S. Court in

Richmond, ruled that one-time football placekicker hopeful at Duke University, Heather Mercer, could legally pursue a discrimination case against Duke University and its football coach Fred Goldsmith. As an all-state high school kicker from Yorktown Heights, New York, Mercer had helped her team win the state championship in 1993. She then tried to walk on at Duke in the fall of 1994. Mercer was turned away for two seasons, but when she kicked the game-winning 28-yarder in the annual Blue-White intrasquad scrimmage in 1995, Coach Goldsmith told her she had earned a place on the team. But over the summer, it seemed, Goldsmith had a change of heart and allegedly told Mercer that she should be "entering beauty pageants" instead of playing football at Duke. Mercer graduated in 1998 without ever playing for the team, thus ending her dream to start as the team's placekicker. Mercer sued Duke for violating her right to play for the team. While Mercer remained sidelined at Duke, Liz Heaston suited up as a placekicker during her junior year at Willamette University (WU). According to WU's sports information director Cliff Voliva, the team's regular kicker was injured in their season's second week, and All-American soccer team star Heaston stepped in to fill the role.

Heather Mercer won a $2 million suit against Duke in 2001, but the decision was overturned by the U.S. Court of Appeals later that same year. As part of a sporting blacklash against female athletes in the National Collegiate Athletic Association (NCAA), the University of Minnesota refused to allow junior Mary Nystrom to try out for a position as a kicker/punter for its football team in 2003, citing the lawsuit by Heather Mercer against Duke as its justification (i.e., they were afraid of being sued if Mary did not qualify to join the team). Interestingly enough, under Title IX provisions, a university can automatically disqualify a woman from a male team if the sport in question is a contact sport (a debate that curiously did not arise in the Mercer case). But in 2005, Katie Hnida played as a reserve kicker for the University of Colorado football team, illustrating once again that the place of women on a men's sports team remains hotly contested and multiply defined.

KEY EVENTS

We must not forget that in the veritable birthplace of organized sports—ancient Greece—women were prohibited from participating in, or even watching (unless one was a virgin or prostitute), the Olympic Games. Instead, the Greeks' ancient Heraea Games is arguably the first sanctioned (and recorded) women's athletic competition to be held. Staged just prior to the men's Olympic contests, the Heraea Games are dated as early as the tenth century B.C.E. Like the men's Olympic contents, Heraea originally consisted of foot races only, involving only the most physically gifted women. The Stadium of Olympis was made available for them but the length of the course was shortened by about one-sixth. The ancient practice of changing the rules (i.e., time, distance) of a contest to accommodate for women is a social practice that remains until this day. Heraea champions were adorned with olive crowns, cow or ox meat from an animal sacrificed to Hera, and were lauded with statues at Hera's temple.

Women were not included in the first modern Olympic Games in 1894 because the all-male International Olympic Committee (IOC) deemed them unwelcome to participate in international athletics, and there is debate whether women were actually included in the 1900 Games in Paris. In 1900, the World Exhibition in Paris precisely coincided, to the days, with the staging of the Games in Paris (from May 14 to October 28). The two events were considered by athletes and audiences as virtually inseparable. For women athletes, this created a noteworthy opportunity because the organizers of the World Exhibition seemed unconcerned about the social taboo of women competing in the masculine world of sports. To this day there is still confusion as to which events participated in by women were Olympic and which were World Fair events. Consensus among historians is that women participated in three sports: tennis, yachting and golf. However, programs from the Paris Exposition show that women also

WOMEN'S PARTICIPATION AT THE SUMMER OLYMPIC GAMES IN THE TWENTIETH CENTURY

Year	Sports	Events	Countries	Athletes
1900	2	3	5	19
1904	1	2	1	6
1908	2	3	4	36
1912	2	6	11	57
1920	2	6	13	77
1924	3	11	20	136
1928	4	15	26	290
1932	3	14	18	127
1936	4	15	26	328
1948	5	19	33	385
1952	6	25	51	518
1956	6	26	39	384
1960	6	29	45	610
1964	7	33	53	683
1968	7	39	54	781
1972	8	43	65	1058
1976	11	49	66	1247
1980	12	50	54	1125
1984	14	62	94	1567
1988	17	86	117	2186
1992	19	98	136	2708
1996	21	108	169	3626
2000	25	132	199	4069

participated in ballooning, croquet, and equestrian events. While it is unclear which events were considered fully Olympic in 1900, the Games slowly began to include more female athletes over the course of the century. Still, the Olympics are heavily slanted toward the representation of males and masculinity (nearly 60% of Olympians at the Games are male) with the bulk of media coverage devoted to men's Olympic sports (in North America, men's Olympic sports receive upward of 90% of television coverage). Further, it was not until 1981 that the IOC included even one woman on its board. Other forms of lingering essentialism existed at the Games; for example, between 1928 and 1956 the women's 800-meter running race was only held once because it was actually declared unsafe for women and thus banned until 1960. Women did not participate in wrestling (among the most ancient sports played at the Games) until 2004, and women are still not allowed to box at the Games.

During the early twentieth century, track and field, regarded as the premier Olympic (male) sport, provided the biggest metaphorical hurdle of all for women at the Olympics. As one of the earliest resistance or feminist movements in North American sports history, women established their own Olympic Games during the early 1920s following the lead of their organizer, Alice Milliat of France. A translator by profession, a rower and sports administrator by avocation, Milliat was founder and president of La Fédération Sportive Féminine Internationale (FSFI). She started the Women's Games in direct response to the repeated refusal of the IOC and the International Amateur Athletic Federation (IAAF) to put women's track and field on the program of the Olympic Games. The first "Women's Olympic Games" were held as a one-day event in Paris in 1922 in front of 20,000 spectators. The second Games were held in Gothenberg, Sweden, in 1926. The success of the Games drew attention from the IOC and the IAAF. Representatives from the two organizations met with Milliat, and in exchange for FSFI's name changing of their Games to the "Women's World Games," the IOC and IAAF would place 10 track and field events on the 1928 Olympic program in Amsterdam (though they later reduced this number to five). Angered by the apparent "selling out" to the IOC, the British Women's Athletics Association balked at the IOC's gesture of inclusion and boycotted the Amsterdam Games it was the only feminist boycott in Olympic history. The Women's Olympic Games have often escaped collective memories about twentieth-century sports, but they were incredibly important as an international focal point for feminist efforts to improve women's sporting opportunities.

Fast-forwarding over several decades of women's amateur sports in North America, the most significant breakthrough at the professional level occurred in 1997, when the National Basketball Association (NBA) announced the establishment of the Women's NBA (WNBA). The WNBA began its first season on June 21, 1997, receiving only marginal attention, media coverage, or public accolade. Not the only league of its kind (the Women's Pro Basketball League, and American Basketball League [ABL] had also been in operation), the WNBA struggled for legitimacy in a male-dominated professional sports culture in North America. When the ABL collapsed in 1999 and marquee players were signed to WNBA teams, the overall quality and style of the game improved, drawing larger audience numbers. The 1999 player lockout in the NBA also served to bolster WNBA ratings and attendance figures.

When the WNBA entered into its 11th season in 2007, it became the only team-oriented women's professional sports league to exist for more than 10 consecutive seasons and proof that women's professional sports could be financially viable in the United States. Still, the relative low pay (for U.S. professional athletes), sexism, and homophobia often directed toward players; the lack of media exposure of the league; and the general public indifference to the sport have served as stark reminders that not all is equal in professional basketball. Even the rules in the WNBA contain some interesting illustrations that essentialism may still be at work in sports. The three-point line is closer to the basket than in the NBA, the ball is smaller, and games are 40 minutes rather than 48 minutes.

Apart from Olympic sports and the WNBA's legitimacy as an authentic professional sports league, women's participation in boxing continues to be a flashpoint issue in North American sports cultures. Women's boxing has roots in the United Kingdom dating back to the eighteenth century and, in the United States, at least back to the 1880s. By the 1890s, carnivals and open fairs on the East Coast of the United States were advertising "Lady Boxing Attractions" and featured side-show circuit celebrities such as Anna Lewis and Hattie Stewart, Mabel Hatfield and Dolly Adams. Controversy and comedy resulted in 1892 when Hessie Donahue sparred a few rounds with then men's heavyweight champion John Sullivan as part of a staged exhibition. Donahue landed a strong punch on Sullivan, knocking him out for over a minute. Twelve years later, and amidst considerable public debate about women's roles in this incredibly barbaric and contrafeminine sport, women's boxing first appeared in the Olympic Games at a demonstration bout in 1904. Boxing relatively disappeared from the landscape of women's sports until the 1970s. During the 1980s, women's boxing resurfaced in California, but the real resurgence of women's boxing came during the 1990s. Boxers including Stephanie Jaramillo, Delia Gonzalez, Laura Serrano, Christy Martin, Deirdre Gogarty, Laila Ali, Jackie Frazier-Lyde, Lucia Rijker, Ada Velez, Ivonne Caples, Bonnie Canino, and Sumya Anani, all world champions, have helped to redefine a woman's "place in the ring." Still, enduring cultural stereotypes about women's involvement in the sport cloud it because neoconservative sports critics decry women's boxing as patently and genetically unnatural.

Noteworthy trailblazers into the world of men's sports include a handful of athletes who have ventured directly onto the playing field with men. Manon Rheaume gained notoriety in 1992 and 1993 when she became the first woman to play in the National Hockey League (NHL). Rheaume, a goaltender, played three exhibition games for the Tampa Bay Lighting. In 2003, Wickenheiser became the first woman to suit up in a men's professional hockey league at a position other than goalie when she played for HC Salamat in Finland. During this season, she also became the first woman to score a goal playing in a men's professional league. Her transition to the league did not proceed smoothly, though. Wickenheiser was initially signed to play in Italy, until the Italian Winter Sports Federation ruled that women were ineligible to play in a men's league. She also turned down an offer from Phil Esposito to play for the Cincinnati Cyclones of the ECHL. However, Finland's Hockey Federation unanimously supported letting women play in a men's league, allowing her to debut with Salamat on January 10, 2003. That same year, golfing phenomenon Annika Sorenstam played on the PGA tour at the Colonial Open. While Babe Zaharias had already broken the gender line in golf by playing at the 1954 Los Angeles Open, Sorenstam's involvement at the Colonial Open became a flashpoint of debate about gender segregation in sports. So hotly contested was her involvement in the tournament that high-profile players including Vijay Singh stated that she did not belong on the men's tour and that if she was paired with him in the first round of play he would withdraw from the tournament. In 2008, another milestone in women's sports occurred when auto racer Danica Patrick became the first woman to win an Indy Car event.

FUTURE PROSPECTS

There is hardly any question as to whether or not sports continue to be a physical and social arena wherein ideologies regarding biological determinism abound. Women's involvement in sports, especially those sports replete with physical contact and masculine mythology, has ostensibly challenged, while in certain cases unintentionally punctuated, long-standing essential ideologies about natural social divisions between men and women. Predicting the future of women's amateur or professional sports or women's competition against men in sports has proven difficult for sports experts. What is certain is that women on the continent continue to struggle for access and recognition in sports as culturally legitimate athletes, unencumbered by discriminatory ideologies and practices.

See also Gender and Educational Opportunities; Gender and Game Rules; Homophobia; LGBT Sports Leagues; Marketing Athlete Sexuality; Media Coverage of Women's Sports; Ubersexuality; Women and the Apologetic; Women Coaches and Owners; Women Sportscasters.

Further Reading: Cahn, S. (1996). *Coming On Strong: Gender and Sexuality in Twentieth Century Women's Sport*. Cambridge: Harvard University Press; Festle, M. (1996). *Playing Nice: Politics and Apologies in Women's Sport*. New York: Columbia University Press; Lenskyj, H. (2003). *Out of Bounds: Women, Sport and Sexuality*. Toronto: Women's Press of Canada; Scranton, S. (2001). *Gender and Sport: A Reader*. London: Routledge.

Michael Atkinson

WOMEN SPORTSCASTERS

Sportscasters commonly broadcast on television or radio and even electronically on the Internet (i.e., Webcasts). However, unlike television sports reporters, radio announcers must be able to give an image to the audience through their words and energy alone using vivid descriptions of the action on the field. The roles of a sportscaster vary from play-by-play announcer to sideline reporter to anchor. Sportscasters are journalists similar to writers in the print media and announcers in the electronic media. The main difference between print media and sports announcers is that radio and television announcers entertain people with action and commentary, which demands on-the-spot urgency.

BACKGROUND

It is important to note the connection between the early 1900s female print sports journalists and the transition to radio and television sportscasters. Much of women's sports history has been documented based on the work of early women sportswriters whose columns, beginning in the late 1920s, appeared in major newspapers across Canada and the United States. Women journalists were expected to present a specifically feminine view of the world and were hired quite simply to attract women readers. Alexandrine Gibb and Phyllis Griffiths were two pioneers in Canadian women's sports writing. The importance of these columns cannot be overestimated. For over 30 years, from the late 1920s until the immediate postwar period, Gibb and Griffiths were a major source of information about Canadian women's sports on a daily, weekly, monthly, and yearly basis.

Often several journalists wrote about the same event, or series of events, so that it was possible to cross-check the information from one source to another. Not surprisingly, many reports were biased and expressed unique view points because women sportscasters' job description included not only commenting on the sporting events that took place but also doing so in a manner controversial enough to engage its readers. Lorena Hickok was a pioneer journalist in the United States and wrote about baseball, football, and boxing in the early 1900s for a captivated audience.

It is doubtful that many men read these columns, except perhaps male team owners and managers involved in the early days of softball and ice hockey. Generally, women sports columnists wrote for other women or the "girls" as some called their loyal readers. The content of the articles consisted of as much gossip and information as commentary and analysis of sports. Women's sports reports were hidden in a little corner of the sports page, and sometimes this was the only space where women, their sports, and their accomplishments were recognized. These early female writers became pioneers in breaking down barriers associated with media and sports. Sports reporting was considered a predominately masculine pursuit; however, these pioneers helped create more opportunities for women to be involved in sportscasting.

DID YOU KNOW?

In 1948, the first ever prime-time television show focusing on women athletes debuted on the National Broadcasting Company (NBC) television network. The show was hosted by a female sportscaster and the program, *Sportswomen of the Week,* featured interviews with outstanding women athletes.

KEY EVENTS

Female radio pioneer Judith Cary Waller is credited with producing the first ever play-by-play coverage of a college football game in 1924. Fifteen years later, on May 17, 1939, a Columbia University baseball game became the first televised sports event in the United States. Women held only minor roles in the television sports business until the mid-1970s when women writers began publishing features on women athletes and women's sports in national magazines across North America, which eventually transferred to the television medium. During the increased media attention to women's sports in the 1970s, the two most obvious changes in how women athletes were represented in the media were the explicit, sexualized descriptions of their physical appearance and their treatment as sex objects. This increased sexualization created struggles for females who tried to break ground in sportscasting because women were not viewed to be good enough to be part of the male sports domain.

Several prominent women athletes tried to help improve women's positioning in the sports arena; for example, Billie Jean King insisted that a woman commentator be hired for the "Battle of the Sexes" tennis match against Bobby Riggs in 1973. Despite criticism, women slowly infiltrated the sportscasting role. Jane Chastain is considered a true pioneer among female sportscasters. After 12 years of local and small-time television sportscasting, she was hired by CBS Sports Network in 1974. At first, she covered women's bowling but was eventually promoted to work on the National Football League (NFL) broadcasts. The efforts of television companies to provide a combination of play-by-play commentary and entertainment led them to hire popular retired athletes and coaches to be announcers. Former elite female athletes have been part of the Summer and Winter Olympics coverage; yet, it is fair to suggest that opportunities for women to broadcast men's games since the late 1990s have remained relatively sparse.

Reporter's work schedules tend to focus on covering men's sports, so including regular coverage of women's sports has required changes in institutionalized patterns of sports media work. The vast majority of sports media personnel are still men, and the highest-status assignments in sports media are considered to

PEOPLE

Donna de Varona was the youngest American to compete in the Olympics in 1960 when she was 13 years old. She had great success as a swimmer and was quite popular with the media. During one of her races, an underwater cameraman photographed her below the surface, which turned out to be the beginning of her presence in the sportscasting field. Upon retiring from swimming, she was hired by *ABC's Wide World of Sports* and covered 17 Olympic Games (Winter and Summer). She won an Emmy for her story on a swimmer in the Special Olympics. Additionally, she was the founding member and the first president of the *Women's Sport Foundation*. Donna de Varona is an excellent example of a pioneer in women's sportscasting.

be those that deal with men's sports. Even women reporters and announcers know that their upward mobility in the sports media industry demands that they focus on men's events in much the same ways that men cover them. If they insist on covering only women's events, they will not advance up the career ladder in media organizations (Coakley and Donnelly, 2004).

Many consider one of the major challenges for women sportscasters to be the player interviews postgames in the locker room setting. Women reporters who cover men's sports are more readily accepted in the locker rooms of men's teams than they were in the past, although male athletes and coaches have been very protective of this "masculinized space." Changes have occurred partly because men have discovered ways to maintain privacy, such as using towels and robes and having designated interview times—just as women athletes have always done when male reporters cover their events.

FUTURE PROSPECTS

A television network in Canada provides an example of including more women sportscasters. Hockey is the most popular televised sport in Canada, and as a result, the coverage of hockey tends to reflect the traditional gender values that are important to many people in the culture. On the "Coach's Corner" segment of the Canadian Broadcast Centre's (CBC) *Hockey Night in Canada,* sportscaster Don Cherry presents a stereotypical form of masculinity. It was a great leap forward when the program hired former Canadian Women's Hockey National team member and captain, Cassie Campbell. She did a few play-by-play commentaries, but she currently occupies the interviewer role. Despite the progress and attempt to include women journalists, there was a backlash by certain segments of Canadian society regarding Campbell's media role. Critics used Internet social networking Web sites, such as Facebook, to create specific, homophobic and misogynists groups in order to discuss how it was not "right" to have a woman in such a position. Despite many female sportscasters possessing journalism degrees and being highly educated, the North American media often sexualizes or trivializes their roles in delivering sports news. Women sportscasters are regularly featured on "top 10 hot lists," and many are asked to pose nude for *Playboy.* By continuing to focus on the sexual appeal of the female sportscasters, women journalists are consequently disrespected and not taken seriously.

Sportscasters play a critical role in helping to construct the meanings associated with people's experiences of sports. They also help people enjoy and understand sports through their informative and engaging dialogue. However, strides still need to be taken to ensure that women sportscasters receive equal opportunities and are not subjected to sexual exploitation and sexism in the workplace.

See also Gender and Game Rules; Media Coverage of Women's Sports; Women Coaches and Owners.

Further Reading: Coakley, J., and Donnelly, P. (2004). *Sports in Society: Issues and Controversies.* Toronto, ON: McGraw-Hill Ryerson; Creedon, P. (Ed.) (1994). *Women, Media* *and Sport: Challenging Gender Values.* Thousand Oaks, CA: Sage Publications; Hall, A. (2002). *The Girl and the Game, a History of Women's Sport in Canada.* Peterborough, ON: Broadview Press; Nelson, M. B. (1995). *The Stronger Women Get, the More Men Love Football: Sexism and the American Culture of Sports.* New York: Avon Books.

Charlene Weaving

X

X GAMES

The X Games are regarded as the Olympic Games of extreme sports. Developed in the United States in the early 1990s, the X Games is now a sports mega event that attracts youth audiences worldwide. The X Games bring together athletes who participate in stereotypically risky sports that are often variants of two or more mainstream sports. Like the Olympics, the X Games is split into summer and winter competitions. The Summer X Games consist of events such as Bike Stunts, Moto X, Speed Climb, Moto X Freestyle, Wakeboard, Bungee jumping, Skysurfing, Skateboard Street, Aggressive In-line Skate, and Downhill BMX; the Winter X Games consist of events such as Snowmobiling, Ice climbing, Skiboarding, Snowboarding, Ski Slopestyle, Skier X M&W Practice, Skiing Superpipe Practice, Moto X Big Air, UltraCross, Snowmobile Cross, and Snowmobile HillCross.

BACKGROUND

Throughout the late 1980s, surfers, BASE jumpers, kite surfers, hang gliders, beach volleyball players, ultimate Frisbee enthusiasts, skateboarders, BMX riders, rock climbers, windsurfers, and even street lugers all became more publicly visible alternative athletes. Each developed particular athletic preferences and practices, unique styles of language and dress, music preferences, and other group preferences. Each one of these new sports offered alternatives to mainstream sports for youths in particular. They rejected mainstream sports values and ethics such as competition and the domination of others through sports. Referred to as *alternative, resistant, whiz, extreme, edge,* or *postmodern* youth sports, each was categorized as fundamentally different from dominant sports such as football, baseball, and basketball.

The bulk of new extreme sports enthusiasts in the late 1980s rejected parent-controlled, heavily competitive, rule-bound, commercial, authoritarian, and exclusionary forms of organized sports. Skateboarders, in particular, were looked at as the youth sports heroes of the 1970s and 1980s because they used free forms of athleticism and performed wild tricks in open public as their "sport." The skaters rejected white, hypermasculine, and middle-class jock cultures, preferring instead to explore the different social possibilities of sports through highly individualized, creative, rebellious, and personally authentic skateboarding tricks and techniques performed in a variety of public spaces. Most of the participants in skateboarding, as in many of the other new sports, only loosely affiliated with one another; few (if any) national or international sports federations existed; and only rarely (perhaps with the exception of surfing) were mega competitions between participants held. Groups such as skateboarders were identified as the urban rebels of the 1990s and were often targeted by police and other control agents for disrupting social spaces such as parking lots, public parks, and shopping malls. The persistent targeting by authorities encouraged a generation of young skateboarders to wear the slogan "skateboarding is not a crime" across their T-shirts.

But by 1990, skateboarding and a range of the other new youth sports were no longer solely outsider activities. The sports, the clothing styles, and the music preferences of the outsiders found their way into popular culture as part of a developing youth style of grunge, edge, or neopunk style. Growing numbers of young North Americans were developing an appetite for cool sports and new sports lifestyles as they became increasingly showcased in the media as extreme sports. The sports network ESPN capitalized on this new consumer trend and innovated what became known as the Extreme Games in 1995, which later shortened to the X Games.

KEY EVENTS

In building on the surging popularity of alternative sports cultures in 1993, executives at ESPN television decided to devote significant resources to the creation of an international gathering of action-sport athletes. By 1994, at a press conference at Planet Hollywood in New York City, ESPN announced to the world that the first Extreme Games would be held in Rhode Island in June of 1995. From June 24 through July 1, 1995, the Extreme Games were held in Newport and Providence, Rhode Island. Athletes (predominantly from the United States and Canada) competed in 27 events in 9 sport categories: Bungee Jumping, Eco-Challenge, In-line Skating, Skateboarding, Skysurfing, Sport Climbing, Street Luge, Biking, and Water Sports. The first iteration of the Extreme Games drew a massive 198,000 spectators—surprising for an upstart sports event—and even attracted seven corporate sponsors all looking to cash in on the youth market at the Extreme Games: Advil, Mountain Dew, Taco Bell, Chevy Trucks, AT&T, Nike, and Miller Lite Ice. Due to the enthusiastic response from the athletes, organizers, spectators, and sponsors, ESPN decided to hold the event again the following year instead of every two years as they originally announced.

In January 1996, the event name "Extreme Games" officially changed to the X Games. The primary reasons ESPN executives cited for the change were to allow easier translation to international audiences and better branding opportunities. Later that year, approximately 200,000 spectators watched the events of the first Summer X Games in Newport, Rhode Island. A press conference was held during these Games announcing that Snow Summit Mountain Resort in Big Bear Lake, California, would host the first-ever Winter X Games in 2007,

X GAMES DATES AND LOCATIONS

Summer X Games

1995—"Extreme Games," Providence and Newport, Rhode Island
1996—Providence and Newport, Rhode Island
1997—San Diego, California
1998—San Diego, California
1999—Pier 30 and 32, San Francisco, California
2000—Pier 30 and 32, San Francisco, California
2001—First Union Center, Philadelphia, Pennsylvania
2002—First Union Center, Philadelphia, Pennsylvania
2003—Staples Center and LA Coliseum, Los Angeles, California
2004—Long Beach Marine Stadium, Los Angeles, California
2005—Staples Center, Los Angeles, California
2006—Long Beach Marine Stadium, Los Angeles, California
2007—Long Beach Marine Stadium, Los Angeles, California
2008—Long Beach Marine Stadium, Los Angeles, California

Winter X Games

1997—Snow Summit Mountain Resort, Big Bear Lake, California
1998—Crested Butte, Colorado
1999—Crested Butte, Colorado
2000—Mount Snow, Vermont
2001—Mount Snow, Vermont
2002—Aspen, Colorado
2003—Aspen, Colorado
2004—Aspen, Colorado
2005—Aspen, Colorado
2006—Aspen, Colorado
2007—Aspen, Colorado
2008—Aspen, Colorado

which would include competitions in snowboarding, ice climbing, snow mountain bike racing, super-modified shovel racing, and a crossover multisport event. From January 30 through February 2, 1997, the inaugural Winter X Games were televised to 198 countries and territories in 21 different languages. This was the first year that ABC Sports worked in conjunction with ESPN to broadcast the X Games.

In March of 1997, the Games took an interesting turn. Due to the booming popularity of extreme sports worldwide and the number of competitors wishing to compete in the X Games, organizers decided to create the X Trials, a money-making qualifying event for the X Games. Additional X Games qualifying events such as the B3 and EXPN Invitational (EXPN became a sister Internet site/channel of ESPN in 1997) were held each summer through 2002 in U.S. cities, including Orlando, Louisville, St. Petersburg, Virginia Beach, Richmond, Lake Havasu, Nashville, and Bristol. Also in 1997, the X Games brand was further extended into new commercial zones as the X Games Xperience road show/exhibition traveled to Disneyland Paris.

The first-ever international X Games qualifying event was held in early 1998 and served as another indicator of the events' continued ascent into popularity. The first Asian X Games was held that year and featured 200 athletes from the Pacific Rim competing in Phuket, Thailand, for a limited amount of spots at X Games IV in San Diego. By this stage in its history, the Games had transformed from a rebel sport showcase to a full-fledged corporate-media machine. As further evidence of the trend, the inaugural "Action Sports and Music Awards" were held on April 7, 2001, to a packed crowd of 6,000 at the Universal Amphitheatre in Los Angeles. The event united what were now being called action sports athletes, musicians, and Hollywood celebrities, presenting the most highly commercialized evening in the history of action sports. Celebrities LL Cool J, Rebecca Romjin-Stamos, and Chris Klein hosted the event, which included performances from the original members of Black Sabbath and Ben Harper and the Innocent Criminals. By this point in the history of the X Games, even the most staunch of its advocates were criticizing organizers and participants for selling out to corporate agenda and losing sight of the initial social outsider cultural meaning of the Games.

The commercial flavor and content of the X Games brand continued through 2001 as ESPN and the Mills Corporation announced a licensing agreement to build state-of-the-art public X Games skate parks at several Mills retail centers across the country. The skate parks, designed by the industry's top course designers, were intended to offer public facilities for skateboarding, bike stunt riding (BMX), and in-line skating. ESPN extended its brand into South America in 2002, as it, along with corporate partners, hosted the inaugural Latin X Games Qualifier in Rio De Janeiro, Brazil. The second annual ESPN Action Sports and Music Awards were held on April 13, 2002, at the Universal Amphitheatre in Los Angeles. A month later, on May 10, 2002, Touchstone Pictures and ESPN presented the major motion picture *ESPN's Ultimate X* in cinema multiplexes across the United States. The film chronicled the highlights and stories of athletes in the

X Games VII. The X Games juggernaut continued only a few days later, when ESPN announced that a new event, the X Games Global Championship would be held. Six teams of the world's top athletes were grouped together by their region of origin to compete in the four-day event, May 15–18, 2003. The Summer X Games of that year (X Games VIII) was the most-watched X Games ever; nearly 63 million people tuned in on ESPN, ESPN2, EXPN, and ABC Sports. In December of that year, average viewership for the Winter X Games VII across the three networks that carried coverage—ESPN, ESPN2, and ABC Sports—set an all-time record as well.

Between 2004 and 2008, the X Games commercial juggernaut continued to flourish and expand its market opportunities. More events, participants, spectators, and companies were involved than ever before. In 2004, ESPN held a 41-day X Games tribute at Disney's California Adventure in Anaheim, California, titled X Games Xperience. Guests of the newest theme park inside the Disneyland Resort were immersed in an array of activities inspired by ESPN's X Games events, including interactive games such as Moto X Big Air. The X Games of 2006 were aired on television 24 hours a day, each day of the event, on ESPN, ESPN2, ABC, ESPN Classic, EXPN, ESPN360, Mobile ESPN, ESPN International, and iTunes.

Critics have argued that the X Games and other imitations of it have effectively neutralized any of the free, different, or rebel aspects of the sports it brought together in the early 1990s. As the X Games and its images are now inserted in comic books, video games, music videos, fast-food packing, and footwear, there is a strong argument to be made that little is "alternative" about these sports. The ways in which ESPN have interlaced the Games with corporate products and agendas seemingly stand in the face of the spirit of the original sports. As the rule structures, participants, and staging of the sports are all directly manipulated or assembled by corporate interests, the very nature of participation has been taken out of the hands of the participants themselves. In the process, however, the X Games has evolved into one of the most profitable global sports brands on the planet and provides evidence that media conglomerates have the power to change the face of twenty-first-century sports.

FUTURE PROSPECTS

Youth sports continues to be a social battleground where young people wage resistance to mainstream cultural expectations through athletics, but these forms of resistance almost inevitably become co-opted into the mainstream. If history is a predictor of future resistance through youth sports, one can expect that every form of rebel sport will indeed follow the pattern of so many of its predecessors and be assimilated into cultural events like the X Games. To this end, one could argue that the socially rebellious sports of today will be the highly commercialized and globally mainstream sports of tomorrow.

See also Adventure Racing; Cool Pose; Parkour (Free Running); Skateboarding; Snowboarding; Yoga and Alternative Fitness.

Further Reading: Andrews, D. (2006). *Sport-Commerce-Culture.* New York: Peter Lang. Rinehart, R., and Sydnor, S. (2003). *To the Extreme: Alternative Sports, Inside and Out.* Albany, NY: SUNY Press.

Michael Atkinson

YOGA AND ALTERNATIVE FITNESS

Yoga is a physical cultural practice that originated in India around 3300 B.C.E. The term *yoga,* which is a Sanskrit term meaning "to yoke" (bring together, or join), refers to the idea that through certain physical movements, breathing techniques, inner reflection, and spiritual awareness, people's minds and bodies can be aligned with higher energies and forces. Yoga is a practice designed to cultivate and shape one's body, to calm the mind and discover a sense of place in the universe. There are many schools of yoga practice now popular in the West, including hatha yoga, jnana yoga, astanga/ashtanga yoga, karma yoga, bhakti yoga, raja yoga, and kundalini. There has been a relative boom in yoga practices in North America over the past 40 years and a mixing and matching of yoga philosophies to match practitioners' needs. At the onset of the twenty-first century, a movement started in North America and elsewhere to transform the historically religious and personal practice of yoga into a competitive sport with its own "Olympics."

BACKGROUND

The bases of traditional Indian yoga are recognized by historians as stemming from the text, *Yoga Sutras of Patanjali.* Pantanjali wrote the Sutras as a derivation of Samkhya religious philosophy. In the *Yoga Sutras,* Patanjali prescribes adherence to eight "limbs" or steps of yoga (the sum of which constitute the Ashtanga Yoga tradition) as a technique for quieting one's mind and achieving the ultimate goal of yoga practice: detachment *(kaivalya).* The *Yoga Sutras* form the theoretical and philosophical basis of Raja Yoga as well and are considered to be the most organized and complete definition of that discipline. The *Sutras* not only provide yoga with a philosophical basis, they also clarify many important concepts that are common to all traditions of Indian thought, such as karma. Although Patanjali's work does not cover the many types of yogic practices that have become prevalent in the West, its succinct form and availability causes it to be sought out as a canonical text for contemporary yoga practitioners. Westerners that have become enamored with yoga in the recent past have especially studied the *Sutras* to understand the spiritual essence of the practice.

The modern discovery of yoga in the West and its insertion into popular culture is indeed difficult to trace. Certainly, neoliberalist tendencies (i.e., finding ways to improve your own life rather than relying on others to do so) in the United States of the 1960s played a role in encouraging people to explore new spiritual practices such as yoga. Yoga cultures, for example, emerged in California during the 1960s and 1970s as part of the burgeoning counterculture movements such as hippie, beatnik, and others. Cities such as San Francisco, Los Angeles, San Diego, and others became focal points for yoga during the time, catering to people who sought to expand their minds and achieve non-mainstream (i.e., non-Judeo-Christian) spirituality through physical practice. Early practitioners were exposed to a range of yoga techniques and philosophies, including the styles of Sri K. Pattabhi Jois's *vinyasa* style and B.K.S. Iyengar's traditional yoga. Several students of Californian yoga during this period, such as David Swenson, went on to become key figures in the mass popularization of the practice in the 1990s. The Californian yoga culture of the time even spawned its own unique countercultural and controversial variants on the practice including naked yoga, which was introduced to the rest of the world through the 1968 Hollywood film *Bob & Carol, Ted & Alice*.

The minor upsurge in yoga's popularity in the late 1960s and early 1970s is certainly attributable to neoliberalist social factors and trends outside of California as well. Books such as Dr. Eric Berne's *I'm Ok, You're Ok* (1969) introduced "transactional analysis" to an increasingly pop psychology–hungry West. Self-realization (inner exploration and self-awareness) traditions from India were explored in a growing number of holistic lifestyle centers in the United States and championed through the 1980s by public figures including actress Shirley MacLaine. Perhaps most notably, the Maharishi Mahesh Yogi introduced transcendental meditation to the Western world as a technique for achieving inner peace. Transcendental meditation (TM) practices achieved notoriety in 1968 when the Beatles experienced a highly publicized TM session with Maharishi Mahesh Yogi. The Yogi then appeared on a *Time* magazine cover on October 13, 1975, as the leader of a new spiritual revolution in the United States.

Alongside weight loss and fitness crazes in the 1970s and 1980s, more (especially women) sought out yoga as a low-impact means of losing weight. Health advocates pitched yoga to people seeking to lose weight, relieve stress, and gain a more positive self-image but who were uncomfortable working out in male-dominated gyms. With the corporate expansion of the fitness industries over the course of the 1990s and early 2000s, more gyms in North America offered a variety of yoga classes in their training schedules to accommodate growing numbers of yoga fans. While not entirely separate from spiritually oriented subcultures of yoga practitioners in the West, many gyms progressively removed overt forms of religious/spiritual instruction from the classes in order to appeal to the interests of their body fitness–focused members. Over the course of a very short period, local yoga centers and yoga classes in gyms or fitness studios charged $10–50 per class rather than the traditional karma fee (i.e., members pay a donation, whatever they feel is appropriate to pay).

Like so many other counterculture or outsider athletic practices in the twentieth century, as yoga became increasingly popular it was co-opted and commercialized as a mainstream form of athleticism. Because of the difficult nature of some yoga forms and asanas (poses or movements), practitioners in some cultural yoga pockets became increasingly competitive about how far one could push their bodies. Yoga has been acknowledged as a competitive sport in parts of India for well over 2,000 years and is showcased at major Indian yoga tournaments such as the National Yoga Championships, India Yoga Cup, the Holy International Sport Yoga Championship, and National World Yoga Championships. These events and others are organized and overseen by major governing bodies in the world of athletic yoga, including the Yoga Federation of India, International Sport Yoga Federation, International Yoga Federation, Indian Yoga Federation, Yoga Confederation of India, North India Yoga Federation, South North Yoga Federation, World Yoga Congress of Pondicherry, World Yoga Society of Calcatta, and the Vivekanda Kendra Yoga Foundation.

The contemporary movement toward a sports-like yoga in North America raises its own set of controversies and debates. For example, North Americans' traditional constructions of sports do not typically include practices such as yoga, in any of its forms. Equally, yoga purists on the continent have argued that despite the roots of athletic yoga in India, the heart of yoga (in India, the West or elsewhere) flatly eschews any notions of competition, self or ego aggrandizement through competition, or concern with notions of being judged in accordance to how well one is practicing. These foci distract the practitioner from finding "yoga" (the union/connection) with the mind, body, and universe by encouraging the practitioner to focus his/her practice on extrinsic rewards.

KEY EVENTS

The birth of modern, competitive athletic yoga is almost single-handedly attributed to the efforts of yoga guru Bikram Choudury. Bikram, born in 1946, started his journey in yoga at the age of 5 in India, studying under legendary guru Bishnu Ghosh in Calcutta. Bikram quickly became a national athletic yoga champion in traditional hatha yoga and retired from active competition undefeated. He went on to open several schools of yoga with Ghosh in India and then in Japan. In his youth, Bikram also competed internationally as a marathon runner and weightlifter. He immigrated to the United States in 1973 and founded the first Yoga College of India there. He introduced a rather militaristic and simple no-nonsense yoga to Westerners that stresses only 26 asanas and two breathing exercises to be completed in a room kept at a temperature above 100 degrees Fahrenheit. By claiming this to be the only authentic variety of yoga to exist on earth outside of India, Bikram highlighted the physical and mental benefits of his system. He drew followers and developed a star-studded clientele in California.

Through the 1990s and 2000s, Bikram became globally known as the "bad boy" of yoga. He lived an opulent lifestyle, professed to be the yoga instructor "of the stars," and developed almost a cult following in sports cultures for his "hot yoga" system's uncanny ability to heal athletes with potentially career-ending injuries. He created the Self Realization Fellowship as a movement designed to teach inner peace to people, and he published *Autobiography of a Yogi* (2007), in which he claims to be the world's leading authority on yoga. He has come under criticism, though, for developing a market chain of his schools in the West and elsewhere, operating his college of instruction as a franchise. He will only allow people to use either his name or reference to his technique if they have graduated his college. While controversial to some as a "pervert" of the spiritual essence of yoga, Bikram is one of a handful of figures that has redrawn the face of yoga in the West. He helped to establish the first athletic yoga competitions in the United States, and he was heavily influential in bringing the International Yoga Championships to the United Sates in 2003. He is also among the leading lobbyists to have yoga included at the Olympic Games as an official sport.

Bikram's yoga developed at a time when yoga practices underwent a set of commercializing processes. With their insertion into mainstream health and fitness clubs during the 1990s, yoga was exposed to entirely new generations of workout fanatics. Through this process, the format of yoga changed; traditional 2-hour classes were condensed to 45- or 60-minute time slots, essential preparatory (chanting, breathing, meditation) aspects were removed from yoga in many cases, and essential asanas in series were eliminated to allow for delivery in a condensed time frame. New schools of yoga instruction emerged, and international yoga federations grew in number to accredit increasing numbers of people who sought out yoga teaching as a profession. Rather than taking years to become a yoga instructor, it is now possible to receive a teaching certificate in as little as a weekend. Such courses tend to be incredibly expensive for participants and lucrative for instructors and their schools. Yoga traditions have been fused with others including Pilates, boxing, tai chi, capoeira, aerobics, and other athletic forms and sold to people as weight-loss and body-toning practices. Additionally, a series of yoga industries have developed in order to further commodify the practice, such as clothing companies (like lululemon athletica), instructional manual publishers, yoga mat and other classroom equipment producers, DVD and yoga music producers, and a range of others. Classes at gyms and private yoga centers are also tapping into the sports market by offering "yoga for runners," "yoga for golfers," or yoga for practically any other brand of athlete.

At the same time, Westerners in the athletic branch of yoga practice have pressed for their sport to be taken seriously by wider audiences. Competitions such as the Yoga Olympiad in Texas and the Yoga Asana Competition in New York present the practice as a blend between gymnastics, bodybuilding, and dance. A yoga competition (which includes competitors of all ages cleaved into male and female categories) pits people against one another on a stage. Each participant performs a 2- or 3-minute routine of moves (normally 5 or 6 asanas in total), and they are judged on how perfectly they perform the moves in relation to their age, experience, body shape, and physical abilities. Questions, of course, are raised about the arbitrariness of judging, potential personal biases in the judging practice, and the difficulty of assessing perfection in any asana. Such arguments are not dissimilar to those made about Olympic sports that are judged, such as figure skating (especially after the 2002 "Skate Gate" judging controversy), diving, and rhythmic gymnastics.

Critics of the yoga-sport model also argue that spotted competitions do not make a practice a sport. Very similar to debates about bodybuilding, the claim is levied that while an incredible amount of training and physical/athletic skill is required to practice most yoga disciplines well, yoga does not have the structured set of rules, standards of play, standardized teaching methods, or other cultural features of competition that categorize something as a sport. Such may be a very white, Western construction of sport, and there may be a degree of inferential ethnocentricism to the argument.

The proliferation of yoga in gyms and in athletic competition formats has changed the culture of yoga in North America. Until the 1990s, women did by no means exclusively populate yoga classes, but they were the majority patrons. As the athletic-power-competitive features of yoga were marketed to wider populations through the turn of the century, however, new male consumers flooded gym settings to explore the muscle-building and recovery-enhancing aspects of the practice. With many of the reflexive and meditative aspects (largely associated with yoga as an emotion-oriented feminine practice") removed in mega-gym classes, males were able to experience the rigors of yoga without feeling stigmatized in the setting. Arguably, it is one of the few examples in North America during the twentieth century of males colonizing a predominantly female athletic culture.

FUTURE PROSPECTS

Some most likely expect yoga's current popularity in the West to diminish in the near future. However, in reviewing the history of how yoga has grown as a physical cultural practice over the past five decades in North America, assessments of its trendiness or faddish nature might be ill-conceived. Yoga should continue to be a social battleground where debates about what constitutes "true sport" will be waged. With its diverse patronage, yoga appears to be a typical postmodern sport wherein boundaries between religion, economics, ethnicity, gender, medical science, and athletics are either erased or merged.

See also Adventure Racing; Parkour (Free Running); Skateboarding; Snowboarding; Surfing and New Water Sports; Ultraendurance Sports; X Games.

Further Reading: Choudhury, B. (2007). *Bikram Yoga: The Guru Behind Hot Yoga Shows the Way to Radiant Health and Personal Fulfillment.* New York: HarperCollins.

Michael Atkinson

BIBLIOGRAPHY

Abrams, R. "Before the flood: The history of baseball's antitrust exemption." *Marquette Sports Law Journal* 9: 307–313 (1999).
Abrams, R. "Game-fixing in the national game." *Florida Entertainment Law Review* 1 (2006): 1–40.
Acker, J. "The future of 'gender and organizations': Connections and boundaries." *Gender, Work and Organization* 4 (1998): 195–206.
Acosta, R., and Carpenter, L. *Women in Intercollegiate Sport: A Longitudinal, National Study—Thirty-One Year Update.* Retrieved March 27, 2008, from http://www.acostacarpenter.org.
Agar V. Canning. 54 W.W.R. 302 (M.Q.B); affd. 55 W.W.R. 384 (C.A.) (1965).
Althusser, L. *Lenin and Philosophy and Other Essays.* London: New Left Books, 1971.
Amis, J., and Bettina, T. *Global Sport Sponsorship:* New York: Berg, 2005.
Anderson, C., and Bushman, B. J. "Effects of violent games on aggressive behavior, aggressive cognition, aggressive affect, physiological arousal, and prosocial behavior: A meta-analytical review of the scientific literature." *Psychological Science* 12 (2001): 353–359.
Anderson, E. *In the Game: Gay Athletes and the Cult of Masculinity.* Albany: SUNY Press, 2005.
Anderson, K. "Snowboarding: The construction of gender in an emerging sport." *Journal of Sport and Social Issues* 23 (1999): 55–79.
Andrews, D. "The facts of Michael Jordan's blackness: Excavating a floating racial signifier." *Sociology of Sport Journal* 13 (1996): 125–158.
Andrews, D. *Michael Jordan Inc: Corporate Sport, Media Culture and Late Modern America.* Albany: SUNY Press, 2001.
Andrews, D. *Sport-Commerce-Culture.* New York: Peter Lang, 2006.

Appadurai, A. "Disjuncture and difference in the global cultural economy." *Theory, Culture & Society* 7 (1990): 295–310.

Armstrong, G. *Football Hooligans: Knowing the Score.* Oxford: Berg, 1998.

Armstrong, L. *It's Not About the Bike: My Journey Back to Life.* New York: Berkley Trade, 2000.

Asinof, E., and Gould, J. *Eight Men Out.* New York: Holt, 2000.

Associated Press. *Text of President Bush's State of the Union Address.* Retrieved October 22, 2006, from http://www.post-gazette.com/pg/04021/263842.stm#drugs.

Atkinson, M. "It's still part of the game: Violence and masculinity in Canadian ice hockey." In *Sport, Rhetoric, Gender and Violence: Historical Perspectives and Media Representations,* edited by L. Fuller. New York: Palgrave MacMillan, 2006.

Atkinson, M. "Playing with fire: Masculinity, health and sports supplements." *Sociology of Sport Journal* 24 (2007): 165–186.

Atkinson, M., and Young, K. "Terror games: Media treatment of security Issues at the 2002 Winter Olympic Games." *OLYMPIKA* 11 (2003): 53–78.

Atkinson, M., and Young, K. "Reservoir dogs." *International Review for the Sociology of Sport* 40 (2005): 335–356.

Atkinson, M., and Young, K. *Deviance and Social Control in Sport.* Champaign, IL: Human Kinetics, 2008.

Baccigaluppi, J., Mayugba, S., and Carnel, C. *Declaration of Independents: Snowboarding, Skateboarding and Music: An Intersection of Cultures.* San Francisco: Chronicle Books, 2001.

Baker, W. *Playing with God: Religion and Modern Sport.* Cambridge: Harvard University Press, 2007.

Bale, J. *Running Cultures.* London: Frank Cass, 2003.

Bandura, A. *Aggression: A Social Learning Analysis.* Englewood Cliffs, NJ: Prentice Hall, 1973.

Bandura, A. *Social Foundations of Thought and Action.* Englewood Cliffs, NJ: Prentice-Hall, 1986.

Barnes, J. *Sport and the law in Canada.* Toronto, ON: Butterworths, 1988.

Basich, T., with Gasperini, K. *Pretty Good for a Girl: The Autobiography of a Snowboarding Pioneer.* New York: HarperCollins, 2003.

Bass, A. *In the Game: Race, Identity and Sports in the Twentieth Century.* London: Palgrave Macmillan, 2005.

Bauman, Z. *Culture as Praxis.* London: Sage, 1999.

Beal, B., and Weidman, L. "Authenticity in the skateboarding world." In *To the Extreme: Alternative Sports, Inside and Out,* edited by R. Rinehart and S. Sydnor, 337–352. New York: SUNY Press, 2003.

Beal, B., and Wilson, C. "Chicks dig scars: Commercialization and the transformations of skateboarders' identities." In *Understanding Lifestyle Sports: Consumption, Identity and Difference,* edited by B. Wheaton. London: Routledge, 2004.

Beamish, R., and Ritchie, I. *Fastest, Highest, Strongest: A Critique of High-Performance Sport.* London: Routledge, 2006.

Bean, B. *Going the Other Way: Lessons from a Life In and Out of Major League Baseball.* Washington, D.C.: Marlowe and Company, 2004.

Beck, K. "Infectious diseases in sports." *Medicine and Science in Sports and Exercise* 32 (2000): S431–S438.

Bell, E., and Campbell, D. "For the love of money." *The Observer* (May 23, 1999), 22.
Bem, S. "The measurement of psychological androgyny." *Journal of Consulting and Clinical Psychology* 42 (1974): 155–162.
Benedict, J. *Public Heroes, Private Felons*. Boston: Northeastern University Press, 1997.
Benedict, J. *Athletes and Acquaintance Rape*. Thousand Oaks, CA: Sage, 1998.
Benedict, J. *Pros and Cons: The Criminals Who Play in the NFL*. Grand Central Press, 1998.
Benedict, J. *Out of Bounds: Inside the NBA's Culture of Rape, Violence & Crime*. New York: HarperCollins, 2004.
Berkovits, S. "Gambling on Las Vegas: Bringing professional sports to sin city." *Gaming Law Review* 9 (2005): 220–231.
Bernstein, A. "Things you can see from there, you can't see from here." *Journal of Sport and Social Issues* 24 (2000): 351–369.
Berryman, J., and Park, R. *Sport and Exercise Science: Essays in the History of Sports Medicine*. Urbana: University of Illinois Press, 1992.
Birrell, S., and Cole, C. "Double fault: Renee Richards and the construction and naturalization of difference." *Sociology of Sport Journal* 7 (1990): 1–21.
Birrell, S., and Cole, C. *Women, Sport and Culture*. Champaign, IL: Human Kinetics, 1994.
Birrell, S., and Theberge, N. "Ideological control of women in Sport." In *Women and Sport: Interdisciplinary Perspectives,* edited by D. Costa and S. Guthrie, 341–360. Champaign, IL: Human Kinetics, 1994.
Bissinger, H. *Friday Night Lights*. Cambridge: Da Capo Press, 1999.
Blehm, E. *Agents of Change: The Story of DC Shoes and its Athletes*. New York: Regan Books, 2003.
Blumberg, A. "Launch." *Transworld Snowboarding* (January 2002), 16.
Booth, D. *Australian Beach Cultures: The History of Sun, Sand and Surf*. London: Frank Cass, 2001.
Borden, I. *Skateboarding, Space & the City: Architecture and the Body*. Oxford: Berg, 2001.
Boutilier, M., and SanGiovanni, L. "Politics, public policy, and Title IX: Some limitations of liberal feminism." in *Women, Sport and Culture,* edited by S. Birrell and C. Cole. Champaign, IL: Human Kinetics, 1994.
Brackenridge, C. "He owned me basically: Women's experience of sexual abuse in sport. *International Review for the Sociology of Sport* 32 (1997): 115–130.
Brackenridge, C. *Spoilsports: Understanding and Preventing Sexual Exploitation in Sport*. London: Routledge, 2001.
Brackenridge, C. "Women and children first? Child abuse and child protection in sport." *Sport in Society* 7 (2004): 322–337.
Branigan, J. *The Reign of the Greyhound*. New York: Howell Book House, 1997.
Bridges, J. *Making Violence Part of the Game*. Commack, NY: Kroshka Books, 1999.
Bridges, P. "Romain DeMarchi." *Snowboarder Magazine* (November 2004): 94–105.
British Broadcast Corporation. *Jump London*. Originally aired September 9, 2003.
Brooke, M. *The Concrete Wave: The History of Skateboarding*. Toronto: Warwick Publishing, 1999.
Brooks, D., and Althouse, R. *Diversity in Sport Management: The Student Athlete's Experience*. Morgantown, WV: Fitness Information Technology, 2007.

Burke, M. "Can Sport Cope with a Wimpy Virus? Using Questions Not Asked in HIV and Sport Discourses to Resist Discrimination." *Journal of the Philosophy of Sport* 29 (2002): 54–65.

Burki, R., Elassasser, H., and Abegg, B. *Climate Change and Winter Sports: Environmental and Economic Threats.* Paper presented at the 5th World Conference on Sport and Environment, Turin, Italy, December 3, 2003.

Bursytn, V. *The Rites of Men.* Toronto: University of Toronto Press, 1999.

Burton, J. "Snowboarding: The essence is fun." In *To the Extreme: Alternative Sports, Inside and Out,* edited by R. Rinehart and S. Sydnor, 401–406. New York: SUNY Press, 2003.

Burton, J., and Dumaine, B. "My half-pipe dreams come true." *Fortune Small Business* 12 (2002): 64.

Butler, J. *Bodies That Matter: The Discursive Limits of Sex.* New York: Routledge, 1993.

Cagan, J., and deMause, N. *Field of Schemes: How the Great Stadium Swindle Turns Public Money into Private Profit.* Monroe, WI: Common Courage Press, 1998.

Cahn, S. *Coming on Strong: Gender and Sexuality in Twentieth-Century Women's Sport.* Cambridge: Harvard University Press, 1994.

Cahn, S. "From the muscle moll to the butch ballplayer: Mannishness, lesbianism, and homophobia in U.S. women's sports." *Feminists Studies* 19 (2003): 343–368.

Califia, P. *Sex Changes: The Politics of Transgenderism.* San Francisco: Cleis Press, 1997.

Cameron, L. *Body Alchemy: Transsexual Portraits.* San Francisco: Cleis Press, 1996.

Canseco, J. *Juiced: Wild Times, Rampant 'Roids, Smash Hits, and How Baseball Got Big.* New York: Harper Entertainment, 2005.

Canseco, J. *Vindicated: Big Names, Big Liars, and the Battle to Save Baseball.* New York: Simon Spotlight Entertainment, 2008.

Cantelon, H. "Sport and politics." In *Canadian Sport Sociology,* edited by J. Crossman, 172–186. Toronto: Nelson, 2003.

Carlson, A. "Suspect sex." *Lancet* 366 (2005): S39–S40.

Carpenter, L. "Letters home: My life with Title IX." In *Women in Sport: Issues and Controversies,* edited by G. Cohen. Newbury Park, CA: Sage Publications, 1993.

Carpenter, L., and Acosta, R. *Title IX.* Champaign, IL: Human Kinetics, 2004.

Carrier, R. *The Hockey Sweater.* Toronto: Tundra Books, 1979.

Cashmore, E. *Encyclopedia of Race and Ethnic Studies.* London: Routledge, 2003.

Cashmore, E. *Tyson: Nurture of the Beast.* London: Polity, 2005.

Cauldwell, J. *Sport, Sexualities and Queer Theory.* London: Routledge, 2007.

Cheslock, J., and Anderson, D. "Lessons from research on Title IX and intercollegiate athletics." In *Title IX 30 Years Later: Sporting Equality,* edited by R. Simon, 127–145. New Brunswick, NJ: Transaction Publishers, 2005.

Choudhury, B. *Bikram Yoga: The Guru Behind Hot Yoga Shows the Way to Radiant Health and Personal Fulfillment.* New York: Collins, 2007.

Clark, T. *Art and Propaganda in the Twentieth Century.* New York: Calmann and King, 1997.

Coakley, J. *Sports and Society: Issues and Controversies.* New York: McGraw-Hill Ryerson, 2004.

Coakley, J., and Donnelly, P. *Sports in Society: Issues and Controversies* (Canadian edition). Toronto: McGraw-Hill Ryerson, 2004.

Coase, R. "The problem of social cost." *Journal of Law and Economics* 3 (1960): 1–44.

Coe, R. *A Sense of Pride: The Story of Gay Games II*. San Francisco: Pride Publications, 1988.

Cohen, J., and Semerjian, T. Z. "The collision of trans-experience and the politics of women's ice hockey." *International Journal of Transgenderism* (in press).

Cohen, L., and Felson, M. "Social change and crime rate trends: A routine activity approach." *American Sociological Review* 44 (1979): 588–608.

Cole, C. "American Jordan: PLAY, consensus and punishment." *Sociology of Sport Journal* 13 (1996): 366–397.

Collingwood, T. *Helping at Risk Youth Through Physical Fitness Training*. Champaign, IL: Human Kinetics, 1997.

Collins, T., and Vamphew, C. *Mud, Sweat and Beers*. Oxford: Berg, 2002.

Connor, T. *Still Waiting for Nike To Do It*. San Francisco: Global Exchange, 2001.

Conway, R. *Game Misconduct: Alan Eagleson and the Corruption of Hockey*. Toronto: Macfarlane Walter & Ross, 1995.

Coubertin, P. *Olympism: Selected Writings*. Lausanne: International Olympic Committee, 2000.

Coulter-Parker, N. "Going over board." *Women's Sport and Fitness* 19 (1997): 56–58.

Couser, G. *Recovering Bodies: Illness, Disability, and Life Writing*. Madison: University of Wisconsin Press, 2007.

Coyle, C. "The Siege at Summit." *Transworld Snowboarding* (September 2002): 128–135.

Crawford, G. *Consuming Sport: Fans, Sport and Culture*. London: Routledge, 2004.

Creedon, P. *Women, Media and Sport: Challenging Gender Values*. Thousand Oaks, CA: Sage Publications, 1994.

Criscuolo, P. "Reassessing the ticket scalping dispute: The application, effects, and criticisms of current anti-scalping legislation." *Seton Hall Journal of Sport Law* 5 (1995): 189–192.

Cromwell, J. *Transmen and FTMs*. Chicago: University of Illinois Press, 1999.

Crossett, T. *Outsiders in the Clubhouse: The World of Women's Professional Golf*. Albany: SUNY Press, 1995.

Curry, P. *Ecological Ethics: An Introduction*. London: Routledge, 2006.

David, P. *Human Rights in Youth Sport*. London: Routledge, 2005.

Davis, J. *Skateboard Roadmap*. New York: Carlton Books, 1999.

Davis, L. *The Swimsuit Issue and Sport: Hegemonic Masculinity and Sports Illustrated*. Albany: SUNY Press, 1997.

Deemer, S. "Snow business is booming in sunny Orange County." *Los Angeles Business Journal* (January 24, 2000). Retrieved January 21, 2008, from http://www.allbusiness.com/north-america/united-states-california-metro-areas/442072-1.html.

De la Chapelle, A. "The use and misuse of sex chromatin screening for 'gender verification' of female athletes." *Journal of the American Medical Association* 256: 1920–1923 (1986).

Delaplace, J.-M. *George Hébert: Sculpter du Corps*. Paris: Vuibert, 2005.

Discrimination Against Women Hearings on Section 805 of H.R. 16,098 Before the Special Subcomm. Of the House Comm. On Edu. & Labor, 91st Cong. (1970). In E. Staurowsky,

"Title IX and College Sport: The Long Painful Path to Compliance and Reform," *Marquette Sports Law Review* 14 (2003): 100.

Dorsch, K., and Paskevich, D. "Stressful experiences among six certification levels of ice hockey officials." *Psychology of Sport and Exercise* 8 (2007): 585–593.

Dresser, C. "Snowboarding Japan: A guide for the young professional." *Transworld Snowboarding* (November 2004): 125–127.

Dubin, C. *Commission of Inquiry into the Use of Drugs and Banned Practices Intended to Increase Athletic Performance.* Ottawa: Canadian Government Publishing Centre, 1990.

Dugard, M. *Surviving the Toughest Race on Earth.* Whitby, ON: Ragged Mountain Press, 1999.

Duncan, M., and Messner, M. "The media image of sport and gender." In *MediaSport*, edited by L. Wenner, 170–185. New York: Routledge, 1998.

Duncan, M., and Messner, M. *Gender in Televised News and Sports Highlight Programs, 1989–2004.* Los Angeles: AAFLA, 2005.

Dunlap, R. "Environmental sociology: A personal perspective on its first quarter century." *Organization and Environment* 15 (2002): 10–29.

Dunning, E. *Sport Matters.* London: Routledge, 1999.

Dunning, E., Murphy, P., Waddington, I., and Astrinakis, A. *Fighting Fans: Football Hooliganism as a World Problem.* Dublin: University College Dublin Press, 2002.

Duquette, J. *Regulating the National Pastime: Baseball and Antitrust.* Westport, CT: Praeger, 1999.

Duthie, K. (Producer/Director), and Duthie, K., and Wilson, D. (Writers). *100% Woman.* (Motion picture). Canada: Artemis Pictures, 2004.

Edwards, G. "Attack of the flying tomato." *Rolling Stone* (March 9, 2006): 43–45.

Edwards, W. "Senate faces women's rights class." *Chicago Tribune* (February 17, 1972), A1: 26.

Eitzen, S. *Fair and Foul: Beyond the Myths and Paradoxes of Sport.* Boulder, CO: Rowman and Littlefield, 1999.

Elias, N. *The Civilizing Process.* Oxford: Blackwell, 2004.

Elias, N., and Dunning, E. *Quest for Excitement: Sport and Leisure in the Civilizing Process.* New York: Basil Blackwell, 1986.

Elias, N., and Scotson, J. *The Established and the Outsiders.* London: Frank Cass & Company, 1965.

Eng, H. "Queer athletes and queering in sport." In *Sport, Sexualities and Queer Theory*, edited by J. Cauldwell. London: Routledge, 2007.

Entine, J. *Taboo: Why Black Athletes Dominate Sports and Why We Are Afraid to Talk About It.* New York: PublicAffairs, 2000.

Euchner, C. *Playing the Field: Why Sports Teams Move and Cities Fight to Keep Them.* Baltimore: The Johns Hopkins University Press, 1993.

Evans, A. "Blacks as key functionaries: A study of racial stratification in professional sport." *Journal of Black Studies* 28 (1997): 43–59.

Evolution of the Draft and Lottery 2007. Retrieved August 12, 2007, from http://www.nba.com/history/draft_evolution.html.

Fainaru, M., and Williams, L. *Game of Shadows.* New York: Gotham, 2006.

Fee, B. "Terje Haakonsen interview." *Snowboardermag.com*. Retrieved March 28, 2008, from http://www.snowboardermag.com/magazine/features/terje-haakonsen-interview-part2.

Feller, A., and Flannigan, T. "HIV-infected competitive athletes: What are the risks? What precautions should be taken?" *Journal of General Internal Medicine* 12 (1997): 243–246.

Ferguson-Smith, M. "3.3.2 gender verification." In *Oxford Textbook of Sports Medicine*, edited by Harries, 329–336. Oxford: Oxford University Press, 1998.

Feshbach, S., and Singer, D. *Television and Aggression: An Experimental Field Study*. San Francisco: Jossey-Bass, 1971.

Festle, M. *Playing Nice: Politics and Apologies in Women's Sports*. New York: Columbia University Press, 1994.

Fields, S. *Female Gladiators: Gender, Law, and Contact Sport in America*. Champaign: University of Illinois Press, 2005.

Finley, P., Fountain, J., and Finley, L. *Sport Scandals*. Westport, CT: Praeger, 2008.

Fixx, J. *The Complete Book of Running*. New York: Random House, 1977.

Florida Statute § 817.36. *Resale of Tickets of Common Carriers, Places of Amusement*, 2004.

Ford, N., and Brown, D. *Surfing and Social Theory*. London: Routledge, 2006.

Forrest, D., and Simmons, R. "Outcome uncertainty and attendance demand in sport: The case of English soccer." *The Statistician* 51 (2002): 229–241.

Fort, R., and Quirk, J. "Cross-subsidization, incentives, and outcomes in professional team sports leagues." *Journal of Economic Literature* 33 (1995): 1265–1299.

Foucault, M. *Discipline and Punish: The Birth of the Prison*. London: Penguin Books, 1977.

Francis, L. "Title IX: Equality for women's sports?" In *Ethics in Sport*, edited by W. Morgan, K. Meier, and A. Schneider, 247–266. Champaign, IL: Human Kinetics, 2001.

Frank, A. *At the Will of the Body: Reflections on Illness*. Boston: Houghton, 1991.

Frank, A. *The Wounded Storyteller: Body, Illness, and Ethics*. Chicago: The University of Chicago Press, 1995.

Frank, A. "Illness and autobiographical work: Dialogue as narrative destabilization." *Qualitative Sociology* 23 (2000): 135–156.

Freud, S. *Civilization and its Discontents*. London: W.W. Norton and Company, 1930.

"Fuzak urges review of Title IX issue." *Chicago Tribune* (September 17, 1975): G3.

G, S. "Transgender Olympians." *Eros Zine*. Retrieved July 15, 2006, from http://www.eros-london.com/articles/2004-06-01/transolympics.

Galton, F. *Hereditary Genius*. London: MacMillan & Co, 1865.

Gavora, J. *Tilting the Playing Field: Schools, Sports, Sex and Title IX*. San Francisco: Encounter Books, 2002.

Gavora, J. "A conservative critique of Title IX, 2002." In *Title IX: A Brief History with Documents*, edited by S. Ware, 124–128. Boston: Bedford/St. Martin's, 2007.

Gavora, J. "Tilting the playing field: Schools, sports, sex and Title IX." In *Equal Play: Title IX and Social Change*, edited by N. Hogshead-Makar and A. Zimbalist, 197–217. Philadelphia: Temple University Press, 2007.

Genetic Technologies Limited. *Your Genetic Sports AdvantageTM, Version 1A*. Retrieved February 24, 2006, from http://www.genetictechnologies.com.au.

Gillett, J., Cain, R., and Pawluch, D. "Moving beyond the biomedical: The use of physical activity to negotiate illness." *Sociology of Sport Journal* 19 (2002): 370–384.

Goffman, E. *Asylums.* New York: Anchor, 1961.

Gorn, E., and Goldstein, W. *A Brief History of American Sport.* Champaign: University of Illinois Press, 2002.

Grant, C., and Darley, C. "Equity: What price equality?" In *Women in Sport: Issues and Controversies,* edited by G. Cohen. Newbury Park: Sage Publications, 1993.

Graves, L., Stratten, G., Ridgers, N., and Cable, N. "Comparison of energy expenditure in adolescents when playing new generation and sedentary computer games: A cross sectional study." *British Medical Journal* 335 (2007): 1282–1284.

Green, J. *Becoming a Visible Man.* Nashville: Vanderbilt University Press. 2004.

Greene, K., Berger, J., Reeves, C., Moffat, A., Standish, L., and Calabrese, C. "Most frequently used alternative and complementary therapies and activities by participants in the AMCOA study." *Journal of the Association of Nurses in AIDS Care* 10 (1999): 60–73.

Griffin, P. *Strong Women, Deep Closets: Lesbians and Homophobia in Sport.* Champaign, IL: Human Kinetics, 1998.

Griffin, R. *Sports in the Lives of Children and Adolescents.* London: Praeger, 1998.

Grusky, O. "Managerial succession." *American Journal of Sociology* 69 (1963): 72–76.

Gurr, T. *Why Men Rebel.* Princeton, NJ: Princeton University Press, 1970.

Guttmann, A. *Sports Spectators.* New York: Columbia University Press, 1985.

Guttmann, A. *Women's Sports: A History.* New York: Columbia University Press, 1991.

Guttmann, A. *The Olympics: A History of the Modern Games.* Chicago: University of Chicago Press, 2002.

Gutman, D. *Baseball Babylon: From the Black Sox to Pete Rose, the Real Stories Behind the Scandals that Rocked the Game.* New York: Penguin Books, 1992.

Hackbart v. Cincinnati Bengals, Inc. and Charles Clark, 601 F.2d 516; 444, U.S. 931 (1979).

Hagerman, E. "The cool sellout." *Outside Magazine* (November 2002). Retrieved March 27, 2008, from http://outside.away.com/outside/features/200211/200211/cool_sellout_2.html.

Halberstam, J. *In a Queer Time and Place: Transgender Bodies, Subcultural Lives.* New York: New York University Press, 2005.

Hall, A. *The Girl and the Game, a History of Women's Sport in Canada.* Peterborough, ON: Broadview Press, 2002.

Hall, S. "The local and the global: Globalization and ethnicity." In *Culture, Globalization and the World-System,* edited by A. King, 19–39. London: Macmillan, 1991.

Hanford, G. *A Report to the American Council on Education on an Inquiry into the Need for and Feasibility of a National Study for Intercollegiate Athletics.* Washington, D.C.: American Council on Education, 1974.

Hanford, G. "Controversies in college sport." *Annals of the American Academy of Political and Social Science* 445 (1979): 66–79.

Hannerz, U. *Transnational Connections: Culture, People, Places.* London: Comedia, 1996.

Happel, S., and Jennings, M. "Assessing the economic rationale and legal remedies for ticket scalping." *Journal of Legislation* 16 (1989): 1–14.

Haraway, D. *Simians, Cyborgs, and Women: The Reinvention of Nature.* London: Free Association Books, 1991.

Hardin, M., and Shain, S. "Strength In numbers? The experiences and attitudes of women in sports media careers." *Journalism & Mass Communication Quarterly* 82 (2005): 804–819.

Hardt, M., and Negri, A. *Empire.* Cambridge: Harvard University Press, 2000.

Hargreaves, J. *Sporting Females: Critical Issues in the History and Sociology of Women's Sports.* London: Routledge, 1994.

Harris, D. *The League: The Rise and Decline of the NFL.* New York, Bantam Books, 1986.

Hartmann, D. "Notes on midnight basketball and the cultural politics of recreation, race and at-risk urban youth." *Journal of Sport and Social Issues* 25 (2001): 339–371.

Hartmann, D. *Race, Culture and the Revolt of the Black Athlete: The 1968 Olympic Protests and their Aftermath.* Chicago: University of Chicago Press, 2004.

Harvey, R. "Snowboarding in the Olympics." *Los Angeles Times* (February 8, 1998).

Heino, R. "What is so punk about snowboarding?" *Journal of Sport and Social Issues* 24 (2000): 176–191.

Held, D., McGrew, A., Goldblatt, D., and Perraton, J. *Global Transformations: Politics, Economics and Culture.* Stanford: Stanford University Press, 1999.

Hemingway, E. *Death in the Afternoon.* New York: Scribner, 1932.

Herrnstein, R., and Murray, C. *The Bell Curve.* New York: Free Press, 1994.

Heywood, L., Dworkin, S., and Foudy, J. *Built to Win: The Female Athlete as Cultural Icon.* Minneapolis: University of Minnesota Press, 2003.

Higgs, R., and Braswell, M. *Unholy Alliance: Sacred and Modern Sports.* Macon: Mercer University Press, 2004.

Hise, R. *The War Against Men.* Oakland, CA: Elderberry Press, 2004.

Hoberman, J. *Mortal Engines: The Science of Performance and the Dehumanization of Sport.* New York: Free Press, 1992.

Hoberman, J. *Darwin's Athletes: How Sport has Damaged Black Athletes and Preserved the Myth of Race.* Boston: Houghton Mifflin, 1997.

Hoberman, J. *Testosterone Dreams: Rejuvenation, Aphrodisia, Doping.* Los Angeles: University of California Press, 2005.

Hoff-Sommers, C. *The War Against Boys: How Misguided Feminism is Harming our Young Men.* New York: Simon and Schuster, 2001.

Hogshead-Makar, N., and Zimbalist, A. *Equal play: Title IX and social change.* Philadelphia: Temple University Press, 2007.

Horne, J. *Sport in Consumer Culture.* New York: Palgrave Macmillan, 2006.

Horrocks, R. *Masculinity in Crisis: Myths, Fantasies and Realities.* Basingstoke: St. Martin's Press, 1994.

Howe, D. *Sport, Professionalism and Pain: Ethnographies of Injury and Risk.* London: Routledge, 2004.

Howe, D. *The Cultural Politics of the Paralympic Movement: Through the Anthropological Lens.* London: Routledge, 2008.

Howe, S. *(SICK) A Cultural History of Snowboarding.* New York: St. Martin's Griffin, 1998.

Howell, C. *Blood, Sweat and Cheers.* Toronto: University of Toronto Press, 2001.

Howell, O. "The creative class and the gentrifying city: Skateboarding in Philadelphia's Love Park." *Journal of Architectural Education* 59 (2005): 32–42.

Hughes, K. "Surfboarding shifts to the ski slopes and cultures clash." *The Wall Street Journal* (March 1988). Retrieved March 10, 2003, from http://global.factiva.com/en/arch/display.asp.

Hughes, R., and Coakley, J. "Positive deviance among athletes: The implications of overconformity to the sport ethic." *Sociology of Sport Journal* 8 (1991): 307–325.

Humphrey, S., and Kahn, A. "Fraternities, athletic teams, and rape." *Journal of Interpersonal Violence* 15 (2000): 1313–1322.

Humphreys, D. "Snowboarders: Bodies out of control and in conflict." *Sporting Traditions* 13 (1996): 3–23.

Humphreys, D. "Selling out snowboarding." In *To the Extreme: Alternative Sports, Inside and Out*, edited by R. Rinehart and S. Sydnor, 407–428. New York: SUNY Press, 2003.

Jennings, K. *Balls and Strikes: The Money Game in Professional Baseball*. New York: Praeger, 1990.

Johnson, J. *Making the Team: Inside the World of Sports Initiations and Hazing*. Halifax: Canadian Scholars' Press, 2004.

Kampion, D. *Stoked: A History of Surf Culture*. Salt Lake City, UT: Gibbs Smith Inc, 2003.

Katz, D. *Just Do It: The Spirit of Nike in the Corporate World*. Cincinnati, OH: Adams Media Corporation, 1995.

Katz, J. *Seductions of Crime*. New York: Basic Books, 1988.

Katz, J. *The Macho Paradox*. Naperville, IL: Sourcebooks, 2006.

Keim, M. *Nation-Building at Play: Sport as a Tool for Re-integration in a Post-apartheid South Africa*. Oxford, UK: Meyer and Meyer, 2003.

Kelling, G., and Wilson, J. "Broken windows." *Atlantic Monthly* 249: 29–38 (1982).

Kelly, D., Pomerantz, S., and Currie, D. "Skater girlhood and emphasized femininity: 'You can't land an ollie properly in heels.'" *Gender and Education* 17 (2005): 129–148.

Kennedy, S. *Why I Didn't Say Anything: The Sheldon Kennedy Story*. Toronto: Insomniac Press, 2006.

Kerr, J. *Understanding Soccer Hooliganism*. Buckingham: Open University Press, 1994.

Kerr, J. *Rethinking Violence and Aggression in Sport*. London: Routledge, 2004.

Kimmel, M., and Messner, M. *Men's Lives*. Boston: Allyn & Bacon, 2001.

King, S. "The politics of the body and the body politic: Magic Johnson and the ideology of AIDS." *Sociology of Sport Journal* 10 (1993): 270–285.

King, S. "Consuming compassion: AIDS, figure skating, and Canadian identity." *Journal of Sport and Social Issues* 24 (2000): 148–175.

King, S. "An all-consuming cause: Breast cancer, corporate philanthropy, and the market for generosity." *Social Text* 19 (2001): 115–143.

Klein, N. *No Logo*. London: Flamingo, 2001.

Knight Commission on Intercollegiate Athletics. *A Call to Action: Reconnecting College Sports and Higher Education*. Retrieved December 18, 2007, from http://www.knightcommission.org/about/a_call_to_action_letter_of_transmittal.

Knight Commission on Intercollegiate Athletics. *Keeping Faith with the Student-Athlete: A New Model for Intercollegiate Athletics*. Retrieved December 18, 2007, from http://www.knightcommission.org/about/keeping_faith_letter_of_transmittal.

Knorr, C. *The End of Baseball as We Knew it: The Players Union.* Champaign: The University of Illinois Press, 2005.

Kocher, L. "1972: 'You can't play because you're a girl'; 2004: 'You can't play because you're a boy.'" In *Title IX 30 Years Later: Sporting Equality,* edited by R. Simon, 147–163. New Brunswick, NJ: Transaction Publishers, 2005.

Kurlantzick, L. "Thoughts on professional sports and the anti-trust laws: Los Angeles Memorial Coliseum Commission v. National Football League." *Connecticut Law Review* 15 (1983): 183–208.

Kutner, L., and Olson, C. *Grand Theft Childhood.* New York: Simon & Schuster Adult Publishing Group, 2008.

Lapchick, L., Brenden, J., and Wright, B. *The 2006 Racial and Gender Report Card of the Associated Press Sports Editors.* Orlando: University of Central Florida, 2006.

Lapchick, R. *On the Mark: Putting the Student Back in Student-Athlete.* Lanham, MD: Lexington Books, 1987.

Lapchick, R. *100 Pioneers in Sport.* Morgantown, WV: Fitness Information Technology, 2007.

Lee, S., Barton, E., Sweeney, H., and Farrar, R. "Viral expression of insulin-like growth factor-I enhances muscle hypertrophy in resistance-trained rats." *Journal of Applied Physiology* 96 (2004): 1097–1104.

Lenskyj, H. *Inside the Olympic Industry: Power, Politics, and Activism.* Albany: SUNY, 2000.

Lenskyj, H. *Out on the Field: Gender, Sport and Sexualities.* Toronto: Women's Press, 2003.

Lenskyj, H. *Best Games Ever? The Social Impacts of Sydney 2000.* New York: SUNY Press, 2004.

Levitt, H. *The Marketing Imagination.* London: Collier-Macmillan, 1983.

Lewis, M. *Moneyball: The Art of Winning and Unfair Game.* New York: W.W. Norton and Company, 2006.

Lidz, F. "Lord of the board." *Sports Illustrated* (December 19, 1997): 114–119.

Lineberry, W. *Breaking and Implementing the Parent Code in Sports.* Longwood, FL: Xulon Press, 2005.

Long, J. "Full count: The real cost of public funding for major league sports." *Journal of Sports Economics* 6 (2005): 119–143.

Lopez, E. *Genetic Modification and Egalitarianism: Distinguish and Distribute.* UCSC Center for Biomolecular Science & Engineering, 2004. http://www.cbse.ucsc.edu/pdf_library/GeneModifEgal_Lopez061604.pdf.

Lorenz, K. *On Aggression.* San Diego: Harcourt Brace, 1963.

Lowe, M. *Women of Steel: Female Bodybuilding and the Struggle for Self-Definition.* New York: New York University Press, 1998.

Lowe, S. *The Kid on the Sandlot: Congress and Professional Sports, 1910–1992.* Bowling Green, OH: Bowling Green State University Popular Press, 1995.

Loy, J., and McElvogue, J. "Racial segregation in American sport." *International Review for the Sociology of Sport* 5 (1970): 5–24.

MacArthur, D., and North, K. "A gene for speed? The evolution and function of alpha-actinin-3." *BioEssays* 26 (2004): 786–795.

Majors, R. *Cool Pose: The Dilemmas of Black Manhood in America.* New York: Simon & Schuster, 1992.

Maloney, M. "An examination of the role that intercollegiate athletic participation plays in academic achievement: Athletes' feats in the classroom." *Journal of Human Resources* 28 (1993): 555–570.

Mangan, J. *Athleticism in the Victorian and Edwardian School.* London: Routledge, 1996.

Marais, J., and de Speville, L. *Adventure Racing.* Champaign, IL: Human Kinetics, 2004.

Margolis, B., and Pilivalin, J. "Stacking in Major League Baseball: A multivariate analysis." *Sociology of Sport Journal* 16 (1999): 16–34.

Markula, P. "The technologies of the self: Feminism, Foucault and sport." *Sociology of Sport Journal* 20 (2003): 87–107.

Markula, P. "The dancing body without organs: Deleuze, femininity and performing research." *Qualitative Inquiry* 12 (2006): 3–27.

Marsh, P. *Aggro: The Illusion of Violence.* London: Dent, 1978.

Martens, R., and Seefeldt, V. *Guidelines for Children's Sport.* Washington, D.C.: American Alliance for Health, Physical Education, Recreation and Dance, 1979.

Martin v. Daigle. 1 N.B.R. (2d) 755, 6 D.L.R. (3d) 634 (N.B.C.A) (1969).

Marx, K. *Das Capital,* vol. 1. New York: Penguin, 1863/1992.

Mason, D. "What is the sports product and who buys it? The marketing of professional sports leagues." *European Journal of Marketing* 33 (1999): 402–418.

McBride, J. *War, Battering, and Other Sports: The Gulf between American Men and Women.* Atlantic Highlands, NJ: Humanities Press, 1995.

McDonagh, E., and Papano, L. *Playing with the Boys: Why Separate is Not Equal in Sports.* Don Mills, ON: Oxford University Press, 2008.

McDonald, M. "Beyond the pale: The whiteness of sports studies and queer scholarship." In *Sport, Sexualities and Queer Theory,* edited by J. Cauldwell. London: Routledge, 2007.

McDonough, E. "Escaping antitrust immunity—Decertification of the National basketball Players Association." *Santa Clara Law Review* 37 (1997): 821–863.

Mechikoff, R., and Estes, S. *A History and Philosophy of Sport and Physical Education.* Madison, WI: Brown & Benchmark Publishing, 1993.

Melucci, A. *Challenging Codes: Collective Action in the Information Age.* Cambridge: Cambridge University Press, 1991.

Messner, M. *Taking the Field: Women, Men and Sports.* Minneapolis: University of Minnesota Press, 2002.

Messner, M. *Out of Play: Critical Essays on Gender in Sport.* Albany: SUNY Press, 2007.

Messner, M., and Solomon, N. "Social justice and men's interest: The case of Title IX." *Journal of Sport and Social Issues* 31 (2007): 162–178.

Miah, A. *Genetically Modified Athletes.* Routledge, 2004.

Miah, A., and Rich, E. "Genetic tests for ability? Talent identification and the value of an open future." *Sport, Education and Society* 11 (2006): 259–273.

Miller, D. *The Official History of the Olympic Games and the IOC.* London: Mainstream Publishing, 2008.

Miller, M. *A Whole Different Ballgame: The Inside Story of the Baseball Revolution.* New York: Birch Lane Press, 1991.

Miller, P. *Sport and the Color Line: Black Athletes and Race Relations in Twentieth Century America.* London: Routledge, 2003.

Miracle, A., and Rees, C. *Lessons of the Locker Room.* New York: Prometheus Books, 1994.
Mitchell, N., and Ennis, L. *Encyclopedia of Title IX and Sports.* Westport, CT: Greenwood Press, 2007.
Monaghan, L. *Bodybuilding, Drugs and Risk.* London: Routledge, 2001.
Monaghan, L. "Vocabularies of motive for illicit steroid use among bodybuilders." *Social Science & Medicine* 55 (2002): 695–708.
Morley, D., and Robins, K. *Spaces of identity: Global media, electronic landscapes and cultural boundaries.* London: Routledge, 1995.
Namaste, V. *Invisible Lives: The Erasure of Transsexual and Transgendered People.* Chicago: The University of Chicago Press, 2000.
Nathanson, P., and Young, K. *Spreading Misandry.* Montreal: McGill-Queen's University Press, 2000.
Nelson, M. *The Stronger Women Get, the More Men Love Football: Sexism and the American Culture of Sports.* New York: Avon Books, 1995.
"NGSA: Women's participation ranked by percent change 2003." *National Sporting Goods Association: Research and Statistic* (2005). Retrieved January 12, 2005, from http://www.nsga.org/public/pages/index.cfm?pageid=155.
Noakes, T. *Lore of Running.* Champaign, IL: Human Kinetics, 2003.
Nuwer, H. *Wrongs of Passage.* Bloomington: Indiana University Press, 2002.
Nuwer, H. *The Hazing Reader.* Bloomington: Indiana University Press, 2004.
Olsen-Acre, H. "The use of drug testing to police sex and gender in the Olympic Games." *Michigan Journal of Gender and Law* 13 (2006–2007): 207–236.
O'Reilly, J., and Cahn, S. *Women and Sports in the United States: A Documentary Reader.* Boston: Northeastern University Press, 2007.
Oxfam International. *Offside: Labour Rights and Sportswear Production in Asia.* Oxford: Oxfam, 2006.
Palzkill, B. "Between gym shoes and high-heels: The development of a lesbian identity and existence in top class sport." *International Review for the Sociology of Sport* 25 (1990): 221–234.
Paolo, David. *Human Rights in Youth Sport.* London: Routledge, 2004.
Pascall, B. *Eliminating Violence in Hockey.* Special Report Commissioned by Ian Waddell, Minister Responsible for Sport, British Columbia, Canada, 2000.
Pemberton, C. *More than a Game: One Woman's Fight for Gender Equity in Sport.* Boston: Northeastern University Press, 2002.
Perryman, M. *Hooligan Wars.* London: Mainstream, 2001.
Person, D., and Shaw, S. *Life Extension.* New York: Warner Books, 1982.
Pope, H., Phillips, K., and Olivardia, R. *The Adonis Complex: The Secret Crisis of Male Body Obsession.* Boston: Free Press, 2000.
Porto, B. *A New Season: Using Title IX to Reform College Sports.* Westport, CT: Praeger, 2003.
Pound, R. *Inside the Olympics.* New York: John Wiley and Sons, 2004.
Powell, S. *Souled Out? How Blacks are Winning and Losing in Sports.* Champaign, IL: Human Kinetics, 2007.
Prebish, C. *Religion and Sport: The Meeting of Sacred and Profane.* Westport, CT: Greenwood Press, 1992.

Pronger, B. *The Arena of Masculinity: Sports, Homosexuality and the Meaning of Sex.* Toronto: University of Toronto Press, 1990a.

Pronger, B. "Gay jocks: A phenomenology of gay men in athletics." In *Sport, Men, and the Gender Order Critical Feminist Perspectives,* edited by M. Messner and D. Sabo, 141–152. Champaign, IL: Human Kinetics, 1990b.

Putnam, R. *Bowling Alone: The Collapse and Revival of American Community.* New York: Simon and Schuster, 2000.

Putney, C. *Muscular Christianity: Manhood and Sports in Protestant America.* Cambridge: Harvard University Press, 2001.

"Question and answer." *Transworld Snowboarding* (January 19, 2006). http://www.transworldsnowboarding.com/article_print.jsp?ID=1000027333.

R v. Cey. 48 C.C.C. (3d) 480 (Sask C.A.) (1989).

R v. Ciccarelli. O.J. No 2388 (O.P.C) (1988).

R v. Green. O.R. 591, 2 C.C.C. (2d) 442, 16 D.L.R. (3d) 137 (Prov. Ct.) (1971).

R v. Maki. 3 O.R. 780, 1 C.C.C. (2d) 333, 14 D.L.R. (3d) 164 (Prov Ct.) (1970).

R v. McSorley. B.C.J. No. 0116 (B.C.P.C) (2000).

R v. Neeld. B.C.J. No. 57676–01 (B.C.P.C) (2000).

R v. Prénoveau. R.L 21 (C.s.p) (1971).

R v. Starrat. 1 O.R. 227, 5 C.C.C. (2d) 32 (C.A) (1980).

R v. Watson. 26 C.C.C. (2d) 150 (O.P.C) (1975).

Rader, B. *American Sports: From the Age of Folk Games to the Age of Televised Sports.* Englewood Cliffs, NJ: Prentice Hall, 1996.

Rainey, D. "Sources of stress, burnout and intention to terminate among basketball referees." *Journal of Sport Behavior* 22 (1999): 19–40.

Randall, L. "The culture that Jake built." *Forbes* (March 27, 1995): 45–46.

Raspberry, W. "Smothering a Civil Rights Bill." *Washington Post* (April 5, 1985): A17.

Reed, R. *The Way of the Snowboarder.* New York: Harry N. Abrams, 2005.

Reese, R. *American Paradox.* Durham, NC: Carolina Press, 2004.

Rhoden, W. *Forty Million Dollar Slaves.* Pittsburgh: Three Rivers Press, 2007.

Rhoden, W. *Third and a Mile.* New York: ESPN, 2007.

Richards, T., and Blehm, E. *P3: Pipes, Parks, and Powder.* New York: Harper Collins, 2003.

Rinehart, R. "Emerging/arriving sport: Alternatives to formal sports." In *Handbook of Sports Studies,* edited by J. Coakley and E. Dunning, 504–519. London: Sage, 2000.

Rinehart, R. " 'Babes' and boards: Opportunities in new millennium sport?" *Journal of Sport and Social Issues* 29 (2005): 232–255.

Rinehart, R., and Sydnor, S. *To the Extreme: Alternative Sports, Inside and Out.* Albany: SUNY Press, 2003.

Ritchie, I. "Sex tested, Gender verified: Controlling female sexuality in the age of containment." *Sports History Review* 34 (2003): 80–98.

Robbins, P. *Anorexia and Bulimia.* Hillside: Enslow Publishers, 1998.

Robinson, L. *Crossing the Line: Violence and Sexual Assault in Canada's National Sport.* Toronto: McClelland & Stewart, 1998.

Roche, M. "The Olympics and global citizenship." *Citizenship Studies* 6 (2002): 165–181.

Rogol, A., and Yesalis, C. "Anabolic-androgenic steroids and athletes: What are the issues?" *Journal of Clinical Endocrinology and Metabolism* 74 (1992): 465–469.

Rosenthal, C., Morris, L., and Martinez, J. "Who's on first and what's on second? Assessing interest group strategies on Title IX." *Women in Sport and Physical Activity Journal* 13 (2004): 65–86.

Rosentraub, M. S. *Major League Losers: The Real Cost of Sports and Who's Paying for it.* New York: Basic Books, 1997.

Ross, C. *Race and Sport: The Struggle for Equality on and Off the Field.* Jackson: University of Mississippi Press, 2005.

Rushton, J-P. *Race, Evolution and Behavior.* Port Huron, MI: Charles Darwin Research Institute, 1997.

Sabo, D., Miller, K., Farrell, M., Melnick, M., and Barnes, G. "High school athletic participation, sexual behavior and adolescent pregnancy: A regional study." *Journal of Adolescent Health* 25 (1999): 207–216.

Sack, A., and Staurowsky, E. *College Athletes for Hire: The Evolution and Legacy of the NCAA's Amateur Myth.* Westport, CT: Praeger, 1998.

Sandoz, J. *Whatever it Takes: Women on Women's Sport.* New York: Farrar, Straus and Giroux, 1999.

Sankaran, G., Volkwein-Caplan, K., Volkwein, K., and Bonsall, D. *HIV/AIDS in Sport: Impact, Issues, and Challenges.* Champaign, IL: Human Kinetics, 1999.

Savage, H. *American College Athletics.* New York: Carnegie Foundation, 1929.

Savulescu, J., and Foddy, B. "Comment: genetic test available for sports performance." *British Journal of Sports Medicine* 39 (2005): 472.

Sawyer, R., Thompson, E., and Chicorelli, A. "Rape myth acceptance among intercollegiate athletes: A preliminary examination." *American Journal of Health Studies* 18 (2000): 19–26.

Schmidt, M., and Berri, D. "On the Evolution of Competitive Balance: The Impact of an increasing Global Search." *Economic Inquiry* 41 (2003): 692–704.

Schwartz, M., and DeKeseredy, W. *Sexual Assault on the College Campus.* Thousand Oaks, CA: Sage, 1997.

Scranton, S. *Gender and Sport: A Reader.* London: Routledge, 2001.

Scraton, P. *Hillsborough: The Truth.* London: Mainstream, 1999.

Seagrave, K. *Ticket Scalping: An American History.* McFarland and Co, 2005.

Seale, C. "Sporting cancer: Struggle language in news reports of people with cancer." *Sociology of Health and Illness* 23 (2001): 308–329.

Semerjian, T. Z., and Cohen, J. " 'FTM means female to me': Transgender athletes performing gender." *Women in Sport and Physical Activity Journal* 15 (2006): 28–43.

Senn, A. *Power, Politics and the Olympic Games.* Champaign, IL: Human Kinetics, 1999.

Shaw, S. "The Construction of Gender Relations in Sport Organisations." Unpublished PhD dissertation. De Montfort University, England, 2000.

Sherowski, J. "Women on the verge: The future of female supershredding is now." *Transworld Snowboarding* (November 2003): 146.

Shogan, D. *The Making of High Performance Athletes: Discipline, Diversity, and Ethics.* Toronto: University of Toronto Press, 1999.

Simon, R. *Title IX 30 years Later: Sporting Equality.* New Brunswick, NJ: Transaction Publishers, 2005.

Simpson, V., and Jennings, A. *Dishonored Games: Corruption, Money and Greed at the Olympics.* New York: SPI Books, 1992.

Smith, A. *National Identity.* London: Penguin, 1991.

Smith, E. *Race, Sport and the American Dream.* Durham: Carolina Press, 2007.

Smith, L. *Nike is a Goddess: The History of Women in Sport.* Cornwall: Atlantic Press, 1995.

"Snowboarding and the Olympics." Retrieved July 17, 2007, from http://www.burton.com/company/default.asp.

Sokolove, M. *Warrior Girls: Lifted Spirits and Broken Bodies in the Wake of Title IX.* New York: Simon and Schuster, 2008.

Sontag, S. *AIDS and Its Metaphors.* London: Anchor Books, 1989.

Sowell, R. "What does sport have to so with AIDS?" *Journal of the Association of Nurses in AIDS Care* 16 (2005): 1–2.

Staffo, D. "Strategies for reducing criminal violence among athletes." *The Journal of Physical Education, Recreation & Dance* 72 (2001): 239–255.

Standish, L., Greene, K., Bain, S., Reeves, C., Sanders, F., Wines, R., Turet, P., Kim, J., and Calabrese, C. "Alternative Medicine Use in HIV-Positive Men and Women: Demographics, Utilization Patterns, and Health Status." *AIDS Care* 13 (2001): 197–208.

Staurowsky, E. "Women coaching male athletes." In *Sport, Men, and the Gender Order: Critical Feminist Perspectives,* edited by M. Messner and D. Sabo, 163–170. Champaign, IL: Human Kinetics, 1990.

Stebbins, R. *Tolerable Differences: Living with Deviance.* Whitby, ON: McGraw-Hill, 1996.

Stryker, S. "My words to Victor Frankenstein above the village of Chamounix: Performing transgender rage." In *The Transgender Studies Reader,* edited by S. Stryker and S. Whittle, 244–256. New York: Routledge, 2006.

Suggs, W. *A Place on the Team: The Triumph and Tragedy of Title IX.* Princeton: Princeton University Press, 2005.

Sundgot-Borgen, J. "Eating disorders among male and female elite athletes." *British Journal of Sports Medicine* 33 (1999): 434.

Susan S., and Whittle, S. *The Transgender Studies Reader.* New York: Routledge, 2006.

Sutliff, M., and Freeland, D. "HIV-infected sports participants engaging in contact limits of confidentiality testing and disclosure with sports: Legal and ethical implications.". *Journal of Sport and Social Issues* 19 (1995): 415–431.

Suzuki, D. *The Sacred Balance: Rediscovering our Place in Nature.* Vancouver: Greystone Books, 2000.

Sykes, H. "Transsexual and transgender policies in sport." *Women in Sport and Physical Activity Journal* 15 (2006): 3–13.

Symons, C., and Hemphill, D. "Transgendering sex and sport in the Gay Games." In *Sport, Sexualities and Queer/Theory,* edited by J. Cauldwell, 109–128. London: Routledge, 2006.

Tamburinni, C., and Tännsjö, T. *Genetic Technology and Sport: Ethical Questions.* London: Routledge, 2005.

Taylor, B., and Trogdon, J. "Losing to win: Tournament incentives in the National Basketball Association." *Journal of Labor Economics* 20 (2002): 23–41.

Teton, L. "Lindsey Jacobellis treated harshly by NBC for snowboard cross gaff." *Snowboardsecrets.com* (February 19, 2006). Retrieved February 18, 2008, from http://snowboardsecrets.com/articles/jacobellis.htm.

Theberge, N. "The construction of gender in sport: Women, coaching, and the naturalization of difference." *Social Problems* 40 (1993): 301–313.

Theberge, N. *Higher Goals: Women's Ice Hockey and the Politics of Gender.* Albany: SUNY Press, 2000.

"The principles of snowboarding" (August 2002). Retrieved January 18, 2004, from http://www.boardtheworld.com.

Thompson, S. "Sport, gender, feminism." In *Theory, Sport & Society,* edited by J. Maguire and K. Young, 105–128. London: JAI, 2002.

Thorpe, H. "Beyond 'decorative sociology': Contextualizing female surf, skate, and snowboarding." *Sociology of Sport Journal* 23 (2006): 205–228.

Thorpe, H. "Snowboarding." In *Berkshire Encyclopedia of Extreme Sport,* edited by Douglas Booth and Holly Thorpe, 286–294. Great Barrington, MA: Berkshire Publishing, 2007.

Tilly, C. *From Mobilization to Revolution.* Reading: Addison-Wesley, 1978.

Todd, J., and Todd, T. "Significant events in the history of drug testing and the Olympic movement: 1960–1999." In *Doping in Elite Sport: The Politics of Drugs in the Olympic Movement,* edited by W. Wilson and E. Derse. Champaign, IL: Human Kinetics, 2001.

Tuaolo, E. *Alone in the Trenches: My Life as a Gay Man in the NFL.* Naperville, IL: Sourcebooks, 2006.

United States Department of Education, Institute of Educational Sciences. Table 270: First-professional degrees conferred by degree-granting institutions, by sex of student, control of institution, and field of study: Selected years, 1985–86 through 2005–06. *Digest of Education Statistics.* (2007, June). Retrieved from http://nces.ed.gov/programs/digest/d07/tables/dt07_270.asp.

van Hilvoorde, I., Vos, R., and de Wert, G. "Flopping, klapping and gene doping: Dichotomies between 'natural' and 'artificial' in elite sport." *Social Studies of Science* 37: 173–200 (2006).

Wachs, F., and Dworkin, S. "There's no such thing as a gay hero: Sexual identity and media framing of HIV-positive athletes." *Journal of Sport and Social Issues* 21 (1997): 327–347.

Wackwitz, L. "Verifying the myth: Olympic sex testing and the category 'woman.'" *Women's Studies International Forum* 26 (2003): 553–560.

Waddell, T., and Schapp, D. *Gay Olympian: The Life and Death of Tom Waddell.* New York: Alfred A. Knopf, 1996.

Waddington, I. *Sport, Health and Drugs: A Critical Sociological Perspective.* London: Taylor and Francis, 2000.

Wallerstein, I. *The Modern World-System: Capitalist Agriculture and the Origins of the European World-Economy in the Sixteenth Century.* New York: Academic Press, 1974.

Walton, L. "How the NBA Draft Process Works." Retrieved August 12, 2007, from http://www.hoopsvibe.com/nba/nba-draft/nba-draft-news/how-the-nba-draft-process-works-ar43263.html.

Walton, T. *Pinned by Gender Construction?: A Critical Media Analysis of Girls' and Women's Wrestling.* Unpublished Ph.D. dissertation, University of Iowa, 2002.

Walton, T. "Reaganism and the dismantling of civil rights in the 1980s: A Title IX retrospective." Paper presented at the Annual Conference of the North American Society for the Sociology of Sport, Montreal, Canada (2003).

Walton, T. "Title IX: Forced to wrestle up the backside." *Women in Sport and Physical Activity Journal* 12 (2003): 5–26.

Walton, T. "Title IX: 30 years of controversy." Paper presented at the Annual Conference of the North American Society for Sport History, Columbus, Ohio, 2003.

Walton, T., and Helstein, M. "Triumph of backlash: Wrestling community and the 'problem' of Title IX." *Sociology of Sport Journal* 25 (3) (2008): 159–187.

Wann, D., Melnick, M., Russell, G., and Pease, D. *Sports Fans: The Psychological and Social Impacts of Spectators.* London: Routledge, 2001.

Ward, C. *All Quiet on the Hooligan Front: Eight Years that Changed the Face of Football.* London: Headline Books, 1997.

Ware, S. *Title IX: A Brief History with Documents.* Boston: Bedford/St. Martin's, 2007.

Weinstein, M., Smith, M., and Wiesenthal, D. "Masculinity and hockey violence." *Sex Roles* 33 (1995): 831–847.

Weistart, J. "League control of market opportunities: A perspective on competition and cooperation in the sports industry." *Duke Law Journal* 1984 (1984): 1013–1070.

West, A., and Brackenridge, C. *A Report on the Issues Relating to Women's Lives as Sports Coaches in the United Kingdom, 1989/90.* Sheffield, UK: Sheffield City Polytechnic and PAVIC Publications, 1990.

Whanell, G. *Fields in Vision: Television Sport and Cultural Transformation.* London: Routledge, 1992.

Wheaton, B. *Understanding Lifestyle Sports.* London: Routledge, 2004.

Whitehead, S. *Men and Masculinities: Key Themes and New Directions.* Cambridge, UK: Polity Press, 2002.

Wiegman, O., and Schie, E. "Video game playing and its relations with aggressive and pro-social behaviour." *British Journal of Social Psychology* 37 (1998): 367–378.

Wiggins, D., and Miller, P. *Unlevel Playing Field: The African American Athlete's Experience.* Syracuse, NY: Syracuse University Press, 2003.

Wiggins, K. *Glory Bound: Black Athletes in a White World.* Syracuse, NY: Syracuse University Press, 1997.

Will, G. "A train wreck called Title IX." In *Women and Sports in the United States: A Documentary Reader,* edited by J. O'Reilly and S. Cahn, 346–347. Boston: Northeastern University Press, 2007.

Willard, M. "Séance, tricknowlogy, skateboarding, and the space of youth." In *Generations of Youth: Youth Cultures and History in Twentieth-Century America,* edited by J. Austin and M. Willard, 327–346. New York: New York University Press, 1998.

Williams, L. "Racist jokes in White House reported in a book." *New York Times* (October 21, 1987): A16.

Williams, M. *The Ergogenics Edge.* Champaign, IL: Human Kinetics, 1999.

Williams, P., Dossa, K., and Fulton, A. "Tension on the slopes: Managing conflict between skiers and snowboarders." *Journal of Applied Recreation Research* 19 (1994): 191–213.

Williams, R. *Marxism and Literature.* Oxford: University of Oxford Press, 1977.

Williams, R. *Promise Keepers and the New Masculinity: Private Lives and Public Morality.* Lanham: Lexington Books, 2001.

Wilson, B. "Good Blacks and bad Blacks: Media constructions of African American athletes in Canadian basketball." *International Review for the Sociology of Sport* 32 (1997): 177–189.

World Anti-Doping Agency. *The 2004 Prohibited List International Standard* Lausanne: WADA, 2004.

World Anti Doping Agency. *The Stockholm Declaration,* 2005. Retrieved May 1, 2008, from http://www.wadaama.org/en/dynamic.ch2?pageCategory.id=530.

World Anti-Doping Association. *The World Anti-Doping Code.* Retrieved May 1, 2008, from http://www.wada-ama.org/rtecontent/document/code_v3.pdf.

World Anti-Doping Association. *The World Anti-Doping Code. The 2008 Prohibited List International Standard.* Retrieved May 1, 2008, from http://www.wada-ama.org/rtecontent/document/2008_List_En.pdf.

Wright, A. *Surfing California.* Redondo, CA: Mountain and Sea, 1973.

Wughalter, E. "Ruffles and flounces: The apologetic in women's sports." *Frontiers: A Journal of Women Studies* 3 (1978): 11–13.

Yang, N., MacArthur, D., Gulbin, J., Hahn, A., Beggs, A., Easteal, S., and North, K. "ACTN3 Genotype is associated with human elite athletic performance." *American Journal of Human Genetics* 73 (2003): 627–631.

Yesalis, C., and Bahrke, M. "History of doping in sport." *International Sports Studies* 24: 42–76 (2002).

Yost, M. *Tailgaiting, Sacks and Salary Caps: How the NFL Became the Most Successful Sports League in History.* New York: Kaplan Business, 2006.

Young, K. "Violence, risk, and liability in male sports culture." *Sociology of Sport Journal* 10 (1993): 373–396.

Young, K. "From sports violence to sports crime: Aspects of violence, law, and gender in the sports process." In *Paradoxes of Youth and Sport,* edited by M. Gatz, M. Messner, and S. Ball-Rokeach. New York: SUNY Press, 2002.

Young, K. "Standard deviations: An update on North American sports crowd disorder." *Sociology of Sport Journal* 19 (2002): 237–253.

Young, K. *Sporting Bodies, Damaged Selves: Sociological Studies of Sport-Related Injury.* Oxford: Elsevier, 2004.

Young, K., and K. Wamsley. "State complicity in sports assault and the gender order in 20th century Canada: Preliminary Observations." *Avante* 2 (1996): 51–69.

Young, N. *The Complete History of Surfing.* Salt Lake City, UT: Gibbs Smith Inc, 2008.

Zarkos, J. "Raising the bar: A man, the flop and the Olympic gold medal." *Sun Valley Guide* 17 (2004): 28.

Zimbalist, A. *Unpaid Professionals: Commercialism and Conflict in Big-Time College Sports.* Princeton: Princeton University Press, 2001.

Zimbalist, A. "What to do about Title IX." In *Title IX 30 Years Later: Sporting Equality,* edited by R. Simon, 71–76. New Brunswick, NJ: Transaction Publishers, 2005.

Zimbalist, A. "Title IX by the numbers." In *Equal play: Title IX and Social Change,* edited by N. Hogshead-Makar and A. Zimbalist, 302–305. Philadelphia: Temple University Press, 2007.

Zirin, D. *What's My Name, Fool: Sports and Resistance in the United States.* Boston: Haymarket Books, 2005.

ABOUT THE EDITOR AND CONTRIBUTORS

Michael Atkinson is Senior Lecturer in the School of Sport and Exercise Science, Loughborough University, UK. His research relates to bodies, violence, animals, deviance, and gender in sports cultures. He is coauthor of *Deviance and Social Control in Sport* with Kevin Young (2008).

Harvey Abrams is a researcher, writer, consultant, and sports historian who has published widely on the history of the Olympic Games. He has been a wrestling coach, FILA referee at U.S. Olympic Freestyle Wrestling trials, a member of the International Olympic Academy, founder of the Philadelphia Amateur Wrestling Club and founder of the International Institute for Sport and Olympic History.

David Andrews is Professor of Physical Cultural Studies in the Department of Kinesiology at the University of Maryland and an affiliate faculty member of the Departments of American Studies and Sociology. He is assistant editor of the *Journal of Sport and Social Issues* and an editorial board member of the *Sociology of Sport Journal, Leisure Studies, Quest,* and *Sport Management Review.* His research focuses on critical analysis of sports as an aspect of contemporary commercial culture.

Becky Beal is Associate Professor of Kinesiology at California State University, East Bay, Hayward, CA. Her research interests focus on the cultural dynamics of extreme sports, and she is regarded as one of the leading authorities on skateboarding cultures.

Rob Beamish is the Head of the Department of Sociology at Queen's University, Kingston, Ontario. He has written extensively and critically on high-performance sports from the perspective of the athlete. His latest book, *Fastest, Highest, Strongest: A Critique of High-Performance Sport,* is coauthored with Ian Ritchie.

Peter Donnelly is Professor and Director of the Centre for Sport Policy Studies in the Faculty of Physical Education and Health at the University of Toronto. He has been editor of the *Sociology of Sport Journal* and International Review for the Sociology of Sport and served as President of the North American Society for the Sociology of Sport. His research interests include sports politics and policy issues (including the area of sports), sports subcultures, and mountaineering (history).

Laura L. Finley teaches in the Department of Women's Studies at Florida Atlantic University and was formerly Director of Social Change at Women in Distress, the only domestic violence agency in Broward County, Florida. Dr. Finley is the author of *Juvenile Justice* (2007) in Greenwood's Historical Guides to Controversial Issues in America series and editor of *Encyclopedia of Juvenile Violence* (Greenwood Press, 2006).

Vanessa Heggie is Lecturer in the Department of History and the Philosophy of Science at the University of Cambridge, UK. Her areas of research interest relate to the history of medicine (1800–2000); the history of health, diet, exercise, and alcohol; sports medicine and sports science; maternalism, district nursing, and infant welfare; food and feeding—school meals, coffee houses; vegetarianism and health fads; degeneration and eugenics; masculinity and physicality; and gender testing in sports.

Joseph Maguire is Professor in the School of Sport and Exercise Science, Loughborough University, UK. He is a past President of the International Sociology of Sport Association and is presently an executive board member of the International Council for Sports Science and Physical Education. His research interests include violence, pain and injury, sports and the body/emotions, sports and the media, and globalization.

Daniel S. Mason is a Professor with the Faculty of Physical Education and Recreation and an adjunct professor with the School of Business at the University of Alberta, in Edmonton, Canada. His research takes an interdisciplinary approach and focuses on the business of sports and the relationships between its stakeholders, including all levels of government, sports teams and leagues, the communities that host teams, agents, and players' associations.

Fred Mason is Assistant Professor in the Faculty of Kinesiology at the University of New Brunswick. He undertook a Bachelor of Physical Education (Recreation) and Bachelor of Arts (Sociology) at the Memorial University of Newfoundland, a Master's degree in Sociology at Ottawa, and a PhD in Sociology at the University of Western Ontario. Fred's research interests vary across the sociology and history of sports, with a general focus on sports and the media, social constructions of gender in historical and sociological perspectives, the history of disability sports, sports-related tourism writing and promotion in the late nineteenth century, and sports in literature and film.

Andy Miah is Reader in New Media and Bioethics at the University of West Scotland and Fellow in visions of Utopia and Dystopia at the Institute for Ethnics and Emerging Technologies. His research is informed by an interest in applied philosophy, technology, and culture, and he writes broadly about emerging technological cultures, particularly the development of human enhancement technologies. This includes the implications of pervasive wireless connectivity and the convergence of technological systems and the modification of biological matter through nanotechnology and gene transfer.

Emma Rich is Senior Lecturer in the School of Sport and Exercise Science at Loughborough University, UK. Her research centers on gender and physical education/sports, equity, inclusion and identity in physical education, and social constructions of health. Dr. Rich is currently undertaking a number of research projects exploring the relationships between education and ill health, with a particular focus on eating disorders. She is coauthor of *The Medicalisation of Cyberspace* with Dr. Andy Miah (2008).

Parissa Safai is Assistant Professor in the sociocultural study of physical activity and health at the School of Kinesiology and Health Science at York University. Her research interests focus on sports at the intersection of risk, health, and health care including sports' "culture of risk"; the development and social organization of sports and exercise medicine; and the social determinants of athletes' health.

Amanda N. Schweinbenz is an Assistant Professor in the School of Human Kinetics at Laurentian University in Sudbury, Ontario, Canada. Her primary areas of research include sports history, gender and sports, women's international rowing, and the Olympic Games.

Tamar Z. Semerjian is Associate Professor of sports psychology in the Department of Kinesiology at San José State University. Her research focuses on marginalized populations and their sports and exercise experiences, incorporating theoretical perspectives from both cultural studies and social psychology of sports. She has published work based on her research with older adults, individuals with spinal cord injuries, and transgender athletes.

Brian P. Soebbing is a Ph.D. candidate in the Faculty of Physical Education and Recreation at the University of Alberta. His main research interests include competitive balance and uncertainty of outcome in professional and amateur sports leagues. Secondary interests include sports betting, public policy and stadiums, and strategic decisions of professional and amateur sports leagues.

Holly Thorpe is Lecturer in Sport and Leisure Studies at the University of Waikato, New Zealand. Her research interests include social theory, gender, and physical youth cultures. Her work has appeared in a number of journals including *Sport in Society, Sociology of Sport Journal, Sport and Social Issues,* and *Junctures.* She is also coeditor (with Douglas Booth) of the *Berkshire Encyclopedia of Extreme Sports* (2007).

Theresa Walton is Assistant Professor in Exercise, Leisure and Sport at Kent Sate University. Drawing on critical cultural studies, her teaching and research scholarship focuses on investigations of power relationships and the ways those relationships are both resisted and maintained within mediated sports narratives. In particular, she examines media discourse of Title IX, women's amateur wrestling, and elite distance running.

Charlene Weaving is Assistant Professor in the Human Kinetics Department at St. Francis Xavier University, in Antigonish, Nova Scotia, Canada. She researches women athletes and sexuality. In 2007, she won the Outstanding Teaching Award for the Faculty of Science.

INDEX

AAP. *See* Athlete Assistance Program
Aaron, Hank, 68
AAS. *See* Anabolic androgenic steroids
ABA. *See* American Basketball Association
Abidjan, 400, 402
ABL. *See* American Basketball League
Abrams, Roger, 25, 162
Absolutely Radical, 394
Abuse, 303; emotional, 366; partner, 312–17; referee, 354–59; sexual, 348–53
Academic misconduct, 1–7
Acosta, R. Vivian, 171
ACTN3 genetic test, 189–90
Acuff, Amy, 258
Adams, Dolly, 497
Adams, Jack, 375
Adams, Jeff, 252–53
Addiction, gambling, 195
Adidas, 125–26, 129–30
Adventure racing, 7–11
Advertising, 266–71; guerrilla, 340
Aerobics, 512
Afghani PKK, 434
AFL. *See* American Football League
Africa, 48–50; soccer tragedies in, 400–402
African Americans, 66–69; coaches, 348; quarterbacks and, 347; sports leagues, 344–45; underrepresentation of, 345
Agassi, Andre, 81–82
Age Discrimination Act, 171
Agee, Stacy, 180
Age limits, 105–6
Agenda 21, 123

Aggression: A Social Learning Analysis (Bandura), 318
Agricultural Revolution, 327
AIA. *See* Athletes in Action
AIAW. *See* Association for Intercollegiate Athletics for Women
AIDS. *See* HIV/AIDS
Ainsleigh, Gordy, 457
Air Jordan, 75
AIS. *See* Androgen Insensitivity Syndrome
Alaska Mountain Wilderness Classic, 9
Alcohol, 247–53; missile throwing and, 292; prohibition of, 334
Alexander, Kris, 486
Alexander, Victoria, 350–51
Alexander the Great, 13
ALF. *See* Animal Liberation Front
Ali, Laila, 497
Ali, Muhammad, 71, 344, 427; ubersexuality and, 452
Alioto, Joseph, 242–43
All-American Girls Professional Baseball League, 181, 182
All-American Girls Softball League, 181
Allemansrätten, 328–30
Allen, Jared, 250
Allen, Johnny, 356
Almonte, Danny, 53–54
Alomar, Roberto, 355–56
Alone in the Trenches: My Life as a Gay Man in the NFL (Tuaolo), 299
Alpine Ironman, 9
Alter, Hobie, 388, 421

539

Index

Alvarez, Wilson, 479
Amaechi, John, 213
Amateur athletes: drafts of, 103–9; Olympics and, 414; skateboarding and, 389
Amateurs, 201
American Basketball Association (ABA), 72–74; antitrust violations and, 26–27; Haywood, Spencer, and, 109
American Basketball League (ABL), 30, 496–97
American Football League (AFL), 26
American Gladiators, 333
American Health Foods Business index, 131
American National Labor Committee, 128–29
American Physical Education Association, 493
Americans with Disabilities Act, 50, 226
American Women's National Physique Championship, 484
Amla, Hashim, 431
Amnesty International, 265–66
Amphetamines, 414
Anabolic androgenic steroids (AAS), 412
Anabolic steroids, 19, 21, 412–18; BALCO and, 480–81; Canseco and, 479; ergogenics and, 135; Johnson, Ben, and, 58; sports medicine and, 405; Turinabol and, 45
Anani, Sumya, 497
Anderson, Brady, 479
Anderson, Greg, 416
Anderson, Jamal, 383
Andrews, David, 67
Androgen Insensitivity Syndrome (AIS), 282
Androgyny, 482–84
Anheuser-Busch, 85
Animal blood sports, 12–18
Animal Liberation Front (ALF), 16
Animal Place, 14
Annan, Kofi, 367
Anorexia athletica, 115
Anorexia nervosa, 111–17
Anquetil, Jacques, 55
Antiauthoritarianism, 385
Antidoping, 18–22
Anti-Racketeering Act, 193
Antiscalping laws, 438–40
Anti-sports movement, 3
Antitrust violations, 22–29
Antwaan, Randle El, 363
Apartheid, 62–63
Apologetic, female, 482–87
ARA. See Australian Rogaining Association
Arbitration, salary, 32–33
Archidamos, 489
Arena Football League, 335; corporate branding and, 79
Arguello, Martin Vassallo, 164–65
Armstrong, Lance, 406; comeback of, 223–24; endorsements of, 81–82; EPO and, 141

Arndt, Judith, 297
Arrests: avoiding, 89; DUIs and, 250
Artest, Ron, 89, 291, 319
Ashe, Arthur, 70
Asians, 67
Aspromonte, Ken, 292–93
Assault cases, 91; referee abuse and, 359
Association for Intercollegiate Athletics for Women (AIAW), 158, 176
Association of Tennis Professionals (ATP), 165
Astacio, Pedro, 315
Astaphan, Jamie, 406
The Astronauts, 422
Asylums (Goffman), 192
Atari, 466; virtual sports and, 472
Athens, 434–35
Athlete Assistance Program (AAP), 200
Athlete performance, 43–51
Athletes: corporate branding of, 81–82; domestic violence and, 312–17; with eating disorders, 116–17; ethnic, 65–71; fan violence and, 317–21; nonathletes *v.*, 3; openly gay, 295–99; sexual abuse among, 377–83; transsexual, 443–48; young, 366–70
Athletes in Action (AIA), 364
Athlete unions. See Unions
athletic therapists, 403
Atkinson, Ron, 431
Atlanta Braves, 264–65
Atlantic Monthly, 311
ATP. See Association of Tennis Professionals
Auburn University, 4, 478
Australia, 2000 Olympics, 64
Australian Rogaining Association (ARA), 8
Autobiography of a Yogi (Choudury), 512
Avalanche Snowboards, 390–91
Aylott, Nigel, 10

Badjocks.com, 381
Baer, Ralph, 465
Bagger, Mianne, 446
Baillet-Latour, Henri de, 231
Bailo, Kent, 174–75
Baiting, 12
"Baja," 422
Baker, Dick, 395
Baker, Jack, 243
Balck, Viktor, 230
BALCO. See Bay Area Laboratory Co-Operative
Bandura, Albert, 318
Baranova-Masolkin, Natalia, 142
Barclay Center, 87
Barefoot, Chuck, 390
Barkley, Charles, 163, 263
Barnett, Gary, 352
Barnett, Marilyn, 296
Barnett, Tim, 315

Barnstable, Dale, 6
Barr, George, 356
Barton, John, 48
Baseball: cheating and, 56; virtual, 472. *See also* Major League Baseball
Baseball Babylon (Gutman), 162
BASE jumping, 455, 503
Basketball: gender and, 179; midnight, 369; taunting and, 426
BASL. *See* Big Apple Softball League
Basso, Ivan, 141
Bateer, Mengke, 67
"Battle of the Sexes," 500
Bay Area Laboratory Co-Operative (BALCO), 58–59, 415–17, 480–81
Baylor University, 5
BCA. *See* Black Coaches and Administrators
BCCI. *See* Board of Control for Cricket in India
Beach Boys, 420
Bean balls, 427
Bean, Billy, 298
Beardall, Alan, 48
Beard, Ralph, 6
Beat Generation, 419
Bechler, Steve, 137
Beckham, David, 339, 371; endorsements of, 81–82; ubersexuality and, 453–54
Beckham, Victoria, 453–54
Beecher, Catherine, 493
Beecher, Lyman, 361
Beer, 292
Behavior: crowd, 322; deviant, 1
Belfour, Ed, 252
Belichick, Bill, 59
Bell, Albert, 56
The Bell Curve (Herrnstein & Murray), 43
Belle, Albert, 320
Belle, David, 307–10
Bell, T. H., 173
Benedict, Jeff, 313, 316, 349, 353
Benkert, Karoly Maria, 208
Bensimhon, Ron, 340, 435
Bergman-Osterberg, Martina, 490
Berne, Eric, 510
Bertuzzi, Todd, 94
Beta-blockers, 405
Betfair, 164–66
Bettman, Gary, 31, 376; draft lotteries and, 107–8
Bevacqua, Kurt, 320
Bias, Len, 252
Big Apple Softball League (BASL), 244–45
Bigarexia, 114
Bike Stunts, 503
Biking, 504. *See also* Mountain biking
Bill of Rights for Young Athletes, 366–67
Billups, Chauncey, 351
Biodiversity, 120
Bioethics, 186–87

Biological determinism, 492
Biology, 43–51
Biomechanics, 403–4
Bird, Larry, 69
Bird, Sue, 179–80, 257
Birkenhead Park, 327–28
Bisexuality, 208
Bissinger, Buzz, 362
Black Coaches and Administrators (BCA), 144–45
Black Power, 62
Black Sabbath, 506
Black September, 61, 432
Black Sox scandal, 56–57, 162, 193
"Blades of Steel," 469
Blair, Tony, 184
Bleiler, Gretchen, 397
Bliss, David, 5
Blood boosting, 19
Blue Chips, 426, 478
Blunt, 396
Board of Control for Cricket in India (BCCI), 270
Bob & Carol, Ted & Alice, 510
Bodybuilding: ephedra and, 137; ergogenics and, 132; GM and, 189; women and, 484–86
Bodychecking, 179
Body dysmorphia, 114
Body Glove, 392
Bohemians, 419
Bonds, Barry, 315, 416, 429, 479–80; BALCO and, 59
Bone density, 283
Bookies, 192
Boone, Bret, 479
Bosman, Jean-Marc, 239
Bossard family, 56
Boston, David, 250
Boston Marathon, 55; cheating and, 57
Boston Red Sox: stadium, 87; taunting and, 425–26
Botero, Santiago, 141
Bouchard, Claude, 49
Boulerice, Jess, 93
Bourdais, Sebastian, 89
Bowen, Lori, 486
Bowe, Riddick, 153, 316
Boxing, 512; racial profiling and, 344; women's, 497
Boycotts, of Olympics, 62, 286, 288
Boy Scouts, 37–38
Brackenridge, Celia, 377
Brackins, Charlie, 347
Bradley, Bill, 193–94
Branding. *See* Corporate branding
Brashear, Donald, 92–94
Bratcher, Roger, 355
Bray, Alberta, 280
Bressoles, Claire, 280

Briscoe, Marlin, 347
Bristol, Dave, 356
British United Provident Association (BUPA), 223
Broadcasting rights, 266–71, 337; corporate branding and, 77
Brookes, William Penny, 229
Brown, Bruce, 421
Brown, Jim, 71, 316
Brown, Ralph, 382
Brown, Roger, 73
Brown, Willie, 243
Brundage, Avery, 231, 280–81, 287; anabolic steroids and, 414
Bruschi, Teddy, 222
Brushbacks, 427
Bryant, Kobe, 352, 372; age limits and, 105; endorsements of, 81–82; rape case, 75
Bryden, Rod, 202
BSkyB, 269
Buddhism, 423
Budweiser Stadium, 85
Bulimia, 111
Bullfighting, 16–17
Bungee jumping, 455, 503–4
BUPA. *See* British United Provident Association
Burgoyne, Tom, 262
Burke, Glenn, 297
Burleson, Nate, 382
Burnett, Mark, 9
Burroughs, Jeff, 292
Burroughs, William, 419
Burstyn, Varda, 295
Burton Boards, 390, 394
Burton, Isaac, Jr., 195
Busch Stadium, 85
Bush, George H. W., 69, 369
Bush, George W., 415–16
Bushnell, Nolan, 465–66
Bushwackers, 218
Butowski, Alexei de, 230
Buzinski, Jim, 245
Byers, Walter, 159
Byrne, Mike, 355

CAAWS. *See* Canadian Association for the Advancement of Women in Sport
CADA. *See* Canadian Amateur Boxing Association
Cade, Robert, 136
Caffeine, 135, 249
Calgary Flames, 325
Callot, Ernest, 230
Camden, James, 355
Caminitti, Ken, 252–53
Campanella, Roy, 427
Campbell, Cassie, 501
Campbell, Clarence, 292
Canada, corporate stadiums of, 86

Canadian Adventure Racing Association, 11
Canadian Amateur Boxing Association (CADA), 364
Canadian Anti-Doping Organization, 21
Canadian Association for the Advancement of Women in Sport (CAAWS), 214
Canadian Breast Cancer Foundation, 223
Canadian Cancer Society, 225
Canadian Center for Ethics in Sports, 137, 251
Canadian Criminal Code, 90–91
Canadian Football League (CFL): corporate branding and, 79; NFL *v.*, 337; video review and, 458
Canadian Hockey Association (CHA), 307, 366, 380
Canadian Imperial Bank of Commerce (CIBC), 223
Canadian Somali Youth Basketball League, 41
Cancer, 223–27
Candlestick Park, 85–87
Can I Kiss You? program, 353
Canino, Bonne, 497
Cannon, Robert, 30
Canseco, Jose, 315, 479–80
Caples, Ivonne, 497
Capoeira, 512
Carlos, John, 62, 70–71, 170; cool pose of, 72
Carmouche, Sylvester, 54–55
Carpenter, Jake Burton, 390, 394
Carpenter, Linda Jean, 171
Carragher, Brian, 93, 357
Carrier, Roch, 362
Carter, Jimmy, 288
Cash, Norm, 56
Castellani, Valentino, 435
Caurla, Lea, 280
CBAs. *See* Collective bargaining agreements
CBS. *See* Columbia Broadcasting System
CDC. *See* U.S. Centers for Disease Control
CEDAW. *See* Convention on Elimination of All Forms of Discrimination Against Women
Celebration rule, 428
Centennial Olympic Park, 432
Centrality hypothesis, 345
Ceriani, Marco, 140
CFL. *See* Canadian Football League
Chad, Norman, 105
Chamberlain, Wilt, 67
Chambers, Chris, 250
Chambers, Dwain, 59
Chambliss, Chris, 152, 320
The Chantays, 420
Chariots of Fire, 49
CHA. *See* Canadian Hockey Association
Chastain, Brandi, 259
Chastain, Jane, 500
Chatham, Matt, 153
Cheating, 53–59
Cheerleaders, 261

Cheevers, Gerry, 320
Cheng, Lydia, 486
Cherry, Don, 501
Chicago Black Sox scandal, 25
Chicago Housing Authority, 39–40
Chicago White Sox, 56–57. *See also* Black Sox scandal
China, 2008 Olympics, 65
Chivalry, 413
Chmura, Mark, 352
Choudury, Bikram, 511
Chouinard, Bobby, 315
Christianity, 2, 360–65
Christie, Linford, 58
Chuter, Penelope Ann, 490
Chylak, Nestor, 293
CIBC. *See* Canadian Imperial Bank of Commerce
Ciccarelli, Dino, 93
Cicotte, Eddie, 57
CIST. *See* Labour Sports Confederation
City College of New York, 55
Civil Rights Act, 171
Civil Rights Restoration Act, 174
Clapham, Vic, 458
Clarett, Maurice, 106
Clark, Grubby, 421
Clark, Kelly, 393, 397
Clay, James, 355
Clayton Act, 23–24, 27; Rozelle Rule and, 28
Cleaves, Michael, 6, 352
Clemens, Roger, 417, 479
Clemente, Roberto, 143
Clery Act, 352
Cleveland Indians, 264–65
Climate change, 118
Clinton, Bill, 369
Coaches: African American, 348; ethnic, 143–48; screening, 380; screening of, 366; sexual abuse and, 378–82; taunting and, 428; women, 159–60, 488–91
Coase, Ronald, 104
Coase Theorem, 104
Cobb, Ty, 57, 313, 321
Cocaine, 252–53
Cockfighting, 13
Coffin, Thomas, 50
Cohen, Sasha, 257
Colangelo, Jerry, 439
Cold War, 198; anabolic steroids and, 414, 416; sex testing and, 280
Collecovision, 472
Collective bargaining agreements (CBAs), 27, 32–33, 376–77; unions and, 30
Collective protests, 60–65
College sports, corporatization of, 87
College Sports Council, 176
Colorado Rockies, 363–64
Colored Hockey League of the Maritimes, 344–45

Color line, 143
Columbia Broadcasting System (CBS), 26; broadcasting rights and, 268
Columbine High School, 475
Comcast, 338
Comebacks, 222–23
Comisky, Charles, 162
Comité International Sports des Sourds, 98
Commercialization: corporate branding and, 78; of ethnic athletes, 65–71; publicity and, 341; of snowboarding, 396–97; of surfing, 423; video games and, 469–70
Commons, 327
Commonwealth Games, 272
Community Softball League (CSL), 242–43
Community spending, 330
Competition Act of Canada, 24
Competition codes, 1
Competitive balance, 104
The Complete Book of Running (Fixx), 456
"Computer Space," 465
Comrades Marathon, 457–58
Contagion theory, 322–23
Conte, Victor, 58, 415, 480
Contrology, 98
Convention on Elimination of All Forms of Discrimination Against Women (CEDAW), 409
Convention on the Rights of Persons with Disabilities (CRPD), 410
Convention on the Rights of the Child, 409
The Convention on the Rights of the Child, 367
Converse Shoes, 69
Conway, Russ, 32
Cook, James, 418
Cool Boarders, 393
Cool pose, 72–76
Cooney, Terry, 356
Cooper, Chris, 59
Copeland, Royal S., 193
Cordero, Wil, 315
Corporate branding, 76–83; stadiums and, 84. *See also* Endorsements
Corporatization, 469–70
Corrales, Diego, 316
Corso, Gregory, 419
Costas, Bob, 262
Cost certainty, 33
Costin, Michael, 303–5
Coubertin, Pierre de, 229–31, 285, 431, 492; vision of, 412–14
Coupland, Douglas, 466–67
Crawford, Jerry, 356
Cricket, 333, 365; broadcasting rights, 270; labor migration and, 237; match fixing and, 165–66; video review and, 459
Cricket Australia, 165
Crime(s), 38–40, 88–90; National Midnight Basketball League and, 369; parkour and, 311–12; scalping and, 436–39

Crowd behavior, 322
CRPD. *See* Convention on the Rights of Persons with Disabilities
Cuff, Leonard A., 230
Culpepper, Daunte, 382, 470
"The Curse of the Bambino," 425–26
Curt Flood Act, 28–29
Curtius, Ernst, 229
Cycling: cheating and, 55; EPO and, 139–40

Dabney, Ted, 465
Dahl, Steve, 293
Dakides, Tara, 397
Dalai Lama, 65
Dallas Cowboys: cheerleaders, 261; drugs and, 251
Dana Point, California, 421–22
Daneyko, Ken, 252
Danton, Mike, 380–81
Darwin, Charles, 44
Daviault, Patrick, 93, 357
Davis, Al, 27–28
Davis, Gail, 8
Davis, Terrell, 383
Davydenko, Nikolay, 164–65
Day, Todd, 351
Deaflympics, 98
Death in the Afternoon (Hemingway), 16
Death penalty rule, 5
de la Hoya, Oscar, 372; endorsements of, 81–82
de Lima, Vanderlei, 155, 435
Demers, Jacques, 58
Dempsey, Rick, 320
Dennehy, Partick, 5
Dennison, Paul, 48
Department of Education (DOE), 171
de Quesada, Alejandro, 136
Desailly, Marcel, 431
Desjardins, Eric, 58
Des Sables Marathon, 457
de Varona, Donna, 500
Diagoros, 489
Dianabol, 414
Diaz, Laz, 155
Dickey, Eldridge, 347
Didrickson, Babe, 231
Diet, 49; eating disorders and, 115; ergogenics and, 131–33; video games and, 468
Diggers, 439
Disability sports, 97–103
Disco, 293
Discovery Channel, 9
Discrimination: genetic, 190; homophobia and, 211–12; racial profiling and, 346; religious, 364; sexual, 377–78. *See also* Gender
Disneyfication, 154
Diversity, 60–61
DNA, 46
Doctors, 403–7
DOE. *See* Department of Education
Dogfighting, 12–13
Dokic, Damir, 212
Dokic, Jelena, 212
D'Oliviera, Basil, 63
Dominguez, Lourdes, 252–53
Domi, Tie, 320
Domitrz, Mike, 353
Donaghy, Tim, 165
Donahue, Hessie, 497
Donoghue, Charles, 262
Doping, 18–22; EPO and, 46–47; gene, 46–47, 185–87; Olympics and, 44–45; sports medicine and, 18, 406. *See also* Antidoping
Dotson, Carlton, 5
Dover, Robert, 297
Downhill BMX, 503
Drafts: of amateur athletes, 103–9; lotteries, 106–8; restrictions, 32
Dream Team, 69
Dress codes, 362
Driving under the influence arrests (DUIs), 250
"Dr. J and Larry Bird Go One on One," 368
Drugs, 247–53; at-risk youth and, 38; Bush, George W., and, 415–16; sports medicine and, 403–7; testing, 19; whistle-blowers and, 477–82. *See also* Doping; *specific drugs*
Dubin, Charles, 21, 412
Duke University, 352–53, 494
Dumaresque, Michelle, 447
Dumervil, Elvis, 89
Dungy, Tony, 148, 362
Dunlap, Carla, 486
Duplizer, Imke, 297
Dwyer, Kelly, 315

Eagleson, Alan, 31, 32
"Earl Weaver Baseball," 468
Earnhardt, Dale, Jr., 372
Earth Summit, 123–24
EA. *See* Electronic Arts
EA Sports, 468–69
East Germany, 44–45
Eating Attitudes Test, 112
Eating Disorder Inventory, 112
Eating disorders, 111–17
eBay.com, 441
Eco-Challenge, 9–11
Eco Flag, 123–24
Edstrom, J. Sigfried, 231
Education: curricula, 1–2; eating disorders and, 118; gender and, 171–77
Edwards, Phil, 421
Ekecheiria, 284
Electronic Arts (EA), 468–69
Ellis Park Stadium, 400

The Endless Summer, 388, 420, 421
Endorsements, 68, 77, 81–82; skateboarding and, 385; sponsorships *v.*, 81; Woods, Tiger, and, 374. *See also* Corporate branding
End-zone celebrations, 75, 427–28
Energy conservation, 123–24
English Premier League, 269–70; corporate branding and, 76
English public school (EPS) system, 78
Engquist, Ludmila, 222
Enron, 85
Entertainment, 333; home, 465
Entine, Jon, 44
Environmental impacts, 117–25
Ephedra, 137
EPO. *See* Erythropoietin
EPS system. *See* English public school system
Equal opportunity, 174
Equal Pay Act, 158
Equal Rights Amendment, 172
Equipment: corporate branding of, 81–82; third world manufacturing of, 125–31
Equity Fights AIDS, 245
Ergogenics, 131–38
Erving, Julius, 67, 73
Erythropoietin (EPO), 20, 46–47, 138–43, 186, 415; sports medicine and, 405
Escobar, Andres, 219
Escotada, 17
ESPN: broadcasting rights and, 268; Eco-Challenge and, 9; fantasy league, 470; snowboarding and, 393; X Games and, 384, 504–7
ESPN's Ultimate X, 506
Esposito, Phil, 184, 497–98
Essentialism, 492
Estalella, Bobby, 59
Ethics: drugs and, 251–52; GM and, 187–88
Ethnic athletes, 65–71
Ethnopharmacology, 132
Euro 2000 Cup, 217
European Sports Charter, 409
European Sports for all Charter, 408–9
European Union (EU), labor migration, 237–39
Evangelische Kirchengemeinde Duisburg-Neumuhl, 128
Evans, David, 353
Evert, Chris, 255, 487
Evolution, 48
Ewald, Manfred, 20, 45
Ewing, Patrick, 108, 383
Exclusivity, 328–29
Exercise: industry, 256; video games and, 468
Exercise for Ladies (Walker), 493
Extreme Adventure Hidalgo, 10
Extreme Games. *See* X Games
Extremity Games, 99

Faber, Katelyn, 352
"Fab Five" scandal, 5
Facebook, 501
Fainaru-Wada, Mark, 58, 480
Faith Days, 364
False negatives, 282
False positives, 282
Family Violence Prevention Fund, 317
The Famous Chicken, 262
Fans: field invasions and, 151–56; fighting with athletes, 317–21; missile throwing and, 289–93; referee abuse and, 354–59; taunting and, 428–29; violence and, 155
Fantasy leagues, 470–71
Fantasy Online Sports, 470
FA. *See* Football Association
Fashanu, Justin, 298
Fashion, 483–84
Faulk, Marshall, 470
Favre, Brett, 428
Fay, David, 180
FBI, 352–53
Federal Baseball Club v. National League, 24–25
Federal League of Baseball Players (FLBP), 24–25
Fédération Internationale de Basketball (FIBA), 368
Federation of Gay Games (FGG), 167
Fédération Sportive Féminine Internationale (FSFI), 496
Feminism, 276, 483; ubersexuality and, 451
Ferrari, 59
Ferrari, Michele, 406
Festina cycling team, 140–41
FGG. *See* Federation of Gay Games
FHM, 257
FIBA. *See* Fédération Internationale de Basketball
Field invasions, 151–56
FIFA. *See* International Federation of Association Football
Filmmakers, 396
Finley, Charlie, 34–35
Finnerty, Colin, 353
Finney, Charles G., 361
Firestone, Bruce, 107–8
Fitness, 456; alternative, 509–13; yoga and, 510
Fixx, Jim, 456
FLBP. *See* Federal League of Baseball Players
Floating signifiers, 67
Fonda, Jane, 256–57
Football Association (FA), 359
Football Spectators Act, 216–17
Force, Ashley, 257
Force, Jim, 8
Ford, Alexander Hume, 420
Ford, Whitey, 56
Ford Motor Corporation, 224–25
Foreman, George, 344, 427; ubersexuality and, 452

Foucan, Sébastien, 307–10
Foucault, Michel, 210
Fox: broadcasting rights and, 268; NHL and, 338
Foxhunting, 13; ban on, 17
Fox, Terry, 224–25
France, Bill, 334
Franchise free agency. *See* Free agency
Francis, Bev, 486
Francisco, Frank, 319
Franks, Herman, 56
Fraser, Kerry, 58
Fraternity Gang Rape (Sanday), 349
Fraud, 437–38; academic, 6–7
Frazier, Joe, 344
Frazier-Lyde, Jackie, 497
Free, H. James, 136
Free agency, 27; Coase Theorem and, 104; v. drafting amateur athletes, 103; Rozelle Rule and, 28; unions and, 31
Freedom, 434
Free market expansion, 127
Free running. *See* Parkour
Freeth, George, 420
French, Jonta, 316
Freud, Sigmund, 322
Fricano, Marion, 427
Friday Night Lights (Bissinger), 362
Frontiere, Georgia, 490
FrontRunners, 243
Frost, David, 380–81
FSFI. *See* Fédération Sportive Féminine Internationale
Fuhr, Grant, 252
Funding equity, 156–60
Fusil, Gerald, 9
Fuzak, John, 172–73

GAG'M. *See* Global Anti-Golf-Movement
Gagnon, Pierre, 93, 357
Galbraith, Jeff, 392
Galen, 403
Galindo, Rudy, 297
Gallagher, Ed, 296
Galton, Francis, 44
Gambling, 161–66; addiction, 195; government and, 191–97; greyhounds and, 15–16; online, 195–96
Gamboa, Tom, 155
Game of Shadows (Fainaru-Wada & Williams), 480
Gangelhoff, Janice, 4, 478
Garabaldi, Denise, 417
Garcia, Karim, 89
Garnett, Kevin, 372
Gaston, Cito, 145
Gatorade, 136–37
Gaumont, Philippe, 142
Gavora, Jessica, 175–76

Gay and Lesbian International Sports Association, 169
Gay Bowl, 245
Gay Games, 167–70, 214, 242; transsexual athletes and, 446
Gay Softball World Series (GSWS), 244
GDR. *See* German Democratic Republic
Gear, 257, 259
Geipel, Ines, 20, 45
Gender: education and, 171–77; female sexuality and, 253–54; journalism and, 276; race and, 181; rules and, 177–85; segregation, 448; sexuality and, 483–84; skateboarding and, 387
Gender binary, 443
Gender dysphoria, 208
Gender identity, 209
Generation D, 471
Generation X, 466–67
Gene therapy, 46–47
Genetic manipulation (GM), 185–91
Genetics, 44–50; anorexia nervosa and, 112; discrimination and, 190; testing, 278; transgenders and, 444
Genetic Technologies, 190
Gentrification, 459–63
German Democratic Republic (GDR), 415
Gervin, George, 73
Gesamtkunstwerke, 413
Getmein.com, 441
Ghosh, Bishnu, 511–12
Giamatti, A. Bartlett, 163
Giambi, Jason, 416, 479; BALCO and, 59
Giambi, Jeremy, 59
Giannoulas, Ted, 262
Gibb, Alexandrine, 499
Gibson, Althea, 67
Gibson, Hanna, 12
Gibson, Missy, 257
Gidget, 420, 422
Gilbert, Gale, 351–52
Gilmore, Artis, 73
Ginsberg, Allen, 419
Ginseng, 132–33
Giove, Missy, 447
Giro d'Italia, 139–40
Givens, Robin, 71; domestic violence and, 314–15
Givins, Ernest, 428
Global Anti-Golf-Movement (GAG'M), 63–64, 121–22
Globalization, 130–31
GM. *See* Genetic manipulation
GNU Snowboards, 391
Goals 200: Educate America Act, 40
Goebbels, Joseph, 413
Goffman, Erving, 192
Gogarty, Deirdre, 497
Going the Other Way (Bean), 298

Gold Club, 382–83
Goldenpalace.com, 340, 435
Golden State Warriors, 265
Goldman, Ronald, 315
Goldsmith, Fred, 494
Golf, environmental impact of, 119–22
Gonzalez, Delia, 497
González, Juan, 479
Gooden, Dwight, 252–53
Goodenow, Bob, 31
Good-faith bargaining, 31
Goodheart, George, 48
Gordon, Jeff, 81–82
Gore, Al, 118
Go Sisters, 370
Government: gambling and, 191–97; sponsorships, 197–202
Grabau, Charles, 305
Graf, Steffi, 155
Graham, Marvin, 183
Graham, Trevor, 58, 415, 480–81
Gramsci, Antonio, 255
Gravity Games, 393
Great North Run, 223
Green, Edith Starrett, 158
Green, Jon, 319
Greenpeace, 17
Greyhounds, 14–16
GRIDS. *See* HIV/AIDS
Griffin, Pat, 211–12, 214–15
Griffith-Joyner, Florence, 255
Griffiths, Phyllis, 499
Grooming, 378–79
Grove City College v. Bell, 173
Groza, Alex, 6
GSWS. *See* Gay Softball World Series
Gudex, Niki, 257
Guest, Kelly, 137
Guide to Sport, Environment and Sustainable Development (IOC), 125
Gulbis, Natalie, 257, 259
Gulick, Luther, 361
Gundlach, James, 4, 478
Gurr, Ted, 318
Guth-Jarovsky, Jiri, 230
Gutierrez, Jose, 141
Gutman, Dan, 162
Guttman, Ludwig, 99
Gymnasiums, 327–28
Gymnastics, 114

Haakonsen, Terje, 392–93
Habitat for Humanity, 208
Hackbartt v. Cincinnati Bengals, 91, 95
Hackney, Darrell, 250
Hahn, Billy, 6
Hall, Matthew, 297
Hamas, 434
Hamill, Dorothy, 255
Hamilton, Bethany, 222
Hanlon, Ned, 24–25
Hannah, David, 364
Hantuchova, Daniela, 257
Harare stadium, 400
Haraway, Donna, 473
Hardaway, Tim, 213
Hare coursing, 14
Hargrove, Mike, 292–93
Harper, Ben, 506
Harris, Eric, 475
Harrison, Lorrin, 421
Harris, Sidney, 93
Harvey, Doug, 30–31, 375
Haskins, Clem, 4, 478
Hatch, Orrin G., 173
Hatfield, Mabel, 497
Hat tricks, 289–90
Hawkins, Connie, 26, 73
Hawkins, Trip, 468
Hawk, Tony, 385, 388–89
Haywood, Spencer, 109
Hazing, 203–8; group sex and, 379
Heart failure, 140
Heaston, Liz, 494
Heatley, Dany, 250
Hébert, George, 308–9
Hébertism, 308–9
Hegemony, 255, 450–51
He Got Game, 426, 478
Heiberg, Gerhard, 433
Heisman Trophy, 71
Hemingway, Ernest, 16
Henderson, Devery, 152
Henderson, Hollywood, 252–53
Henderson, Thomas, 251
Henrich, Christy, 114
Henry, Eltonio Waylon, 355
HEP. *See* Human exceptionalism paradigm
Heraea Games, 494
Herbert, Charles, 230
Heredia, Angel, 480–81
Hereditary Genius (Galton), 44
Herrnstein, Richard, 43
Hester, Carl, 297
Heteronormativity, 241
Heterosexism, 209, 297–98
Hezbollah, 434
HGP. *See* Human Genome Project
Hickok, Lorena, 499
Hicks, Michael, 93–94
Hicks, Thomas, 18
Higginbotham, Leon, 26
High-performance sports, 404–5
Hilgendorf, Tom, 292–93
Hilleman, Richard, 469
Hingis, Martina, 252–53
Hippocrates, 403
Hirschbeck, John, 355

548 | Index

Hitler, Adolf, 231, 285–87; anabolic steroids and, 413; Schott and, 490
HIV/AIDS, 38, 169–70, 226; Ashe, Arthur, and, 70; Johnson, Earvin, and, 69; openly gay athletes and, 296–97; young athletes and, 369–70
Hnida, Katie, 352, 494
Hoberman, John, 44, 404
Hobson, Butch, 252–53
Hockey: assault cases, 91; criminal violence and, 92–94; gender and, 179, 183–84; homophobia and, 245; missile throwing and, 289–90; parental misconduct and, 306–7; postevent riots and, 324–25
Hockey Night in Canada, 337; women sportscasters and, 501
The Hockey Sweater (Carrier), 362
Hoffman, Bob, 132
Hoffman, Phillip, 421
Hoffman, Walter, 421
Hollis, Wilbur, 347
Holmes, Oliver Wendell, 25
Holyfield, Evander, 71, 91, 153, 344
Holy International Sport Yoga Championship, 511
Home Run Derby, 339
Home run record, 479–80
Homophobia, 208–15, 333, 501; Gay Games and, 242; hockey and, 245
Homosexuality, 208, 279; open, 295–99
Hooliganism, 215–19; alcohol and, 249; postevent, 321–26; tragedy and, 398–402
Hoop Dreams, 426
Hooton, Don, 417
Hoppner, Manfred, 20, 45
Horan, Cornelius, 155
Hormonal therapy, 443
Horn-Miller, Waneek, 259
Hornung, Paul, 195
Horse racing: gambling and, 193; publicity, 339
Hostages, 61
Howe, Susanna, 396
Hubris, 55
Hughes, Thomas, 2, 360–61
Hull, Bobby, 373–74
Humane Society, 13
Human exceptionalism paradigm (HEP), 118–21
Human genome, 185
Human Genome Project (HGP), 46, 49
Human rights violations, 127
Human Rights Watch, 128
Hunter, Catfish, 34–35
Hunter, C. J., 481; BALCO and, 59
Huntington, Henry, 420
Hurlbut, Tim, 153
Hyperconsumerism, 341
Hypermasculinity, 426, 491–92; rejection of, 504. *See also* Ubersexuality

IAAF. *See* International Association of Athletics Federation
ICC. *See* International Cricket Council
Identity politics, 240–41
IFBB. *See* International Federation of Body Builders
IFLA. *See* International Fair Labor Association
IIHF. *See* International Ice Hockey Federation
Illness, 221–27
I'm Ok, You're Ok (Berne), 510
Impasse standard test, 35–36
Inanimate Hare Conveyor, 15
INAS-FID. *See* International Sports Federation for Persons with Intellectual Disability
An Inconvenient Truth, 118
Independent Women's Forum, 176
India, 511
Indiana Family Institute, 362
Indian Premier League (IPL), 270
India Yoga Cup, 511
Industrial Revolution, 327
Infantization, 275–76
Injury: reports, 165; skateboarding and, 387
In-line Skating, 503–4
Inner-city, 37
Innocent Criminals, 506
Inside Out: Straight Talk from a Gay Jock (Tewksbury), 213
Instant replay systems. *See* Video review
Instinct theory, 318
The Institute for Diversity and Ethics in Sport (TIDES), 148
Institute for the Study of Youth Sports, 366
Intent to injure, 91
Interactional group structure, 345
Inter-continental movement, 236
Internal Revenue Service, 417
International Association of Athletics Federation (IAAF), 18, 480, 496; prosthetics and, 50–51, 102–013; sex testing and, 282–83
International Association of Skateboard Companies, 385
International Association of Ultra Runners, 457
International Cricket Council (ICC), 63
International Cycling Union (UCI), 19
International Fair Labor Association (IFLA), 129
International Federation of Association Football (FIFA): corporate branding and, 76; doping and, 19; hooliganism and, 216–17; Right to Play and, 368; South African suspension by, 62
International Federation of Body Builders (IFBB), 486
International Ice Hockey Federation (IIHF), 179

International Labor Rights Research and Education Fund, 128
International Labour Organization, 130
International Movement Against Bullfights, 17
International Olympic Committee (IOC), 228–33; broadcasting rights and, 268–69; Carlos, John, and, 70–71; doping and, 19, 21–22; drugs and, 250–51; environmental impact and, 125; Medical Commission, 186, 414; militarism and, 285–87; NSMs and, 62; Olympic Charter, 409–11; Right to Play and, 368; sex testing and, 282–83; Smith, Tommie, and, 70–71; snowboarding and, 392–93; transsexual athletes and, 444–45; virtual sports and, 473; women and, 495–96
International Sport Organization for the Disabled (ISOD), 99
International Sports Federation for Persons with Intellectual Disability (INAS-FID), 99
International Tennis Federation (ITF), 164
International Yoga Championships, 512
Internet: gambling and, 195–96; ticket distribution and, 441; video games and, 470–71; women sportscasters and, 501
INTERPOL, 216–17
Intra-continental movement, 236
IOC. *See* International Olympic Committee
IPL. *See* Indian Premier League
Irish Council against Bloodsports, 14
Irving, Julius, 26
Irvin, Ken, 382
Irvin, Michael, 251
ISOD. *See* International Sport Organization for the Disabled
Issel, Dan, 73
ITF. *See* International Tennis Federation
Iverson, Allen, 75, 316
Iyengar, B.K.S., 510

Jackass, 388
Jackson, Bo, 68
Jackson, Don, 263
Jackson, Janet, 153
Jackson, Joe, 57
Jackson, Mark, 163
Jackson, Stephen, 291, 319
Jacobellis, Lindsey, 397
Jacobs, Regina, 59
Jaksche, Jorg, 481
James, Gloria, 372
James, Graham, 366, 380
James, LeBron, 105, 372
Jan and Dean, 420
"Jane Fonda's Workout," 256–57
Jaramillo, Stephanie, 497
Jeffrey, Patrick, 297
Jeffries, Willie, 146
Jenapharm, 20, 44–45
Jensen, Knud, 18–19, 414

Jeter, Derek, 81–82, 372
Jet skiing, 423
Jewell, Richard, 432–33
Jews, 285–87, 365; Black September and, 432
Jimenez, Jose Maria, 140
Johnson, Ben, 19, 21, 58, 406; anabolic steroids and, 415
Johnson, Billy, 427–28
Johnson, Eddie, 348
Johnson, Earvin, 68, 69, 226
Johnson, Keyshawn, 428
Johnson, Robert, 146
Johnstone, Lance, 382
Jois, Sri K. Pattabhi, 510
Jonathan, Stan, 291, 320
Jones, B. Todd, 349
Jones, Dean, 431
Jones, Kitty, 8
Jones, Marion, 480; BALCO and, 59; EPO and, 141–42
Jordan, Michael: corporate branding and, 76; endorsements of, 69–70, 81–82; Nike Corporation and, 74–75; PLAY campaign and, 41
Journalism, 271–77
Joyner-Kersey, Jackie, 67
Joyner, Wally, 291
Judkins, Robin, 9
Juiced: Wild Times, Rampant 'Roids, Smash Hits and How Baseball Got Big (Canseco), 479
Jump London, 309
Junta, Thomas, 303–5
Jurges, Billy, 356
Justice, Do It Nike, 128–29
Juventus, 164; soccer tragedies and, 399

Kahanamoku, Duke Paoa, 420–21
Kaplan, Steve, 383
Kaptain, John, 320
Karalahti, Jere, 252
Karl, George, 163
Karras, Alex, 195
Karrimor International Mountain Marathon, 8–9
Kass, Danny, 393, 394, 397
Katz, Jack, 323
Kefauver, Estes, 193
Kelly, Craig, 392
Kelly, Paul, 31
Kemeny, Ferenc, 230
Kendall, Florence, 48
Kendall, Henry, 48
Kenkuis, Johan, 297
Kennedy, Lincoln, 291
Kennedy, Robert, 193
Kennedy, Sheldon, 366, 380
Kenya, 48–50
Kerouac, Jack, 419
Kick AIDS Out!, 370

Kidd, Jason, 315–16
Kidd, Joumana, 316
Kinesiology, 48
King, Billie Jean, 296, 500
Kingerly, Jeff, 263
King, Larry, 296
Kingsley, Charles, 360–61
Kissing Bandit, 154
Kitchen, William, 94
Kite surfing, 423, 455
Klebold, Dylan, 475
Klein, Chris, 506
Klippel-Traunay-Weber Syndrome, 50
Klobukowska, Ewa, 282
Knight, Phil, 129
Knoblauch, Chuck, 417
Kohne, Kathy, 422
Kohner, Frederick, 422
König, Karin, 20, 45
Kopay, David, 296
Kournikova, Anna, 82, 258–59, 274
Kouros, Yiannis, 457
Krebbs, Charles, 48
Kreuter, Chad, 291, 320
Kuhn, Bowie, 163
Kuhn, Rick, 195
Kyniska, 489

Labor, 126; migration, 235–40
Labour Sports Confederation (CSIT), 408
Lack of consent, 91
Ladies Professional Golf Association (LPGA), 259–60; transsexual athletes and, 446
LAF. *See* Lance Armstrong Foundation
Lagat, Bernard, 142
Lamaze, Eric, 252–53
Lance Armstrong Foundation (LAF), 223–24
Landing Officer, 54–55
Landis, Floyd, 141
Landis, Kenesaw Mountain, 57, 162, 356
Lapchick, Richard, 148
Larkai, Dzaflo, 6
La Russa, Tony, 250
La Salle University, 6
Lasorda, Tommy, 262
Laval University, 49
Lavender U. Joggers, 243
Laycock, John, 8
Laycoe, Hal, 291–92
League Against Cruel Sports, 17, 64
Leagues: black, 344–45; fantasy, 470–71; gender and, 178–79; Jewish, 365; LGBT, 240–46; Muslim, 365
Learning theory, 318
le Bon, Gustav, 322
LeClair, John, 250
Lee, Spike, 316
Leghzaoui, Asmae, 142
Lemieux, Mario, 107, 222

Lesbian, gay, bisexual and transgender (LGBT), 167–70; definition, 209; rights, 60–61; sports leagues, 240–46
Lesbians, 209–11
Leskinen, Kristi, 257
Lessons of the Locker Room (Miracle & Rees), 3
Lett, Leon, 251
Levitt, Arthur, 376
Lewis, Anna, 497
Lewis, Carl, 58, 67; anabolic steroids and, 415
Lewis, Jamal, 252–53
Lewis, Ray, 470
Lewis, Sherman, 347
Leyritz, Jim, 250
LFC. *See* Liverpool Football Club
LGBT. *See* Lesbian, gay, bisexual and transgender
Libman, Alyn, 444
Life Extension (Pearson & Shaw), 133
Ligget, Phil, 140
Li, Huiquan, 142
Lindeberg, Johan, 259
Lindsay, Ted, 30–31, 375
Linkage policies, 463
Liston, Sonny, 427
Little League, 301
Little League World Series, 53–54
Liverpool Football Club (LFC), 399–400
Livestrong, 223–24
LL Cool J, 506
Loaded, 257
Lobbyists, 158
Lockouts, 376–77
Lohman, Britney, 250
Lombardi, Vince, 53
London, Jack, 420
Long, Andrew, 93
Looney, Ed, 195
Loots, Riann, 89
Lopez, Rick, 381
Lorde, Audrey, 208
Lorenz, Konrad, 318
Lorz, Fred, 55
Louganis, Greg, 297
Louis Bullock, 5
Louis, Joe, 344
Love Boat scandal, 382–83
Love Park, 386
Lovett, Robert, 47–48
LPGA. *See* Ladies Professional Golf Association
Lucchesi-Palli, Mario, 230
Luxury taxes, 33

Maccabi USA, 365
Mackey, John, 28
MacLaine, Shirley, 510
MacTavish, Craig, 263
Madden, John, 468–69, 470
"Madden curse," 470

"Madden NFL Football," 468–69
Madlock, Bill, 356
Magerkurth, George, 356
Maglie, Sal, 427
Magnavox Odyssey, 465
Maharishi Mahesh Yogi, 510
Major League, 264
Major League Baseball (MLB): amateur drafts, 104–5; antitrust violations and, 23–24; broadcasting rights, 337; cocaine and, 252–53; corporate branding and, 77, 79; doping and, 22; endorsements and, 68; gambling and, 161–63; Gatorade and, 136; publicity, 339; race and, 146; referee abuse in, 355–56; religious expression and, 363; Ruth, Babe, and, 425–26; salaries, 371–72, 374; strikes and, 376; unions and, 29–37; urban planning and, 461; video review and, 459; whistle-blowers and, 479
Major League Baseball Players Association (MLBPA), 34–35; formation of, 30
Major League Soccer (MLS): amateur drafts, 104; corporate branding and, 79; Gatorade and, 136; salaries, 371
"Malaria No More," 454
Maleeva, Manuela, 155
Malibu, 422
Malone, Moses, 73
Managers, ethnic, 143–48
Mancebo, Francisco, 141
Man in the Middle (Amaechi), 213
Manion, Jim, 486
Manley, Effa, 490
Manley, John, 202
Mann Act, 382
Mantha, Moe, 205–7
Mantle, Mickey, 163
Marathon of Hope, 224–25
Marathons, 455
Marginal Revenue Product, 29
Marijuana, 247–53
"Mario Brothers," 466
Maris, Roger, 479
Martens, Rainier, 366–67
Martin, Billy, 292
Martin, Casey, 50
Martin, Christy, 497
Martin, Ed, 5
Martinez, Conchita, 297
Martinez, Dave, 479
Martinez, Pedro, 89
Martinez-Patino, Maria, 282
Mascots, 260–66
Match fixing, 164–66
Match racing, 339
Materazzi, Marco, 89
Mathare Youth Sports Association, 370
Mattis, Doug, 297
Mauresmo, Amelie, 297
Maxim, 257; hottest women in sports, 485

Maxwell, Vernon, 320
Mays, Willie, 67; gambling and, 162–63
McElhiney, Ashley Renée, 490
McEwen, John, 59
McGill University, 207
McGinnis, George, 73
McGowan, Jack, 242–43
McGraw, John, 56
McGwire, Mark, 68, 479–80
McKinnie, Bryant, 382
McLaren racing team, 59
McLish, Rachel, 485–86
McMahon, Vince, 335–36
McMichael, Lokelani, 257
McNabb, Donovan, 470
McNally, Dave, 35
McNamee, Brian, 417
McPherson, Adrian, 195
McSorley, Marty, 58, 92–94
Media: broadcasting rights, 266–71; eating disorders and, 114; IOC and, 232–33; parkour and, 311; publicity and, 336–41; rape and, 350; snowboarding and, 396–97; women sportscasters, 498–501; women's sports and, 181, 271–77
Meditation, 510
Medwick, Joe, 291
Megarexia, 114, 417
Meier, Garry, 293
Melbourne University Mountaineering Club, 8
Mellanby, Scott, 290
Men: women competing with, 491–98; in women's sports, 278–84
Men Can Stop Rape, 353
Mentors in Violence Prevention (MVP), 317
Mercer, Heather, 494
Mercer, Ron, 351
Merkel, Texas, 382
Messersmith, Andy, 35
Methandieone, 414
Metrosexuals, 484
Mexico, 1968 Olympics, 61–62, 287–88
Michaels, Cass, 427
Mickelson, Phil, 81–82, 372
Middleton, Frank, 263
Midnight Basketball League, 40
Mighty Ducks, 82, 339–40
The Mighty Ducks, 82, 340
Migration, labor, 235–40
Milbury, Mike, 291
Militarism, 284–89
Millennium Development Goals, 367
Miller, James, 153–54
Miller, John, 6
Miller, Marvin, 30, 34
Miller, Reggie, 383
Milliat, Alice, 496
Mills Report, 195–96
Milovick, Dimitrije, 390

Mink, Patsy, 183
Miracle, Andrew, 3
Misconduct, academic, 1–7
Missile throwing, 289–93
Mitchell, George, 417
Mitts, Heather, 257
MLBPA. *See* Major League Baseball Players Association
MLB. *See* Major League Baseball
MLS. *See* Major League Soccer
Modern Language Association, 265–66
Moggi, Luciano, 164
Monday Night Football, 323, 337; taunting and, 428
Monfort, Charlie, 363
Monopolies and Restrictive Practices Act, 24
Monroe, Mike, 107
Montgomery, Tim, 59, 480
Moody, D. L., 361
Moon, Warren, 250, 315
Moore, Carl, 8
Moore, Mewelde, 382
Moore, Steve, 94
Moriah, 395
Morris, Michael, 231
Morrison, Tommy, 226
Mosely-Braun, Carol, 40
Mosley, Shane, 59
Moto X, 503
Mountain biking, 7
Muldowney, Shirley, 183
Mulroney, Brian, 21
Multiuse facilities, 460
Munich, 432
Murderball, 103
Murdoch, Don, 252
Murdoch, Rupert, 269, 338
Murray, Charles, 43
Muscle Testing and Function (Goodheart), 48
Musial, Stan, 427
Muslims, 181, 365; terrorism and, 434–35
Mutombo, Dikembe, 383
MVP. *See* Mentors in Violence Prevention
Myers, Mel, 347

NAACP, 147; mascots and, 265–66
NADOs. *See* National antidoping organizations
NAGAAA. *See* North American Gay Amateur Athletic Alliance
Nagra, Pardeep, 364
Naismith, James, 361
Namath, Joe, 452–53
Naming rights, 83
Nandrolone, 137
NASCAR, 334–35; corporate branding and, 77, 79, 82; video review and, 459
NASDAQ, 394–95
NASO. *See* National Association of Sports Officials

National Alliance for Youth Sports (NAYS), 302–3
National antidoping organizations (NADOs), 22
National Association of Base Ball Players, 162, 344
National Association of Midnight Basketball, 40
National Association of Sports Officials (NASO), 354, 356–57
National Association of Ticket Brokers, 441
National Basketball Association (NBA): age limits, 105; amateur drafts, 104–6; antitrust violations and, 23, 26–27; cool pose and, 72–75; domestic violence and, 313; draft lotteries and, 106–7; drugs and, 251–52; gambling and, 163; Gatorade and, 136; lockout, 376; Podoloff and, 6; postevent riots and, 324; publicity, 337; race and, 144, 147–48; salaries, 371–72; sexual assault and, 349; tanking in, 108; unions and, 29–37; video review and, 458–59; virtual sports and, 473
National Basketball Players Association (NBPA): antitrust violations and, 23; formation of, 30
National Coalition Against Domestic Violence, 313
National Collegiate Athletic Association (NCAA), 4; age limits and, 105–6; alcohol abuse and, 248; broadcasting rights, 337; cheating and, 55; domestic violence and, 316–17; EA Sports and, 469; field invasions and, 152; gender rules and, 179; gift rules, 372; mascots and, 265–66; online gambling and, 196; scandals, 4–6; sexual assault and, 349; Title IX and, 159, 172–75; transsexual athletes and, 446; video review and, 458–59; whistle-blowing and, 478; women's media coverage and, 275
National Education Association, 265–66
National Football League (NFL): age limits, 106; amateur drafts, 104–5; antitrust violations and, 23, 27–28; broadcasting rights, 268, 337; CFL *v.*, 337; corporate branding and, 82; doping and, 22; drugs and, 251; EA Sports and, 469; end-zone celebrations and, 75; mascots and, 261; PASPA and, 194; race and, 144, 146–48; religious expression and, 362–63; salaries, 371; Sports Broadcasting Act and, 26; strikes and, 35–36; taunting and, 427–28; ubersexuality and, 452–53; unions and, 29–37; urban planning and, 462; video review and, 458; virtual sports and, 473; women sportscasters and, 500
National Football League Players Association (NFLPA), 36; formation of, 30; Rozelle Rule, 28
National Gay Flag Football League (NGFFL), 245

National Greyhound Association (NGA), 15
National Hockey League (NHL): African Americans and, 345; amateur drafts, 104; antitrust violations and, 26; cheating and, 57–58; corporate branding and, 79; criminal violence and, 92–93; draft lotteries and, 107–8; drugs and, 252; EA Sports and, 469; Fox and, 338; gambling and, 195; government sponsorship and, 201–2; lockout, 376–77; missile throwing and, 290; NHLPA and, 375; publicity, 337–38; salaries, 371–73; taunting and, 428–29; unions and, 29–37; video review and, 358; women in, 497–98
National Hockey League Players Association (NHLPA): Eagleson and, 32; formation of, 30–31, 375
National Hot Rod Association (NHRA), 183
National Institute of Mental Health, 349
National Institutes of Health, 46
National Midnight Basketball League, 369
National Negro League, 344
National Recreation and Parks Association (NRPA), 40
National Soccer League (NSL), 333
National World Yoga Championships, 511
National Yoga Championships, 511
National Youth Sports Safety Foundation, 306
Native Americans, 264–65
Nattress, Ric, 252
Natural Method, 308–10
Navratilova, Martina, 212, 296, 297, 484, 487
NAYS. *See* National Alliance for Youth Sports
Nazis, 285–87, 413
"NBA Jam," 469
NBA. *See* National Basketball Association
NBC, 267–68; Olympic broadcasting rights, 337; snowboarding and, 393; women sportscasters on, 499
NBPA. *See* National Basketball Players Association
NCAA. *See* National Collegiate Athletic Association
Neagle, Denny, 363
Neal, Gary, 6, 352
Necessary Roughness, 478
Nelson, Jeff, 89
NEP. *See* New ecological paradigm
Nettles, Graig, 56
New ecological paradigm (NEP), 119
New England Patriots, 59
New Right, 173–74
News Corporation, 269–70, 338
New social movements (NSMs), 60. *See also* Social movements
Newson, Andy, 8
Newton, Nate, 251
Newton, Rob, 297
New York Knicks, 108
New York Times, 478

New York Yankees: field invasions, 152; stadium, 87; taunting and, 425–26
New Zealand Snowboarder, 396–97
"NFL Blitz," 469
NFL Network, 268
NFLPA. *See* National Football League Players Association
NFL. *See* National Football League
NGA. *See* National Greyhound Association
NGFFL. *See* National Gay Flag Football League
NHLPA. *See* National Hockey League Players Association
NHL. *See* National Hockey League
NHRA. *See* National Hot Rod Association
Nidal, Abu, 434
Niekro, Joe, 54–55
Nielson, Roger, 428–29
Nifong, Mike, 353
Nike Corporation, 376; Jordan, Michael, and, 69, 74–75; NSMs and, 63; PLAY campaign and, 41; recycling and, 124–25; sexual abuse and, 379–80; skateboarding and, 388; snowboarding and, 394; Swoopes and, 212; third world manufacturing and, 125, 128–30
Nilsmark, Catrin, 259–60
9/11, 433
Nintendo Entertainment System, 466
Nintendo Wii, 466, 471
NIT, 55
Nixon, Richard, 171
Noakes, Tim, 49, 456
Nolan, Ted, 430
No Mas Violencia, 17
Nomo, Hideo, 67
Nonathletes, athletes *v.*, 3
Nongovernmental organizations, 121
North American Gay Amateur Athletic Alliance (NAGAAA), 213, 244
North American Snowboard Association (NASBA), 391, 394
North American Soccer League, 339
NRPA. *See* National Recreation and Parks Association
NSL. *See* National Soccer League
NSMs. *See* New social movements
Nudity, 325. *See also* Streaking
Nystrom, Mary, 494
Nyungah Circle of Elders, 64

Oakland Raiders, 27–28
Oakley, Charles, 250
Obesity, 3, 137; video games and, 468
OCR. *See* Office for Civil Rights
O'Dell, Ann, 315
O'Dowd, Dan, 363
Office Depot, 85
Office for Civil Rights (OCR), 171
Officials: protection for, 358; violence against, 354–59

554 | Index

Offord, Willie, 382
Ogi, Adolf, 367
Ohio High School Athletic Association (OHSAA), 372
OHL. *See* Ontario Hockey League
OHSAA. *See* Ohio High School Athletic Association
Olmstead, Frederick Law, 327
Olsen, Mike, 391
Olsen, Neil, 281
Olson, Knut, 8
Olympic Job Opportunities Program, 201
Olympic Revue, 230
Olympics: BALCO and, 59; Black September and, 61; boycott of, 62; broadcasting rights, 337; broadcasting rights and, 267; cheating and, 55; in China, 2008, 65; corporate branding and, 76–77; doping and, 18–22, 44–45; Dream Team, 69; environmental impact of, 124; ergogenics and, 132; *FHM* and, 257; Gay games *v.*, 168–70; gender rules and, 179; gene doping and, 186; government sponsorship of, 200; IOC and, 228–33; marathon and, 455; in Mexico, 1968, 61–62; militarism and, 284–89; NSMs and, 61–65; openly gay athletes and, 297; scandals and, 232; sex testing and, 282–83; snowboarding and, 392–93; sports for all and, 409–11; terrorism and, 430–36; trademark infringement, 169–70; vision of, 412–14; women and, 495–96; women sportscasters and, 500; women's sports coverage, 272; yoga and, 512
Olympism, 228
On Aggression (Lorenz), 318
O'Neal, Jermaine, 291, 319
O'Neal, Shaquille, 372
O'Neil, Buck, 145
Ontario Hockey League (OHL), 93, 205–7
OPCY. *See* Oriole Park at Camden Yards
Ordaz, Gustavo, 61–62, 288
O'Reilly, Terry, 291, 320
Organized Crime Control Act, 193
Orienteering, 7–8
Oriole Park at Camden Yards (OPCY), 461
Orr, Scott, 469
Orser, Brian, 297
Orthodox Bungalow Baseball League, 365
Osborne, Tom, 351
Outgames, 169, 214
Out of Bounds: Inside the NBA's Culture of Rape Violence & Crime (Benedict), 313, 349
Outward Bound, 208
Owen, Mickey, 291
Owens, Terrell, 340, 428
Owners: ethnic, 143–48; women, 488–91
Oxfam, 130

Paddling, 7
Pain, 387
Painkillers, 405
Pallone, Dave, 296–97, 356
Palmeiro, Rafael, 417, 479–80
Palmer, Shaun, 392
Panathlon Charter on the Rights of the Child in Sport, 367
Pantani, Marco, 140
Paphitis, Theo, 218
Paralympics, 61, 98–100; Pistorius and, 50–51
Parche, Günther, 155
Parent misconduct, 301–7; referee abuse and, 355
Parents Association for Youth Sports (PAYS), 302–3
Parkour, 307–12
Parks, 327–30
Parrish, Robert, 314
Partner abuse, 312–17
PASPA. *See* Professional and Amateur Sports Protection Act
Patanjali, 509–10
Patrick, Danica, 254, 257, 498
Patrick, Owen, 14–15
"Patterns of Global Terrorism Report," 435
PAYS. *See* Parents Association for Youth Sports
Payton, Gary, 163
Pearl, Bruce, 478
Pearson, Durk, 133
Pele, 339
Pension, 375
People for the Ethical Treatment of Animals (PETA), 14, 16–18
Perez, Pascual, 320
Performance enhancing drugs. *See* Doping
Perot, Ross, 3
Perry, Gaylord, 56
PETA. *See* People for the Ethical Treatment of Animals
Peter, Christian, 351
Peterson, Kelsey, 381
Pettigrew, Antonio, 480–81
Pettitte, Andy, 417
PGA. *See* Professional Golfers' Association
Pheidippides, 455
Pherenike, 489
"Phevos and Athena," 434
Philadelphia Phillies, 262
Philadelphia World Hockey Club v. Philadelphia Hockey Club, 26
Phillips, Laurence, 315
Phillips, Neil, 8
Phillips, Rod, 8
Philly Phanatic, 262
Photographers, 396
Physical exertion, 333
Physiology, 403–4
Physiology and Calisthenics for Schools and Families (Beecher), 493

Pichler, David, 297
Pilates, 98, 512
Pilates, Joseph, 98
Pillar, Jeff, 320
Pink Flamingo Relay, 168
Pisidorus, 489
Pistorius, Oscar, 50–51, 102–3
Pit Bulls, 12
Placekickers, female, 494
"The Play," 154
Playboy, 257–58, 501
PLAY campaign, 41
Player-fan fighting, 317–21
Player mobility, 33
Play movement, 38
Pobar, Art, 421
Podoloff, Maurice, 6
Point-shaving, 195
Poker, 335
Police, 355
Pollard, Frederick, 347
Pollard, Fritz, 145, 147
Pollentier, Michel, 55
Pollution, 121, 123–24
Pond, Gardner, 243
"Pong," 466; virtual sports and, 472
Pop culture, 331, 420
Pope, Herb, 250
Poppen, Sherman, 390, 394
Portland, Rene, 297
Pound, Dick, 47
Powers, Ross, 393, 394
Presidential Commission on Status of Women, 158
President's Council on Bioethics, 185
President's Council on Physical Fitness and Sports, 132
Primal Quest, 10–11
Probert, Bob, 252
Professional and Amateur Sports Protection Act (PASPA), 193–94
Professional Golfers' Association (PGA): Gatorade and, 136; genetics and, 50; Woods, Tiger, and, 374
Professional Snowboard Tour of America (PSTA), 392
Profiling. *See* Racial profiling
Profit, 34
The Program, 478
Prohibition, 334
ProLine, 202
Promise Keepers, 364
Prosthetics, 50–51, 102–3; illnesses and, 224
Prostitution, 363, 382
Protests, 61–65
Protests. *See* Collective protests
Proud Hockey Parent, 307
Pseudosports, 331–36
PSTA. *See* Professional Snowboard Tour of America

Public funds, 330
Publicity, 336–41
Public School Athletic League, 3
Public spaces, 327–30; skateboarding and, 385
Puckett, Kirby, 349
Pumping Iron II: The Women, 486
Pyle, Norris, 167, 242

Quarterbacks, black, 347
Queer politics, 241
Queer Theory, 443
Questioning, 208, 209

Race, 44, 48–49; coaching and, 143–48; ethnic athletes and, 65–71; gender and, 181; managers and, 143–48; mascots and, 264–65; owners and, 143–48; stacking and, 343–48; taunting and, 430; terrorism and, 431
Race, Evolution and Behavior (Rushton), 43
Racial-genetic theory, 48–49
Racial profiling, 343–48
Raid Gauloises, 9–10
Randall, Marcus, 152
Rape, 348–53, 380–82
Rathbun, Bill, 433
Ratjen, Hermann, 280–82, 445
Ratner, Harvey, 107
Raye, Jimmy, 347
Reagan, Ronald, 173–74
Rebagliati, Ross, 250
Recruiting, illegal, 478
Recycling, 124–25
Red Brigades, 435
Red Bull, 135
Reddick, Bob, 8
Redmond, Kathy, 351
Reece, Gabrielle, 258
Reese, Pee Wee, 427
Rees, Roger, 3
Referee abuse, 354–59
Rehabilitation Act, 171, 226
Religion, 360–65; surfing and, 422
Religious Right, 173–74
Rentzel, Lance, 251
Repoxygen, 47, 186
Resource mobilization, 60
Restraint, 1
Retton, Mary Lou, 255
Reverse anorexia, 114
"Revolutionary Struggle," 434
Rheaume, Manon, 183–84, 497–98
Richard, Maurice, 291–92, 362
Richardson, Luke, 93
Richards, Renee, 445
Richards, Todd, 397
Ride Snowboards, 394
Ride Wild Surf, 420
Riggs, Bobby, 500

Right to Play, 368
Rijker, Lucia, 497
Rios, Armando, 59
Riots, postevent, 321–26
Risk, 406, 455
Risk society, 38–39
Rivera, Marco, 317
Robbins, Barrett, 59
Robert, Dominique, 10
Roberts, Ian, 297
Roberts, Mark, 153, 340
Roberts, Morganna, 154
Robertson, Oscar, 27
Robinson, Frank, 67, 146–47
Robinson, Glenn, 316
Robinson, Jackie, 143, 346–47, 427
Robinson, Laura, 379
Robinson, Will, 146
Rock climbing, 7
Rodeo, 459
Rodman, Dennis, 66–67, 75, 340
Rodriguez, Alex, 371–72
Rodriguez, Fernando, 381
Rodríguez, Iván, 479
Rogaining, 7–8
Rogers, Don, 252
Roger's Media, 338
Rogge, Jacques, 232
Rolling Stone, 393
Romanowski, Bill, 59
Romano, Yossi, 432
Romijn-Stamos, Rebecca, 506
Rooney, Dan, 148
Rooney Rule, 148
Rosas, Eduardo Delgado, 10
Rosenbloom, Carroll, 490
Rosenthal, Sam, 194
Rose, Pete, 57, 356; gambling and, 161, 163; Roberts, Morganna, and, 154
Rose, Richard, 155
Routine activities theory, 378
Rowing, 113
Royal, Darrell, 173
Royal Society for the Protection of Animals, 64
A Royal Sport: Surfing in Waikiki (London), 420
Roy, Patrick, 315, 429
Royster, Jerry, 320
Rozelle, Pete, 195
Rozelle Rule, 28
Rugby, 333; labor migration and, 237; video review and, 459
Ruiz, Rosie, 57
Rules: celebration, 428; gender and, 177–85; of reason, 25
Rule violation. *See* Cheating
"Rumble in the Jungle," 427
Run for the Cure, 223
Runner's World, 249

Running: alcohol and, 249; cross-country, 7; environmental impact of, 121; ultraendurance, 454–59
Running of the Bulls, 340
Rusconi, Marco, 140
Rushton, J. Philippe, 43
Russell, Arthur, 230
Russell, Bill, 67, 145–46, 147
Rutgers University, 353
Ruth, Babe, 320–21, 425–27
R. v. Cey, 92
R. v. McSorley, 95

Sabbath day, 365
Sage Orienteering Club, 8
Salanson, Fabrice, 140
Salaries, 371–77; arbitration, 32–33; gender and, 180
Salary caps, 30–31, 375–76; CBAs and, 33
Sale, Jamie, 257
Salming, Borje, 252
Salt Lake City, 433–34
Samaranch, Juan Antonio, 232, 415
Sanday, Peggy R., 349
Sanders, Bev, 390–91
Sanders, Chris, 390–91
Sanders, Deion, 68
Sanderson, Derek, 253
San Diego Chicken, 262
San Francisco Renaissance, 419
Santiago, Benito, 59
Sapp, Warren, 428
Saskin, Ted, 31
Saunders, Tony, 479
Sawyer, Diane, 298
Sbeih, Adham, 142
Scalping, 436–42
Scandals: academic misconduct and, 4–7; Black Sox, 56–57, 162, 193; EPO, 140–41; "Fab Five," 5; Love Boat, 382–83; Olympics and, 232; third world manufacturing and, 126
Scarsdale Diet, 133
Scheffield, Gary, 416
Schilling, Curt, 480
Schinegger, Eric, 280
School sports. *See also* Academic misconduct
Schott, Marge, 490
Schreiner, Anja, 486
Schreyer, Edward, 225
Schroeder, Patricia, 40
Schwartz, Jeff, 293
Schwarzenegger, Arnold, 486
Scott, Barbara Ann, 254
Scousers, 429–30
SCREAM. *See* Students Challenging Reality and Educating Against Myths
Scully, Gerald, 29
Seabiscuit, 339
Sears, 466

Index

SEA. *See* Snowboard European Association
Seefeldt, Vern, 366–67
Sega, 466
Segregation, 346; gender, 448
Seidel, Guenter, 297
Seles, Monica, 155
Self Realization Fellowship, 512
Selig, Bud, 376, 479
Seligmann, Reade, 353
Septien, Rafael, 251
Serie A soccer league, 164
Sermon, John, 140
Serrano, Laura, 497
Severson, John, 421
Sevilla, Oscar, 141
Sex, group, 379
Sex testing, 278–83
Sexual assault, 313–15, 348–53; among athletes, 377–83; on young athletes, 366
Sexual Assault Services and Crime Victim Assistance, 353
Sexual harassment, 211, 377–78
Sexuality, female, 253–60
Sexual status, 168
Shackleford, A. J., 319
Sharapova, Maria, 254
Shaun Palmer Pro-Snowboarder, 393
Shaw, Sandy, 133
Sheffield, Gary, 59
Shelby, John, 320
Shell, Arthur, 147
Sherman Antitrust Act, 23–24, 26, 27; Rozelle Rule and, 28
Shih, David, 335
Shires, Dana, 136
Shockey, Jeremy, 471
Shorter, Frank, 456
Shriver, Eunice Kennedy, 101
Sidewalk men, 437
Simmons, Roy, 297
Simon, Randall, 263
Simpson, Lisa, 352
Simpson, Nicole Brown, 315
Simpson, O. J., 315
Sims Snowboards, 390, 394
Sims, Tom, 390, 394
Simulated sports, 333
Singh, Vijay, 184, 498
Skateboarding, 383–89; X Games and, 504
Skateboard Street, 503
Skate parks, 385–86
Ski Slopestyle, 503
Skydiving, 455
Sky Sport, 269–70
Skysurfing, 503–4
Slamball, 333
Slam dunk: ABA and, 73; competition, 75
Sloane, William Milligan, 230
Smith, Doug, 315
Smith, Eddie, 355

Smith, Lovie, 148
Smith, Owen Patrick, 14–15
Smith, Raymond, 59
Smith, Steven, 195
Smith, Tim, 355
Smith, Tommie, 62, 70–71, 170; cool pose of, 72
Smith, Troy, 315
Smoot, Fred, 382
SMU. *See* Southern Methodist University
Snowboarder Magazine, 392
Snowboard European Association (SEA), 391–92, 394
Snowboarding, 389–98, 455, 503
Snowmobiling, 503
Snurfer, 390, 394
Snyder, Dan, 250
Soccer, 333; hooliganism and, 215–19; labor migration and, 238; taunting, 429–30; tragedies, 398–402
Social Darwinism, 344
Socially contested sports, 333
Social movements, 60–65
Social safety net, 196
Society for the Prevention of Cruelty to Animals (SPCA), 16
Society for the Study of the Indigenous Languages of the Americas, 265–66
Sockalexis, Louis, 264
Sommers, Christina Hoff, 175
Sony PlayStation, 466, 472
Sorenstam, Annika, 180, 184, 498
Sosa, Sammy, 68, 479–80
South Africa: FIFA suspension, 62; ICC and, 63
South African War, 458
Southern Methodist University (SMU), 6
Soviet Union, 62
Space Jam, 69
SPCC. *See* Sports Parent Code of Conduct
Speak Out, 366
Special Olympics, 99, 101–2
SPIEGEL, 481
Spiers, Bill, 320
Spitting, 355
Spitz, Mark, 432
Sponsorships: drugs and, 248; endorsements v., 81; government, 197–202; snowboarding, 397; of X Games, 504–5
Sport Canada, 198–99
Sport Climbing, 504
Sport for Development and Peace, 367–68
Sportization, 78
Sport Medicine Council of Canada, 404–5
Sports Action, 194
Sports Broadcasting Act, 26
Sportscasters, women, 498–501
Sports deviance, 54
Sports for all, 407–11
Sports for the People, 409

Sports Illustrated, 259; anabolic steroids and, 415; salaries and, 371; swimsuit issue, 256–58, 274
Sports-media nexus, 66
Sports medicine, 403–7
Sports Parent Code of Conduct (SPCC), 304–6
Sports spaces, private *v.* public, 326–30
Sportswomen of the Week, 499
Sport Without Borders, 368
Sprague, Matt, 167, 242
Sprewell, Latrell, 75
Springstein, Thomas, 47
Sprint Capitol Club, 480
Stackhouse, Jerry, 383
Stacking, 343–48
Stadium(s): Canadian, 86; construction of, 460; corporate, 83–87; environmental impact of, 120; private *v.* public, 330; rebranded, 80; terrorism and, 431; ticket distribution, 436–42; tragedies, 401
Staffordshire Bull Terriers, 12
Stanford University, 154
Stanozolol, 19, 58
Stanton, Elizabeth Cady, 313
Starks, John, 383
Stebbins, Robert, 192–93
Stephens, Helen, 281
Stephens, Sandy, 347
Stereotyping, 274; profiling and, 344
Stern, David, 75, 105; draft lotteries and, 106–8; gambling and, 163; missile throwing and, 291; race and, 144
Steroids. *See* Anabolic steroids
Stevens, Jenny, 351
Stevens, Jerramy, 250
Stevens, Kevin, 252
Stewart, Hattie, 497
Stewart, Rollen Frederick, 340
Stockholm Consensus, 446
Stoudemire, Amare, 371
Stratton Mountain, 391
Strawberry, Darryl, 252
Streaking, 153; publicity and, 340
Street Luge, 504
Strikes, 375–76; NFL and, 35–36
Stringer, Corey, 137
Strode, Willy, 347
Stubblefield, Dana, 59
StubHub, 441
Students Challenging Reality and Educating Against Myths (SCREAM), 353
Suicide Six, 391, 394
Sullivan, John, 497
Super Bowl: broadcasting rights and, 267; corporate branding and, 76; field invasions, 153
Supplements, 131; false claims of, 135–36. *See also* Ergogenics
Surcharge fees, 442
Surf, 421

Surfer magazine, 421
Surfers Against Sewage, 118
"Surfin' Bird," 422
Surfing, 388, 418–23
Suzuki, Ichiro, 67
Sweeney, Lee, 186–87
Swenson, David, 510
Switzer, Peter, 242
Swoopes, Sheryl, 212
Symbolism, 413

TAFISA. *See* Trim and Fitness International Sports for all Association
Tagliabue, Paul, 428
Tai chi, 512
Tait, Blyth, 297
Taliban, 433
Tanking, 108
Tarde, Gabriel, 322
Tarnower, Herman, 133
Tarshment, 422
Tattoos, 453
Taunting, 75, 425–30
Taxes, luxury, 33
Taylor, Beck, 108
Taylor, Maurice, 5
Taylor, Peter, 8
Taylor, Travis, 382
Taylor Report, 218
Team names, 178–79
Tehami, Abbes, 57
Tejada, Miguel, 479
Television, 336–37. *See also* Media
Tennis: gambling and, 164–65; video review and, 459
Terrorism, 430–36
Testing: ACTN3 genetic, 189–90; anabolic steroid, 414–15; chromosomal, 445–46; drug, 19; false negatives, 282; false positives, 282; HIV/AIDS, 226; sex, 278–83; urine, 55
Tetrahydrogestrinone (THG), 58, 480
Tetter, Hannah, 397
Tewksbury, Mark, 213
Texas Child Protective Services, 382
TGHA. *See* Toronto Gay Hockey Association
Thatcher, Margaret, 217, 400
Theodosius I, 228–29
THG. *See* Tetrahydrogestrinone
Thie, John, 48
Third world manufacturing, 125–31
Thomas, Deon, 478
Thomas, J. J., 393, 394
Thomas, Tammy, 59
Thompson, Cliff, 292
Thompson, David, 73
Thompson, Jenny, 259
Thrower, Willie, 347
Thurman, Tracey, 313
Ticket distribution, 436–42

TicketLiquidator, 441
Ticketmaster, 437, 440–41; surcharge fees, 442
TicketReserve.com, 441
Ticketron, 440
TicketWeb, 441
TIDES. *See* The Institute for Diversity and Ethics in Sport
Tilden, Bill, 296
Tilting the Playing Field (Gavora), 175–76
Timberlake, Justin, 153
Time, 259
Time4Media, 396
Time Magazine, 391
Time Warner, 338
Title IX, 156–60, 171–77, 182–83; female sexuality and, 255
Title IX (Acosta & Carpenter), 171
T-Mobile, 481
TM. *See* Transcendental meditation; Transgender Menace
Tocchet, Rick, 195
Tom Brown's Schooldays (Hughes), 2, 360–61
Tomlin, Mike, 148
Tomlinson, Jane, 225–26
Toronto Gay Hockey Association (TGHA), 245
Torre, Joe, 317
Tort law, 90
Toth, Kevin, 59
Tour de France: Armstrong, Lance, and, 223; cheating and, 55; doping and, 21–22; EPO and, 139–40
Tourism, 459, 462
Tracy, Paul, 89
Trainers, 403–7
Training, 456; virtual, 473; women and, 487
Transcendental meditation (TM), 510
Transgender Menace (TM), 168
Transgenders, 209, 280. *See also* Transsexuals
Transitioned, 209
Transsexuals, 443–48
Transworld Snowboarding, 396
Trash talking, 426
Traum, Dick, 224
Traylor, Robert, 5
Trespassing, 329
Tressel, Jim, 106
Trim and Fitness International Sports for all Association (TAFISA), 408
Trogdon, Justin, 108
Truces, 284–85
Tuaolo, Esera, 299
Tucson Orienteering Club, 8
Turf clubs, 194
Turinabol, 45
Turner, Pamela Joan, 381
24-second shot clock, 74
Two Oceans Marathon, 457–58
Tyson, Mike, 71, 91, 344, 350; domestic violence and, 314–15; taunting and, 429

Ubersexuality, 449–54
UCI. *See* International Cycling Union
Ueberroth, Peter, 163
UEFA. *See* Union of European Football Association
UK Sport, 368
Ullrich, Jan, 141
UltraCross, 503
Ultraendurance running, 454–59
Ultramarathons, 455
UNESCO. *See* United Nations Educational, Scientific and Cultural Organization
UNICEF. *See* United Nations Children's Fund
Union of European Football Association (UEFA), 164, 239; Right to Play and, 368
Unions, 29–37; labor migration and, 239–40; salaries and, 375
United Nations: environmental impact and, 123; militarism and, 285; terrorism and, 431; young athletes and, 367–68
United Nations Children's Fund (UNICEF), 367; Beckham, David, and, 454
United Nations Educational, Scientific and Cultural Organization (UNESCO), 367, 409
United States of American Snowboarding Association (USAASA), 392
United States, Olympic boycott, 62
United States Tennis Association (USTA), 445
Universal Declaration of Human Rights, 408
University of Arkansas, 351
University of California (Berkeley), 154
University of Colorado, 352, 494
University of Kentucky, 6; gambling and, 195
University of Michigan, 5
University of Minnesota, 4
University of Moncton, 93, 357
University of Nebraska, 351
University of New Haven, 6
University of Prince Edward Island (UPEI), 93, 357
UPEI. *See* University of Prince Edward Island
Urban planning, 459–63
Urine samples, 55
USAASA. *See* United States of American Snowboarding Association
USADA. *See* U.S. Anti-Doping Agency
U.S. Anti-Doping Agency (USADA), 58–59, 480
U.S. Centers for Disease Control (CDC), 131
U.S. Department of Energy, 46
U.S. Department of Housing and Urban Development, 39–40
USGA. *See* U.S. Golf Association
U.S. Golf Association (USGA), 180, 446
U.S. Justice Department, 23–24
USOF. *See* U.S. Orienteering Federation
U.S. Olympic Committee (USOC), 201
U.S. Orienteering Federation (USOF), 8
USTA. *See* United States Tennis Association

Vanbiesbrouck, John, 290
Van Standifer, G., 40, 369
Vassar College, 493
Vassar, Matthew, 493
Vectrex, 472
Veeck, Mike, 293
Velez, Ada, 497
Venationes, 12
Verity, Andrew, 48
Vermeuleun, Katie, 258
Vick, Marcus, 89
Vick, Michael, 470
Video games, 311, 465–71; snowboarding and, 393; types, 467
Video review, 358–59
Videotaping, cheating and, 59
Vietnam Labor Watch, 63, 127
Vikelas, Demetrius, 229–30
Vincent, Troy, 363
Vinoukorouv, Alexandre, 141
Violence: at-risk youth and, 38; criminal, 88–95; domestic, 312–17; fans and, 155; hooliganism and, 216–19; legal v. illegal, 90; mascots and, 263; against officials, 354–59; parental misconduct and, 303–7; player-fan, 317–21; postevent, 321–26; sexual abuse and, 379; soccer tragedies and, 398–402; terrorism and, 432–36; third world manufacturing and, 127; video games and, 469–70; virtual sports and, 474–75
Virtual sports, 472–75
Voet, Willy, 140–41
volenti non fit injuria, 91
Voliva, Cliff, 494
Votaw, Ty, 260

WADA. *See* World Anti-Doping Agency
Waddell, Tom, 167–70, 214, 241–42, 296
Wakeboarding, 423, 503
Walker, Antoine, 351
Walker, Donald, 493
Wallace, Ben, 89, 291, 319
Wallace, Jaymee Lane, 381–82
Wallemberg, Ettore, 435
Waller, Judith Cary, 500
Walsh, Stella, 280–81
Walt Disney Company, 339–40; corporate branding and, 82; publicity and, 338; X Games and, 384
Wang, Zhizhi, 67
Wanninger, Rick, 480
The War Against Boys (Sommers), 175
Washington, Desiree, 315, 350
Washington, George, 13
Washington, Kenny, 347
Waste management, 123–24
Water conservation, 123–24
Water sports, 504
Way, Danny, 385

WDNAAF. *See* Women's Division of the National Amateur Athletic Federation
Weather Underground, 433
Weaver, Earl, 356
Webber, Chris, 5
Webb, Marcus, 351
Webster, Steen, 396–97
Weider, Ben, 486
Weider, Joe, 135–36
Weight loss: cheating and, 54; yoga and, 510
Weinberg, Moshe, 432
Weston, Mary Louise Edith, 280, 283
WHA. *See* World Hockey Association
Wheatley, Tyrone, 59
Wheeler, Rashidi, 137
Whiskey Rebellion, 334
Whistle-blowers, 4, 477–82
Whitehead, Willie, 428
White, Kelli, 59, 417
White Men Can't Jump, 426
White, Reggie, 363
White Ribbon Campaign, 316
White, Shaun, 393, 394, 397
Why Men Rebel (Gurr), 318
Wickenheiser, Hayley, 183–84
Wide World of Sports, 337, 500
Wiggins, Alan, 320
Wiggins, Jermaine, 382
Wilander, Mats, 252–53
Wilhite, Gerald, 428
Williams, Erik, 251
Williams, Harvey, 315
Williams, Kevin, 382
Williams, Lance, 58, 480
Williams, Moe, 382
Williamson, Troy, 382
Williams, Pat, 382
Williams, Paul, 89
Williams, Richie, 250
Williams, Roland, 363
Williams, Venus, 184
Wimbledon Open, 184; Ashe, Arthur, and, 70
Windsurfing, 423
Winterstick, 390
Wire Act, 193
Wirtz, Bill, 32
Witt, Katarina, 258
WNBA. *See* Women's National Basketball Association
WOC. *See* World Orienteering Championship
Wolfe, John, 351–52
Women: apologetic and, 482–87; bodybuilding and, 484–86; boxing, 497; coaches, 159–60, 488–91; funding equity and, 156–60; journalists, 276; *Maxim* and, 485; media coverage and, 271–77; in men's sports, 491–98; men v., 278–84; naked, 325; objectification of, 253–60, 261; owners, 488–91; skateboarding and, 387; sportscasters, 498–501; training and, 487

Women's Division of the National Amateur Athletic Federation (WDNAAF), 157–58
Women's liberation movement, 172
Women's National Basketball Association (WNBA), 179–80, 496–97
Women's Professional Football League (WPFL), 180
Women's rights, 60–61
Women's Sport Foundation, 214–15, 500
Woods, Ickey, 428
Woodson, Charles, 291
Woods, Tiger, 374; corporate branding and, 76; endorsements of, 81–82; salary, 371–72
Wood, Stuart, 8
World Anti-Doping Agency (WADA), 18, 21–22, 140–41; AAS and, 412; anabolic steroids and, 415; drugs and, 247–53; EPO and, 47; genetic discrimination and, 190; GM and, 186; Guest, Kelly, and, 137; Johnson, Ben, and, 58
World Anti-Doping Code, 22; anabolic steroids and, 415; GM and, 185
World Championship Wrestling league, 340
World Conference on Doping in Sport, 21
World Cup 1998, hooliganism and, 219
A World Fit for Children, 367
World Hockey Association (WHA), 253, 373; antitrust violations and, 26
World Motor Sports Council, 59
World Orienteering Championship (WOC), 8
World Series of Poker, 335
World systems theory, 126
"World Tour Golf," 368
World Trade Organization, 434
World War II, 198, 404; CSIT and, 408
World Wrestling Federation, 335
WPFL. *See* Women's Professional Football League
Wrestling, eating disorders and, 113
Wrestling, professional, 333
Wright, Elmo, 428

Wrigley, Phillip, 181
Wymer, Dave, 252

Xbox, 472
XFL football, 270, 333, 335–36
X Games, 384, 388–89, 394, 503–7; Eco-Challenge and, 9; snowboarding and, 393
X Trials, 506

Yahoo!, 470
Yao Ming, 67
Yegorova, Olga, 142
YMCA. *See* Young Men's Christian Association
Yoga, 509–13
Yoga Asana Competition, 512–13
Yoga Olympiad, 512–13
Yoga Sutras of Patanjali (Patanjali), 509–10
Yoonew.com, 441
York Barbell, 132
Young, Jerome, 481
Young Men's Christian Association (YMCA), 2; at-risk youth and, 37–38; government funding of, 199; religious expression and, 361; sports spaces and, 327
Your Physique, 135
Youth: at-risk, 37–42; sports, 199–200
Youth Education Through Sports, 370

Zaharias, Babe, 184, 498
Zanette, Denis, 140
Zanoli, Michel, 140
Zappas, Evangelis, 229
Zeigler, Cyd, 245
Zeigler, John, 31, 32
Zheng Yongji, 142
Zidane, Zinedene, 89
Ziegler, John, 414
Zimbalist, Andrew, 176
Zimmer, Don, 89
Zubiaur, Jose, 230